Cultural Studies and Education

Perspectives on Theory, Methodology, and Practice

Cultural Studies and Education

Perspectives on
Theory, Methodology, and Practice

Edited by

RUBÉN A. GAZTAMBIDE-FERNÁNDEZ

HEATHER A. HARDING

TERE SORDÉ-MARTÍ

Harvard Educational Review

Reprint Series No. 38

Library of Congress Control Number 2003115029

ISBN 0-916690-41-5

Published by the Harvard Educational Review,
an imprint of the Harvard Education Publishing Group

Harvard Educational Review
8 Story Street
Cambridge, MA 02138

Cover Design: Anne Carter
Cover Art: Victor Cervantes

The typeface used in this book is Adobe Garamond.

To our parents and to cultural workers
around the world

Contents

INTRODUCTION

At the Crossroads of Education and Cultural Theory

This book portrays the intersection of two impressive currents in contemporary intellectual life, cultural studies and educational research. Despite important contributions from a number of scholars, commerce between these two fields has, until recently, been disappointingly scarce. Yet as the rich array of essays in this volume suggests, fruitful collaborations between cultural and educational studies have begun to appear. Moreover, these essays suggest that such collaborations can greatly enrich both fields. For education scholars and practitioners in particular, encounters with various aspects of the cultural studies enterprise have already begun to open up new approaches and insights in their research and their schools.

Over the last two decades, cultural studies has emerged as a potent intellectual force, crossing the boundaries of academic disciplines in the humanities and the social and behavioral sciences. Despite some resistance from traditional academic disciplines, specialized departments, academic programs, and research centers that are pursuing scholarly work in cultural studies are proliferating in universities around the world. As a field, cultural studies is difficult to define, largely because scholars within it draw from an amalgam of disciplinary perspectives while resisting traditional academic demarcations. It can generally be characterized as a scholarly movement that draws on theories of culture from various disciplines, such as literature, anthropology, sociology, and psychoanalysis, to understand issues regarding cultural phenomena — including academic culture itself.[1]

In the mid-1950s, British cultural and social theorists like Raymond Williams, Richard Hoggart, and E. P. Thompson began to suggest that the study of working-class culture could yield a theory of cultural practice as a force for political change.[2] Drawing on Marxist theory,[3] these "cultural populists"[4] faced a range of theoretical dilemmas as they attempted to cross disciplinary boundaries to study the cultural practices of their own social groups. These challenges were accentuated by dramatic shifts in scholarly discourse and radical transformations in the nature of social inquiry itself.[5] The work of Frankfurt School critical theorists like Max Horkheimer and Theodor Adorno,[6] who fiercely questioned the traditions of the Enlightenment,[7] and the work of theorists associated with postmodernism, like Michel Foucault and Jacques Derrida,[8] were especially influential in the development of cultural studies.

By the mid-1970s, a field of "cultural studies" solidified its status in the academy with the creation of the Birmingham Center for Cultural Studies, founded by a new generation of scholars building on the work of Williams, Hoggart, and Thompson, and led by cultural theorist Stuart Hall.[9] Since then, cultural studies has oscillated between offering interpretations of meaning through "readings" of cultural practices[10] and focusing on how communities engage products of popular culture and develop new cultural formations.[11] Some scholars have also studied the institutions and the practices through which culture enters a market of cultural goods.[12] While the initial focus of cultural studies was on working-class culture, it soon became clear that other axes of difference, such as race and gender, were also important dimensions of cultural production in need of particular attention.[13] Cultural studies scholars have drawn from and been an important force behind the development of other critical theoretical frameworks emerging at the margins of the academy, such as queer and postcolonial theories. As an intellectual tradition, cultural studies has sought to illuminate issues of power by understanding the role of culture in social and economic oppression while reconceptualizing culture as an important form of resistance.

Although many schools of education have yet to recognize the tremendous opportunities that cultural studies opens for understanding the intersection of culture and education, some education scholars doing field research and working in educational theory draw from similar theoretical perspectives and often frame educational research in conceptual ways analogous to those of cultural studies.[14] Despite this parallel, the communication and exchange between scholars working in these two fields has not always been fluid.[15] Given the dominant disciplinary discourses and specializations within the field of education (e.g., developmental psychology, sociology, and economics), cultural studies remains unfamiliar to many students of education, who often find works in this scholarly tradition difficult to access and easy to dismiss. This is due in part to the wide range of theoretical traditions applied in cultural studies, which are not always clearly articulated and which require familiarity with multiple disciplinary discourses and methodologies. At the same time, scholars doing work in cultural studies often have a reductive view of education and educational research, and fail to recognize the crucial overlap between the two fields of inquiry.

Given this context, this book aims to serve three purposes. First, it is an introduction for educators and education researchers to some of the theoretical debates and analytic frameworks that have shaped the field of cultural studies. Second, it offers an introduction to and examples of three areas of inquiry in which education and cultural studies overlap. Third, these examples illustrate how education scholars have dealt with the conceptual challenges of cultural studies and how an educative perspective offers unique contributions to the broader debates in cultural theory. The essays in this book are a sample of a growing literature in cultural studies of education, which will introduce readers in both fields to the ways scholars draw from these theoretical perspectives to study the intersection of education and culture.

This collection is organized into four parts. The first gathers three essays dealing with central theoretical issues that are at the heart of the conceptual frameworks of cultural studies. These essays raise questions about the uses of theory, the purposes of research, and the relationship between the two. Framed in a larger debate about modernism, the nature of science, the production of knowledge, and the postmodern challenge to these concepts, each of these essays introduces the reader to contemporary theoretical discourses and to how these debates influence scholarship in education. The chapters in the rest of the book present conceptual frameworks that represent different angles on education and culture, but remain situated in the same larger theoretical context. While these chapters are certainly not exhaustive, they do provide a window into important concepts and perspectives. Most importantly, they illustrate the relevance of these debates to educational research, theory, and practice.

Part One sets the theoretical context for the three remaining parts of the book — Gender and Queer Studies, Postcolonial and Ethnic Studies, and Popular Culture and Youth Studies — each of which introduces the reader to a specific area within cultural studies of education. While it would be erroneous to suggest, for instance, that gender and sexuality are the same thing, or that popular culture is only relevant to young people, we believe that the organization of this book offers a heuristic tool for introducing newcomers to cultural studies of education and to the conceptual frameworks that support this work. Each part is introduced with a brief, accessible introduction that, in addition to summarizing the main ideas of each article, opens the door for readers into the theoretical traditions that inform the chapters in each section. These introductions will be of special interest to readers who are new to these areas of study and provide a coarse description of issues and debates concerning theory, research methodology, and practice, as well as references for further study.

Part Two contains three essays that focus on gender and queer studies. During its inception, cultural studies had a strong masculine bias.[16] Male scholars populated the field, and their analysis tended to ignore gender as an important force shaping cultural phenomena. Women quickly responded to the masculine bias in early cultural studies by bringing a feminist lens that has had a significant influence on the field.[17] They noted that ignoring gender left large analytic vacuums and raised crucial questions about the gender bias of the frameworks gaining relevance in cultural studies. This gender dynamic has also been noted in the field of education, where men have traditionally assumed dominant roles in both research and public leadership, while women comprise the majority in the teaching profession.[18]

Feminist theory has been central to the development of cultural studies of education, not only by offering a way to address issues about the role of women in education, but also in developing a more comprehensive and thorough understanding of gender as a crucial dimension of cultural phenomena and power relations. This gender analysis, which has tended to view sexuality in terms of a one-dimensional male/female dichotomy, has led directly to a more complex view that considers the experiences of lesbian, gay, bisexual, and transgender people as another important piece of the cultural puzzle in education.[19] Queer theory, with its roots in a feminist reinterpretation of psychoanalysis,[20] has opened the doors for raising questions about sexuality, desire, and a deeper understanding of the psychosexual dynamics of teaching and learning.[21] The three essays in Part Two address issues that are central to these perspectives, and to how they are deeply intertwined with other identity categories and forms of oppression.

Part Three introduces the theoretical perspective of postcolonial and ethnic studies. Taking an intimate tone, this critical perspective emerged in the mid-twentieth century from the work of scholars like Frantz Fanon, who experienced the effects of colonialism firsthand.[22] Colonialism remains central to the idea of globalization and continues to shape the life chances of many people.[23] However, postcolonial theory has been embraced as a theoretical framework for understanding race and ethnicity broadly, particularly when considering the experiences of migration and its attendant cultural transformation. Despite these developments, postcolonial theory continues to reject, on the one hand, Eurocentrism and imperialism, and on the other, monolithic and one-dimensional views of ethnicity, race, and the idea of "the native."[24] In this sense, postcolonial theory offers a theoretical framework to understand different experiences of oppression, from African Americans, Latinos, and other minorities in the United States, to the Romà in Europe, the first nations of North America, and the indigenous communities of South America and the Pacific Islands.

Ethnic studies, which is closely related to postcolonial theory, puts at the center of analysis the role that race and ethnicity as social constructs play in defining social locations and determining opportunities. Race and ethnicity are not just variables to be considered and analyzed in the research process; they are the experiential lens that filters the study of culture by and for people who experience themselves as members of various racial or ethnic groups[25] — including, more recently, Whiteness as a racial experience.[26] Ethnic studies focuses on race and ethnicity as sociopolitical mobilizing principles that can empower racial and ethnic groups to end oppression. The recent institutionalization of ethnic studies, while counter to the anti-academic roots of cultural studies, represents an important victory in the struggles of ethnic minorities for recognition on many university campuses.[27] Still, heated debates over multiculturalism, which has its roots in ethnic studies, continue to rage in contemporary educational discourse.[28]

Popular culture has also been an important area of inquiry in social science since critical theorists like Horkheimer, Adorno, and Benjamin first drew their attention to the culture industry.[29] Drawing from and challenging their early work, the study of popular culture has focused on how different groups within various social categories develop patterns in the process of both consuming and producing symbolic culture, in particular the kinds of symbolic culture that emerge at the level of mass consumption.[30] The study of popular culture in education has developed slowly, triggered primarily by the interest in the different kinds of cultures and engagements with mass media that students bring to their education.[31]

In his chapter in Part Three, which was first published in the *Harvard Educational Review* in 1994,[32] Henry Giroux invites educational researchers and cultural theorists to realize the enormous potential that each of their fields offers for the expansion of the other. This essay has become one of the most widely cited in the burgeoning study of popular culture within education. Yet, much of the most exciting and engaging work in popular culture is happening within cultural studies programs, far away from schools of education because, as Giroux suggests, these institutions have been slow to embrace the tremendous opportunities that the study of popular culture offers. Giroux calls for educators to be "informed by [the] emphasis on popular culture as a terrain of significant political and pedagogical importance."[33] Central to the development of this idea has been the work of Paul Willis,[34] who offers an overview and analysis of his contributions to the study of youth culture over the past twenty-five years in the concluding chapter of this book.

Despite almost three decades of development and expansion, cultural studies remains an elusive and roguish field of inquiry. Some of the authors in this collection may even raise questions about their inclusion in a book about "cultural studies." But their reservations would actually confirm the trajectory of this intellectual endeavor over these thirty years, one filled with struggles over boundaries, ambivalence about status and legitimacy, and deliberate uncertainty about what exactly constitutes cultural studies. While we do not seek to define, it is our hope that the chapters in this book and the brief introductions that frame each section will provide an entry into the theoretical discourses and areas of study encompassed here. We hope that readers who are new to these important approaches to the study of education will be able to explore areas of interest in depth, and gain some sense of direction and clarity about the aims, purposes, and methods that drive the various approaches to cultural studies of education.

Rubén A. Gaztambide-Fernández
Heather A. Harding
Tere Sordé-Martí
Editors

Notes

1. The edited volumes by Simon During, ed., *The Cultural Studies Reader* (London: Routledge, 1999) and Larry Grossberg, Cary Nelson, and Paula Treichler, eds., *Cutural Studies* (New York: Routledge, 1992) offer excellent collections of essays that have been fundamental to the development of the field and a much more thorough introduction than we can provide in this limited space.

2. Richard Hoggart, *The Uses of Literacy: Aspects of Working-Class Life with Special References to Publications and Entertainments* (London: Chatto and Windus, 1957); E. P. Thompson, *The Making of the English Working Class* (London: Gollancz, 1963); Raymond Williams, *Culture and Society: 1780 / 1950* (New York: Columbia University Press, 1958); Raymond Williams, *The Long Revolution* (New York: Columbia University Press, 1961); Raymond Williams, *Marxism and Literature* (Oxford, Eng.: Oxford University Press, 1977).

3. The work of Italian Marxist scholar Antonio Gramsci has been particularly influential in the development of cultural studies. See especially Antonio Gramsci, *Selections from Cultural Writings* (Cambridge, MA: Harvard University Press, 1985); Antonio Gramsci, *Selections from the Prison Notebooks,* trans. Quintin Hoare and Geoffrey Nowell Smith (New York: International, 1971).

4. A term coined by Jim McGuigan, *Cultural Populism* (London: Routledge, 1992).

5. For an excellent historical overview of the development of cultural studies, see Jeffrey Alexander, "Analytic Debates: Understanding the Relative Autonomy of Culture," in *Culture and Society: Contemporary Debates*, ed. Jeffrey Alexander and Steven Seidman (London: Cambridge University Press, 1990). For an analysis of the roots of cultural theory, see Jere Paul Surber, *Culture and Critique: An Introduction to the Critical Discourses of Cultural Studies* (Boulder, CO: Westview Press, 1998).

6. David Held, *Introduction to Critical Theory: Horkheimer to Habermas* (Berkley: University of California Press, 1980); Jay Martin, *The Dialectical Imagination: A History of the Frankfurt School and the Institute of Social Research* (Berkeley: University of California Press, 1996).

7. See, for example, Max Horkheimer and Theodor W. Adorno, *Dialectic of Enlightenment,* trans. John Cumming (New York: Continuum, 2001).

8. See, for instance, Jacques Derrida, *A Derrida Reader* (New York: Columbia University Press, 1991); Michel Foucault, *Discipline and Punish: The Birth of the Prison,* trans. A. Sheridan (New York: Vintage, 1979); Michel Foucault, "What Is an Author?" in *Language, Countermemory, Practice: Selected Essays and Interviews by Michel Foucault,* ed. Donald F. Bouchard (Ithaca, NY: Cornell University Press, 1977). See also the introduction to Part One of this volume for discussion of postmodernism.

9. Paul Gilroy, Lawrence Grossberg, and Angela McRobbie, eds., *Without Guarantees: In Honour of Stuart Hall* (New York: Verso, 2000); Grossberg et al., *Cutural Studies.*

10. These authors draw heavily on the literary theory of such authors as Mikhail M. Bakhtin, *The Dialogic Imagination,* trans. Caryl Emerson and Michael Holquist (Austin: University of Texas Press, 1981); Julia Kristeva, *The Kristeva Reader* (New York: Columbia University Press, 1986); Williams, *Marxism and Literature.* See, for example, Stuart Hall and Tony Jefferson, eds., *Resistance through Ritual: Youth Subcultures in Post-War Britain* (London: Unwin Hyman, 1989); Dick Hebdige, *Subculture: The Meaning of Style* (London: Methuen & Co., 1979); Glenn Hudak, "The 'Sound' Identity: Music-Making and Schooling," in *Sound Identities: Popular Music and the Cultural Politics of Education,* ed. Cameron McCarthy et al. (New York: Peter Lang, 1999).

11. See, for example, Andy Bennett, *Popular Music and Youth Culture: Music, Identity and Place* (New York: St. Martin's Press, 2000); David Buckingham, *After the Death of Childhood: Growing Up in the Age of Electronic Media* (Cambridge, Eng.: Polity Press, 2000); Nadine Dolby, *Constructing Race: Youth, Identity, and Popular Culture in South Africa* (Albany: State University of New York Press, 2001); Anne Haas Dyson, *Writing Superheroes: Contemporary Childhood, Popular Culture, and Classroom Literacy* (New York: Teacher's College Press, 1997); Sunaina Marr Maira, *Desis in the House: Indian American Youth Culture in New York City* (Philadelphia: Temple University Press, 2002); Cameron McCarthy et al., eds., *Sound Identities: Popular Music and the Cultural Politics of Education* (New York: Peter Lang, 1999); Janice Radway, *Reading the Romance: Women, Patriarchy, and Popular Literature* (Chapel Hill: University of North Carolina Press, 1991); John Springhall, *Youth, Popular Culture, and Moral Panics: Penny Gaffs to Gangsta-Rap, 1830–1996* (New York: St. Martin's Press, 1998); Paul Willis, *Common Culture: Symbolic Work at Play in the Everyday Cultures of the Young* (Boulder, CO: Westview Press, 1990); Paul Willis, "Labor Power, Culture and the Cultural Commodity," in *Critical Education in the New Information Age,* ed. Manuel Castells et al. (Lanham, MD: Rowman & Littlefield, 1999); Paul Willis, *Learning to Labour: How Working Class Kids Get Working Class Jobs* (Farnborough, Eng.: Saxon House, 1977).

12. This work responded critically to Theodor Adorno's assessment of "the culture industry." Theodor W. Adorno, *The Culture Industry: Selected Essays on Mass Culture* (London: Routledge, 1991). See, for example, Jody Berland, "Angels Dancing: Cultural Technologies and the Production of Space," in *Cultural Studies,* ed. Larry Grossberg, Cary Nelson, and Paula Treichler (New York: Routledge, 1992); Simon Frith, *Performing Rites: On the Values of Popular Music* (Cambridge, MA: Harvard University Press, 1996); Keith Negus, *Popular Music in Theory: An Introduction* (Hanover, NH: Wesleyan University Press, 1996); Roy Shuker, *Understanding Popular Music* (London: Routledge, 1994).

13. Paul Gilroy, *The Black Atlantic: Modernity and Double Consciousness* (Cambridge, MA: Harvard University Press, 1993); Paul Gilroy, *"There Ain't No Black in the Union Jack": The Cultural Politics of Race and Nation* (London: Hutchinson, 1987); Angela McRobbie, ed., *Gender and Generation* (Hampshire, Eng.: Macmillan, 1984); Radway, *Reading the Romance.*

14. See, for example, Dolby, *Constructing Race;* Maira, *Desis in the House;* McCarthy et al., *Sound Identities.*

15. Henry A. Giroux and Patrick Shannon, eds., *Education and Cultural Studies: Toward a Performative Practice* (New York: Routledge, 1997).

16. For a discussion of cultural studies from a feminist perspective, see the essays in Kathleen Weiler, ed., *Feminist Engagements: Reading, Resisting, and Revisioning Male Theorists in Education and Cultural Studies* (New York: Routledge, 2001).

17. See, for example, Madeleine Arnot, *Reproducing Gender? Essays on Educational Theory and Feminist Politics* (London: Routledge, 2002); McRobbie, *Gender and Generation;* Weiler, *Feminist Engagements.*

18. For an analysis of the "feminization" of teaching, see Madeleine Grumet, *Bitter Milk: Women and Teaching* (Amherst: University of Massachusetts Press, 1988).

19. See William Pinar, ed., *Queer Theory in Education* (Mahwah, NJ: Lawrence Erlbaum, 1998).

20. For an introduction to this line of analysis, see Monique Wittig, "The Straight Mind," in *Critical Theory: A Reader,* ed. Douglas Tallack (New York: Harvester Wheatsheaf, 1995).

21. James T. Sears and Debbie Epstein, eds., *A Dangerous Knowing: Sexuality, Pedagogy and Popular Culture* (London: Cassell, 1999); Peter Taubman, "Gender and Curriculum: Discourse and the Politics of Sexuality," *Journal of Curriculum Theorizing* 4, No. 1 (1982), 12–87.

22. Frantz Fanon, *Black Skin, White Masks,* trans. Charles Lam Markman (New York: Grove Press, 1967); Frantz Fanon, *The Wretched of the Earth,* trans. Constance Farrington (New York: Grove Press, 1963). See also Albert Memmi, *The Colonizer and the Colonized,* trans. Howard Greenfeld (Boston: Beacon Press, 1991).

23. Michael Hardt and Antonio Negri, *Empire* (Cambridge, MA: Harvard University Press, 2000).

24. See the essays in Edward Said, *Reflections on Exile and Other Essays* (Cambridge, MA: Harvard University Press, 2000). See also Homi Bhabha, *The Location of Culture* (London: Routledge, 1997); Homi Bhabha, ed., *Nation and Narration* (London: Routledge, 1990); Edward Said, *Orientalism* (New York: Pantheon Books, 1978). In education, the work of Cameron McCarthy has been especially important. See Cameron McCarthy, *The Uses of Culture: Education and the Limits of Ethnic Affiliation* (New York: Routledge, 1998).

25. Chela Sandoval, *Methodology of the Oppressed* (Minneapolis: University of Minnesota Press, 2000); Linda Tuhiwai Smith, *Decolonizing Methodologies: Research and Indigenous Peoples* (London: Zed Books, 1999); Sofía Villenas, "The Colonizer /Colonized Chicana Ethnographer: Identity Marginalization, and Co-Optation in the Field," *Harvard Educational Review* 66 (1996), 711–731. Also see the chapter by Dolores Delgado Bernal in this volume.

26. Michelle Fine, Christine Sleeter, and Lois Weis, eds., *Off White: Readings on Race, Power, and Society* (New York: Routledge, 1997).

27. Robert Rhoads, *Freedom's Web: Student Activism in an Age of Cultural Diversity* (Baltimore: Johns Hopkins University Press, 1998); David Yamane, *Student Movements for Multiculturalism* (Baltimore: Johns Hopkins University Press, 2001).

28. Amy Binder, "Friend and Foe: Boundary Work and Collective Identity in the Afrocentric and Multicultural Curriculum Movements in American Public Education," in *The Cultural Territories of Race: Black and White Boundaries,* ed. Michèle Lamont (Chicago: University of Chicago Press, 1999); Cameron McCarthy, "After the Canon: Knowledge and Ideological Representation in the Multicultural Discourse on Curriculum Reform," in *Race, Identity, and Representation in Education,* ed. Cameron McCarthy and Warren Crichlow (New York: Routledge, 1993). See also other chapters in section three of Cameron McCarthy and Warren Crichlow, eds., *Race, Identity, and Representation in Education* (New York: Routledge, 1993). The chapter by McCarthy in this volume discusses and challenges both sides of this debate.

29. Theodor W. Adorno, "Cultural Criticism and Society," in *Critical Theory: A Reader,* ed. Douglas Tallack (New York: Harvester Wheatsheaf, 1995), Adorno, *The Culture Industry;* Horkheimer and Adorno, *Dialectic of Enlightenment.* In "The Work of Art in the Age of Mechanical Reproduction," Walter Benjamin offers a more nuanced and less pessimistic view and has been extremely influential in the study of contemporary art and popular culture. In *Illuminations: Walter Benjamin Essays and Reflections,* ed. Hannah Arendt (New York: Schocken Books, 1968)

30. See, for example, Manuel Castells et al., *Critical Education in the New Information Age* (Lanham, MD: Rowman & Littlefield, 1999); Willis, *Common Culture.*

31. See the Special Issue on Popular Culture and Education published by the *Harvard Educational Review* 73 (2003) for a contemporary view of this growing field of inquiry. See also Toby Daspit and John A. Weaver, eds., *Popular Culture and Critical Pedagogy: Reading, Constructing, Connecting* (New York: Garland, 1999).

32. Henry A. Giroux, "Doing Cultural Studies: Youth and the Challenge of Pedagogy," *Harvard Educational Review* 64 (1994).

33. Giroux, "Doing Cultural Studies."

34. Willis, *Common Culture;* Willis, *Learning to Labour.*

PART ONE

Theoretical Context:
Debating (Post)modernism

INTRODUCTION

Theoretical Context:
Debating (Post)modernism

Rationality, objectivity, universality, and the capacity for human progress — concepts that are central to the idea of modernity as it emerged from the Enlightenment — have been the object of rich intellectual exchange in the last half-century. Theorists associated with postmodernism argue that these ideas have run out of substance, as the complexities of contemporary society and culture have challenged the basic assumptions on which these concepts are built.[1] But while postmodern theorists argue that modernity has come to an end, others suggest that it still has much to offer as they call for a reorientation of its basic premises.[2] Despite their differences, both theoretical camps have challenged the basic elements and definitions on which traditional science, including educational research, is grounded. The controversies around these basic elements frame the context in which cultural studies emerged as an academic field and its relationship to education scholarship. It would be impossible to escape this complex theoretical labyrinth upon entering cultural studies. The three articles in Part One introduce some of these debates and offer a glimpse of the dense theoretical maze that informs the other three parts of this volume.

Since the publication of Jean-Francois Lyotard's *The Postmodern Condition*, the attacks on modernity formulated from the earlier works of Nietzsche and Heiddeger became known as postmodern. Postmodern theories took as their primary target the metanarratives that characterized the modern views of humanity, namely, that humanity is a coherent whole with a linear history, progressing toward an ever-improving social order based on the accumulation of knowledge about nature and society through objective, scientific methods. Postmodernism questioned modernity's basic premises by arguing that these narratives were simply a collection of tools for maintaining a hegemonic status quo. Some postmodern theorists propose irrationality, relativism, and chaos as alternatives to the modernist view of reality, suggesting that there is no such thing as universal laws of truth.[3] Most relevant to the field of cultural studies has been the proposition, drawn mostly from the work of Michel Foucault,[4] that power is a central force behind the production of scientific knowledge, and that behind any claim to truth, knowledge, and morality are various relations of domination. From this perspective, modernist views of human emancipation are seen by postmodernists as naïve and self-defeating. Drawing on this view of power, many postmodern theorists have turned away from traditional science and toward cultural production as the site where power dynamics are enforced and the illusion of a democratic society is constructed.[5] At the same time, some postmodern theorists see culture and cultural work (including research as a form of cultural practice, as presented in Patti Lather's chapter)[6] as essential in struggles for equity and freedom.[7]

Despite the severe attacks from postmodern theorists, some scholars have sought to recuperate and reorient the project of modernity. Critical theorists like Jürgen Habermas defend the original premises of modernity, including the possibility of achieving justice, equality, and freedom through the communicative nature of the human "lifeworld," and have called for the recuperation of instrumental rationality as a form of seeking truth and freedom.[8] Anthony Giddens offers a reconceptualization of social change that accounts for both the reproductive force of social structures and the processes of resistance of social actors.[9] The capacity for individuals and social movements to work toward freedom from social oppression through the reflexive use of reason is at the heart of this amended modernity, as is the importance of understanding culture as a site for the formation of a democratic civil society.[10] While the three chapters in this section do not represent the entire range of theoretical debates, they do discuss, directly or indirectly, the major issues introduced above and represent differing positions. Patti Lather and Gary Thomas are aligned with postmodern theory, and Ramón Flecha presents a modernist view through the lens of communicative action, offering a good introduction to this view of modernity.

Gary Thomas exemplifies the postmodern challenge to the stability of basic premises in modern science and advocates a relativist approach. He starts his chapter by confronting the multiple and sometimes contradictory uses and definitions of theory. Thomas questions the power that theory has over educational research, even the need for it, and proposes a more anarchic approach to scientific production. According to Thomas, when ideas develop into complex theoretical frameworks, they constrain public access and creativity of thought, ignoring alternative explanations and keeping them on the margins. Given the centrality of theory in debates about culture and society, Thomas offers a unique entrance by challenging the function of this defining feature.

Research is another central aspect of both cultural and educational studies. A range of methodological approaches have developed in both fields that draw on various traditions from the social and natural sciences, as well as the humanities. In the second chapter of Part Two, feminist and postmodern theorist Patti Lather articulates a view of research methodology that takes as its primary concern the radical transformation of society through the active engagement of participants in the research process. Lather defines "research as praxis" in terms of empowerment, reciprocity, and a dialectic process of theory-building in which research "subjects" are active participants. Recognizing the "failure to probe the methodological implications of critical theory," Lather frames her discussion in the context and the language of contemporary debates about the relationship between research, politics, and social change. As a solid and rigorous alternative to the scientistic paradigm that dominates educational research today, the view of "research as praxis" invites education scholars to consider the "catalytic validity" of their work and the extent to which it works to improve rather than reproduce participants' living conditions.

To conclude this section, European sociologist Ramón Flecha offers an analysis of how particular theoretical perspectives end up reproducing old and producing new forms of racism, particularly in educational practice. Reflecting on the changing multicultural reality of Europe, Flecha offers a theoretical framework that identifies both modern and postmodern forms of racism. In defining their main features, Flecha makes connections between the two philosophical traditions and these different kinds of racism. According to Flecha, while educators tried to confront modern racism with a postmodern view, the latter was not capable of mitigating the former, and actually reinforced new forms of racism. Drawing on Habermas,[11] Flecha calls for a dialogic approach to fight both forms of racism.

The debates between modernists and postmodernists continue to rage. These debates underlie the various theoretical frameworks and approaches to the study of culture and education that inform the rest of the chapters in this book. It is therefore crucial to be somewhat familiar with some of the terms of the debates, many of which will emerge throughout the rest of the book. We encourage readers to consult some of the original works that sparked these important intellectual debates, many of which are cited in the notes to this introduction, in order to get a more complete view of the issues and arguments and to develop new ideas.

Notes

1. Jacques Derrida, *A Derrida Reader* (New York: Columbia University Press, 1991); Michel Foucault, *Power/Knowledge: Selected Interviews and Other Writings* (New York: Pantheon Books, 1980); Jean-François Lyotard, *The Postmodern Condition: A Report on Knowledge*, trans. Geoff Bennington and Brian Massumi (Minneapolis: University of Minnesota Press, 1984). See also the collection of essays and excerpts in Thomas Docherty, ed., *Postmodernism: A Reader* (New York: Columbia University Press, 1993).
2. Fundamental in this tradition are the works of Ulrich Beck, ed., *The Reinvention of Politics: Rethinking Moderninty in the Global Social Order* (Cambridge, Eng.: Polity Press, 1997)' Ramón Flecha, Jésus Gomez Alonso, and Lidia Puigvert, eds., *Contemporary Sociological Theory* (New York: Peter Lang, 2003); Anthony T. Giddens and Jonathan H. Turner, eds., *Social Theory Today* (Stanford, CA: Stanford University Press, 1987); Jürgen Habermas, *The Theory of Communicative Action, Vol. 1: Reason and the Rationalization of Society* (Boston: Beacon Press, 1984).
3. Paul Feyerabend, *Against Method* (London: Verso, 1993).
4. Michel Foucault, *Language, Counter-Memory, Practice: Selected Essays and Interviews by Michel Foucault*, trans. Donald F. Bouchard and Sherry Simon (Ithaca, NY: Cornell University Press, 1977); Foucault, *Power/Knowledge*.
5. Jean Baudrillard, *The Gulf War Did Not Take Place* (Bloomington: Indiana University Press, 1995); Jean Baudrillard, *Simulacra and Simulation*, trans. Sheila Faria Glaser (Ann Arbor: University of Michigan Press, 1994).
6. See also her expansion of this view of research in Patti Lather, *Getting Smart: Feminist Research and Pedagogy with/in the Postmodern* (New York/ London: Routledge, 1991).
7. See the analysis of postmodernism as the outgrowth of capitalism in Frederic Jameson, *Postmodernism, or, the Cultural Logic of Late Capitalism* (Durham, NC: Duke University Press, 1991).
8. Habermas, *Communicative Action;* Jürgen Habermas, *The Theory of Communicative Action, Vol. 2: Lifeworld and System, a Critique of Functionalist Reason* (Boston, MA: Beacon Press, 1987).
9. Giddens and Turner, *Social Theory Today.*
10. Manuel Castells et al., *Critical Education in the New Information Age* (Lanham, MD: Rowman & Littlefield, 1999).
11. Habermas, *Communicative Action.*

What's the Use of Theory?

GARY THOMAS

Theory holds a central place in educational inquiry. Tutors exhort students to embed their work in it; grant-giving bodies demand that research proposals be contextualized in it; conferences on educational research assert and reassert its importance; complete journals are devoted to its discussion. Some commentators (such as Garrison, 1988) have even claimed that what they call "atheoretical" research in education is impossible. Nontheoretical research seems a taboo for the research community in education.

The allure of theory is puzzling, given that a developing theme of contemporary commentary on methods of inquiry has concerned theory's fragility, not its utility. Despite the emergence of strong anti-theoretical strands in postmodern thought, the reputation of theory in education persists with its lustre untarnished. My aim in this article is therefore to examine the tenacity with which education adheres to theory.

I seek reasons for this tenacity in the absence of a community language system by which educational researchers and academics understand theory; the word has a multiplicity of meanings popularly constructed for it. My thesis is that lack of definition has resulted in "theory" coming loosely to denote, simply, intellectual endeavor. Many kinds of thinking and heuristics have come to be called theory. But why should they be entitled to this guise? It is like wanting to call a pig a cat. A cat certainly is a more elegant animal than a pig, but this is no reason to call one's pig a cat. The point I try to make in this article is that theory, if it is to be used and defended seriously, cannot describe just any kind of intellectual endeavor.

I contend that the allure of theory — and the desire of educationists to call their ideas "theory" — rests historically on the success of theory in other fields.[1] It was from this success that theory drew its epistemological legitimacy. Many educationists appeared to have at the back of their minds the idea that theory represented the clearest distillation of intellectual endeavor, the conceptual and epistemological cream of the various disciplines from which it had been borrowed. But my argument is that these successes provide no good reason for contemporary education's romance with theory. The domains in which theory has been useful find no congruence in education. Indeed, those domains in which theory is valuable are more limited than one might imagine. I plead here for more methodological anarchy, just as Feyerabend (1993), the iconoclastic philosopher of science, pleaded for in scientific research.

Harvard Educational Review Vol. 67 No. 1 Spring 1997

Theory's acquired potency for bestowing academic legitimacy is troublesome, for it means that particular kinds of endeavor in educational inquiry are reinforced and promulgated, while the legitimacy of atheoretical kinds is questioned or belittled.[2] Educational inquiry is thus distorted; within educational research, strange interstices are created by the hegemony of theory. I argue that theory of any kind is thus a force for conservatism, for stabilizing the status quo through the circumscription of thought within a hermetic set of rules, procedures, and methods. Seen in this way, theory — far from being emancipatory as some have claimed (e.g., Carr, 1995) or a vehicle for "thinking otherwise" (Ball, 1995) — is in fact an instrument for reinforcing an existing set of practices and methods in education.

This article is divided into several parts. I first look at the problem of the meaning of theory in education by outlining a number of ways in which the word is used, and how ideas about theory are thereby confused; in particular, the distinction between grand theory and personal theory is drawn.[3] I then suggest that theory circumscribes methods of thinking about educational problems and that it inhibits creativity among researchers, policymakers, and teachers. I make this case both for personal theory and for grand theory, and give case studies of theory-construction and theory-use that have influenced practice in education. I finally make a case for "ad hocery" rather than theory, arguing that creativity and progress are rarely the fruit of theory and more often the fruit of anarchy in thought.

What Is Theory in Education?

Debate about theory is rarely accompanied by any discussion about its meaning. Any superficial examination (or, indeed, detailed examination) of educational literature discloses little consensus about the meaning of theory, as I shall show. There is no bond between theory and the constellation of meanings it has acquired. The reader or listener, when encountering the word, is forced to guess what is signified by the word through the context in which it is applied.

But the problem of the reader or listener is different from that facing the reader who has to interpret the meaning of red in reading about a red rose or a red herring. There, context tells the reader or listener something unequivocal. Yet context helps little when we find "theoretical" in educational discourse: a theoretical article has no a priori distinction from a theoretical view, a theoretical background, or a theoretical position. I have no way of knowing what the speaker intends to convey when the signifier "theoretical" is used in any of these contexts. The relation of signifier to signified is dangerously unstable, given the importance attached to theory in education. It is this relation I shall attempt to disentangle in the first part of this article.

Defining theory is a problem and, given the significance attached to it, this is serious, since the message from commentators such as Ball (1995) is that while theory is essential, we must be discriminating in our selection of it. "Will any theory do?" he asks, and answers himself emphatically, "I think not!" warning against "theory by numbers" (p. 268). Others have made similar warnings: the historian Namier (1955) has dismissed general social theories as "flapdoodle."

This is confusing for students of education, for education abuts a range of different kinds of theory: learning theory, attribution theory, Freudian theory, Rawls's theory of justice, critical theory, or Marxist theory, to name a few. Even chaos theory is taken by LeCompte (1994) to be a valid source from which to draw. Sociologists such as Glaser and Strauss (1967), who have questioned the traditional development of theory and its uses, have nonetheless shown a loyalty to the notion of theory, and have attempted to develop Grounded Theory. More recently, students of education have been encouraged to develop their own personal or practical theories (e.g., Carr, 1995; McIntyre, 1995).

To begin to understand how students of education might divine the meaning of theory, given these many and varied usages, one can consult a popular textbook on educational research. Cohen and Manion's (1989) textbook claims that while theories in the natural sciences "are characterized by a high degree of elegance and sophistication," educational theory is "only at the early stages of formulation and . . . thus characterized by great unevenness" (pp. 15–16).

These comments, if unpacked, exaggerate rather than attenuate the definitional burden that I set out to lighten. The opposition of "elegance and sophistication" with "unevenness" betrays the expectations of the writers about the nature of theory. Indeed, the positing of this opposition falls into the trap of what Medawar (1974) has called "poetism," namely, the adoption of a theory because of its elegance, attractiveness, or romantic appeal.[4] Theory in its purest form, they seem to be saying, should be precise and succinct, like scientific theory. Cohen and Manion's (1989) placing of "thus characterized" between "only at the early stages of formulation" and "unevenness" reveals their judgment that unevenness is undesirable. Unevenness will with time, they appear to say, be ironed out. The conclusion to be drawn by the reader is that evenness in theory — and by extension smoothness and elegance — is desirable.

"Unevenness" perhaps is serving as a euphemism for confusion, which makes itself manifest in two definitions of theory Cohen and Manion offer. The first, from Kerlinger (1970), says that theory is "a set of interrelated constructs, definitions, and propositions that presents a systematic view of phenomena by specifying relations among variables, with the purpose of explaining and predicting the phenomena" (Cohen & Manion, 1989, p. 15). The other, from Mouly (1978), says that "theory is a convenience — a necessity, really — organizing a whole slough of facts, laws, concepts, constructs, principles into a meaningful and manageable form"(Mouly, 1978, p. 15). This latter is similar to O'Connor's "a set or system of rules or a collection of precepts which guide or control actions of various kinds," quoted by Hirst (1993, p. 149).

Now, the definitions of Kerlinger on the one side and Mouly and O'Connor on the other do not simply lack congruence. Rather, they describe intellectual processes as different as chalk and cheese. The first acknowledges theory's traditionally held purposes of explanation and prediction in science, while the latter could be said to take a toolshed view: theory is a repository, a way of tidying the various bodies of knowledge and analytical instruments that might be used in education.

However, it is true to say that each definition does provide a satisfactory descriptive account of a way in which the word "theory" is sometimes used in education. If this is the case, there is a serious problem. "Theory" as a word must be one thing or another. It cannot — if it is to be used seriously to describe a particular kind of intellectual construction in education — have two or more meanings, unless the context in which it is used can universally and unequivocally distinguish those meanings. If we are to understand what "pipe" means, the word must refer only to that class of objects normally thought of as pipes; it must not also refer to dogs, vacuum cleaners, and trees. And if "pipe" does happen to be inconvenient enough to refer, as my dictionary tells me it does, to a musical wind instrument, to a tube, or to the note of a bird, I can be confident that the context — sentence, paragraph, or longer passage — will finish the job and furnish the right meaning. I cannot be so sure with "theory." For it is my contention that the context cannot distinguish the strong colors of meaning that alter with various uses of "theory," since the users themselves are rarely aware of the meaning they intend.[5]

Indeed, the situation is far more complex than Cohen and Manion (1989) describe. The broad-ranging definitions they offer are insufficient to explain what is popularly meant by theory in education, and a further disentangling of meanings is necessary. In another textbook definition, Bryman and Cramer (1994) state: "Theories in the social sciences can vary between abstract general approaches (such as functionalism) and fairly low-level theories to explain specific phenomena (such as voting behaviour, delinquency, aggressiveness)" (p. 2). Note the opposition of adjectives such as "abstract" and "low-level," and compare this to the opposition of "elegance" with "unevenness" in Cohen and Manion's definition. There seems to be the feeling that theories that are to be awarded high marks are those that are refined, parsimonious, elegant, and capable of wide application. On the other hand, theories that still need a bit of work done on them are those that are only capable of applicability in a narrow range of cases.

However, an examination of textbook definitions does not complete a deconstruction of popular meaning. There is a widely held view, for instance, that theory is anything that isn't practice; a simple theory-practice continuum is implied. Theory is at one end of the continuum; practice is at the other. When theory is used as the opposite of practice, it seems to be used to convey not specific theories, such as child development theory or Marxist theory, but, more generally, book-learning and speculation. This undifferentiated nexus of mental activities appears to be put forward as the opposite of doing and learning on the job. The notion is a powerful one, shared by academics. Skinner (1990), for example, even suggests that those whom he calls the "anti-theorists" of postmodernism are in fact "the grandest theorists of current practice."[6] This perplexing assertion is supported by no more than the fact that these individuals (Wittgenstein, Feyerabend, Foucault, Derrida) have done a lot of critical thinking, and thinking has apparently come to be congruent with theorizing. If "theory" can mean any kind of intellectual endeavor (and "theorizing" any kind of thinking), then one would be forced to accept that any conjoining of words is a theoretical enterprise, and even that this article is a theoretical one.

Defenders of theory in education also take the expansive view that theory means any kind of structured reflection. Carr (1995), for example, suggests that the ambit of theory encompasses a wide range of critical activity concerned with "intellectual resources" (p. 36). The problem, he feels, is attributable to the fact that educational theory has in the past been seen as an attempt to derive practical principles from general philosophical beliefs, and more recently to a Hirstian belief that educational theory should draw on various forms of knowledge, particularly history, philosophy, and the social sciences. Carr says that this is mistaken — that educational theory does not have to conform to conventional criteria of academic legitimacy, but should rather demonstrate "a capacity to explore a particular range of problems in a systematic and rigorous manner" (p. 32). In dismissing the relevance and utility of traditional notions of theory, there seems to be the attempt here to rescue the word "theory" from its past and apply it to simple critical reflection and thinking. But why do this when "theory" is so epistemologically encumbered? Why not use simpler terms that are less semantically loaded?

The foregoing only begins to unravel the multiple meanings of theory in educational discourse. A useful overview is provided by Chambers (1992), who asserts that he can distinguish no fewer than nine meanings for the word. First, he says, there is theory contrasted with fact; here theory is used simply to mean a hunch, a loose explanatory idea. Second, there is theory as the opposite of practice, as I described earlier. Third, theory may be used to mean evolving explanation; he gives Bruner's Theory of Instruction as an example. What is meant here is an accumulating body of knowledge that, in contrast to scientific theory, has become more diffuse (not more precise and succinct) as it has tried to accommodate more facts. Bannister and Fransella (1986) liken such theories to stalactitic growths that have accumulated over the years. This kind of theory is closest to the grand theory to which Wright Mills (1959) objected.

Fourth, he identifies practical theory, meaning reflective practice; this is probably what Carr (1995) refers to above, and what Hirst (1993) refers to when he says, "Any adequate account of educational theory must, I now consider, reject more firmly than I once saw certain central tenets of rationalism in favour of a more complex theory of rational action" (p. 152).

Fifth, theory is taken to have a cluster of meanings surrounding the idea of a hypothesis, model, or heuristic. Sixth, theory may mean presupposition: a set of orienting principles or epistemological antecedent assumptions. Seventh, Chambers suggests that people may be talking about what he calls normative theory, a clearly developed argument that has evolved under the pressure of rigorous criticism; he gives Rousseau's individualism as an example. Eighth, there is empiricist theory, which seems to be the equivalent of craft knowledge, or the accumulation of technical knowledge through doing (see Naughton, 1981, for a discussion of craft knowledge). Last, there is scientific theory, the most complex of all, comprising interrelated sets of propositions, and rational and empirical connections between concepts.

Chambers's codification is interesting as an unusually detailed acknowledgment of the diversity of uses of the word "theory" in education, and it is valuable as such. However, before proceeding with his list some refinement is necessary: whether certain of the categories are legitimate descriptions of usage is open to question, and he misses one important category.

For my purposes here, I shall query several of his categories, conflate others, and add one. The first and fifth uses he identifies — theory as hunch and theory as hypothesis — may be conflated as looser and tighter versions of the same notion. The third and seventh uses — theory as evolving explanation, and normative theory — may also be conflated.

Grounded theory (Glaser & Strauss, 1967), which does not find a neat fit in any of the above categories, needs to be added as a notion now widely drawn upon in educational research. Its omission is surprising, given that it represents a distinguished inductivist position stretching back to John Stuart Mill and beyond. The central difference between grounded theory and other kinds of intellectual endeavor labeled theory is the temporal placing of the intellectual organization; in most theorizing one might say that presupposition exists, while what occurs in grounded theory might be called "postsupposition" and an iterative visiting of the data to refine the theory.

If the foregoing critique of Chambers's typology is accepted, four broad uses of theory in education are left remaining. Those four uses are:

1. Theory as the opposite of practice. Theory is thinking and reflecting (as opposed to doing). This encompasses personal theory, Carr's (1995) notion of structured reflection, Hirst's (1993) rational action (both referred to above), and McIntyre's (1995) practical theorizing.
2. Theory as hypothesis. Theory is an idea that may be followed up, embracing looser or tighter hypothesizing, modeling, heuristics, and thought experiments (Hoffman, 1973). Grounded theory may be taken to be the same idea in reverse: the distillation of explanatory notions from data.
3. Theory as developing explanation. This category embraces the broadening bodies of knowledge developing in particular fields, which may or may not have come to be associated with labels such as learning theory, management theory, or Piagetian theory.
4. Scientific theory. In line with the expectations of most rationalist epistemologists, theory here exists as ideas formally expressed in a series of statements. It is part of the process of normal science critically described by Kuhn (1970). Involved in it is Popper's (1968, 1969) notion of radical theory developed in such a way that it is falsifiable.[7]

Perhaps the clearest description of common usage comes if these four categories are further conflated to form two separate continua. One of these continua represents theory versus practice (see Fig. 1), where at the left extreme, theory in its purest form is an elegant description of knowledge. Incorporated along the length of this continuum is the notion of the hunch or hypothesis, which has crystallized out of practical experience; at the other end of the continuum, at the right, is practice or doing.

Thus, at the far left of the continuum (enter the rationalist epistemologists), theory exists in the form of ideas formally expressed in a series of statements, (as, for instance, in Kelly's Construct Theory).[8] Toward the center-left, and less formal, there may be theories such as attribution theory that seek to account for behavior under an overarching idea (that idea in attribution theory being the dispositional-situational divide). Toward the center, theory may be used to mean an idea — based on observation and open to being tested — about some aspect of the way the world works. Here the word is used in the loosest sense (as it might be used in action research, or in practical theory), almost as an alternative to "hypothesis." To the right of the line would be practical knowledge in its various forms: craft knowledge, apprenticeship, and "learning by Nellie," learning on the job.

The other continuum may be described as theory as plural versus theory as singular. Certain theories are, in fact, single formally stated ideas or loosely stated hypotheses. Or they may have the precise, succinct character of scientific theory. The common element in these diverse notions is that of singularity. At the other end of the extreme, theory in education may comprise broadening bodies of knowledge or collations of cognate knowledge.

FIGURE 1

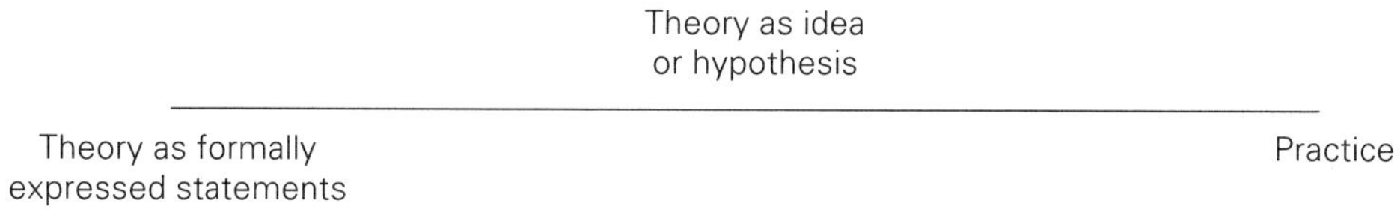

Theory as idea
or hypothesis

_____

Theory as formally   Practice
expressed statements

If these continua are now presented orthogonally, the position of various theories (and other epistemological tools with more or less right to call themselves theory) may be situated within the resulting frame (see Fig. 2).

Thus, for instance, Kelly's Construct Theory, a unitary and formal theory, might be placed in the top left corner, while half-way down and nearer the center one might place attribution theory, a reasonably tight collection of ideas with a single explanatory theme. Along the bottom left we might draw sausage shapes representing the more amorphous and ill-defined learning theory or child development theory.

This looseness — this straying along and between the continua I have described — is a cause for serious concern. If use and interpretation of the word slips arbitrarily this way and then that, its potential utility (assuming for a moment that it might have any utility) is compromised: its possible usefulness as a construct (I am thinking particularly of the newer conceptions of which Carr, 1995, and McIntyre, 1995, write) may be diluted by its association with heuristics of dubious worth. Or, as Hirst (1990) has indicated, the ambiguity that arises from lack of definition leads to any practical enterprise — any attempt at theory-practice integration — being too open-ended to be of value.

Conversely, and worse, its possible lack of utility may be camouflaged. It is one of the shibboleths of educational research that theory, and its construction, development, and testing, are valuable, if not essential. But if the morphology of theory is in-constant — if it takes on a number of shapes and hues in people's understanding — its chameleon-like nature will allow it to escape serious scrutiny.

However, perhaps the most serious problem concerning theory is its encouragement to particular kinds of thinking and to the discouragement of diversity in thought. To argue the point I shall take very different kinds of theory from my taxonomy above — personal on one side and grand on the other, both central to contemporary theorizing in education — and argue that they suffer the same problems in that they discourage a diversity of thought.

I shall return to these later. First, I wish to examine why education has come to be in such thrall to theory, and why its confidence in theoretical endeavor is misplaced.

The Problem with Theory

Although theory currently occupies a wholly new (and ill-defined) place in the affections of academics and researchers, its place at the summit of epistemological activity probably rests historically on its supposed success in science. It is as though the new disciplines — of education, psychology, and sociology — in their adolescent years suffered from a collective inferiority complex about their epistemological pedigrees, and to inoculate themselves against potential criticism sought to assume the epistemological clothes (with theory as the essential garment) of the disciplinary giants. The non-contiguity of scientific theory and educational theory (and the impossibility of emulating scientific theory in education) is discussed interestingly by Hirst (1993), Chambers (1992), and others, and I shall return to it briefly later. To spend too long now discussing the non-contiguity itself would be to distract from my main point here, which is simply to establish the genealogy of the allure of theory. My argument is that education has come to be in thrall to theory.

Being in thrall to theory means that education is preoccupied with the paraphernalia of theory and its development, and that it eschews alternative currents of thought that offer it much. While educationists have occasionally bounced up against these currents of thought and considered them cursorily, they appear to have dismissed their potential. Dismissed is perhaps too positive a word. They have sniffed at them, as a dog sniffs at a tree in the street, and have passed on uninterested.

One of those currents of thought is articulated in the work of Feyerabend, though it is an insistent theme through much twentieth-century thought on inquiry and is, surprisingly, linked with the work of Foucault, whose relevance to this discussion I examine below. I therefore first concentrate on the work of Feyerabend, but also link that work with the work of Wittgenstein, Foucault, and others who have come to be associated latterly with postmodern thought.

Feyerabend's position is not simply that theory is of no use, or that its users should be more fastidious in their verbal hygiene. It is that the trappings of theory are harmful, actively destructive of thought and progress. His field is the philosophy of science. If his arguments are true for science, how much more true are they for education and the social sciences?

Why, then, is theory harmful? The answer is that theory structures and thus constrains thought. Thought actually moves forward, Feyerabend says, by "a maze of interactions . . . [by] accidents and conjunctures and curious juxtapositions of events" (Feyerabend, 1993, p. 9). The naive and simple minded rules that methodologists use cannot hope to provide the progress for which we wish. He quotes Einstein as saying that the creative scientist must seem to the systematic epistemologist to be an "unscrupulous opportunist." Holton (1995) also draws on Einstein, saying that the essence of scientific method is in the seeking "in whatever manner is suitable, a simplified and lucid image of the world. There is no logical path, but only intuition" (p. 168). In other words, Feyerabend (1993) concludes, "the only principle that does not inhibit progress is *anything goes*" (p. 14).

Alongside Feyerabend, it is worth examining in some detail Foucault's views here. Looking at an entirely different set of issues and problems, Foucault emerges with an analysis that is directly comparable to Feyerabend's. Foucault concentrates on areas more directly akin to education, psychiatry, sociology, and economics. His conclusions, though, are remarkably similar.

"He [Foucault] rejects the traditional units of analysis and interpretation . . . as well as the postulated unities in science — theories, paradigms and research

FIGURE 2

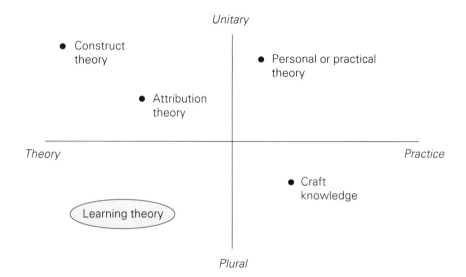

programmes" (Philp, 1990, p. 69). I have noted that theory and theorizing, if they are to mean anything, must mean more than simply intellectualizing or thinking. Clearly, thinking and reflecting are meritworthy. But theory and theorizing, in almost any of the forms I identified in the earlier typology, are about the construction of ideas into a framework. The problem with such frameworks, in looser or tighter forms — in either the mental model notion of theory or in grand theory — is that once they exist they constrain thought within their boundaries. The refreshing and enlightening aspect of Foucault's work is its homelessness, its theoretical and method-ological anarchy. In, for instance, *Discipline and Punish* (Foucault, 1985), he cuts a swathe through the theoretical understandings that have guided psychological and so-ciological conceptions of deviance.

The point I am making is not about the veracity or interest of Foucault's substan-tive position here. It is, rather, about his techniques for approaching and thinking about the problem. It is not by coincidence or by serendipity that he comes to such insights. It is by deliberately walking theoretically unarmed into the territory he ex-plores. It is, he says, the rules and constraints, the archive, of particular discourses that forces thought into stereotypical channels. Assumptions and certainties should be questioned as we try to "breach self-evidence . . . [to] construct around the singular event a 'polyhedron' of intelligibility" (Foucault, 1981, p. 4).

Douglas (1975) contrasts Foucault and Durkheim. She makes the point that for both Foucault and Durkheim, "controls, boundaries, prohibitions and privileges" were crucial. The difference between them, she says, was that whereas Durkheim ven-erated the system of controls, Foucault savagely denounced it. Her conclusion, similar to Foucault's, is that this system of controls — in which I would place theory at the apex — is a means of controlling what is permitted to count as knowledge.

Against Personal or Practical Theory

Foucault's target is surely not simply the homogenizing certainty of grand theory (which I examine in the following section), but also the system of rational ideas and accepted methodologies that lies at the root of latter-day theorizing — that loose nexus of ideas that might be called structured reflection or practical theory — in education.

If this is the case, it is ironic that Ball (1995) should draw heavily on the vocabulary of Foucault in championing contemporary notions of theory. He asserts that the role of theory should be to liberate us from the "discourses, dispositifs and epistemes from which we wish to escape" (p. 269). But Foucault would surely have denounced theory in favor of "eventalization" (see Foucault, 1981). Here again, then, is the problem of definition. Ball invokes Foucault but fails to define theory. For Ball, theory "unleashes criticism." But why call the unleashing of criticism "theory"? By calling it theory there is the problem of confusion with the host of other meanings locked into science and grand theory with which Ball and many others would quarrel.

When Foucault gave one of his too-rare interviews into his own thinking, it was clear that his distaste was for that bundle of received methods for thinking and analyzing — methodology, relevant literature, existing criticism — in which most accepted academic work, from the scientific to the structured reflective, is located.

Looking both at student essays and academic articles in education, one of the dangers of this structured reflection (as it represents theory in education) is in its conformity to the archive, its desire not to be anarchic or radical, but rather to cleave to the structure of established and respectable methodologies, literatures, rules, and procedures. One can understand this conservatism on the part of students, since one of the commonest criticisms of the student dissertation is that the work is inadequately located in theory. Students, if they are wise, do as they are told by their supervisors.

Foucault's peculiar affinity with Feyerabend lies in his predilection for anarchy in thought, for his distaste for theory. Unusual and different opinion, local and specific knowledge should be given free play. "Rupture, and discontinuity" (Philp, 1990, p. 70) should be afforded more status than the structure of theory. We should rediscover fragmented, local, and specific knowledge. Progress comes through "critique," through those who "fight, those who refuse and resist what is." It comes through "conflict and confrontation" (Foucault, 1981, p. 13). This is in contrast to the often anodyne reflections that pass as theorizing in education.

It is the placement of personal educational theory within the archive that surely makes it so often anodyne. It is thus also at the political level that personal theory or practical theory should be seen as suspect. Carr (1995) suggests in "confronting the postmodernist challenge" that educational theory can "best defend Enlightenment ideals by seeking to multiply and extend emancipatory educational practices" (p. 127). However, the view of personal theory — presumably encouraged following postgraduate training or continuing professional development — as "emancipatory" could not be further from a Foucaultian view of codified discourse defending the status quo.

Foucault is just one proponent (a brilliant one) of this view, yet the view is proffered from postmodern thinkers in a wide variety of disciplines. It is important for my argument to establish the increasing rootedness of this thought; that Feyerabend and Foucault were not merely mavericks. From the philosophical traditions of Nietzsche and Heidegger, to the contributions of figures such as Barthes and Lacan in literary and psychoanalytic thought, the broad theme is one which emphasizes the situated-ness of thought and the fragmentary nature of knowledge. The common theme is the ephemeral, and the construction of meaning by the individual. The same theme even infects contemporary science as physicists realize that the phenomena they study be-come increasingly transitory, fragile, or in other ways vulnerable in the face of obser-vation and measurement. Thus, Stewart (1990), for example, talks of "quantum inde-terminacy" in explaining the fact that events such as the decay of the radioactive atom are now held to be determined by chance, not law.

Some commentators find the general mood created by this collection of post-modern ideas too anarchic. Brooker (in Selden & Widdowson, 1993), for instance, suggests that this mood is one of "radical indeterminacy, [with] a tone of self-con-scious parodic skepticism towards previous certainties in personal, intellectual and political life" (Brooker, 1991, cited in Selden and Widdowson, 1993, p. 175). This may have given rise in education to an impression of postmodernism's "easy oppos-itionalism" (Green, 1994) — an undisciplined contrariness. It has led to a fear of ni-hilism, a fear that systematic inquiry will be rejected.

There may indeed have been some nihilism associated with the flotsam and jetsam of postmodern criticism, but this should not detract from the wholly legitimate cri-tiques of theory that such criticism implies. Smith (1995) suggests that postmodern-ism is not, or, rather, should not be, a guise for nihilism. He argues for a new vision of practice liberated from theory, a view seen also in Polanyi's "tacit knowing" (see Polanyi, 1969) and Oakeshott's (1989) views on the development of practice distinct from theory. The key theme is mistrust in procedure; we should be concerned, Oakeshott says, to consider the role of "procedures, methods and devices," and we should notice how in recent times these procedures and devices have broken loose from their subordination as a means of "finding out" and have "imposed themselves on our understanding of the transaction itself, with unfortunate consequences" (p. 63). The problem with theory — particularly theory as the word is used in education — is that it accretes these procedures and "correct" methodologies. It pays too much heed to that which is established.

Against Grand Theory:
The Cases of Piaget, Habermas, and Chomsky

The anti-theoretical thrust of late-twentieth-century thought has ostensibly been in-visible — or at least it has appeared only wraithlike — to educationists. Wright Mills (1959) warned how inimical a search for theory was to the development of imagina-tion. His warning specifically concerned the enervating effects of the search for grand theory, and I give here some support for this thesis in education by analyzing some grand theory that has influenced education significantly.

I start with Piagetian Theory because it provides good examples of many of the problems to which I have referred. In the formidable and powerful figure of Piaget one also sees a forceful construction, reinforced by the solid status of theory, of the power/knowledge nexus to which Foucault alludes and the dangerous fixity of theo-retical knowledge within an institution committed to certain ideas. One can see the process clearly in an account from Gruber and Vonèche (1977) in which the accretion of funds and power to the International Centre for the Study of Genetic Epistemology is described. One can almost hear the hushed tones in which discussion about *Le Patron* is conducted.

We should be concerned about the methods and the consequences of theory, since those consequences are in the real world of classrooms and the real lives of teachers and children. Theories are not simply the playthings of bored academics. Piaget's thinking has been responsible for many of the ideas in discovery learning and, for instance, the idea that a child had to pass through stage x before proceeding to stage y. Some of those ideas have been helpful, but the power of the theory has meant that others — which, without the legitimization and lustre of theory, would not have made it to the light of day — have been wholly destructive. (In terms of destructiveness, one can think of the notion of "readiness" for reading, which his interpreters have imputed from his ideas.) It is surely not too soon to say that certain elements of the theory proffer a serious misrepresentation of the way children think. This has happened for two main reasons: due to unrealistic expectations about the place and limits of theory in education, and because of the understandable fascination of professional and academic communities by a particularly powerful nexus of theoretical knowledge. I shall examine these briefly.

In the accumulating body of knowledge surrounding Piagetian theory is the realization that there are not simply odd observations for which Piaget has not been able to account. Rather, it now appears that many of his ideas were wholly mistaken. Donaldson (1978) summarizes well the arguments against Piaget's conclusions, for instance those of McGarrigle and Donaldson (1974), and others. And Nisbett (1993), in relation to Piagetian theory, now states that

> psychological theories that hold that there are no rules, or no domain — independent rules, for problem solving are not tenable. . . . Psychological and educational positions, as well as philosophical positions, that assume a universal adult competence with respect to reasoning must give way to the recognition that adult inferential competence is highly variable and highly dependent on educational history. (p. 7)

Indeed, a significant amount of evidence continues to accumulate steadily against the conclusions and explanations Piaget draws from his theory. Yet its resilience and its putative solidity as a basis for further study continues, because of the status of theory as received knowledge. I have referred to some of the evidence against Piaget. One can, of course, continue, and in that continuation one is struck by the simplicity of the ideas and experiments that have challenged Piagetian theory. It is almost as though educationists, in continuing defense of Piaget, were hypnotized by the theoretical power nexus that surrounded him, finding it difficult to accept a challenge to what became almost canonical. The significant worry in all of this is that what invariably characterized those challenges was a more positive and optimistic view of children's capabilities than that which inhered in Piagetian theory. Bower's (1982) most important experiment, for instance, conjoined commonsense logic with measures of infants' heart rates to demonstrate that infants' supposed egocentricity is in fact an artefact of their undeveloped motor system, not their knowledge of the world. Wason and Johnson-Laird (1972) and others subsequently have shown that logic — even in college students — is more elusive than Piaget imagined, while paradoxically logic can be shown to exist in young children (Hughes, 1975) if the circumstances are propitious. The paradoxical (and wholly age-inappropriate) appearance and disappearance of logical thought appears to depend more on social and other circumstances than on the passing of developmental marker-posts. Indeed, the success of very young children in the use of deictic shifters (words like "I" and "you" that change their meaning depending on who is uttering and who is listening) is elegant enough proof of the young child's ability to decenter, without recourse to any experiments.[9]

Convinced by the elegance of his theory, Piaget (and others subsequently) found it legitimate to ask eight-year-old children questions such as, "Are there more primroses on this table or more flowers?" [as a demonstration that formal operations do not occur until the conditions are correct] (Piaget, 1973, p. 23). Not surprisingly, the ingenuous, eager to please youngsters would give a helpful response such as, "It's the same thing because there are six on one side and six on the other" (p. 23). This seems to me to be a perfectly reasonable response, and a far more polite one than would be obtained from a confident adult confronted with a similar question. If someone came into my garden and asked me, "Do you have more lupins in your garden or more plants?" I should think that they were suffering from some fairly serious thought disorder, probably schizoid in origin. However, the baffled response from the youngsters is taken as support for Piaget's theory. Adherents of this theory, contrary to all expectations about falsifiability, seem to find it legitimate to give in support of Piaget's theory the fact that children cannot answer silly questions.

The elegance and significance of the theory meant that the absurdity of such question wording was not challenged until relatively recently. Indeed, questions of this kind even made their way into serious tests such as the British Ability Scales.[10] It seems that the power of a good theory is enough to subvert the reason even of hardened psychological scientists.

Many of Piaget's conclusions arise from a theory-first view of the world. The theory is foremost and the experiment is ostensibly designed to support (rather than refute) the theory. In Kuhn's terms, the data are products of the activity and artifacts of the scientific culture in which the experiment is set. As Bryant (1984), the Oxford psychologist whose work twenty years ago was among the first seriously to challenge Piagetian orthodoxy, has pointed out, the failure of young children to perform adequately in Piagetian experiments is likely due to children's being flabbergasted by the task they are being asked to complete. There are more straightforward and more parsimonious explanations for children's behavior that are simply unconsidered, since the children's behavior is taken as confirmation of a powerful theoretical explanation. The work of Bryant and Kopytynska (1976), for instance, shows that Piaget's supposition that young children would not take the logical path of measuring a tower using available equipment is the case because they reasonably consider that the evidence of their eyes is satisfactory evidence. If the top of the tower is not actually visible, however, children will use available measuring tools. The experiments are self-validating; they produce a world in which they are true.

Others have shown Piagetian conclusions to be mistaken as well. Elkind (1967) and Gelman (1982) in their well-known work have shown that children are quite able to conserve (that is, to hold on to the idea of a constant amount, in spite of presentation) if given the right circumstances. To this day, work continues to show the same thing: that children's thinking is characterized by adaptability and plasticity rather than fixity. Glenn (1993) and Lawson (1992) are just two of the many who recently have shown that children's learning is dependent on context and use of language. Bryant (1984) sums up the situation:

> In fact every one of the many claims that Piaget made for some glaring logical gap in young children is now hotly disputed, and in every case some evidence has been produced which appears to show that young children can manage the logical move in question. (p. 255)

The purpose of presenting this discussion is not to harangue Piagetians. It is, rather, to demonstrate the power and resilience of theory, of a totalizing discourse in Foucault's terms. Despite being shown to be mistaken, Piagetian theory has influenced (and is still influencing) two generations of early childhood educators. Even after the questioning of the last twenty-five years, it is still revered. Dadds (1992), for instance, is still able to claim that it would be "absurd and arrogant" to discount Piaget's contribution, apparently because "Piaget was a great researcher, a great thinker and a great theoretician" (p. 132).

The central point I wish to make is that theory has achieved this influence through what Feyerabend (1993) calls the transformation of ideas into "obstacles to thought":

> The theory becomes acceptable as a topic for discussion; it is presented at meetings and large conferences . . . [it] enters the public domain. There are introductory texts, popularisations; examination questions start dealing with problems to be solved in its terms. Scientists and philosophers, trying to show off, drop a hint here and there, and this often quite uninformed desire to be on the right side is taken as a further sign of the importance of the theory. . . . [But] problematic aspects which were originally introduced with the help of carefully constructed arguments now become basic principles; doubtful points into slogans; debates with opponents become standardized [and] only serve as a background for the splendour of the new theory. (p. 30)

Feyerabend here describes an academic socialization of knowledge. Strong connections can be drawn between the "archive" and "totalizing discourse" of Foucault and the paradigm of Kuhn (1970). Kuhn describes the way that the paradigm is used consensually. It is what is agreed to be correct rather than the product of compelling justifications. If experiments are done that confirm the paradigm, all is well and good, and knowledge is gained. However, if experiments fail to confirm existing theory in the paradigm, it is taken to be because of the incompetence or stupidity of the scientist or some problem in the design or interpretation of the experiment. Thus Finn (1992) accuses those who interpret and criticize Piaget of "clichéd description" and "malign misinterpretation." Even those who have followed Piaget (but emerged with mistaken and attack-prone conclusions) are accused by Finn of a process akin to raiding a goodie-bag for support for their ideals (such as discovery learning). But it should surely come as no surprise, given the creed-like status that is ascribed to knowledge when it achieves such theoretical heights, that supporters may willfully misinterpret it.

Indeed, those who have found the theory wanting are taken to be guilty of a process that is familiar to Kuhn; Finn (1992) says that "precociously successful conservation" may be noted (as it has often been in the critique of Piaget), but he puts this down to the "specifically advantageous situations" in which children have been placed. The problem, as Kuhn predicts, is taken to be in the design of the challenging experiment or in its interpretation. Although Kuhn's target is the influence of "existing custom, convention, inherited knowledge, current procedures and current interpretations" (Barnes, 1990, p. 89) in science, the defenses of Piaget give ample evidence for the same process in education.

Not only has Piaget's theory influenced education, it has also influenced other theories, themselves with their own influences on the world. Webs of theories arise, with each strand of the web depending on other strands, which in turn depend on others. Never mind that the original strand may be wildly off the mark or even hopelessly wrong. For instance, Habermas (see Giddens, 1990, for a readable overview) relies extensively on Piaget's notion that the child gradually decenters, and the conception of decentering has been one of the most conclusively attacked aspects of Piaget's work.[11] Habermas relies heavily on Freud's psychoanalysis (itself now mortally wounded) as a vehicle for demonstrating the reconcilability of the positivist and hermeneutic traditions. Habermas sought to show that the interpretive elements of psychoanalysis (e.g., via the analysis of dreams) and its simultaneous assumption of impersonal, anonymous forces (e.g., in the unconscious forces of the id) were signal evidence of the assumptions of two supposedly irreconcilable traditions (positivist and hermeneutic) in fact complementing one another.

Looking at Habermas's position and his reliance on both Piaget and Freud, it is possible to see that a vast intellectual superstructure — interestingly, one that argues for modernism and against postmodernism — is constructed on what is now recognized to be, at best, shaky foundations. If the theories on which the arguments are based can be shown to be mistaken, then all the conclusions drawn from arguments based on those theories must be without value. In both cases the fault lies with theory being taken to be the substantial representation of our best knowledge.

Let us move on to Chomsky and his "theory of mind" (Chomsky, 1980, p. 50). Chomsky argues in his theory for physiological correlates to thought. He tries to make the point by drawing on a passage from Wittgenstein, who takes the opposite view, that mental capacities lack locally structured vehicles. Wittgenstein illustrates his point by drawing an analogy with the contents of a plant's seed, arguing for the anarchy in the germ:

> I mean this: if I talk or write there is, I assume, a system of impulses going out from my brain and correlated with my spoken or written thoughts. But why should the system continue further in the direction of the centre? Why should this order not proceed, so to speak, out of chaos? The case would be like the following — certain kinds of plants multiply by seed, so that a seed always produces a plant of the same kind as that from which it was produced — but nothing in the seed corresponds to the plant which comes from it; so that it is impossible to infer the properties or structure of the plant from those of the seed that comes out of it — this can only be done from the history of the seed. So an organism might come into being even out of something quite amorphous, as it were causelessly; and there is no reason why this should not really hold for our thoughts, and hence for our talking and writing. (quoted in Chomsky, 1980, p. 49)

Clearly Wittgenstein is not arguing for the complete absence of physiological correlates for thought. He is arguing from analogy that there is no necessary central or localized form of organization that corresponds to the thought. It is this that jars Chomsky, because it contradicts his theory.

Subsequent genetic science shows Wittgenstein to be right and Chomsky to be wrong; there are no obvious (or indeed covert) connections between the coded message in the seed and its phenotypic effects. Indeed, pleiotropy is a key feature of geneticists' current understanding of the way that the coded message has its effects; Dawkins (1982) defines pleiotropy thus:

> The phenomenon whereby a change at one genetic locus can bring about a variety of apparently unconnected phenotypic changes. For instance, a particular mutation might at one and the same time affect eye color, toe length, and milk yield. Pleiotropy is probably the rule rather than the exception, and is entirely to be expected from all that we understand about the complex way in which development happens. (p. 292)

Further evidence against Chomsky's simple Language Acquisition Device, against the notion of simple mapping of language to neurological hard-wiring, comes from the application of insights from quantum physics to the workings of the brain (see Penrose, 1994). Penrose points to the strong likelihood that the cytoskeleton — that is, the level of interconnections of microtubules below that of neurons (which are explicable in terms of classical-level physics) — operates at a level where quantum laws rather than classical-level laws apply. With quantum laws applying, with multiple possibilities and, ultimately, with what Penrose calls "non-computability," the likelihood of Chomsky's "device," localized in some discrete organizational center, seems even more remote.

Back in the world of classical physics, Chomsky's theory has recently been questioned following the research of those who are looking at the learning of language in nonhuman primates. It now seems very likely that other primates have the mental apparatus to learn language (see, for example, Fouts & Fouts, 1993; White-Miles, 1993). The notion of a brain center exclusive to homo sapiens for the learning of language has had to give way to the notion of plasticity in thinking and learning — to a generalized ability to learn something even as complex as language in the higher primates, albeit at not such a sophisticated level as that developed in humans.

The point of using Chomsky's ideas to exemplify this debate is, as with Piaget and Habermas, to signify the nature of the wrongness of the theory. The "structural theory of mind," if it is wrong, is not simply slightly off the mark; it is fundamentally mistaken. It contains not a germ of truth about it. And yet, partly because of the allure of theory, it has, like Piaget's theory, influenced a generation of educators.

The committed theoriphile might defend the process rather than the actual theories in the examples I have used and point to the value of the cut-and-thrust of discourse in providing better ideas. But the problem with the legitimacy ascribed to theory is that for substantial periods, social, psychological, and educational theory is taken to be the best representation of our knowledge. Even if assumptions are subsequently shown to be mistaken or conclusions flawed, strange loyalty is shown to the ailing theory. It is treated not as tentative or once-useful, but something to be supported, even when the contradictory evidence and challenging arguments assume substantial weight. The legacy in education is not simply the debris of academic debate, but practice in classrooms. Both Piaget and Chomsky can leave the educator with a less-than-optimistic view as to the potential of the teacher, a view that emphasizes the fixedness of development. As Bryant (1984) says in the specific case of Piaget, the message for the teacher is "a pretty bleak one." Although one side of Piaget's theory has been helpful (i.e., the way in which children construct the world for themselves), Bryant avers that "there can be no question that the implications of Piaget's theories about children's logical skills are, as far as teachers are concerned, restrictive and negative" (p. 257).

I reemphasize here that the point is not to attack these specific theories, but rather to challenge the process of theorizing in education. Theory may exist in various forms along the continua I have drawn, and its value, respectability, and putative validity will be determined irrespective of its positioning here, since those who speak of theory and theorizing in education often use the word indiscriminately, with little conscious knowledge of how they are using it from one moment to the next. Perhaps most seriously, though, theory in all forms has acquired a respectability and a glamour. Theorizing, and thought that is located in theory, is taken to be legitimate and acceptable. Even the personal theory favored by Carr surely conforms to Foucault's archive, and we may ask questions about how limiting such a set of theories may be to fertility in thought about education. One might also ask who benefits by the reinforcement of that archive, that notion of correct procedures and processes to structure one's thoughts. And grand theory — theory as totalizing discourse — actually influences policy and practice. Given the nature of theory in education, its veracity is difficult to gauge, yet its influence may be significant. Whether that influence is benign or malign will be open to test; my point is that power has been located in theory and in those who are associated with it. If theory is then seen as the engine of ideas and change, particular kinds of ideas, particular ways of thinking, and particular methods for structuring research have legitimacy bestowed upon them.

Grand Theory and Its Non-Contiguity with Scientific Theory

It is apposite to pause here, since a discussion of grand theory raises again the lack of contiguity between educational and scientific theory. This has been discussed fully elsewhere (by Chambers, 1992, and others), yet several points need to be raised in the light of the foregoing discussion on grand theory.

Theory in properly conducted science (that is, properly conducted according to Popper) is open to attack, tenuous, and devised in such a way that it is falsifiable. By contrast, in education, theory is often taken as creed-like. There is the tendency not only not to treat theory as something to be refuted — or even as tenuous, as a loose statement of where we are now — but to treat it as a sacred text, something to be cherished and protected, as I have tried to show in the case studies of grand theory above. As Bruner (1986) puts it, the aim seems to be to construct "theory that can be . . . carefully guarded against attack" (p. 48). If this criticism is valid, it is, of course, as Kuhn (1970) has noted, one that applies to "normal science," which proceeds by seeking confirmation of established theory rather than its refutation. The fault of "normal science," though, is at least acknowledged; there is no such acknowledgment within education. There is an erroneous expectation that theory drives forward knowledge and ideas, rather than being a for-the-time-satisfactory statement of someone's intellectual leap.

Bruner (1986) also points out that science is marked by what he calls the paradigmatic mode, concerned with formal systems of explanation employing categorization with a language regulated by the requirements of consistency and noncontradiction. Here, development of theory involves "higher and higher reaching for abstraction" (p. 13). The elements in inquiry are linked and the association of theory-making with them is logical. But there are rarely such elements in educational inquiry; the processes of educational and scientific inquiry are non-analogous and there is no need to assume that theory marks the endpoint of educational inquiry.

There are also substantial differences in the notions of theoretical progress, and there are therefore serious dangers in education's use of the word theory here, since scientific development of theory entails well-researched and well-understood processes. To assume that science-like development of theory is occurring in education is mistaken and has potentially damaging effects in the classroom, as I have suggested in the case study of Piaget. To exemplify the progress of theory in science it is worth focusing on two well-known developments: those of the Einsteinian revolution and neo-Darwinian development.

When Einstein's General Theory of Relativity replaced Newton's theory of mechanics, it did so because Newton's theory was unable to account for various paradoxical observations and phenomena at the edges of the measured world. But until the new theory was proposed, Newton's theory had sufficed (and continues to suffice) quite satisfactorily for most scientific purposes. Einstein's theory did not replace the theory of mechanics because the latter was hopelessly and spectacularly wrong. As Feyerabend (1993) puts it, "The trouble is not . . . the result of sloppy procedure. It is created by experiments and measurements of the highest precision and reliability. . . . There is not a single theory that is not in some trouble or other" (p. 39).

Similarly, we are now seeing a replacement of traditional Darwinian theory, a replacement of the notion that the individual is the replicator with the notion that the gene is the replicator. Although neo-Darwinian theory is a revolution in thinking, it retains and cleaves to the central dogma of molecular biology that nucleic acids act as templates for the synthesis of proteins, but never the reverse; in other words, that acquired characteristics are not inherited. It is essentially and fundamentally Darwinian in character.

Both of these examples of the replacement of Newtonian and Darwinian theory are examples of the progress of science (although Kuhn suggests that "normal science" is less clear-cut, less elegantly progressive). The point of giving them is to show the contrast between the progress of these theories in science and the progress (if it can be called that) of theories in education. When theories in education are shown to be wrong, they are shown to be not simply unable to account for a minority of paradoxical observations but mistaken in their fundamentals, as, for example, elements of Piagetian theory have proved to be.

There are, then, a number of differences between theory in education and theory in science, though it is worth pointing out in conclusion to this section that the place of theory in science itself is open to question. Kuhn suggested that there is a rationalist mythology to which accounts of scientific progress cleaved. He exposed the lack of congruity between what really happens in science with this myth. What really happens is a mix of systematic inquiry with the consensual approval of the scientific community. The process of acceptance and change, of the fracture of one paradigm and movement to the next, is social as well as logical. As Feyerabend reminds us, science is far more sloppy and irrational than its methodological image. It depends upon the ad hoc. It seems to be becoming clearer that the forms of organization, notably theory, which seem from a rationalist history to call to us, are not necessarily the best-fashioned tools to employ in creatively thinking about problems or even in systematizing our knowledge. Insights and explanations that emerge from our interaction with the world do not have to crystallize together into theory in order to achieve legitimacy or utility.

Theory Versus "Ad Hocery"

None of this is new. Dewey railed against certain kinds of theory nearly a century ago, but such is the glamor and resilience of theory that few seem to have heard him. This is to such an extent that the journal that is the organ of the John Dewey Society actually calls itself *Educational Theory.* His own views on this matter seem a generation or two ahead of his time and almost postmodern in their orientation. Indeed, Rorty (1991) suggests that "Foucault can be read . . . as an up-to-date version of John Dewey" (p. 193). Take Meiklejohn's (1966) summary:

> It is unwise, Dewey tells us, to philosophize, to have and to use "general theories." . . . "What is needed," Dewey says, "is specific inquiries into a multitude of specific structures and interactions. Not only does the solemn reiteration of categories of individual and organic or social whole not further these definite and detailed inquiries but it checks them. It detains thought within pompous and sonorous generalities wherein controversy is incapable of solution." Such theorizing tends to substitute mere abstract ideas for concrete, specific investigations. (Meiklejohn, 1966, pp. 83–84)

Dewey is saying that investigations should be specific. They should not derive from theory, nor should they be aimed at establishing theory. In particular, he warns that education's predilection for theory may not merely lead to pompous banality, but that it is actually dangerous. It "detains thought" (Meiklejohn, 1966, pp. 83–84).

Garforth (in Dewey, 1966) comes to similar conclusions about Dewey's position, asserting that Dewey concluded that "philosophy's primary purpose is that of rationalizing the possibilities of experience, especially collective human experience; it is practical, not theoretical, in intention" (Dewey, 1966, p. 16). In this, Barrett (1978) is at one with Dewey. Barrett warns specifically of the simplifying tendency of theory in the social and symbolic sciences:

> The greater and more spectacular the theory, the more likely it is to foster our indolent disposition to oversimplify: to twist all the ordinary matters of experience to fit them into the new framework, and if they do not, to lop them off. (p. 149)

So theoretical molds, from wherever they derive, are the Procrustean bed of the educationist; there is the danger that in compacting, trimming, and generally forcing the worlds with which we work into theoretical molds we distort and misperceive those worlds. Education is not alone in this respect; Wright Mills (1959) described and attacked this theoretical tendency in socio-historical analysis, where he suggested that theory (in particular in the philosophies of Compte, Marx, Spencer, and Weber) creates a "trans-historical strait-jacket" into which the evidence of history is coerced.

Naughton (1981) suggests that our aim should not be to establish all-encompassing theories, with their strait-jacketing qualities. He quotes Checkland (1972, 1981) and Popper (1966) in saying that our orientation ought to be toward "piecemeal social engineering." In playing down the importance of theory in understanding people-based problems, Checkland finds not only Popper for company, for even in harder fields, scientific advance is now seen as not so reliant on an epistemology that demands theory and its tidying qualities. Rather, as I have noted from Feyerabend, progress is seen as anarchic, the very antithesis of theory. Kuhn (1970) sees progress as a series of noncumulative developments, and Quinton (in Magee, 1982) suggests that Wittgenstein saw progress as the dissipation of confusion in a piecemeal way. Shouldn't we then in education be less self-conscious about departure from a self-imposed attachment to the orderliness of theory?

Toffler (1985) contends that the postmodern world is characterized by ideas in constant flux. This world, he says, will increasingly be marked by what he calls "ad hocery"; an analogue can clearly be seen in educational research.

These notions — of piecemeal dissipation of confusion, of "ad hocery," of craft knowledge, and of piecemeal social engineering — although from different stables (or from none), are congruent in one important respect. Central to these notions is the belief that Dewey expressed long ago that problem-solving, particularly of the kind engaged in by educationists, requires a different kind of understanding of the world from the one that educational research, and theory deriving from and driving educational research, has traditionally offered. It needs to be less structured, less constrained. Yeats puts it (as one would expect) poetically: "Wisdom is a butterfly/ Not a gloomy bird of prey."

Atheoretical Progress Outside and Inside Education: Where Next?

When breakthroughs in thinking occur, they almost always occur despite theory rather than because of theory. Progress in thinking occurs via "punctuated equilibrium" following individuals' energy, curiosity, ingenuity, and creativity. In almost any leap forward — the invention of the microscope, the discovery of penicillin, the development of nylon, the recent isolation of *Helicobacter pylori* — the story is one of chance discovery (one might say amethodological as well as atheoretical), pursued with creativity and intelligence, despite the rear-guard action of theoreticians who often proclaim that facts cannot be facts because they contravene theory·

Successes appear to arise more often from accident — from the happy process of noticing (Köhler's apes' "Ah ha!") (see Köhler, 1925) — and the unusual conjoining of ideas (sometimes outlandish ideas) than from the employment of theory. Looking at advances in knowledge from Archimedes's "Eureka!" to Einstein's thought experiments, it is probable that the vast majority of successes arise from "Ah ha!" experiences rather than from theory. Einstein (see Hoffmann, 1973), for example, describes how he performed thought experiments in developing the theory of relativity. He would imagine himself sitting on the end of a beam of light to make guesses about how the world around him would change visually as he surfed at the speed of light. Neither theory nor the set of respectable methods associated with it were as valuable as these exercises in imagination. Theory, based as it is on the systematization of existing knowledge, can only provide disjointed, incremental accretion.

In the development of new ideas theory rarely plays a part. Theory systematizes and tidies cognitive leaps; it cannot act as a vehicle for creativity. When inventors and creative thinkers give us an insight into the ways that they think, it is clear that the role of theory is predicated to that of metaphor, inspiration, and even dream. From Watts's invention of lead shot to the pure mathematics involved in Wiles's solution of Fermat's Last Theorem, theory had zero significance. Watts describes the idea for making lead shot coming to him in a drunken dream. Wiles describes the elegant solution to Fermat's Last Theorem (see Millson & Singh, 1996), which had baffled mathematicians for three hundred years, coming to him "almost from nowhere" and against the grain of most of the theoretical work he had been conducting in the seven years he had worked on the problem.

The history of *Helicobacter pylori* is worth outlining in detail as an exemplar of the process of atheoretical progress, and especially of establishment resistance to challenges to theoretically well-established knowledge. Stomach ulcers mystified the medical profession for generations, and until well into the 1980s aetiology remained a mystery. Hypotheses (concerning stress, diet, lifestyle) abounded, but none of these could reliably be established as the cause. One possible cause — the presence of bacteria in the stomach — was discounted because it violated the established theory that no bacterium could tolerate the acidic environment of the stomach. The theory survived resiliently (as theories do) until a remarkable conjunction of events challenged and eventually toppled it. A pathologist noticed that the histology of patients' stomach walls formed a pattern that merited further investigation. One might say that he had a hypothesis (hypothesis is probably too pompous a word — what he had was more like an "Ah ha!"), but certainly not a theory. He and a physician colleague obtained the grudging permission of superiors to try to culture a bacterium from an ulcer patient's stomach. At first the bacterium could not be cultured, until by happy accident (the intervention of a public holiday) incubation was allowed for three days longer than normal. With the extra days, cultures did begin to develop. Thus *H. pylori,* a now-famously slow-growing bacterium, was identified, centuries of suffering ended, and drug companies' profits slumped. The long and heated resistance by the medical and academic establishment to the notion that a cherished theory should not only be challenged, but challenged by such unconventional means, is in itself proof of the effects of "archive" of which Foucault warns.

The important point is that in one hundred years of modern medicine, acceptance of the veracity of the real causative link was obstructed by the assumption that *H. pylori* could not possibly provide an answer because its existence in the stomach violated the theory that bacteria could not survive in such an acid environment! Theory and *H. pylori* survived in symbiosis while possible challenges to them were discounted (see Blaser, 1996, for a fuller account).

The examples I give here are not merely anecdotal, peculiar, singular, or unusual. Naughton (1981) asserts that the notion that there is a one-way traffic of ideas from theory to technology is refuted by history. Technologies flourished long before theories could have informed them. They represent "craft knowledge." Lee (1988) concurs about the validity of craft knowledge or "craft psychology," as she calls it, echoing Dewey in saying that "the critical issue [for human sciences such as psychology and education] is whether the strategy will work under the actual work requirements of daily life" (p. 146).

Conclusion

Theory in education is antagonistic to pluralism in ideas. With commitment to it, fertility is sacrificed to orderliness. What is needed is more "ad hocery," more thought experiments, more diversity. I return to Carr's appeal for theory, where theory is reflection and thought. I agree on the merit of reflection and thought, but why call reflection and thought "theory," when "theory" carries with it the epistemological baggage that it does? Why assert its importance when, in the absence of adequate definition, overzealous and misunderstanding Ph.D. supervisors will exhort their students to locate their work in theory?

In the absence of definition, "theory" has come to denote not merely grand theory, which has its own dangers, but more loosely a safe conceptualization, a packaging of experience and ideas into circumscribed form and language. Teachers and researchers are supposed to have theories, but if academics cannot agree on what a theory is, then it is reasonable to assume that "theory" will come to assume the status of received, acceptable schemata or knowledge. Such a process of legitimizing mental activity is part of the institutional rule-making that buttresses existing forms of what is permitted to count as rational. In short, I suspect that, in encouraging teachers and researchers to develop their own theories, academics are inviting them to conform to Foucault's tacit archive of rules and procedures for thinking — or risk being condemned to silence.

Notes

1. When I write of educationists, I am referring to academics and researchers.
2. See, for example Garrison (1988) and Suppes (1974). Ball (1995) characterizes atheoretical research as "technical rationalist" and contrasts this with theoretically grounded research that concerns "intellectual intelligence." He associates atheoretical technical rationalism with isolation and the neglect of significant ideas and concepts.
3. *Grand theory* is a term coined by C. Wright Mills (1959) to describe the expectation among social scientists that their disciplines should attempt to build systematic theory of "the nature of man and society" (p. 23); he saw this effort as an obstacle to progress in the human sciences. By contrast, personal theory and "practical theorizing," discussed by Carr (1995) and McIntyre (1995), concern using "intellectual resources that will enable educational practitioners to take their activities more seriously" (Carr, 1995, p. 36). At its core is the notion of emancipation from habit and tradition via critical examination of existing belief.

4. Medawar and Medawar (1977) give examples of elegant theory being "profoundly appealing" yet "profoundly unsound" (p. 10). They record that the once attractive but now discredited notion of protoplasm led Victorian biologist Thomas Henry Huxley, in a paper for the *Quarterly Journal of Microscopical Science,* to give a detailed account of an organism dredged from deep in the Atlantic and consisting of naked protoplasm. The new organism was given a Latin name (*Bathybius haeckeli*) after the eminent zoologist Ernst Haeckel, who first proposed the existence of a group of organisms, the Monera, consisting entirely of *Urschleim,* or primitive slime. The whole episode is an example of the consensual construction of supposedly scientific knowledge based on simple, romantic theory.

5. Illich and Sanders (1988) discuss the misuse of words such as "theory," which they say are used without thinking in academic, professional, and lay circles, almost as a "sub-linguistic grunt" (p. 106). They give the word "energy" as a detailed example, recording how its early sixteenth-century English use as "vigor of expression" altered in the nineteenth century, as it acquired a technical meaning culled from physics. Later, concurrent with Marx's ascription of "labor force" to the proletariat, German physicists described a general potential to perform work and called it "energy," and this transferred itself to English. The continual accretion of technical and nontechnical nuance and meaning, and the inaccurate vernacular use of the word in pretending technical expertise or scientific knowledge, is troublesome. These "sub-linguistic grunts" (and I would put theory at the head of the list) are used, they say, "neither with common sense, nor with the senseless precision of science" (p. 106).

6. Skinner (1990) aligns anti-theory with "conceptual relativism" (p. 12). He says that it is the project of these thinkers (Foucault, Feyerabend, Wittgenstein) to demolish the claims of theory and method to organize the materials of experience.

7. "'Normal science' means research firmly based upon one or more past scientific achievements, achievements that some particular scientific community acknowledges for a time as supplying the foundation for its further practice" (Kuhn, 1970, p. 10). It is the conservatism of this process of which Kuhn was critical, as was Popper. Hence the latter's emphasis on developing theory in such a way that it can be falsified. The aim is to avoid ossification; nothing should be allowed to become sacred, so we must develop theory in such a way that it can be knocked down and replaced.

8. Kelly's Construct Theory sees people as self-inventing of their worlds. It has a formal structure with a fundamental postulate and eleven elaborative corollaries. Bannister and Fransella (1986) emphasize this formality and contrast Construct Theory with other putative theories, which they claim do not deserve the name "theory." They say, for instance, that a "theory of memory can be no better than the concept of memory itself" (p. 15).

9. Deixis is the use of words relating to the time and place of utterance, e.g., personal pronouns, demonstrative adverbs, adjectives, and pronouns. The use and understanding of personal pronouns require users to put themselves "in another's shoes" (which is notably lacking in autistic children, though present in normal development from the very early years).

10. The British Ability Scales were devised during the late 1970s to assess ability without necessary recourse to the production of an IQ score. One element, devised on Piagetian principles, involved children answering questions of the kind described above.

11. Habermas maps Piaget's three main developmental stages to three main stages of social evolution: the "mythical," "religious-metaphysical," and "modern." Decentering, and the movement of the child from stage to stage, is seen to be also at the root of the move of small, traditional cultures dominated by myths (which represent concrete thought), eventually to societies that develop forums in which debate and argument are possible, and ultimately to a society in which the development of religion signifies rationality. The linkage of societal development to individual development and its dependence on Piagetian theory is tortuous and is evidence of the "profoundly appealing" yet "profoundly unsound" process of theoretical development about which Medawar (1974) warned. Even if taken metaphorically, Habermas's ideas in this respect already appear at best mistaken and at worst insulting.

References

Ball, S. J. (1995). Intellectuals or technicians? The urgent role of theory in educational studies. *British Journal of Educational Studies, 33,* 255–271.

Bannister, D., & Fransella, F. (1986). *Inquiring man: The psychology of personal constructs.* Beckenham, Eng.: Croom Helm.

Barnes, B. (1990). Thomas Kuhn. In Q. Skinner (Ed.), *The return of grand theory in the human sciences* (pp. 83–100). Cambridge, Eng.: Canto.

Barrett, W. (1978). *The illusion of technique.* New York: Anchor-Doubleday.

Blaser, M. J. (1996). The bacteria behind ulcers. *Scientific American, 274*(2), 92–98.

Bower, T. G. R. (1982). *Development in infancy* (2nd ed.). San Francisco: W. H. Freeman.

Bruner, J. (1986). *Actual minds: Possible worlds.* Cambridge, MA: Harvard University Press.

Bryant, P. E. (1984). Piaget, teachers and psychologists. *Oxford Review of Education, 10,* 251–259.

Bryant, P. E., & Kopytynska, H. (1976). Spontaneous measurement by young children. *Nature, 260,* 773.

Bryman, A., & Cramer, D. (1994). *Quantitative data analysis for social scientists.* London: Routledge.

Carr, W. (1995). *For education: Towards critical educational enquiry.* Buckingham, Eng.: Open University Press.

Chambers, J. H. (1992). *Empiricist research on teaching: A philosophical and practical critique of its scientific pretensions.* Dordrecht, Netherlands: Kluwer.

Checkland, P. B. (1972). Towards a systems based methodology for real-world problem solving. *Journal of Systems Engineering, 3*(2), 87–116.

Checkland, P. (1981). *Systems thinking, systems practice.* Chichester, Eng.: Wiley.

Chomsky, N. (1980). *Rules and representations.* Oxford, Eng.: Blackwell.

Cohen, L., & Manion, L. (1989). *Research methods in education* (3rd ed.). London: Routledge.

Dadds, M. (1992). Monty Python and the three wise men. *Cambridge Journal of Education, 22,* 129–141.

Dawkins, R. (1982). *The extended phenotype.* Oxford, Eng.: Oxford University Press.

Dewey, J. (1966). *Selected educational writings.* London: Heinemann.

Donaldson, M. (1978). *Children's minds.* London: Fontana.

Douglas, M. (1975). *Implicit meanings.* London: Routledge.

Elkind, D. (1967). Piaget's conservation problems. *Child Development, 38,* 15–27.

Feyerabend, P. (1993). *Against method* (3rd ed.). London: Verso/New Left Books.

Finn, G. (1992). Piaget, psychology and education. *Scottish Educational Review, 24,* 125–131.

Foucault, M. (1981). Questions of method: An interview with Michel Foucault. *Ideology and Consciousness, 8,* 3–14.

Foucault, M. (1985). *Discipline and punish: The birth of the prison.* Harmondsworth, Eng.: Penguin.

Fouts, R. S., & Fouts, D. H. (1993). Chimpanzees' use of sign language. In P. Cavalieri & P. Singer (Eds.), *The great ape project: Equality beyond humanity* (pp. 28–41). London: Fourth Estate.

Garrison, J. W. (1988). The impossibility of atheoretical educational science. *Journal of Educational Thought, 22*(1), 21–26.

Gelman, R. (1982). Accessing one-to-one correspondence: Still another paper about conservation. *British Journal of Psychology, 73,* 209–221.

Giddens, A. (1990). Habermas, Jürgen. In Q. Skinner (Ed.), *The return of grand theory in the human sciences* (pp. 121–140). Cambridge, Eng.: Canto.

Glaser, B. G., & Strauss, A. L. (1967). *The discovery of grounded theory: Strategies for qualitative research.* New York: Aldine.

Glenn, S. A. (1993). Onset of theory of mind: Methodological considerations. *Early Child Development and Care, 86,* 39–51.

Green, A. (1994). Postmodernism and state education. *Journal of Education Policy, 9*(1), 67–83.

Gruber, H. E., & Vonèche, J. J. (Eds). (1977). *The essential Piaget.* London: Routledge & Kegan Paul.

Habermas, J. (1973). *Theory and practice.* Boston: Beacon Press.

Hirst, P. H. (1990). Internship: A view from outside. In P. Benton (Ed.), *The Oxford internship scheme: Integration and partnership in initial teacher education.* London: Calouste Gulbenkian Foundation.

Hirst, P. H. (1993). Educational theory. In M. Hammersley (Ed.), *Educational research: Current issues* (pp. 149–159). London: Paul Chapman.

Hoffman, B. (1973). *Albert Einstein.* London: Hart-Davis MacGibbon.

Holton, G. (1995). The controversy over the end of science. *Scientific American, 273,* 168.

Hughes, M. (1975). *Egocentrisms in preschool children.* Unpublished doctoral dissertation, University of Edinburgh.

Illich, I., & Sanders, L. (1988). *ABC: The alphabetization of the popular mind.* London: Penguin.

Kerlinger, F. N. (1970). *Foundations of behavioural research.* New York: Holt, Rinehart & Winston.

Köhler, W. (1925). *The mentality of apes.* New York: Harcourt.

Kuhn, T. (1970). *The structure of scientific revolutions* (2nd ed.). Chicago: University of Chicago Press.

Lawson, A. E. (1992). What do tests of "formal" reasoning actually measure? *Journal of Research in Science Teaching, 29,* 965–983.

LeCompte, M. D. (1994). Defining reality: Applying double description and Chaos theory to the practice of practice. *Educational Theory, 44,* 277–298.

Lee, V. L. (1988). *Beyond behaviorism.* Hillsdale, NJ: Lawrence Erlbaum.

Magee, B. (1982). *Men of ideas.* Oxford, Eng.: Oxford University Press.

McGarrigle, J., & Donaldson, M. (1974). Conservation accidents. *Cognition, 3,* 341–350.

McIntyre, D. (1995). Initial teacher education as practical theorising: A response to Paul Hirst. *British Journal of Educational Studies, 43,* 365–383.

Medawar, P. B. (1974). *The hope of progress.* London: Wildwood House.

Medawar, P. B., & Medawar, J. S. (1977). *The life science.* London: Wildwood House.

Meiklejohn, A. (1966). Knowledge and intelligence. In R. D. Archambault (Ed.), *Dewey on education* (pp. 75–95). New York: Random House.

Millson, P., & Singh, S. (Eds.). (1996). *Fermat's last theorem.* London: BBC.

Mouly, G. J. (1978). *Educational research: The art and science of investigation.* Boston: Allyn & Bacon.

Namier, L. B. (1955). *Personalities and powers.* London: Macmillan.

Naughton, J. (1981). Theory and practice in systems research. *Journal of Applied Systems Analysis, 8,* 61–70.

Nisbet, R. E. (1993). Reasoning, abstraction and the prejudices of 20th-century psychology. In R. E. Nisbett (Ed.), *Rules for reasoning* (pp. 1–12). Hillsdale, NJ: Lawrence Erlbaum.

Oakeshott, M. (1989). Education: The engagement and the frustration. In T. Fuller (Ed.), *The voice of liberal learning: Michael Oakeshott on education.* London: Yale University Press.

Penrose, R. (1994). *Shadows of the mind.* Oxford, Eng.: Oxford University Press.

Philp, M. (1990). Michel Foucault. In Q. Skinner (Ed.), *The return of grand theory in the human sciences* (pp. 65–82). Cambridge, Eng.: Canto.

Piaget, J. (1973). *The child and reality: Problems of genetic psychology.* London: Frederick Muller.

Polanyi, M. (1969). *Knowing and being: Essays by Michael Polanyi.* London: Routledge & Kegan Paul.

Popper, K. R. (1966). *The open society and its enemies.* London: Routledge & Kegan Paul.

Popper, K. R. (1968). *The logic of scientific discovery.* London: Hutchison.

Popper, K. R. (1969). *Conjectures and refutations.* London: Routledge & Kegan Paul.

Rorty, R. (1991). *Essays on Heidegger and others: Philosophical papers. Vol. 2.* Cambridge, Eng.: Cambridge University Press.

Selden, R., & Widdowson, P. (1993). *A reader's guide to contemporary literary theory.* Hemel Hempstead, Eng.: Harvester Wheatsheaf.

Skinner, Q. (Ed.). (1990). *The return of grand theory in the human sciences.* Cambridge, Eng.: Canto.

Smith, G. B. (1995). *Nietzsche, Heidegger, and the transition to postmodernity.* Chicago: University of Chicago Press.

Stewart, I. (1990). *Does God play dice?* Harmondsworth, Eng.: Penguin.

Suppes, P. (1974). The place of theory in educational research. *Educational Researcher, 3*(6), 3–10.

Toffler, A. (1985). *The adaptive corporation.* Aldershot, Eng.: Gower.

Wason, P., & Johnson-Laird, N. J. (1972). *Psychology of reasoning: Structure and content.* London: B. T. Batsford.

White-Miles, H. L. (1993). Language and the orang-utan: The old "person". In P. Cavalieri & P. Singer (Eds.), *The great ape project: Equality beyond humanity* (pp. 42–57). London: Fourth Estate.

Wright Mills, C. (1959). *The sociological imagination.* New York: Holt.

Research as Praxis

PATTI LATHER

> The attempt to produce value-neutral social science is increasingly being abandoned as at best unrealizable, and at worst self-deceptive, and is being replaced by social sciences based on explicit ideologies. (Hesse, 1980, p. 247)

> Since interest-free knowledge is logically impossible, we should feel free to substitute explicit interests for implicit ones. (Reinharz, 1985, p. 17)

> Scientists firmly believe that as long as they are not *conscious* of any bias or political agenda, they are neutral and objective, when in fact they are only unconscious. (Namenwirth, 1986, p. 29)

Fifty years ago the Italian neo-Marxist, Antonio Gramsci, urged intellectuals to adhere to a "praxis of the present" by aiding "developing progressive groups" to become increasingly conscious of their own actions and situations in the world (quoted in Salamini, 1981, p. 73). This essay explores what it means to do empirical research in an unjust world. In it I discuss the implications of searching for an emancipatory approach to research in the human sciences.[1] It is written from the perspective of one who believes that, just as there is no neutral education (Freire, 1973), there is no neutral research (Hall, 1975; Reason & Rowan, 1981; Westkott, 1979). Bearing in mind the words of Gramsci, my objective is to delineate the parameters of a "praxis of the present" within the context of empirical research in the human sciences.[2]

I base my argument for a research approach openly committed to a more just social order on two assumptions. First, we are in a postpositivist period in the human sciences, a period marked by much methodological and epistemological ferment. There has been, however, little exploration of the methodological implications of the search for an emancipatory social science. Such a social science would allow us not only to understand the maldistribution of power and resources underlying our society but also to change that maldistribution to help create a more equal world. Second, research that is explicitly committed to critiquing the status quo and building a more just society — that is, research as praxis[3] — adds an important voice to that ferment.

My exploration of postpositivist, praxis-oriented research draws on three research programs — feminist research,[4] neo-Marxist critical ethnography (Masemann, 1982; Ogbu, 1981), and Freirian "empowering" or participatory research (Hall, 1975, 1981). Each of these research programs opposes prevailing scientific norms as inher-

Harvard Educational Review   Vol. 56   No. 3   August 1986
Copyright © by the President and Fellows of Harvard College

ently supportive of the status quo; each is premised on a "transformative agenda" with respect to both social structure and methodological norms; each is, in other words, concerned with research as praxis (Rose, 1979, p. 279). All three of these post-positivist research programs are examples of what Hesse (1980), borrowing from Althusser,[5] terms the "epistemological break" of developing a critical social science with an openly emancipatory intent (p. 196). After brief overviews of praxis-oriented, new paradigm research and of recent efforts in radical educational theorizing aimed at creating an empirically informed Marxism, the essay focuses on the development of empowering approaches to generating knowledge.

The Postpositivist Era

Research paradigms inherently reflect our beliefs about the world we live in and want to live in (Bernstein, 1976; Fay, 1975; Habermas, 1971; Hesse, 1980). Currently we are in a period of dramatic shift in our understanding of scientific inquiry. Lecourt (1975) has termed this present era "the decline of the absolutes" (p. 49; see also Bernstein, 1983; Smith & Heshusius, 1986). No longer does following the correct method guarantee true results, rather, "method does not give truth; it corrects guesses" (Polkinghorne, 1983, p. 249). It is increasingly recognized that the fact/value dichotomy simply drives values underground. Facts are never theory independent (Hesse, 1980, p. 172); they are as much social constructions as are theories and values. Whereas positivism insists that only one truth exists, Rich (1979) argues: "There is no 'the truth,' [nor] 'a truth' — truth is not one thing, or even a system. It is an increasing complexity" (p. 187). Postpositivism has cleared methodology of prescribed rules and boundaries. The result is a constructive turmoil that allows a search for different possibilities of making sense of human life, for other ways of knowing which do justice to the complexity, tenuity, and indeterminacy of most of human experience (Mishler, 1979).

Broadly speaking, postpositivism is characterized by the methodological and epistemological refutation of positivism (Bernstein, 1976, 1983; Mitroff & Kilmann, 1978); much talk of paradigm shifts (Eisner, 1983; Phillips, 1983; Smith, 1983); and by the increased visibility of research designs that are interactive, contextualized, and humanly compelling because they invite joint participation in the exploration of research issues (Reason & Rowan, 1981; Reinharz, 1979, 1983; Sabia & Wallulis, 1983). Postpositivism is marked by approaches to inquiry which recognize that knowledge is "socially constituted, historically embedded, and valuationally based. Theory serves an agentic function, and research illustrates (vivifies) rather than provides a truth test" (Hendrick, 1983, p. 506). What this means is that "scholarship that makes its biases part of its argument" has arisen as a new contender for legitimacy.[6]

Research programs that disclose their value-base typically have been discounted, however, as overly subjective and, hence, "nonscientific." Such views do not recognize the fact that scientific neutrality is always problematic; they arise from a hyper-objectivity premised on the belief that scientific knowledge is free from social construction (Fox-Keller, 1985; Harding, 1986). Rather than the illusory "value-free" knowledge of the positivists, praxis-oriented inquirers seek emancipatory knowledge. Emancipatory knowledge increases awareness of the contradictions hidden or distorted by ev-

eryday understandings, and in doing so it directs attention to the possibilities for social transformation inherent in the present configuration of social processes.
Admittedly, this approach faces the danger of a rampant subjectivity where one finds
only what one is predisposed to look for, an outcome that parallels the "pointless precision" of hyper-objectivity (Kaplan, 1964). Thus a central task for praxis-oriented researchers becomes the confrontation of issues of empirical accountability — the need
to offer grounds for accepting a researcher's description and analysis — and the search
for workable ways of establishing the trustworthiness of data in new paradigm
inquiry.

Research as Praxis

The foundation of postpositivism is the cumulative, trenchant, and increasingly definitive critique of the inadequacies of positivist assumptions[7] in light of the complexities of human experience (Bernstein, 1976; Cronbach, 1975; Feinberg, 1983;
Giroux, 1981; Guba & Lincoln, 1981; Kaplan, 1964; Mishler, 1979). Postpositivism
argues that the present orthodoxy in the human sciences is obsolete and that new visions for generating social knowledge are required (Hesse, 1980; Reason & Rowan,
1981; Rose, 1979; Schwartz & Oglivy, 1979). Those committed to the development
of a change-enhancing, interactive contextualized approach to knowledge-building
have amassed a body of empirical work that is provocative in its implications for both
theory and, increasingly, method.

Several examples of this work are available. Consider Bullough and Gitlin's (1985)
case study of one middle school teacher, a study designed to encourage rethinking the
meaning of resistance and its place in theories of cultural and economic reproduction
within the context of teachers' work lives. Their research design included the teacher's
written response to a preliminary interpretation of the data, which is an example of
the most common form of an emancipatory approach to research — the submission
of a preliminary description of the data to the scrutiny of the researched. In an earlier
study, Willis (1977) focused on the school-to-work transition in the lives of twelve
working-class British "lads." The most oft-cited example of neo-Marxist critical ethnography, Willis's work both identifies the area of resistance to authority as a corrective to the overly deterministic correspondence theories then popular in neo-Marxist
circles (see Apple, 1980-81; Bowles & Gintis, 1976) and builds into his research design an attempt to take the research findings back to the lads for further dialogue.
McRobbie (1978) conducted a similar study inquiring into the effects of socialization
into femininity on the lives of working-class British females. Finally, a more praxis-
oriented example is Mies's (1984) action-research project in Germany, designed to respond to violence against women in the family. A high visibility street action attracted
people who were then interviewed regarding their experience with and views on wife-
beating. The resulting publicity led to the creation of a Women's House to aid victims
of domestic abuse. A desire for transformative action and egalitarian participation
guided consciousness-raising in considering the sociological and historical roots of
male violence in the home through the development of life histories of the women
who had been battered. The purpose was to empower the oppressed to come to understand and change their own oppressive realities (see also Anyon, 1980, 1981,

1983; Berlak & Berlak, 1981; Everhart, 1983; Hall, 1981; McNeil, 1984; Miller, ; Roberts, 1981; Tripp, 1984).

Such examples are part of a rich ferment in contemporary discourse about empirical research in the human sciences, a discourse that spans epistemological, theoretical, and, to a lesser degree, methodological areas. Within radical educational circles, for example, there have been several calls for eliminating the dichotomy between empirical work and the construction of emancipatory theory (Anyon, 1982; Ramsay, 1983; Wexler, 1982). There are, however, few clear strategies for linking critical theory and empirical research.

This failure to probe the methodological implications of critical theory has led to a number of difficulties for praxis-oriented research. The abundance of theoretically guided empirical work affiliated with the "new sociology of education" attests both to the conceptual vitality offered by postpositivist research programs and to the danger of conceptual overdeterminism. This nondialectical use of theory leads to a circle where theory is reinforced by experience conditioned by theory. Marxism's history of sectarianism and "theoretical imperialism" (Thompson, 1978; see also Bottomore, 1978) gives evidence of the need for open, flexible theory-building grounded in a body of empirical specificities for a priori theory (Hargreaves, 1982; Lather, b). Such work demonstrates the continued relevance of Thompson's assertion that too much of Marxist social theory is an "immaculate conception which requires no gross empirical impregnation"[8] (1978, p. 13; see also Comstock, 1982, p. 371; Kellner, 1975, p. 149; Krueger, 1981, p. 59; Wright, 1978, p. 10).

Additionally, neo-Marxist empirical studies are too often characterized by an attitude toward the people researched that is captured in the words of one research team: "We would not expect the teachers interviewed to either agree with or necessarily understand the inferences which were made from their responses" (Bullough, Goldstein, & Holt, 1982, p. 133). Given the all-male research team and the largely female teacher subjects, one could make much of the gender politics involved in such a statement. But the issue here is the implications of such a stance for the purposes of emancipatory knowledge-building and the empowerment of the researched. One of the central tasks of my argument is to encourage those of us who do critical inquiry to demonstrate how our attitude differs from what Reinharz (1979) has termed the "rape model of research" (p. 95) so characteristic of mainstream social science: career advancement of researchers built on their use of alienating and exploitative inquiry methods.

The difficulties which continue to characterize critical inquiry raise two central questions about the effort to develop a style of empirical research that advances emancipatory knowledge. First, what is the relationship between data and theory in emancipatory research? In grounded theory-building the relationship between data and theory, according to Glasser and Strauss (1967), is that theory follows from data rather than preceding it. Moreover, the result is a minimizing of researcher-imposed definitions of the situation, which is an essential element in generating grounded theory. Given the centrality of a priori theory in praxis-oriented research, it is evident that emancipatory theory-building is different from grounded theory-building. Understanding those differences requires a probing of the tensions involved in the use of a priori theory among researchers who are committed to open-ended, dialectical theory-building that aspires to focus on and resonate with lived experience and, at the same time, are convinced that lived experience in an unequal society too often lacks an awareness of the need to struggle against privilege. Second, growing out of the first question, how does one avoid reducing explanation to the intentions of social actors, by taking into account the deep structures — both psychological and social, conscious and unconscious — that shape human experience and perceptions, without committing the sin of theoretical imposition? This question is tied to both the issue of false consciousness (defined later in this essay) and the crucial role of the researcher vis-a-vis the researched in emancipatory inquiry. An exploration of both of these central questions comprises the remainder of this essay.

For praxis to be possible, not only must theory illuminate the lived experience of progressive social groups; it must also be illuminated by their struggles. Theory adequate to the task of changing the world must be open-ended, nondogmatic, informing, and grounded in the circumstances of everyday life; and, moreover, it must be premised on a deep respect for the intellectual and political capacities of the dispossessed. This position has profound substantive and methodological implications for postpositivist, change-enhancing inquiry in the human sciences.

Empowering Approaches to the Generation of Knowledge

> For persons, as autonomous beings, have a moral right to participate in decisions that claim to generate knowledge about them. Such a right . . . protects them . . . from being managed and manipulated . . . the moral principle of respect for persons is most fully honored when power is shared not only in the application . . . but also in the generation of knowledge . . . doing research on persons involves an important educational commitment: to provide conditions under which subjects can enhance their capacity for self-determination in acquiring knowledge about the human condition. (Heron, 1981, pp. 34–35)

Krueger (1981) notes that "there are hardly any attempts at the development of an alternative methodology in the sense of an 'emancipatory' social research to be explored and tested in substantive studies" (p. 59). Along these lines, Giddens (1979) suggests that the task of a critical social science is to explore the nature of the intersection between choice and constraint and to center on questions of power. Is this not equally true of the research situation itself? Insofar as we have come to see that evolving an empowering pedagogy is an essential step in social transformation, does not the same hold true for our research approaches?

I am arguing for an approach that goes well beyond the action-research concept proposed over thirty years ago by Lewin, which has given rise to "a very active and lively field" in Britain and Australia over the past decade (Tripp, 1984, p. 20). While Tripp (1984) and Grundy (1982) note the existence of some critical and emancipatory teacher-based action research, the vast majority of this work operates from an ahistorical, apolitical value system which lends itself to subversion by those "who are tempted to use merely the technical form as a means of engineering professional teacher development" (Tripp, 1984, p. 20).

An emancipatory social research calls for empowering approaches to research whereby both researcher and researched become, in the words of feminist singer-poet Chris Williamson, "the changer and the changed." For researchers with emancipatory aspirations, doing empirical research offers a powerful opportunity for praxis to the extent that the research process enables people to change by encouraging self-reflection and a deeper understanding of their particular situations. In an attempt to reveal the implications that the quest for empowerment holds for research design, I will focus on three interwoven issues: the need for reciprocity, the stance of dialectical theory-building versus theoretical imposition, and the question of validity in praxis-oriented research.

The Need for Reciprocity

No intimacy without reciprocity. (Oakley, 1981, p. 49)

Reciprocity implies give-and-take, a mutual negotiation of meaning and power. It operates at two primary points in emancipatory empirical research: the junctures between researcher and researched and between data and theory. The latter will be dealt with in the next section of this essay; I here address reciprocity between researcher and researched.

Reciprocity in research design is a matter of both intent and degree. Regarding intent, reciprocity has long been recognized as a valuable condition of research fieldwork, for it has been found to create conditions which generate rich data (Wax, 1952). Everhart (1977), for example, presents reciprocity as "an excellent data gathering technique" (p. 10) because the researcher moves from the status of stranger to friend and thus is able to gather personal knowledge from subjects more easily. He traces his evolution from detachment to involvement in a study of student life in a junior high school where he comes to recognize "the place of reciprocity in productive fieldwork" (p. 8). I argue that we must go beyond the concern for more and better data to a concern for research as praxis. What I suggest is that we consciously use our research to help participants understand and change their situations. I turn now to those who build varying degrees of reciprocity into their research designs for the purpose of empowering the researched.

Laslett and Rapoport (1975), who studied school dropouts in Britain, build a minimal degree of reciprocity into their research designs. They term their approach "collaborative interviewing and interactive research." A central component of their strategy is to repeat interviews at least three times. The repetition is "essential to deal with the feelings roused, often covertly, in order to 'unlock' deeper levels of data content" (p. 973). Furthermore, they urge "giving back" to respondents a picture of how the data are viewed, both to return something to the participants and to check descriptive and interpretive/analytic validity.

A Marxist survey researcher, Carr-Hill (1984), expands the use of reciprocity to identify, through initial interviews, a group of twelve to fifteen people with whom the researcher engaged in a series of open discussions about the mismatch between formal education and the way people live their lives. This resulted in a collectively generated survey given to one hundred people, a survey couched in the language of respondents and "in terms of the social categories through which they perceive the world" (p. 281). Additionally, interested participants attended evaluation seminars where survey results stimulated respondents "to critically analyze their own educational history and its relation to their present life-styles" (p. 281).

A maximal approach to reciprocity in research design can be found in the work of two evaluators involved in a four-year project to assess the curricular reform movements of the 1960s (Kushner & Norris, 1980–1981). The goal of their research was to move people from articulating what they know to theorizing about what they know, a process the researchers term "collaborative theorizing" (p. 27). This methodology is characterized by negotiation: negotiation of description, interpretation, and the principles used to organize the first-draft report. While they admit that final drafts are usually the preserve of the researcher, Kushner and Norris suggest that the attractiveness of this approach is that all participants, within time constraints, are allowed a role in negotiation of the final meanings of the research. Such collaboration, they contend, offers "an opportunity to extend the range of theories and meanings . . . to give participants the dignity of contributing to theorizing about their worlds . . . [and] through sharing meaning-production . . . [to] develop significant understandings of schooling and education" (p. 35).

A final example is provided by Tripp (1983). He explores what it means for interviews to be coauthored and negotiated in a conscious effort to democratize the research situation. In his case studies of alienation and the school-to-work transition, Tripp held one-to-one and group discussions "as a means of developing participants' views" (p. 32). The resulting coauthored statements constituted an agreed-upon account of the views of the participants. Tripp cautions, however, that "the negotiation process must be clearly bounded" (p. 38) because participants often wish to "unsay" their words. In Tripp's view, "the right to negotiate [on the part of research participants] was replaced by the right to comment" (p. 39). Researchers are not so much owners of data as they are "majority shareholders" who must justify decisions and give participants a public forum for critique.

Tripp's research design, however, is not fully interactive. Reciprocity in the negotiation of meaning is limited to the early stages of investigation. No attempt is made to involve research participants in either the interpretation of the descriptive data or the construction of empirically grounded theory. The lack of involvement of research participants in these later stages of the research process makes possible a situation where the entire issue of false consciousness is skirted. False consciousness is the denial of how our commonsense ways of looking at the world are permeated with meanings that sustain our disempowerment (Bowers, 1984; Gramsci, 1971; Salamini, 1981); it is a central issue in any maximal approach to reciprocity.

In order to address this issue, Fay (1977) argues that we must develop criteria/theories to distinguish between people's reasoned rejections of interpretations and theoretical arguments and false consciousness. Fay pinpoints this as a glaring omission, a blackhole,[9] if you will, in critical theory: a lack of knowledge about "the conditions that must be met if people are going to be in a position to actually consider it [critical theory] as a possible account of their lives" (p. 218). Fay is pointing out that the creation of emancipatory theory is a dialogic enterprise. Both the substance of emancipatory theory and the process by which that theory comes to "click" with people's sense of the contradictions in their lives are the products of dialectical rather than top-down impositional practices.

Dialectical practices require an interactive approach to research that invites reciprocal reflexivity and critique, both of which guard against the central dangers to praxis-oriented empirical work: imposition and reification on the part of the researcher. As Comstock (1982) argues, "dialogic education is integral to every research program which treats subjects as active agents instead of objectifying them and reifying their social conditions" (p. 386). Yet, notably more often than in either feminist or Freirian praxis-oriented research, the neo-Marxist researcher's self-perceived role is as "interpreter of the world" (Reynolds, 1980–1981, p. 87), exposer of false consciousness. This nondialectical, nonreciprocal perception of the role of the researcher confounds neo-Marxist researchers' intent to demystify the world for the dispossessed. Respondents become objects — targets of research — rather than active subjects empowered to understand and change their situations. As a result, neo-Marxist praxis-oriented work too often falls prey to what Fay (1977) notes as the irony of domination and repression inherent in most of our efforts to free one another (p. 209). In the name of emancipation, researchers impose meanings on situations rather than constructing meaning through negotiation with research participants.

There are at present few research designs which encourage negotiation of meaning beyond the descriptive level. The involvement of research participants in data interpretation as well as (to take one further step toward maximal reciprocity) theory-building remains largely an "attractive aspiration" (Kushner & Norris, 1980–1981, p. 35). But as Fay (1977) notes, feminist consciousness-raising groups provide a model for how to begin to flesh-out the nature of maximal reciprocity: the involvement of research participants in the construction and validation of knowledge.

Throughout the late 1960s and 1970s, thousands of small grassroots groups formed to provide a way for women to exchange thoughts, experiences, and feelings. From this movement emerged the feminist maxim: the personal is political. What were once thought to be individual problems were redefined as social problems that require political solutions. For Fay (1977), the lesson from these groups is that

> coming to a radical new self-conception is hardly ever a process that occurs simply by reading some theoretical work; rather, it requires an environment of trust, openness, and support in which one's own perceptions and feelings can be made properly conscious to oneself, in which one can think through one's experiences in terms of a radically new vocabulary which expresses a fundamentally different conceptualization of the world, in which one can see the particular and concrete ways that one unwittingly collaborates in producing one's own misery, and in which one can gain the emotional strength to accept and act on one's new insights.
>
> The experience of the Women's Movement confirms that radical social changes through rational enlightenment require some mechanism for ensuring that those conditions necessary for such enlightenment will be established and maintained. (p. 232)

Following Fay (1977), I propose that the goal of emancipatory research is to encourage self-reflection and deeper understanding on the part of the persons being researched at least as much as it is to generate empirically grounded theoretical knowledge. To do this, research designs must have more than minimal reciprocity. The following is a summary of some of the procedures and theory necessary to attain full reciprocity in research:

• *Interviews conducted in an interactive, dialogic manner, that require self-disclosure on the part of the researcher.* An example of self-disclosure can be found in Oakley's (1981) research with women and their experience of motherhood. Arguing the need for interactive self-disclosure, Oakley emphasizes a collaborative, dialogic seeking for greater mutual understanding. This is opposed to mainstream interview norms where interview respondent's questions about the interviewer's own life are deflected (see also Acker, Barry, & Esseveld, 1983; Hanmer & Saunders, 1984).

- *Sequential interviews of both individuals and small groups to facilitate collaboration and a deeper probing of research issues.*
- *Negotiation of meaning.* At a minimum, this entails recycling description, emerging analysis, and conclusions to at least a subsample of respondents. A more maximal approach to reciprocity would involve research participants in a collaborative effort to build empirically rooted theory.
- *Discussions of false consciousness which go beyond simply dismissing resistance to Marxist interpretations as such.* We need to discover the necessary conditions that free people to engage in ideology critique, given the psychological hold of illusion — "the things people cling to because they provide direction and meaning in their lives" (Fay, 1977, p. 214). There is a dialectic between people's self-understandings and researcher efforts to create a context which enables a questioning of both taken-for-granted beliefs and the authority that culture has over us (Bowers, 1984). There, in the nexus of that dialectic, lies the opportunity to create reciprocal, dialogic research designs which not only lead to self-reflection but also provide a forum in which to test the usefulness, the resonance of conceptual and theoretical formulations.

Dialectical Theory-Building versus Theoretical Imposition

> I do not believe that imposing Marxist rather than bourgeois categories is socialist practice. (Carr-Hill, 1984, p. 290)

The goal of theoretically guided empirical work is to create theory that possesses "evocative power" (Morgan, 1983, p. 298). By resonating with people's lived concerns, fears, and aspirations, emancipatory theory serves an energizing, catalytic role. It does this by increasing specificity at the contextual level in order to see how larger issues are embedded in the particulars of everyday life. The result is that theory becomes an expression and elaboration of politically progressive popular feelings rather than an abstract framework imposed by intellectuals on the complexity of lived experience.

Building empirically grounded theory requires a reciprocal relationship between data and theory. Data must be allowed to generate propositions in a dialectical manner that permits use of a priori theoretical frameworks, but which keeps a particular framework from becoming the container into which the data must be poured. The search is for theory which grows out of context-embedded data, not in a way that automatically rejects a priori theory, but in a way that keeps preconceptions from distorting the logic of evidence. For example, Ramsay (1983) aptly criticized Anyon's critical ethnographies (which focus on the effects of class and gender on the structure of U.S. public school classrooms) for telling us more about her predispositions than about the phenomena studied. Anyon's (1980, 1981) *certainty* and *clear-cutness* are particularly problematic, for, as Ramsay notes, "while we would agree that there is no such thing as 'value-free' or objective research, we would argue that there is a need to keep as open a frame of reference as is possible to allow the data to generate the propositions" (p. 316).

Theory is too often used to protect us from the awesome complexity of the world. Yet, "the road to complexity" is what we are on in our empirical efforts (Clark, 1985, p. 65). Moving beyond predisposition requires a set of procedures that illuminates the ways that investigators' values enter into research (Bredo & Feinberg, 1982, p. 439; Feinberg, 1983, pp. 159–160). Anchoring theoretical formulations in data requires a critical stance that will reveal the inadequacies of our pet theory and be open to counter-interpretations. Apple (1980–1981), in cautioning that conceptual validity precedes empirical accuracy, neglects the largely undialectical role that theory plays in most critical ethnography. Empirical evidence must be viewed as a mediator in a constant mutual interrogation between self and theory. Otherwise, neo-Marxist theory will fail to transcend "the hubris of the social sciences" still present in the two emergent alternatives to positivist orthodoxy — the interpretive and critical paradigms (Moon, 1983, p. 28). As Acker, Barry, and Esseveld (1983) note, "An emancipatory intent is no guarantee of an emancipatory outcome" (p. 431). The struggle, of course, is to develop a "passionate scholarship" (Du Bois, 1983) which can lead us toward a self-reflexive research paradigm that no longer reduces issues of bias to canonized methodology for establishing scientific knowledge (Cronbach, 1980; Goddard, 1973, p. 18).

The search for ways to operationalize reflexivity in critical inquiry is a journey into uncharted territory. Sabia and Wallulis (1983) make clear the danger: too often critical self-awareness comes to mean "a negative attitude towards competing approaches instead of its own self-critical perspective" (p. 26). Guidelines for developing critical self-awareness, hence, are rare. Nevertheless, while the methodological implications of critical theory remain relatively unexplored (Bredo & Feinberg, 1982, p. 281), the need for research approaches which advance a more equal world is receiving some attention (Acker, Barry & Esseveld, 1983; Apple, 1982; Comstock, 1982; Fay, 1975, 1977). Various suggestions for operationalizing reflexivity in critical inquiry can be drawn from that small body of work.

First, critical inquiry is a response to the experiences, desires, and needs of oppressed people (Fay, 1975). Its initial step is to develop an understanding of the world view of research participants. Central to establishing such understandings is a dialogic research design where respondents are actively involved in the construction and validation of meaning. The purpose of this phase of inquiry is to provide accounts that are a basis for further analysis and "a corrective to the investigator's preconceptions regarding the subjects' life-world and experiences" (Comstock, 1982, p. 381).

Second, critical inquiry inspires and guides the dispossessed in the process of cultural transformation; this is a process Mao Tse Tung characterized as "teach[ing] the masses clearly what we have learned from them confusedly" (quoted in Freire, 1973, p. 82). At the core of the transformation is "a reciprocal relationship in which every teacher is always a student and every pupil a teacher" (Gramsci quoted in Femia, 1975, p. 41). Thus, critical inquiry is a fundamentally dialogic and mutually educative enterprise. The present is cast against a historical backdrop while at the same time the "naturalness" of social arrangements is challenged so that social actors can see both the constraints and the potential for change in their situations.

Third, critical inquiry focuses on fundamental contradictions which help dispossessed people see how poorly their "ideologically frozen understandings" serve their interests (Comstock, 1982, p. 384). This search for contradictions must proceed from progressive elements of participants' current understandings, or what Willis (1977) refers to as "partial penetrations": the ability of people to pierce through cultural contradictions in incomplete ways that, nevertheless, provide entry points for the process of ideology critique.

Fourth, the validity of a critical account can be found, in part, in the participants' responses. Fay (1977) writes: "One test of the truth of critical theory is the considered reaction by those for whom it is supposed to be emancipatory. . . . Not only must a particular theory be offered as the reason why people should change their self-understandings, *but this must be done in an environment in which these people can reject this reason*" (pp. 218–219, italics in original). The point is to provide an environment that invites participants' critical reaction to researcher accounts of their worlds. As such, dialogic research designs allow praxis-oriented inquirers both to begin to grasp the necessary conditions for people to engage in ideology critique and transformative social action, and to distinguish between what Bernstein (1983) calls "enabling" versus "blinding" biases on the part of the researcher (p. 128).

Fifth, critical inquiry stimulates "a self-sustaining process of critical analysis and enlightened action" (Comstock, 1982, p. 387). The researcher joins the participants in a theoretically guided program of action extended over a period of time.

Earlier in this essay, I argued for reciprocity as a means to empower the researched. Here reciprocity is employed to build more useful theory. Research designs can be more or less participatory, but dialogic encounter is required to some extent if we are to invoke the reflexivity needed to protect research from the researcher's own enthusiasms. Debriefing sessions with participants provide an opportunity to look for exceptions to emerging generalizations. Submitting concepts and explanations to the scrutiny of all those involved sets up the possibility of theoretical exchange — the collaborative theorizing at the heart of research which both advances emancipatory theory and empowers the researched.

A strictly interpretive, phenomenological paradigm is inadequate insofar as it is based on an assumption of fully rational action.[10] Sole reliance on the participants' perceptions of their situation is misguided because, as neo-Marxists point out, false consciousness and ideological mystification may be present. A central challenge to the interpretive paradigm is to recognize that reality is more than negotiated accounts — that we are both shaped by and shapers of our world. For those interested in the development of a praxis-oriented research paradigm, a key issue revolves around this central challenge: how to maximize the researcher's mediation between people's self-understandings (in light of the need for ideology critique) and transformative social action *without becoming impositional.*

Comstock (1982) says that the critical researcher's task is to stimulate research participants into "a self-sustaining process of critical analysis and enlightened action" (p. 387). Doing such work in a nonelitist and nonmanipulative manner means that one wants to be not a "one-way propagandist," but rather like the Cobbett written about by Thompson (1963): Cobbett acknowledged "the aid which he is constantly deriving from those new thoughts which his thoughts produce in their minds." Thompson notes: "How moving is this insight into the dialectical nature of the very process by which his own ideas were formed! For Cobbett, thought was not a system but a relationship" (p. 758).

For theory to explain the structural contradictions at the heart of discontent, it must speak to the felt needs of a particular group in ordinary language (Fay, 1975, p. 98). If it is to spur toward action, theory must be grounded in the self-understandings of the dispossessed even as it seeks to enable them to reevaluate themselves and their situations. This is the central paradox of critical theory and provides its greatest challenge. The potential for creating reciprocal, dialogic research designs is rooted in the intersection between people's self-understandings and the researcher's efforts to provide a change-enhancing context. Such designs would both lead to self-reflection and provide the forum called for by Fay (1977) whereby the people for whom the theory is supposed to be emancipatory can participate in its construction and validation.

In sum, the development of emancipatory social theory requires an empirical stance which is open-ended, dialogically reciprocal, grounded in respect for human capacity, and yet profoundly skeptical of appearances and "common sense." Such an empirical stance is, furthermore, rooted in a commitment to the long-term, broad-based ideological struggle to transform structural inequalities.

Issues of Validity

> The job of validation is not to support an interpretation, but to find out what might be wrong with it. . . . To call for value-free standards of validity is a contradiction in terms, a nostalgic longing for a world that never was. (Cronbach, 1980, pp. 103–105)

What does empirical rigor mean in a postpositivist context?[11] If validity criteria are the products of the paradigms which spawn them (Morgan, 1983), what validity criteria best serve praxis-oriented research programs? The need to systematize as much as possible the ambiguity of our enterprise does not mean that we must deny the essential indeterminacy of human experience — "the crucial disparity between the being of the world and the knowledge we might have of it" (White, 1973, p. 32). My point is, rather, that if illuminating and resonant theory grounded in trustworthy data is desired, we must formulate self-corrective techniques that check the credibility of data and minimize the distorting effect of personal bias upon the logic of evidence (Kamarovsky, 1981).

Currently, paradigmatic uncertainty in the human sciences is leading to the reconceptualization of validity. Past efforts to leave subjective, tacit knowledge out of the "context of verification" are seen by many postpositivists as "naive empiricism." Inquiry is increasingly recognized as a process whereby tacit (subjective) knowledge and propositional (objective) knowledge are interwoven and mutually informing (Heron, 1981, p. 32; Polanyi, 1967). The absence of formulas to guarantee valid social knowledge forces us to "operate simultaneously at epistemological, theoretical and empirical levels with self-awareness" (Sharp & Green, 1975, p. 234). Our best tactic at present is to construct research designs that demand a vigorous self-reflexivity.

For praxis-oriented researchers, going beyond predisposition in our empirical efforts requires new techniques and concepts for obtaining and defining trustworthy data which avoid the pitfalls of orthodox notions of validity. The works of Reason and

Rowan (1981) and Guba and Lincoln (1981) offer important suggestions in this regard. Reason and Rowan advise borrowing concepts of validity from traditional research but caution us to revise and expand those concepts in ways appropriate to "an interactive, dialogic logic" (p. 240). Their notion of validity is captured in the phrase "objectively subjective" inquiry (p. xiii). Guba and Lincoln argue for analogues to the major principles of orthodox rigor. They state that in order to fulfill the minimum requirement for assessing validity in new paradigm research the techniques of triangulation, reflexivity, and member checks should be enlisted. Building on these, I offer a reconceptualization of validity appropriate for research that is openly committed to a more just social order.

First, *triangulation* is critical in establishing data-trustworthiness, a triangulation expanded beyond the psychometric definition of multiple measures to include multiple data sources, methods, and theoretical schemes. The researcher must consciously utilize designs that allow counterpatterns as well as convergence if data are to be credible.

Second, *construct validity* must be dealt with in ways that recognize its roots in theory construction (Cronbach & Meehl, 1955). Our empirical work must operate within a conscious context of theory-building. Where are the weak points of the theoretical tradition we are operating within? Are we extending theory? Revising it? Testing it? Corroborating it? Determining that constructs are actually occurring, rather than they are merely inventions of the researcher's perspective, requires a self-critical attitude toward how one's own preconceptions affect the research. Building emancipatory social theory requires a ceaseless confrontation with and respect for the experiences of people in their daily lives to guard against theoretical imposition. A *systematized reflexivity* that reveals how a priori theory has been changed by the logic of the data becomes essential in establishing construct validity in ways that contribute to the growth of illuminating and change-enhancing social theory.

As an example, Acker, Barry, and Esseveld (1983), in a noteworthy effort to reconstruct "the social relations that produce the research itself" (p. 431), write that "our commitment to bringing our subjects into the research as active participants [has] influenced our rethinking of our original categories . . ." (p. 434). As part of their self-reflexive essay on their research into the relation between changes in the structural situation of women and changes in consciousness, they explore the tension "between letting the data speak for itself and using abstracted categories." They ask, "How do we explain the lives of others without violating their reality?" (p. 429). Contrast this with Willis's (1977) classic ethnography where there is no clear indication how the researcher's perspectives were altered by the logic of the data. Without this account, one is left viewing the role of theory in this research (which is so strongly shaped by a priori conceptions) as being nondialectical, unidirectional, an imposition that disallows counter-patterns and alternative explanations (see also Lather, 1986b; Walker, 1985).

Third, *face validity* needs to be reconsidered. Kidder (1982) contends that although it has been treated lightly and dismissed, face validity is relatively complex and inextricably tied to construct validity. "Research with face validity provides a 'click of recognition' and a 'yes, of course' instead of 'yes, but' experience" (p. 56). Face validity is operationalized by recycling description, emerging analysis, and conclusions back through at least a subsample of respondents: "Good research at the nonalienating end of the spectrum . . . goes back to the subjects with the tentative results, and refines them in light of the subjects' reactions" (Reason & Rowan, 1981, p. 248). The possibility of encountering false consciousness, however, creates a limit on the usefulness of "member checks" (Guba & Lincoln, 1981) in establishing the trustworthiness of data. False consciousness, an admittedly problematic phenomenon (Acker, Barry, & Esseveld, 1983), however, does exist. For reasons illuminated by Gramsci's (1971) theories of hegemony, most people to some extent identify with and/or accept ideologies which do not serve their best interests. Thus, an analysis which only takes account of actors' perceptions of their situations could result in research being incorrectly declared invalid. The link between face and construct validity and the possible false consciousness of research participants is an area that very much needs empirical exploration. Perhaps the best that can be suggested at this point is that, just as reliability is necessary but not sufficient to establish validity within positivism, building face validity into new paradigm research should become a necessary but not sufficient approach to establishing data credibility.

Fourth, given the emancipatory intent of praxis-oriented research, I propose the less well-known notion of *catalytic validity* (Brown & Tandom, 1978; Reason & Rowan, 1981, p. 240). Catalytic validity represents the degree to which the research process reorients, focuses, and energizes participants toward knowing reality in order to transform it, a process Freire (1973) terms conscientization. Of the guidelines proposed here, this is by far the most unorthodox; it flies directly in the face of the positivist demand for researcher-neutrality. The argument for catalytic validity is premised not only within a recognition of the reality-altering impact of the research process, but also in the desire to consciously channel this impact so that respondents gain self-understanding and, ultimately, self-determination through research participation.

Efforts to produce social knowledge that will advance the struggle for a more equitable world must pursue rigor as well as relevance. By arguing for a more systematic approach to triangulation and reflexivity, a new emphasis for face validity, and inclusion of catalytic validity, I stand opposed to those who claim that empirical accountability either is impossible to achieve or is able to be side-stepped in praxis-oriented, advocacy research. Lack of concern for data credibility within praxis-oriented research programs will only decrease the legitimacy of the knowledge generated therein. Praxis-oriented research can only benefit from agreed-upon procedures that make empirical decision-making public and hence subject to criticism. Most important, if we do not develop such procedures, our theory-building will suffer from a failure to protect our work from our passions and limitations. I join Lecourt (1975) in his call for an "ardent text" (p. 49) grounded in "the real motion of knowledge" (p. 79), which is as tied to passion as to "objectivity." The tension between advocacy and scholarship, however, can be fruitful only to the extent that it pushes us toward becoming vigorously self-aware in our efforts to develop a praxis-oriented research paradigm.

Summary

This essay has one essential argument: a more collaborative approach to critical inquiry is needed to empower the researched, to build emancipatory theory, and to move toward the establishment of data credibility within praxis-oriented, advocacy research. The present turmoil in the human sciences frees us to construct new designs based on alternative tenets and epistemological commitments. My goal is to move research in many different and, indeed, contradictory directions in the hope that more interesting and useful ways of knowing will emerge. Rather than establishing a new orthodoxy, we need to experiment, document, and share our efforts toward emancipatory research. To quote Polkinghorne (1983):

> What is needed most is for practitioners to experiment with the new designs and the submit their attempts and results to examination by other participants in the debate. The new historians of science have made it clear that methodological questions are decided in the practice of research by those committed to developing the best possible answers to their questions, not by armchair philosophers of research. (p. xi)

Let us get on with the task.[12]

Notes

1. Polkinghorne (1983) traces the history of the term *human science.* He argues that "behavioral science" retains the specter of behaviorism and its prohibition against including consciousness as a part of scientific study. "Social science" carries connotations of seeking a knowledge characteristic of the natural sciences in its law-seeking mode of inquiry. "Human science," he argues, is more inclusive, using multiple systems of inquiry, "a science which approaches questions about the human realm with an openness to its special characteristics and a willingness to let the questions inform which methods are appropriate" (p. 289).

2. In another article (Lather, 1984), I explore what Gramsci's concept of "developing progressive groups" means in a contemporary context by arguing that women presently constitute a "developing progressive group" ripe with potential for assuming a position at the center of a broad-based struggle for a more equal world.

3. Morgan (1983) distinguishes between positivist, phenomenological, and critical/praxis-oriented research paradigms. While my earlier work used the term *openly ideological,* I find that *praxis-oriented* better describes the emergent paradigm I have been tracking over the last few years (Lather, 1986b). "Openly ideological" invites comparisons with fundamentalist and conservative movements, whereas "praxis-oriented" clarifies the critical and empowering roots of a research paradigm openly committed to critiquing the status quo and building a more just society.

   Praxis-oriented means "activities that combat dominance and move toward self-organization and that push toward thoroughgoing change in the practices of . . . the social formation" (Benson, 1983, p. 338). Praxis, is, of course, a word with a history. In this essay, I use the term to mean the dialectical tension, the interactive, reciprocal shaping of theory and practice that I see at the center of an emancipatory social science. The essence of my argument, then, is that we who do empirical research in the name of emancipatory politics must discover ways to connect our research methodology to our theoretical concerns and commitments. At its simplest, this is a call for critical inquirers to practice in their empirical endeavors what they preach in their theoretical formulations.

4. Feminist research is not monolithic: some researchers operate out of a conventional positivist paradigm, others out of an interpretive/phenomenological one, while others still — an increasing number — use a critical, praxis-oriented paradigm concerned both with producing emancipatory knowledge and with empowering the researched (see Acker, Barry, & Esseveld, 1983; Bowles & Duelli-Klein, 1983; Roberts, 1981; Westkott, 1979).

5. It was actually French philosopher Bachelard who originated the concept of epistemological break, which Althusser then applied to the work of Marx (see Lecourt, 1975). Epistemological break means a rupture in the established way of conceptualizing an issue, a rupture which essentially *inverts* meaning. Hesse (1980), for example, uses the term to characterize those who argue not only *against* the possibility of an "objective" social science but *for* the possibilities inherent in an explicitly value-based social science with emancipatory goals.

6. Phrase used by Jean Anyon in a session of the annual meeting of the American Educational Research Association, Montreal, April 1984.

7. The basic assumptions of positivism are four: 1) the aims, concepts, and methods of the natural sciences are applicable to the social sciences; 2) the correspondence theory of truth which holds that reality is knowable through correct measurement methods; 3) the goal of social research is to discover universal laws of human behavior which transcend culture and history; and 4) the fact-value dichotomy, the denial of both the theory-laden dimensions of observation and the value-laden dimensions of theory. For an overview and critique of each of the three paradigms, the positivist, the interpretive, and the critical/praxis-oriented, see, respectively, Bredo and Feinberg (1982), Carr and Kemmis (1983), and Bernstein (1976).

8. Two examples of the dangers of conceptual overdeterminism leading to theoretical imposition (the lack of a reciprocal relationship between data and theory) in the new sociology of education are correspondence theory, which posited an overly deterministic mirror-image relationship between schools and the needs of corporate capitalism (Apple, 1979; Bowles & Gintis, 1976), and the wishful thinking which saw resistance in every inattentive student and recalcitrant teacher (for critiques, see Bullough & Gitlin, 1985; Giroux, 1983).

9. Sears (1983) first used this term in a conference paper.

10. The inadequacies of an overreliance on rationality in human behavior are eloquently captured in Ascher's letter to de Beauvoir, a letter written to "clear the air" after Ascher had written a biography of de Beauvoir: "I don't think you ever grasped sufficiently the way the unconscious can hold one back from grasping a freedom consciously chosen. Too often I see your sense of freedom being based on a rationalism that denies that murky inner world over which we have as little, or much, control as the world outside us. And, in fact, control would be your word, not mine. For I believe we have to love this deep inner self and try to be in harmony with it" (Ascher, De Salvio, & Ruddick, 1984, p. 93; see also Harding, 1982).

11. Issues of validity in openly ideological research are dealt with much more fully in Lather (1986b).

12. To avoid becoming "an armchair philosopher of research" myself, I am presently engaged in what I see as a long term effort to explore student resistance to liberatory curriculum in an introductory women's studies course (Lather, 1986a). My theoretical concern is with the processes of "ideological consent" (Kellner, 1978, p. 46), especially the enabling conditions which open people up to ideology critique and those which limit these processes (Berlak, 1986).

References

Acker, J., Barry, K., & Esseveld, J. (1983). Objectivity and truth: Problems in doing feminist research. *Women's Studies International Forum, 6,* 423–435.

Anyon, J. (1980). Social class and the hidden curriculum of work. *Journal of Education, 62,* 67–92.

Anyon, J. (1981). Social class and school knowledge. *Curriculum Inquiry, 11,* 3–42.

Anyon, J. (1982). Adequate social science, curriculum investigations, and theory. *Theory into Practice, 21,* 34–37.

Anyon, J. (1983). Accommodation, resistance, and female gender. In S. Walker & L. Burton (Eds.), *Gender and education* (pp. 19–38). Sussex, Eng.: Falmer Press.

Apple, M. (1979). *Ideology and curriculum.* Boston: Routledge & Kegan Paul.

Apple, M. (1980–1981). The other side of the hidden curriculum: Correspondence theories and the labor process. *Interchange, 11*(3), 5–22.

Apple, M. (1982). *Education and power.* Boston: Routledge & Kegan Paul.

Ascher, C., De Salvio, L., & Ruddick, S. (Eds.). (1984). *Between women.* Boston: Beacon Press.

Benson, J.K. (1983). A dialectical method for the study of organizations. In G. Morgan (Ed.), *Beyond method: Strategies for social research* (pp. 331–346). Beverly Hills, CA: Sage.

Berlak, A. (). *Teaching for liberation and empowerment in the liberal arts: Toward the development of pedagogy that overcomes resistance.* Unpublished paper.

Berlak, A., & Berlak, H. (1981). *Dilemmas of schooling: Teaching and social change.* New York: Methuen.

Bernstein, R. (1976). *The restructuring of social and political theory.* New York: Harcourt Brace Jovanovich.

Bernstein, R. (1983). *Beyond objectivism and relativism: Science, hermeneutics, and praxis.* Philadelphia: University of Pennsylvania Press.

Bottomore, T. (1978). Marxism and sociology. In T. Bottomore & R. Nisbet (Eds.), *A history of sociological analysis* (pp. 118–148). London: Hunemann.

Bowers, C. A. (1984). *The promise of theory: Education and the politics of cultural change.* New York: Longman.

Bowles, G., & Duelli-Klein, R. (Eds.). (1983). *Theories of women's studies.* Boston: Routledge & Kegan Paul.

Bowles, S. & Gintis, H. (1976). *Schooling in capitalist America: Educational reform and the contradictions of economic life.* New York: Basic Books.

Bredo, E., & Feinberg, W. (Eds.). (1982). *Knowledge and values in social and educational research.* Philadelphia: Temple University Press.

Brown, D., & Tandom, R. (1978). Interviews as catalysts. *Journal of Applied Psychology, 63,* 197–205.

Bullough, R. & Gitlin, A. (1985). Beyond control: Rethinking teacher resistance. *Education and Society, 3,* 65–73.

Bullough, R., Goldstein, S., & Holt, L. (1982). Rational curriculum: Teachers and alienation. *Journal of Curriculum Theorizing, 4,* 132–143.

Carr, W., & Kemmis, S. (1983). *Becoming critical: Knowing through action research.* Deakin, Australia: Deakin University Press.

Carr-Hill, R. (1984). Radicalizing survey methodology. *Quality and Quantity, 18,* 275–292.

Clark, D. (1985). Emerging paradigms in organizational theory and research. In Y. Lincoln (Ed.), *Organizational theory and inquiry: The paradigm revolution* (pp. 43–78). Beverly Hills, CA: Sage.

Comstock. D. (1982). A method for critical research. In E. Bredo and W. Feinberg (Eds.), *Knowledge and values in social and educational research* (pp. 370–390). Philadelphia: Temple University Press.

Cronbach, L. (1975). Beyond the two disciplines of scientific psychology. *American Psychologist, 30,* 116–127.

Cronbach, L. (1980). Validity on parole: Can we go straight? *New Directions for Testing and Measurement, 5,* 99–108.

Cronbach, L., & Meehl, P. (1955). Construct validity in psychological tests. *Psychological Bulletin, 52,* 281–302.

Du Bois, B. (1983). Passionate scholarship: Notes on values, knowing and method in feminist social science. In G. Bowles and R. Duelli-Klein (Eds.), *Theories of Women's Studies* (pp. 105-116). Boston: Routledge & Kegan Paul.

Eisner, E. (1983). Anastasia might still be alive, but the monarchy is dead. *Educational Researcher, 12*(5), 13-14, 23-24.

Everhart, R. (1977). Between stranger and friend: Some consequences of "long term" fieldwork in schools. *American Educational Research Journal, 14,* 1-15.

Everhart, R. (1983). *Reading, writing and resistance: Adolescence and labor in a junior high school.* Boston: Routledge & Kegan Paul.

Fay, B. (1975). *Social theory and political practice.* London: Allen & Unwin.

Fay, B. (1977). How people change themselves: The relationship between critical theory and its audience. In T. Ball (Ed.), *Political theory and praxis* (pp. 200-233). Minneapolis: University of Minnesota Press.

Feinberg, W. (1983). *Understanding education: Toward a reconstruction of educational inquiry.* New York: Cambridge University Press.

Femia, J. (1975). Hegemony and consciousness in the thought of Antonio Gramsci. *Political Studies, 23,* 29-48.

Fox-Keller, E. (1985). *Reflections on gender and science.* New Haven, CT: Yale University Press.

Freire, P. (1973). *Pedagogy of the oppressed.* New York: Seabury.

Giddens, A. (1979). *Central problems in social theory.* Berkeley: University of California Press.

Giroux, H.A. (1981). *Ideology, culture, and the process of schooling.* Philadlephia: Temple University Press.

Giroux, H.A. (1983). Theories of reproduction and resistance in the new sociology of education: A critical analysis. *Harvard Educational Review, 53,* 257–293.

Glaser, B., & Strauss, A. (1967). *The discovery of grounded theory: Strategies for qualitative research.* Chicago: Aldine.

Goddard, D. (1973). Max Weber and the objectivity of social science. *History and Theory, 12,* 1–22.

Gramsci, A. (1971). *Selections from the prison notebooks of Antonio Gramsci* [1929–1935] (Q. Hoare & G. Smith, Eds. & Trans.). New York: International Publishers.

Grundy, S. (1982). Three modes of action research. *Curriculum Perspectives, 3*(2), 22–34.

Guba, E., & Lincoln, Y. (1981). *Effective evaluation.* San Francisco: Jossey-Bass.

Habermas, J. (1971). *Theory and practice.* Boston: Beacon Press.

Hall, B. (1975). Participatory research: An approach for change. *Prospects, 8*(2), 24–31.

Hall, B. (1981). The democratization of research in adult and non-formal education. In P. Reason and J. Rowan (Eds.), *Human inquiry* (pp. 447–456). New York: Wiley.

Hanmer, J., & Saunders, S. (1984). *Well-founded fear: A community study of violence to women.* London: Hutchinson.

Harding, S. (1982). Is gender a variable in conceptions of rationality? *Dialectica, 36,* 225–242.

Harding, S. (). *The science question in feminism.* Ithaca, NY: Cornell University Press.

Hargreaves, A. (1982). Resistance and relative autonomy theories: Problems of distortion and incoherence in recent Marxist analyses of education. *British Journal of Sociology of Education, 3,* 107–126.

Hendrick, C. (1983). A middle-way metatheory. [Review of *Toward transformation in social knowledge.*] *Contemporary Psychology, 28,* 504–507.

Heron, J. (1981). Experimental research methods. In P. Reason and J. Rowan (Eds.), *Human inquiry* (pp. 153–166). New York: Wiley.

Hesse, M. (1980). *Revolution and reconstruction in the philosophy of science.* Bloomington: Indiana University Press.

Kamarovsky, M. (1981). Women then and now: A journey of detachment and engagement. *Women's Studies Quarterly, 10*(2), 5–9.

Kaplan, A. (1964). *The conduct of inquiry: Methodology for behavioral science.* San Francisco: Chandler.

Kellner D. (1975). The Frankfurt School revisited. *New German Critique, 4,* 131–152.

Kellner, D. (1978). Ideology, Marxism, and advanced capitalism. *Socialist Review, 42,* 37–65.

Kidder, L. (1982, June). Face validity from multiple perspectives. In D. Brinberg and L. Kidder (Eds.), *New directions for methodology of social and behavioral science: Forms of validity in research* (No. 12, pp. 41–57). San Francisco: Jossey-Bass.

Krueger, M. (1981). In search of the "subjects" in social theory and research. *Psychology and Social Theory, 1*(2), 54–61.

Kushner, S., & Norris, N. (1980-1981). Interpretation, negotiation and validity in naturalistic research. *Interchange, 11*(4), 26–36.

Laslett, B., & Rapoport, R. (1975). Collaborative interviewing and interactive research. *Journal of Marriage and the Family, 37,* 968–977.

Lather, P. (1984). Critical theory, curricular transformation, and feminist mainstreaming. *Journal of Education, 166,* 49–62.

Lather, P. (1986a, June). *Empowering research methodologies: Feminist perspectives.* Paper presented at the annual meeting of the National Women's Studies Association, Champaign, IL.

Lather, P. (1986b). Issues of validity in openly ideological research: Between a rock and a soft place. *Interchange, 17,* 63–84.

Lecourt, D. (1975). *Marxism and epistemology.* London: National Labor Board.

Masemann, V. (1982). Critical ethnography in the study of comparative education. *Comparative Education Review, 26,* 1–15.

McNeil, L. (1984, April). *Critical theory and ethnography in curriculum analysis.* Paper presented at annual meeting of American Educational Research Association, New Orleans.

McRobbie, A. (1978). Working class girls and the culture of femininity. In Women's Study Group (Ed.). *Women take issue: Aspects of women's subordination* (pp. 96–108). London: Hutchinson.

Mies, M. (1984). Towards a methodology for feminist research. In E. Altbach, J. Clausen, D. Schultz, & N. Stephan (Eds.), *German feminism: Readings in politics and literature* (pp. 357–366). Albany: State University of New York Press.

Miller, J. (1986). Women as teachers: Enlarging conversations on issues of gender and self-control. *Journal of Curriculum and Supervision, 1,* 111–121.

Mishler, E. (1979). Meaning in context: Is there any other kind? *Harvard Educational Review, 49,* 1–19.

Mitroff, I., & Kilmann, R. (1978). *Methodological approaches to social science.* San Francisco: Jossey-Bass.

Moon, J.D. (1983). Political ethics and critical theory. In D. Sabia & J. Wallulis (Eds.), *Changing social science: Critical theory and other critical perspectives* (pp. 171–188). Albany: State University of New York Press.

Morgan, G. (Ed.). (1983). *Beyond method: Strategies for social research.* Beverly Hills, CA: Sage.

Namenwirth, M. (1986). Science through a feminist prism. In R. Bleir (Ed.), *Feminist approaches to science* (pp. 18–41). New York: Pergamon Press.

Oakley, A. (1981). Interviewing women: A contradiction in terms. In H. Roberts (Ed.), *Doing feminist research* (pp. 30–61). Boston: Routledge & Kegan Paul.

Ogbu, J. (1981). School ethnography: A multilevel approach. *Anthropology and Education Quarterly, 12,* 3–29.

Phillips, D.C. (1983). After the wake: Postpositivistic educational thought. *Educational Researcher, 12*(5), 4–12.

Polanyi, M. (1967). *The tacit dimension.* Garden City, NY: Anchor Books, Doubleday.

Polkinghorne, D. (1983). *Methodology for the human sciences: Systems of inquiry.* Albany: State University of New York Press.

Ramsay, P. (1983). A response to Anyon from the Antipodes. *Curriculum Inquiry, 13,* 295–320.

Reason, P. & Rowan, J. (1981). Issues of validity in new paradigm research. In P. Reason & J. Rowan (Eds.), *Human inquiry* (pp. 239–252). New York: Wiley.

Reinharz, S. (1979). *On becoming a social scientist.* San Francisco: Jossey-Bass.

Reinharz, S. (1983). Experiential analysis: A contribution to feminist research. In G. Bowles & R. Duelli-Klein (Eds.), *Theories of women's studies* (pp. 162–191). Boston: Routledge & Kegan Paul.

Reinharz, S. (1985). *Feminist distrust: A response to misogyny and gynopia in sociological work.* Unpublished manuscript. [Expanded version of Reinharz, S. (1985). Feminist distrust: Problems of context and content in sociological work. In D. Berg & K. Smith (Eds.), *Clinical demands of social research* (pp. 153–172). Beverly Hills, CA: Sage.]

Reynolds, D. (1980-1981). The naturalistic method and educational and social research: A Marxist critique. *Interchange, 11*(4), 77–89.

Rich, A. (1979). *On lies, secrets, and silence: Selected prose, 1966–1978*. New York: Norton.

Roberts, H. (1981). *Doing feminist research*. Boston: Routledge & Kegan Paul.

Rose, H. (1979). Hyper-reflexivity: A new danger for the counter-movements. In H. Nowotny & H. Rose (Eds.), *Counter-movements in the sciences: The sociology of the alternatives to big science* (pp. 277–289). Boston: Reidel.

Sabia, D., & Wallulis, J. (Eds.). (1983). *Changing social science: Critical theory and other critical perspectives*. Albany: State University of New York Press.

Salamini, L. (1981). *The sociology of political praxis: An introduction to Gramsci's theory*. Boston: Routledge & Kegan Paul.

Schwartz, P., & Oglivy, J. (1979, April). *The emergent paradigm: Changing patterns of thought and belief* (Values and Lifestyles Program Report No. 7). Menlo Park, CA: Stanford Research Institute (S.R.I.) International.

Sears, J. T. (1983, October). *Black holes of critical theory: Problems and prospects of ethnographic research*. Paper presented at Fifth Annual Curriculum Theorizing Conference, Dayton, OH.

Sharp, R., & Green, A. (1975). *Education and social control: A study in progressive primary education*. Boston: Routledge & Kegan Paul.

Smith, J.K. (1983). Quantitative vs. qualitative research: An attempt to clarify the issue. *Educational Researcher, 12*(3), 6–13.

Smith, J. & Heshusius, L. (1986). Closing down the conversation: The end of the quantitative-qualitative debate among educational inquirers. *Educational Researcher, 15*(1), 4–12.

Thompson, E.P. (1963). *The making of the English working class*. New York: Pantheon Books.

Thompson, E.P. (1978). *The poverty of theory and other essays*. New York: Monthly Review Press.

Tripp, D.H. (1983). Co-authorship and negotiation: The interview as act of creation. *Interchange, 14*(3), 32–45.

Tripp, D.H. (1984, August). *Action research and professional development*. Discussion paper for the Australian College of Education Project, 1984–1985. Murdock, Australia: Murdock University.

Walker, J.C. (1985). Rebels with our applause: A critique of resistance theory in Paul Willis's ethnography of schooling. *Journal of Education, 167*(2), 63–83.

Wax, R. (1952). Reciprocity as a field technique. *Human Organization, 11*, 34–41.

Westkott, M. (1979). Feminist criticism of the social sciences. *Harvard Educational Review, 49*, 422–430.

Wexler, P. (1982). Ideology and education: From critique to class action. *Interchange, 13*(1), 53–78.

White, H. (1973). Foucault decoded: Notes from underground. *History and Theory, 12*, 23–54.

Willis, P. (1977). *Learning to labor: How working class kids get working class jobs*. New York: Columbia University Press.

Wright, E.O. (1978). *Class, crisis and the state*. London: National Labor Board.

Modern and Postmodern Racism in Europe: Dialogic Approach and Anti-Racist Pedagogies

RAMÓN FLECHA

To make the public more aware of a new wave of racism in Europe, the Council of the European Union declared 1997 the "European Year against Racism." In recognition of this declaration, many European schools have developed and implemented new pedagogies aimed at eliminating racism. Despite their efforts, however, racism continues to manifest itself in new and alarming ways. In response, educators and intellectuals have engaged in deep reflection about how to develop better anti-racist programs and policies to counter this threat to peaceful educational relationships.

One weakness of current anti-racist educational programs and policies is their frequent confusion between dialogic and relativistic approaches. The dialogic approach fosters different people's living together according to rules agreed upon by all through free and egalitarian dialogue. In contrast, the relativistic approach rejects such rules with the argument that they eliminate the identities and differences of oppressed people. This article aims to clarify the differences between relativist and dialogic approaches in educational literature, and between their respective consequences in relation to old and new forms of racism. The older, modern forms of racism are based on arguments of inequality among races and the existence of superior and inferior races. Newer, postmodern forms of racism stress cultural difference among ethnicities and races rather than equality. The first two sections of this article outline the ways in which newer forms of racism challenge European education, and argue for the need to include a dialogic approach in education in order to overcome racism. The argument builds on definitions of modern and postmodern racism and describes how both currently coexist in Europe. It addresses the fact that, although a modern tradition of anti-racist education exists in Europe, the intellectual and educational tools currently in use are insufficient to combat postmodern racism. It further demonstrates that some concepts used to fight modern racism — concepts related to difference and identity — actually promote postmodern racism by failing to include the idea of equality.

Harvard Educational Review   Vol. 69   No. 2   Summer 1999

The third section argues that modern racism is generated primarily by ethnocentric beliefs, and develops the three main characteristics of ethnocentrism as the intellectual base of modern racism. The fourth section addresses the relationship between postmodern racism and its post-structuralist bases by developing the three main characteristics of relativism as the intellectual basis of postmodern racism. It also raises crucial questions for educators by discussing the extent to which authors such as Jacques Derrida, Michel Foucault, and Martin Heidegger are often misread in educational literature. The final section develops the three main characteristics of the dialogic approach by focusing on how this approach differs from the others. It draws from educational and social theories such as those of Paulo Freire and Jürgen Habermas, and includes examples of educational practices that confront both modern and postmodern racism.

The Challenges of New Racism to Current European Education

The Declaration of the European Year against Racism was justified by the growth of racism in European society, particularly the rapid rise of neo-Nazism in the 1990s. In Austria, the neo-Nazi Freiheitliche Partei Österreichs (FPO)[1] won 27.6 percent of the vote in the first elections to the European Parliament, while the first and second parties won 29.6 percent and 29.1 percent respectively. Similarly, Jean-Marie Le Pen's Front National won 15.1 percent of the vote in the 1995 French presidential elections. In the 1994 Belgian city council elections, the extreme right Vlaams Blok won the relative majority of votes in several Flemish cities, including Antwerp, where a coalition of the other parties prevented Vlaams Blok's participation in the government. In 1997, in Norway, the neo-Nazi Progress Party (Fremskrittspartiet) came in second in the general presidential election with 15.3 percent of the votes. Also in 1997, the neo-Nazi Vojislav Seselj, a sociologist who was the first to speak of ethnic purification in the Bosnian War, won 50 percent of the votes in the second round of elections in Serbia.

These ideologies also influence what European youth do and believe. In 1991, the Austrian government launched a campaign against the use of a game for teenagers in which players received points for sending Jews, gays, and lesbians to the gas chamber. In 1988 in Vienna, 20 percent of the surveyed teenagers declared they were close to the extreme right, and 58 percent reported that they supported the idea of one strong person's taking power and imposing order (Cáceres, 1993). The effects of these ideologies on European youth directly challenge educators to develop new programs and new policies to counter these problems, but they are unsure how to stem racism's alarming growth. Hoping for solutions, educators have often turned to programs that actually exacerbate rather than eliminate racism. Today, for example, many European educators emphasize the idea of diversity as a way of opposing growing beliefs in the superiority or inferiority of particular races or ethnicities. They are unaware that those who hold racist beliefs, such as the neo-Nazi groups previously cited, also use the concept of difference to support their programs of hate. Focusing on difference and diversity while excluding the idea of equality obscures the possibility of solidarity and masks the possibility of people's living together in the same space and sharing the same educational institutions.

Educators must clarify this lack of awareness if they are to develop effective tools for the fight against racism. There is an emerging effort for clarification grounded in dialogic perspectives from which current intellectuals contribute to the development of new anti-racist pedagogies. The works of authors like Habermas and Freire are oriented toward a combination of equality and difference, and therefore provide an alternative framework that challenges both ethnocentrist and relativist bases of current European racism. From this perspective, anti-racist educators give support, for instance, to the Gypsy women who claim both the right to education and the right to decide what kind of education would respect their identities. Such thinking replaces the idea that "we are different" with the idea that "we are equal and we are different."

This clarification requires that we engage in an in-depth study of key relativist and dialogic authors. Much educational literature on racism uses the works of authors such as Foucault or Habermas, but its authors have often never read these works directly. They often cite these authors indirectly with no notation of the authors' works, references, or pages.[2] In short, they cite secondary rather than primary sources. In so doing, they extend their confusions to other educators who later develop anti-racist actions with good intentions but very misguided orientations.

The Need for the Dialogic Approach in Current European Education

Europe has been a continent of emigration since 1492; thus, European schools have historically educated primarily European students. As a result, we have developed educational theories and practices based on the assumption that mainstream European culture is the universal norm. Only in the twentieth century has this emigration process reversed to become one of immigration (Contreras, 1994).

European schools reflect these changes. As a result of immigration, our educational institutions are receiving an increasing number of people from Africa and Asia. In Spain, for example, between 1988 and 1997 the total number of legal immigrants increased by 69 percent, but the proportion of African and Asian legal immigrants within that percentage rose by 298 percent. Mobility among European populations within the European Union has also increased the multinational composition of schools.[3] Schools have also been deluged by immigrant populations in response to social and political changes in Eastern Europe. Additionally, higher birth rates and the shift from itinerant to settled life have increased the Gypsy population in schools.

As a result of this new multicultural environment, Europeans now face the problem of learning how to live together in the same territories and educational institutions. People can answer this question by using either power claims or validity claims as the basis of their actions (Habermas, 1989a). In essence, they must choose between violence or dialogue (Giddens, 1994). Power claims impose actions on people, while validity claims seek a consensual basis for action through argumentation. Relativistic approaches do not differentiate between these two types of claims because they argue that all claims are generated by power. In contrast, the dialogic approach rejects power claims and instead promotes validity claims.

Using power claims to orient action results in the coexistence of modern and postmodern racism in Europe today. Modern racism occurs when the rules of the dominant culture are imposed on diverse peoples in the name of integration. Postmodern racism occurs when people deny the possibility of dialogue among diverse groups and reject the possibility of different groups living together in the same territory. Today, anti-racist educational programs and policies fight modern racism and its idea of racial inequality, which is still very powerful in our institutions and in ourselves. At the same time, however, many of these anti-racist educational programs promote a seductive image of postmodern racism in spaces where modern racism has already been clearly rejected. Facing the challenges of both modern and postmodern racism, the dialogic approach works so that people from different ethnic backgrounds can live together in the same educational system, using rules that result from a dialogue between them.

Modern racism claims inequality among races. For instance, traditional Western racism has promoted the idea that *Payos* are superior to Gypsies.[4] It considers social and cultural inequalities to be the consequence of biological characteristics of people, rather than the social and political construction of those in power. From the perspective of modern racism, Gypsies have poorer educational achievements and lower social positions because they are lazier or less intelligent, and not because schools are Payo institutions and Gypsies have less power in education and society (Presencia Gitana, 1991).

Modern racism was characteristic of European industrial society. During the 1960s, immigrants were channeled into lower paying jobs. The labor market needed people from other cultures to do the jobs that mainstream citizens considered undesirable, and the perceived inequality of races legitimized this exploitation. The explanation that certain races' lower academic achievement was due to inferior motivation and intelligence justified their future placement in lower status positions.

During the last few decades, this idea of racial inequality has been countered and partially defeated by anti-racist pedagogies. As a result, statements about the superiority or inferiority of one race relative to another are steadfastly avoided in educational literature and curricula. Most European authors (e.g., Molina, 1994) reject the concept of race, which is now considered a biological concept inapplicable to socially constructed human identities.[5] In Europe, classifying people according to race is often associated with ethnic cleansing. The Holocaust still looms large in the memories of many Europeans, and the events in Kosovo are a reminder that such events are not limited to history. Spain, for example, forbids delineation by race in any official document. In place of the concept of race, many European ethnic minorities and social scientists now use the concept of ethnicity, a term that takes into account both biological and cultural aspects of identity.

Many educators also focus on differences among ethnicities. They do so, however, in a society in which ethnic differentiation is rapidly becoming the basis for racist politics as a result of the social, political, and economic inequalities brought about by the shift from an industrial to an informational society (Castells, 1996, 1997, 1998). This transformation has led to a scarcity of stable jobs. In this changing economy, some Europeans regard immigrants as potential job competitors and as social burdens on the public budget. They do not want to treat other ethnic groups as subordinate, but they do want them to be segregated from their children, their community, and their country. When minority children fail, they are blamed for the poor academic performance of their school and sometimes even the educational system; when they succeed, they are considered to be stealing scarce jobs.

Supporters of barriers to immigration or even of expulsion of immigrants have looked for new ways to legitimize their agendas.[6] Postmodern thought has provided the intellectual context to do so, enabling the new racism to shift its focus from overcoming race inequalities to recognizing ethnic and cultural differences. An increasing number of European educators who claim to be anti-racist are angered by statements of racial inferiority. Yet they strongly support the construction of barriers to students from other ethnicities, arguing that such students are too different to be compatible with Europeans and that they cannot preserve their ethnic identities without being assimilated.

Ironically, these educators (Guitart, 1998) use the same arguments as the politicians of growing European neo-Fascism, who also stress the recognition of difference in their political agendas in order to promote exclusion. For instance, Haider, the acknowledged leader of European neo-Nazism, proposed an amendment to the Austrian constitution stating that Austria is not a country of immigration. He based his statements not on claims of racial inferiority, but on the postmodern concept of difference: "If I lived in Istanbul, no one would imagine that I would change the Half Moon for the Cross in my child's school. . . . Those arriving in our country, in our world, should accept the basic principles of our society, of our culture" (Haider, cited in Martí Font, 1993, p. 6).

In Europe today, updated anti-racist pedagogies must be prepared to deal with both modern and postmodern racism. Most pedagogies lack adequate intellectual resources to do so. Only the dialogic perspective — such as that provided by Jürgen Habermas (1984, 1987, 1989a, 1996), Anthony Giddens (1991, 1992, 1994), Ulrich Beck (Beck & Beck-Gernsheim, 1995; Beck, Giddens, & Lash, 1994), and even by rational choice theorists such as Jon Elster (1998) — can provide an appropriate intellectual framework to deal with both forms of racism. We must first differentiate the dialogic approach from the intellectual foundations of contemporary discrimination: ethnocentrism (modern racism) and relativism (postmodern racism).

Ethnocentrism of Modern Racism

Ethnocentrism is the primary basis of modern racism. With reference to multicultural relations, the three main characteristics of ethnocentrism are inequality, Western universalism, and capitalist democracy.

Inequality

Ethnocentrism frequently defends the idea of equality of rights for every human being, while simultaneously creating an atmosphere in which other inequalities can flourish. Western ethnocentrism defines progress according to a Western model and evaluates different people's conditions in relation to such progress. As a result, modern racism presumes that different races have unequal levels of intellectual, cultural, economic, and political progress, rather than simply different ones. For instance, modern racist teachers think Payo students are more motivated than Gypsy students because they assess Gypsies' cultural level as lower than that of the Payos.

This perception of racial inequality runs through most European educational theories and practices. Furthermore, this bias is often disguised when racism is reduced to Nazism, thereby relegating racist perspectives to a few discrete groups of extremists and individuals with outdated visions. Many European anti-racist authors have criticized the Ford Report (Ford, 1991) for falling into this kind of reductionism, since part of the report's emphasis was the relationship between racism and neo-Nazi groups.[7] Such an emphasis can lead to the incorrect assumption that only neo-Nazis are racist, instead of looking at racism as a more widespread, pervasive problem inherent in European societies and cultures.

For educators, the challenge of an anti-racist pedagogy is not just about how to fight neo-Nazism as an external danger for schools, but also about how to revise cultural and educational theories to overcome racist implications. The majority of these ethnocentrist theories classify a people's intellectual capacities as either inferior or superior, depending on cultural background. Widespread educational and psychological theories often place European students in a superior developmental stage compared to children of other ethnicities. For instance, teachers frequently say that Western teenagers attending compulsory schooling reach the Piagetian stage of formal operations, while adults from other cultures who did not complete schooling, like many Gypsies, remain in the previous, less advanced stage of concrete operations. This represents a misapplication of Piaget's work, for he did not explicitly examine adult development or the role of culture in that development. Yet, teachers use his explorations of White, middle-class children to look at Gypsy families. As a result, they consider Gypsy children to be at an inferior stage of intellectual development as a natural result of cultural difference. In any case, such theories contribute to a bias created in the name of difference and grounded in a belief in racial inequality. An anti-racist pedagogy should therefore include the revision of these theories and a review of their implications.

Western Universalism

European ethnocentrism accepts the idea of people from different ethnicities living in the same territory while it rejects the idea of equal status. From this approach, the whole world is a unique territory for the domination of other subordinated races by a superior race. Immigrants are thus considered suited only for those positions that European people do not want. Ethnocentrism further holds that the relationship between European and developing countries should be based on an exchange of the best that each has to offer, and holds that the best that developing nations have to offer is raw material. For instance, European high technology can be exchanged for these nations' raw resources. This exchange also relates to human resources, as European executives and personnel can be exported to fill top managerial positions in non-Western countries.

Underlying all such ethnocentrist actions, including those within education, is the concept of subordination. Present ethnocentrist politics mix students of different backgrounds in the same schools to reproduce the dominant Western culture. However, the adaptation of Western children to a school culture that generally replicates their own is usually simpler than for non-Western children. This is often interpreted as the result of their higher intelligence and more sophisticated attitudes. In addition,

Western educators see schools in countries that they perceive as "developing" also to have "developing" school systems that seek to apply Western advancements. For instance, when children from Africa come to Europe, schools often consider the fact that they previously attended school in a "developing" country a deficit to be remediated.

When ethnocentrist educators discuss the role of schools in integrating immigrants, they are in fact referring only to the integration of "southern people" — loosely defined as people from developing countries that are situated primarily in the southern hemisphere. In Spain, for example, when ethnocentrist educators talk about integration of minorities, they are thinking about students coming from Morocco or Gambia rather than from the United States or Germany. They seek to assimilate people from cultures considered inferior to European culture, but the same process does not apply to northern foreigners, who are thought to be equal or superior.

For example, Spain has American schools based on the dominant language, culture, and educational system of the United States. It welcomes the development of some elements of the dominant U.S. culture as a convenient contribution to their schools. The same, however, is not true of "southern" culture, language, and educational orientations. Moroccan or Gypsy schools that could teach according to their Arabic or Gypsy languages and practices are rejected. Education in the North American way is considered as fostering success; education in the Moroccan or Gypsy way is considered as closing children into ghettos and impeding cultural integration. Some teachers' groups and mainstream families have asked the Spanish government to establish restrictive quotas in schools that hold the percentage of students considered to be "problems of integration" — that is, Gypsy or immigrant students — to 15 percent. In this respect, the educational system is more restrictive than the market. While there are no Arabic schools in Spain, there are Arab butcher shops that prepare and sell meat that has been slaughtered according to the Islamic tradition. Among their customers are both Islamic and non-Islamic customers who appreciate the product. It seems much easier for many Spaniards to accept the equality of "inferior" people's money than to accept the equality of their ethnicities and cultures.

The way money and power have been handled by different ethnicities in Europe has had a strong influence on whether they are considered superior or inferior. Gypsies, Africans, and Arabs are subordinated in Europe and, currently, even Latin Americans are increasingly discriminated against by Latin Europeans.[8] However, belonging to those ethnicities is far less of a hardship for individuals with money and power, like the Arab millionaires whose presence is well appreciated along the eastern coast of Spain.[9]

Capitalist Democracy

Western ethnocentrist politicians, intellectuals, and media have defended the idea that all societies should evolve toward their integration into the Western capitalist system. They have supported democracies as long as that support does not interfere with their capitalist interests. Algeria provides an example of how such politics create conflicts and violence among people of different cultures. In the early 1990s, Algeria was moving toward becoming a democracy with a growing Islamic influence. In June 1990, the Islamic Salvation Front (ISF) won 54.25 percent of the vote. In December 1991, it won the first round of legislative elections with 47.5 percent of the vote, and it was clear that they were going to win the second and definitive round. The government, pressured by the army, annulled the elections in January 1992. In February, the army declared a state of emergency, and in March it dissolved the ISF.

Western governments never opposed this coup d'état, and most Western media legitimated this anti-democratic process with demagogic but effective arguments (Sales, 1992). Despite popular support for the ISF, the Western media interpreted the 41 percent abstention rate as evidence that only one out of four potential voters backed the ISF. Although Western media did not approve of the army's coup d'état as a legitimate method of taking control of the government, it did approve of its objective of impeding a minority party from gaining power. In other words, in this case the end justified the means, an argument that would have been unacceptable to the Western media if applied to Western democracies. It also would never have been applied to an Arab country if the election's winner had been a pro-Western party. In defending the coup d'état, the Western media explained that democracy cannot be governed by a religious party, ignoring the fact that such an argument would never be applied to Christian parties, such as Germany's CDU, governing Western democracies. These capitalists accept religious parties in democratic governments when they are Christian, but not when they are Islamic.

Western media also blamed Islamists for the violent situation that emerged from the destruction of the democratic process after the coup (Bell Jelloun, 1997). Such biased interpretations can lead mainstream citizens of Western countries to perceive Islamism and Arab culture as inherently anti-democratic, rather than as merely opposed to the anti-democratic defenders of Western ethnocentrism. This demagogic idea creates racism against Islamic people and culture in international relations as well as inside schools. As a result, many European children identify their classmates' Islamic religion with fundamentalist terrorism.

Relativism of Postmodern Racism

Postmodern racism rejects the preceding ethnocentrist assumptions of modern racism by stating that cultures are not inferior or superior; they are simply different. However, it denies the possibility of dialogue between different cultures in order to establish common rules for living together in the same territories. In this way, a postmodern racist perspective rejects Arab people's living in European countries. Postmodern racism has an intellectual basis in the relativist approaches of poststructuralist authors, such as the postmodernism of Jean François Lyotard (1979), the genealogy of Michel Foucault (1968), and the deconstructionism of Jacques Derrida (1967). These approaches are based on Friedrich Nietzsche's works (Habermas, 1987).[10] Regarding the issue of multicultural relations, these neo-Nietzschean thoughts legitimate the three main characteristics of postmodern racism: difference, power, and rebellion against rationalism and democracy.[11]

Difference of Ethnicities

Relativism is based on the notion of difference. It considers ethnicities or cultures not superior or inferior to one another, but different, existing in particular contexts that differ from others. Relativists thus deny both the ethnocentric perception of races as unequal and the affirmation of equality among human beings, ethnicities, and cultures. The deconstructionist concept of difference, as seen in the writings of Derrida (1967), rejects evaluation that attempts to delineate one context as better than another; thus, it is directly linked to relativism. While claiming anti-ethnocentrist radicalism, the deconstructionist perspective actually legitimizes social inequalities both among and within different cultures.

Neo-Nietzschean thought, as found in Derridean deconstructionism, has ambivalent results with respect to racism. On the one hand, its emphasis on difference can shed light on how Western institutions and thoughts exclude other cultures and ethnicities.[12] On the other hand, difference without equality can deconstruct the possibility of dialogue among different cultures. Where there is difference without equality, cultures can only be understood within themselves and any intermingling represents a loss of identity.

For example, Gypsy cultures have frequently prevented female teenagers from attending school because their tradition includes a key family role for women that begins in adolescence. From the relativist position, one could argue that Gypsies should not be expected to adhere to the European concept of equal educational rights for men and women. In focusing on cultural differences, relativists thus deconstruct the principle of equality. They consider school to be a European educational institution imposed on Gypsies through ethnocentrism. Gender equality is therefore presented as a European imposition rather than as a basic human right. This allows relativists then to deconstruct the universal right to schooling, arguing that, in other kinds of educational activities, schools press Gypsies to lose their identity, culture, and way of life.

Such analyses focus on the negative aspects of schooling and ignore the positive ones. For example, many Gypsy women, unsatisfied with the traditional roles imposed on them by Gypsy culture (Wang et al., 1990), use schooling to exercise professional options formerly unattainable. In the same way, many Western women reject the mandatory limitation to traditional female roles in Western culture. Yet, for relativists, these educational opportunities are evidence of the destruction of Gypsy culture rather than of their evolution through change.

Contrary to what relativists suggest, emancipatory perspectives are not simply Western principles imposed on other ethnicities under the flag of universalism. Rather, they are the natural consequence of the struggles and dreams of all people who, regardless of culture and ethnicity, continually strive toward better lives and societies. The relationship between the emancipatory perspectives of Western and Gypsy cultures is not just the effect of the ethnocentric imposition of the former upon the latter, but also a result of dialogue and solidarity between them.

Power

Relativism defends power as a means of regulating human relations. Neo-Nietzschean thought considers power to be creative rather than negative (Foucault, 1975; Levy, 1977). In *Discipline and Punish*, for example, Foucault (1975) states that "we must cease once and for all to describe the effects of power in negative terms: it 'excludes', it 'represses', it 'censors', it 'abstracts', it 'masks', it 'conceals.' In fact, power produces; it produces reality; it produces domains of objects and rituals of truth. The individual and the knowledge that may be gained of him belong to this production" (p. 196). From this perspective, relativists understand society as a space of struggle among opposing forces. They oppose dialogical solutions to violence — for example, conciliation and peace agreements as a solution to war — because cultural relations are perceived as inherently violent.[13]

Unfortunately, many people are unaware that this form of neo-Nietzscheanism does not seek to achieve a better level of living together through dialogue and consensus; instead, it seeks to justify violence in relations among cultures. Relativist critics can then justify oppressive dictatorships that rule through direct violence rather than through dialogue. Using such a perspective, it is possible to deconstruct the international intervention against Nazism in the 1940s and the present international solidarity with people suffering under famine and war as negative rather than positive actions.

In Europe, the issue of international intervention to stop war was a key debate during the Bosnian War. Most Spanish people pressed the United Nations to maintain its commitment to defend the town of Srebenica from the aggression of Serb Chetniks. Opposing this solidarity, relativist authors deconstructed the claim for protection as Western universalism. Srebenica was taken amid scenes of terror before passive UN soldiers.[14]

Relativist authors wrote against those international interventions oriented to substitute violence with dialogue. Some even defended the right of people to wage war and took a position against human rights as a Western imposition. Unfortunately, many actions during the European Year against Racism were partially oriented by those relativist ideas. For instance, during this year an exhibition entitled "The City of Difference" was held in Barcelona. Ironically, the planning of the exhibition was commissioned to one relativist anthropologist who wrote against human rights in favor of the people's right to wage war (Delgado, 1994).

Rebellion against Rationalism and Democracy

Historically, Europeans have seen radical critiques of Western democracies and rationalism open doors to extremism. For example, in the 1930s and 1940s, the radical intellectual philosophy of Heideggerian Nietzscheanism was linked to German Nazism and Italian Fascism. Some authors contend that this relationship is intellectually irrelevant because it was simply the bastardization of Nietzschean thought by politicians such as Hitler to justify their own political agendas. In fact, this link was made by Heidegger himself, the most important Nietzschean of the modern age.

In radical circles, there is a disinclination to recognize any association of important radical intellectuals with Nazism. Many followers of Nietzsche and Heidegger have labeled authors who dare to detail the relationship between Heidegger's works and Nazism as nonintellectual and unintelligent (Farias, 1989). Frequently, Nazism is mistakenly reduced to political dictators, brutal military chiefs, and classical conservative cultural workers rather than linked to the actions of intellectuals. Such simple categorization obscures relevant points necessary to stop the present wave of neo-Nazism and its relation to postmodern racism. This lack of serious scientific analysis opens the door for intellectual fashions like the neo-historical denial of the Holocaust.[15]

Contrary to popular belief, Fascism was not initiated by conservative politicians as a bourgeois action, but by radical intellectuals and anti-bourgeois movements.[16] Before founding the Fascist political movement in Italy, Mussolini was not a conservative politician but a radical school teacher and socialist leader. As director of magazines and newspapers such as *Avanti* (the official publication of the Italian Socialist Party), he was considered a radical intellectual. He was caught up in the irrationalism of futurism, a movement in art that called for the destruction of all traces of the past, including museums, to free Italian painters, writers, and artists from the limitations of tradition. Futurism was one of the key components of Fascism.

In Europe, anti-racist educators should not embrace Nietzschean and Heideggerian undermining of rationalist bases of Western culture and conservative democracy because, by doing so, they promote the irrationalism of Nazi racism. Schools, colleges, and universities should teach that current democracy has resulted not only from an elite imposition of power but also from a long grassroots struggle. For example, students should be taught that common people, such as the *sans culottes* of the French Revolution, fought for democracy. Although they were eventually oppressed in the interest of capitalist democracy, their situation improved in comparison to their lives under absolute monarchy. As radical educators, we should focus our critiques of capitalist democracy toward achieving a better democracy, rather than from a nihilist outlook that leaves the door open to anti-democratic alternatives.

The Living Together of the Dialogic Perspective

From the dialogic perspective, it is possible to create the conditions that allow people from different cultures and ethnicities to live together. In the field of education, the dialogic perspective was originally developed by Paulo Freire (1970, 1996, 1997). Similarly, developments in social sciences during the last two decades have moved, more or less directly, toward this orientation (Beck & Beck-Gernsheim, 1995; Giddens, 1991; Habermas, 1984). Concerning multicultural relations, the three main characteristics of the dialogic perspective are equality of differences, sharing territories, and radicalization of democracy.

Equality of Differences

Like relativism, the dialogic perspective considers cultures and ethnicities to be neither superior nor inferior to one another, but different. Unlike relativism, however, the dialogic perspective emphasizes the need for equal rights among ethnicities as well as among diverse social sectors and people. It aims to promote a transformation to principles such as equality and freedom. Under this view, difference is simply part of equality — the equal right of everybody to live differently.

The dialogic approach aims for an equal position for all ethnicities, groups, and individuals. In education, recognition of difference is important in addressing cultural diversity in schools, and equality is important in allowing everyone to acquire the competencies that allow them to transcend their present societal barriers. Difference is therefore necessary to promote the maintenance and development of one's own culture and identity; similarly, equality is necessary to prevent marginalization and exclusion.

Such a perspective transcends the understanding of culture based on conservative nostalgia for a uniform or homogeneous culture that never was. The orientation toward cultural dialogue and *mestizaje*, or hybridism, are worthy goals because no culture in Europe can survive without communicating with other cultures, taking elements from them, and developing new cultural components from this exchange.[17] In fact, conservative nostalgia for the "original" culture and the "original" identity distorts history by denying that present human identities are the result of this process. It ultimately provokes racism and the rejection of dialogue with others by perceiving dialogue as a threat to the original culture's identity. Hermann Tertsch (1993) writes of a 91-year-old woman who has always lived in the same village, Samorin, but has belonged to different countries. Born in the Austro-Hungarian Empire, she was first Hungarian. Then, during Hitler's regime, she was Slovakian. In 1945, she became Czechoslovakian, and now she is Slovakian again. Yet, she has been oblivious to these changes in identity because, throughout her life, she was too busy working to avoid hunger to participate in the "great historical" events of that region. Her story illustrates that the social construction of national and ethnic identity can distort history when it ignores individuals.

Every culture is already a result of different mestizajes and cannot evolve without new ones. Usually mestizajes have been accomplished through the domination and oppression of some cultures by others, but the equality of differences stance, within the dialogic perspective, demands freer and more egalitarian conditions of dialogue as a forum for a new kind of communication among cultures and the development of new kinds of mestizajes.

An updated anti-racist pedagogy, such as that of Freire, affirms that schools can make a great contribution to promoting the dialogic idea of mestizajes. On the one hand, schools serve people from different ethnicities and different cultures. On the other, they are pressured by the dominant cultural demands of society. As ethnocentric institutions, schools tend toward homogeneity and exclusion of different cultures, but the intercommunication of teachers, students, parents, and communities can lead to the development of dialogic processes within those schools to orient them toward equality of differences.

In Spain, for example, the Learning Communities Project is attempting to develop such a dialogic process. The process of transforming schools into learning communities consists in the reelaboration of a school's project of learning (including curriculum, organization, and rules of the institution) through dialogue and the participation of the whole community — teachers, parents, relatives, associations, volunteers, and local companies. As part of this transformation, the whole community designs a coordinated dialogic process at diverse sites (classrooms, homes, streets) that increases the two dimensions of dialogic learning: the process of learning academically and the process of learning to live together peacefully.

Such an approach takes on the cultural challenge of combating modern and postmodern racism. Communities should be able to learn and experience how communication among cultures enriches all of them, and how it is both possible and beneficial to live together in a shared territory. Students should be able to see themselves not as superior or inferior but as different, not as homogeneous but as equals.

Shared Territories

A dialogic perspective is oriented toward creating conditions for people from different cultures and ethnicities to live together. These conditions are not predetermined, but must be continuously consented to by participants. Dialogue and agreement are the procedural criteria for living together (Habermas, 1984, 1989a, 1994, 1996, 1997), while imposition and direct violence are excluded from the process. Unequal positions in the dialogue are challenged by relevant dissent and social action. Thus, the dialogic or communicative process includes consensus to obtain conditions for living together, and dissent to criticize them when new and more egalitarian conditions are needed (Habermas, 1992).

The dialogic perspective challenges the notion of territory as the exclusive property of one ethnicity, origin, religion, culture, language, or motherland. Habermas (1989b) proposes overcoming this old notion of patriotism by developing instead a patriotism of constitution, based not on territory but on agreement. Instead of racial origins, this perspective relies on consensual rules to organize different people's living together. Unfortunately, conservative approaches try to associate this idea to a consensus built upon unequal positions, as can be found today in many institutionalized democratic spaces. In contrast, the communicative approach is oriented to a dialogue that leaves the floor open for a critical struggle to achieve a more egalitarian consensus.

Within the European multicultural reality, Gypsy people have historically fostered this communicative approach, as seen in their vision of shared territory. Many Gypsies consider themselves a people with no territory and no intention of ever having an exclusive and homogeneous one. They want to share territory with any and all people throughout the world (Presencia Gitana, 1991), a claim they made in a public statement in Spain in the mid–1970s. As a result of the political transition from Franco's dictatorship to democracy, Spain reorganized into seventeen autonomous regions, each of which tried to define itself by creating a separate identity for its territory. At that time, some Gypsies asked for an eighteenth autonomous region without territory. In 1993, Glyn Ford, the president of the European Parliament Commission on racism and xenophobia, echoed this Gypsy concept of non-territoriality in European relations. He noted that the European Union had one more country besides the ones officially recognized — the unrecognized "country of immigrants" that has no exclusive territory, does not look for one, and shares terrain with other European countries.

Opposing the racism and neo-Nazism that are on the rise today, many humanitarian agencies and social organizations are calling for an intercultural and pluricultural Europe to be shared by any and all people living there. It is a call for diverse people to live together with respect for the basic norms agreed to by all. For instance, on February 7, 1993, twenty thousand people marched in Paris in favor of a multiethnic France. Among them were Africans, Arabs, Jews, mainstream Europeans, and people from many other ethnicities asking for one territory where they could maintain, develop, and share their own differences, cultures, and identities. Many danced to the song, "We Are All Descendants of Immigrants."

European education requires a multiculturalism that includes both pluricultural and intercultural solutions.[18] The former is needed to allow all individuals and groups to live their differences; the latter is needed to allow them the opportunity to exchange and share new forms of living and new cultural mestizajes with others. Both pluricultural and intercultural education can happen in shared territories. For instance, schools based on Gypsy culture for those who desire to emphasize their differences could exist alongside other school projects based on cultural exchange.

Radicalization of Democracy

The creation of a critical dialogic option for democracy (Giddens, 1991, 1994) implies the understanding and radical application of the principles of equality and freedom. This alternative also means overcoming any exclusion based on culture, religion, language, or lifestyle.

The ethnocentrism of modern racism identifies democracy with Western democracies, which are limited by their interest in capital. Instead, the critical dialogic position challenges all limitations to democracy and promotes intercultural negotiation around the unique principles of equal rights for all.

The relativism of postmodern racism deconstructs the concept of democracy. By assessing no set of values as superior to another, from this perspective one could argue that democracy is not superior to dictatorship. Such a perspective then leaves room for those who want to impose their beliefs through violence. In contrast, the critical dialogic approach does not deconstruct democracy. Instead, it seeks to extend and radicalize democracy.

The differences in the interpretations of democracy among the ethnocentrist, relativist, and dialogic perspectives can be seen in recent conflicts in Algeria. In January 1995, the Algerian political opposition — composed of the Islamic Salvation Front (ISF), the most influential party in Algeria; the lay National Liberation Front; and other groups — met in exile. They proposed a consensual "national agreement" to the government of Algeria based on the principles of universal suffrage, multipartyism, political alternatives, and the rejection of violence. Their actions reflected a dialogic approach to political conflict.

In response, the dominant ethnocentrist thought of the present Algerian regime opposed that consensus. When the polls indicated an ISF electoral victory, it used the army to stop democratic suffrage with violence. They did so to limit Algerian democracy to one that excluded the possibility of an Islamic government. To justify their actions, they used the relativist argument of the right of people to wage war. They also interpreted the fact that the political opposition had met in a Western nation as proof of foreign interference. The ISF leader, Abdelkader Hachani, did not desire foreign interference, but worked for a dialogue with Western democratic forces. He asked the support of the European Union to encourage a political solution based on a dialogue among Algerians (Azcárate, 1998). In doing so, he was using a dialogic orientation to sustain an alternative to the democracy defined by European ethnocentrism, and to defend an Islamism different from relativist proposals that avoid cultural change.

The evolution of Algeria is crucial for the relations between Europeans and Arabs on both sides of the Mediterranean. Ethnocentrist subordination of democracy as a means of defense from Islamism, as well as relativist deconstruction of democracy in favor of the affirmation of traditional identities, poses a great threat to world peace. Both approaches foster the possibility of war among ethnicities, cultures, and religions. They also signal the destruction of democratic solutions.

These conflicts are not limited to the political arena. Western media transmit these ideas and symbols that create obstacles to the extension and radicalization of democracy. For example, children and educators are bombarded daily by the public acceptance of ethnic war and of limited democracy. Comics, music, television, and even children's literature include symbols of ethnic wars and neo-Nazism.[19] In the process, it is shifting public perception of war and Nazism from terrible reality to provocative spectacle. Even educators who favor peace are increasingly influenced by the relativist denial of the destructive and cruel reality of wars and Nazism. This transformation allows postmodernist intellectuals to discuss war simply as representation, as in J. Baudrillard's book, *The Gulf War Did Not Take Place* (1991).

Postmodernist representational theory therefore undermines the rationalist bases of democracy. It serves to deny the reality of the extermination of Nazi concentration camps, to accept the antidemocratic implications of certain intellectuals and their theories as irrelevant, and even to present Fascist leaders as exceptional persons. For example, in 1994 in Italy, Silvio Berlusconni, the political leader whose career was based on the telecommunications industry rather than on ideas, led the government as head of the rightist Forza Italia party with the support of the neo-Fascist Alleanze Nazionale. During the electoral campaign, TV channel RAI-2 broadcast a series about the young Mussolini. The image it portrayed of the leader was more attractive than the image of terror most people had previously associated with Fascism. Spectators watched a Mussolini associated with human emotions rather than horror. To many children's eyes, the fictionalized and romanticized image of the young Mussolini on TV is much better than that of most political democratic leaders as portrayed in the media in the same country.

At a time of the dramatic rise of new racism and neo-Nazism, an updated anti-racist pedagogy should develop intellectual opposition to the cultural grounds of Fascism. We should not equate radical critiques of present democracy and its rationalist grounds with the fight against racism, because some of those critiques actually promote radical postmodern racism and neo-Nazism. In Europe, we cannot take democracy for granted. New anti-racist pedagogies should be present in all kinds of languages, including comics and music.[20]

Dialogic critiques of current democratic arrangements are part of the democratic, anti-racist struggle. These critiques are oriented toward new and more egalitarian dialogues among people from different ethnicities who live in the same territory.

Conclusion

Given the current socio-political context, educational institutions and educators must seek ways to counter both modern and postmodern racism through anti-racist pedagogies. In accordance with European Union initiatives, many are doing so. Despite these efforts, racism has not stopped growing in Europe, which has led many educators to reflect on the situation. In the process, they are discovering that many of these actions are framed within perspectives that actually foster racism rather than overcome it.

One of the main reasons is that relativism fights modern racism with proposals and actions that promote postmodern racism — the kind of racism that today excludes immigrants and minority groups in a more dehumanized way. For instance, the emphasis on deconstructing dialogue and consensus favors those who argue that our respective cultures and identities would be better maintained if Europeans lived in *our* Europe and Arabs went back to *their* countries. To avoid the homogenization of culture, educators defend identity differences without realizing that neo-Nazi leaders use identical arguments to defend the idea that different groups, ethnicities, or races cannot live together within the same territory.

Many educators' confusion between relativist and dialogic approaches leads them to promote postmodern racism while fighting modern racism. Because both perspectives take a position against modern racism and its ethnocentric foundations, educators understand them as equal. In addition, until the mid-1990s, postmodern thought was the intellectual fashion in Europe. Educators then have adopted relativist orientations of postmodern thought and used them as the theoretical framework of their practices. Educators need to be aware, however, that such relativism is, in fact, the intellectual foundation of postmodern racism. In contrast, the dialogic perspective is the intellectual ground for the overcoming of both modern and postmodern racism.

Educators, therefore, need to include the dialogic perspective in their struggle against cultural inequality. In this way, they will be able to focus on overcoming the growing wave of racism and neo-Nazism in Europe. The dialogic perspective makes it possible for different ethnicities, cultures, nations, and populations to share the same schools and territories through dialogue. One essential criteria of their pedagogies should be to avoid the misrepresentation of Nazi intellectuals as heroes of anti-racist actions. Another criteria should be to avoid theoretical works that could leave room for the legitimization of racist or even neo-Nazi behaviors or forms of discrimination. Instead, educators should base educational theories and pedagogies on works respectful of human rights, democracy, equality, solidarity, and difference. Based on such work, educators will be using their theories, actions, and beliefs to join in the people's struggle to live together in the same schools, different yet equal.

Notes

1. The FPO leader, Joerg Haider, is now the prevailing leader of European neo-Nazism. He considers Austria part of the Greater Germany and had to resign as president of the regional government of Carintia after proposing and trying to apply the same politics of employment as the German Third Reich. Statistical election data in this and subsequent sections is drawn from Gumuzio (1994).

2. Misreadings of original literature have created many problems in education. For instance, in the 1970s, Althusser's reproduction model, as developed by his followers Bourdieu and Passeron, Baudelot and Establet, and Bowles and Gintis, applied Marxist structuralism to education. In *Reading Capital* (1967), Althusser created Marxist structuralism, but he later recognized (Althusser, 1995) that he had written this book without reading Marx's *Das Kapital* himself. A considerable part of educational literature ended up being based on Althusser's misreadings. The same process now is happening in educational literature with authors such as Foucault.

3. In 1999, the European Union included Austria, Belgium, Denmark, Finland, France, Germany, Greece, Ireland, Italy, Luxembourg, Netherlands, Portugal, Spain, Sweden, and the United Kingdom.

4. *Payos* is the way Spanish Gypsies refer to non-Gypsy people.

5. This process is also occurring in regard to gender, as an increasing number of authors are replacing the biological concept of sex with the biological-cultural one of gender.

6. Barriers such as strict annual quotas aim to make immigration into Europe increasingly difficult. Human rights organizations have denounced these quotas. Moreover, the problems of

border control in areas such as the Spain and Africa suggest that controlling immigration is difficult because many prefer to risk their lives than to stay in their countries.

7. This report about racism and xenophobia was issued by a Commission of the European Parliament in 1991.

8. Latin Europeans are European people from Latin cultures such as Italy, Portugal, and Spain.

9. The acceptance of immigration when it also brings money is clear in the case of a Ghanaian immigrant who in 1994 won the largest prize in the history of the lottery in Spain, almost $20 million. The winner was protected by the African community so that the European media could not identify the person. Many of the town's inhabitants who had previously objected to the presence of the African community suddenly developed an interest in knowing them and establishing connections with them.

10. Because of the North American appropriation of Foucault without Nietzsche, it should be noted that Nietzsche created the concept of genealogy, and Foucault then adopted it (Descombes, 1987; Giroux & Flecha, 1992; Rorty, 1991). In *Nietzsche, la Généalogie et l'Histoire* (Foucault, 1968), he acknowledges Nietzsche's influence in his work.

11. There is a trend to include any neo-Nietzschean thought under the label of postmodernism. However, in a more restricted meaning, the genealogy of Foucault and the deconstructionism of Derrida differ from the postmodernism developed by Lyotard in the social sciences.

12. The Derridean concepts of difference and deconstructionism operate within the context of racism and anti-racism. Derrida (1967) developed the concept of *différance*, a neologism that differs from the French word *différence*. The change of the letter "e" for the letter "a" is graphically perceptible, but not orally. There is then a Derridean preference for writing against phonocentrism, which in Derrida is linked to logocentrism. Différance has a double meaning: to differ in space and to defer in time. Any meaning is generated by spacing and timing of this différance.

13. Nietzsche (1887/1956) considers "the coming of democracy, of peace arbitrage instead of wars, [and] of women rights equality" (pp. 290–291) as factors of declining vitality.

14. While I recognize that this episode could be seen as sensationalism, we should not close our eyes to the human suffering that relativist indifference legitimizes. A survivor in Srebenica narrated one mother's fight to save her 14-year-old boy from Serb soldiers (Estarriol, 1995):

> In front of them, in a house, UN soldiers stood watching. They saw how a Chetnik . . . cut off the child's ear. The child began to writhe and yell in pain, while blood streamed down his shoulder . . . the soldier slashed with his knife again and the boy's nose flew off. . . . The child fell down, writhing and screaming. Suddenly the mother threw herself at the Chetnik, took the soldier's hand holding the knife and stabbed it into her own heart (p. 4).

15. Since 1986, intellectual debate has suggested that Nazism was a reaction to Stalinism. As a result, the "truth" of the Nazi genocide has begun to be denied by some sectors of the population. In Germany, neo-historicists propose restoring narrative and oppose what they see as the artifice of theoretical explanation (Habermas, 1992). This perspective makes it impossible to judge any practice outside its particular context. Such deconstructionist perspective could free certain individuals, collectives, and countries from their responsibility and guilt of their collaboration with Nazis. Ernst Nolte (1995), the author who initiated this historical revisionism, also argues that there is no relation between Heidegger's work and the Nazi implications of his life.

As a result of this revisionist debate, in the 1990s, more and more people have questioned the possibility of verifying the genocide in Hitler's concentration camps. A few authors simply deny it, saying, for instance, that gas chambers were only used to wash Jews and not to murder them. In fact, they deny the existence of scientific historical truths (Nolte, 1995). The rise of such revisionism has been so strong that some countries are trying to stop its social consequences. In 1992, for example, Austria approved a ruling that condemns people who deny or justify the Holocaust to a prison term of up to ten years. Other countries have also instituted similar penalties. In Spain, the sentence is between one and two years.

16. In their recent in-depth study, Maia Asheri, Zeev Sternhell, and Mario Sznajder (1994) outline the three sources of fascism: Marinetti's futurism, Sorel's revolutionary trade unionism, and Barrès's tribal nationalism.

17. The Spanish word *mestizaje,* usually translated in English as "hybridism," has a positive intercultural connotation in Spain. It refers to the collective creation of new cultures through interaction among different ethnic groups and people.

18. Although European multiculturalism has several definitions, it is usually understood (Castells et al., 1999) as the recognition of the existence of different cultures in the same territory. Interculturalism is an intervention into that reality that emphasizes the relationship among cultures. Pluriculturalism is another intervention focused on keeping one's own cultural identity. Intercultural education promotes the coexistence in the same school of people from different ethnicities while schools based on one culture tend to be seen as ghettos. Pluricultural education tends to place more value on the possibility that students follow an education that facilitates maintaining and developing their own culture. For instance, the idea of one Gypsy school in Barcelona would be seen as a ghetto solution from an interculturalist perspective and as an opportunity for cultural identity from a pluriculturalist one.

19. There is, however, resistance to these destructive symbols that suggests the transformative possibilities of human action. In April 1992 in Spain, for example, a group of sixth-grade students in Federico García Lorca Public School denounced *Kabuto*, a TV series of animated cartoons, because its heroes were wearing the swastika. That initiative resulted in the TV channel's decision to stop broadcasting the series.

20. In Spain, almost all well-known comic makers published a book of anti-racist cartoons (Torres et al., 1993), coordinated by the Gypsy association Presencia Gitana. The same kind of work is being done by groups like Comilande, an association of young German authors.

    There are also important reactions in the world of music. In 1992, an anti-racist rock festival united 300,000 people in Munich with the slogan, "We are all foreigners." A similar festival, celebrated yearly in Frankfurt, brought together 100,000 people with the slogan, "They today, you tomorrow."

References

Althusser, L. (1967). *Lire le capital.* Paris: Maspero.

Althusser,L. (1995). *The future lasts forever: A memoir.* New York: New Press.

Asheri, M., Sternhell, Z., & Sznajder, M. (1994). *The birth of fascist ideology.* Princeton, NJ: Princeton University Press.

Azcárate, M. (1998, January 18). Argel: Matanzas y oscuridades. *El País*, p. 6.

Baudrillard, J. (1991). *La guerre du golfe n'a pas eu lieu.* Paris: Galilée.

Beck, U., & Beck-Gernsheim, E. (1995). *The normal chaos of love.* Cambridge, Eng.: Polity Press.

Beck, U., Giddens, A., & Lash, S. (1994). *Reflexive modernization: Politics, tradition and aesthetics in the modern social order.* Cambridge, Eng.: Polity Press.

Bell Jelloun, T. (1997, January 30). El silencio de los intelectuales. *El País*, p. 11.

Cáceres, G. (1993, February 7). Haider: El nazi elegante. *El Periódico*, p. 16.

Castells, M. (1996). *The information age: Economy, society and culture. Vol. I: The rise of network society.* Cambridge, Eng.: Blackwell.

Castells, M. (1997). *The information age: Economy, society and culture. Vol. II: The power of identity.* Cambridge, Eng.: Blackwell.

Castells, M. (1998). *The information age: Economy, society and culture. Vol. III: End of the millenium.* Cambridge, Eng.: Blackwell.

Castells, M., Flecha, R., Freire, P., Giroux, H., Macedo, D., & Willis, P. (1999). *Critical education in the new information age.* Boulder, CO: Rowman & Littlefield.

Contreras, J. (1994). *Los retos de la inmigración: Racismo y pluriculturalidad.* Madrid: Talassa.

Delgado, M. (1994, July 27). ¿Es la guerra un derecho de los pueblos? *El Periódico*, p. 7.

Derrida, J. (1967). *De la grammatologie.* Paris: Editions de Minuit

Descombes, V. (1987, March 5). Je m'en Foucault. *London Review of Books*, pp. 20–21.

Elster, J. (Ed.). (1998). *Deliberative democracy.* New York: Cambridge University Press.

Estarriol, R. (1995, July 22). El horror nazi de Srebenica. *La Vanguardia*, p. 4.

Farias, V. (1989). *Heidegger and Nazism.* Philadelphia: Temple University Press.

Ford, J. (1991). *Informe Ford sobre el racismo en Europa.* Madrid: Ministerio de Asuntos Sociales.

Foucault, M. (1968). *Nietzsche, la généalogie et l'histoire.* Paris: Presses Universitaires de France.

Foucault, M. (1975). *Surveiller et punir: Naissance de la prison* Paris: Gallimard.

Freire, P. (1970). *The pedagogy of the oppressed.* New York: Herder & Herder.

Freire, P. (1996). *Pedagogia da autonomia: Saberes necessários à prática educativa.* Sao Paulo, Brazil: Paz e Terra.

Freire, P. (1997). *Pedagogy of the heart.* New York: Continuum.

Giddens, A. (1991). *Modernity and self-identity: Self and society in the late modern age.* Cambridge, Eng.: Polity Press.

Giddens, A. (1992). *The transformation of intimacy: Sexuality, love and eroticism in modern societies.* Cambridge, Eng.: Polity Press.

Giddens, A. (1994). *Beyond left and right: The future of radical politics.* Cambridge, Eng.: Polity Press.

Giroux, H. A., & Flecha, R. (1992). *Igualdad educativa y diferencia cultural.* Barcelona: Roure.

Guitart, J. (1998, August 31). Enseñanza descarta el reparto de alumnos inmigrantes extranjeros entre las escuelas. *El País*, p. 15.

Gumuzio, J. C. (1994, December 29). Sobre la vigencia fascista. *El País,* pp. 4–5.

Habermas, J. (1984). *The theory of communicative action: Vol. I. Reason and the rationalization of society.* Boston: Beacon Press.

Habermas, J. (1987). *The philosophical discourse of modernity: Twelve lectures.* Cambridge, MA: MIT Press.

Habermas, J. (1989a). *The theory of communicative action: Vol. II. Lifeworld and system: A critique of functionalist reason.* Boston: Beacon Press.

Habermas, J. (1989b). *Identidades nacionales y postnacionales.* Madrid: Tecnos.

Habermas, J. (1992). In P. Dews (Ed.), *Autonomy and solidarity: Interviews with Jürgen Habermas.* London: Verso.

Habermas, J. (1994). *Postmetaphysical thinking.* Cambridge, MA: MIT Press.

Habermas, J. (1996). *Between facts and norms: Contributions to a discourse theory of law and democracy.* Cambridge, Eng.: Polity Press.

Habermas, J. (1997, April). *Multiculturalism: Does culture matter in politics?* Paper presented at the University of Barcelona, Spain.

Levy, B. H. (1977, March 12). Non au sexe roi. *Le nouvel observateur, 644,* 92–93, 95, 98, 100, 105, 113, 124, 130.

Lyotard, J. F. (1979). *La condition postmoderne: Rapport sur le savoir.* París: Les éditions de minuit.

Martí Font, J. M. (1993, February 7). No sobrevaloro el fenómeno nazi. *El País*, p. 6.

Molina, F. (1994). *Sociedad y educación: Perspectivas interculturales.* Lleida: Edicions Universitat de Lleida.

Nietzsche, F. (1956). *The genealogy of morals: The birth of tragedy and the genealogy of morals.* New York: Anchor Books Doubleday. (Original work published 1887)

Nolte, E. (1995). *Nietzsche y el nietzscheanismo.* Madrid: Alianza.

Presencia Gitana. (1991). *Informe sobre la cuestión gitana.* Madrid: Author.

Rorty, R. (1991). Moral identity and private autonomy: The case of Foucault. In *Essays on Heidegger and others* (pp. 193–198). Cambridge, Eng.: Cambridge University Press.

Sales, F. (1992, January 23). El círculo Argelino. *El País*, p. 2.

Tertsch, H. (1993). *La venganza de la historia.* Madrid: El País-Aguilar.

Torres, R. (Ed.) (1993). *Vamos a reírnos muy en serio del racismo.* Madrid: Editorial Presencia Gitana.

Wang, K., Díaz, M. T., Engel, M., Grande, G., Martín, M. L., & Pérez Serrano, M. (1990). *Mujeres gitanas ante el futuro.* Madrid: Editorial Presencia Gitana.

PART TWO

Gender and Queer Studies

INTRODUCTION

Gender and Queer Studies

Cultural and educational theories have historically revolved around male heterosexuality. That is to say, when theorists and researchers imagined a human subject at the center of cultural and educational activity, they assumed by and large that the subject had characteristics associated with being male and comported himself by socially acceptable "norms" of sexual behavior.[1] Furthermore, when scholars dealt with nonmale and nonheterosexual subjects, they defined their characters in opposition to a traditional, dominant view of what it meant to be "male." The way that (mostly male) educational theorists and researchers have approached the study of teaching and teachers is illustrative of this pattern.[2]

While feminism is understood largely as a political movement seeking to raise the status and protect the sociopolitical rights of women, feminist theory has also been fundamental to the ways in which gender has been addressed and rethought in cultural and educational theory.[3] Feminism and feminist theory have a long historical trajectory, but without a doubt the social revolutions of the 1960s, when women engaged in civil unrest and claimed a political movement for themselves, were pivotal points in how we understand gender today. In many ways, to speak of gender — to make it visible — is to acknowledge the hierarchy that exists in the dominant, dichotomous view of the sexes, and to point to its attendant oppressive relations. Traditional gender constructs position males as dominant, females as inferior, and deny a more fluid human experience that lives somewhere between (and perhaps beyond) narrow conceptions of tough masculinity and gentle femininity. In addition to demanding a more equal distribution of political power between the sexes, feminism also opened the door for multiple interpretations of being a "woman," and, in the process, of being a "man," pointing toward a more open understanding of these categories and the possibility of moving beyond their boundaries.[4]

Throughout its history, feminism and feminist theory have undergone critical revisions. Two important challenges, both especially relevant to the essays in Part Two, came from women of color and from the lesbian, gay, bisexual, transgender, and transsexual communities, which often embrace the collective term *queer*. From the late 1970s into the 1980s, women of color challenged feminism as a movement dominated by White women who ignored how race and ethnicity marked their gender identities and the privileges that being a White woman entailed.[5] In the 1990s, queer theory represented a challenge to the basic premises of feminist theory by questioning the dominant male/female dichotomy that informed much of feminist theory. Queer theorists questioned the dominant boundaries that constituted male and female subjectivities and called for a more fluid view of sexual identities.[6] Concomitantly, some gender scholars have become increasingly interested in understanding the social, cultural, and psychological dimensions of male heterosexual subjectivities.[7]

Within education, Carol Gilligan's landmark article "In a Different Voice" pointed out that theories of moral development were based on the experiences of men and suggested that they were inadequate in how they accounted for crucial differences in how women made sense of the world.[8] Furthermore, proponents of a feminist methodology called for putting the issues facing women in society front and center in the research agenda and for women to take the lead in investigating their own condition.[9] Despite these developments, some educational researchers draw on feminist theory in ways that reify gender hierarchies and underscore the experience of White, heterosexual women.[10] A worldview that implies the existence of a gender and sexual hierarchy is reproduced through the language of findings and policy, even when provocative questions about injustice and inequality are posed. Whether by expanding the definitions of gender and sexual orientation or through the inclusion of multiple identities, the authors in this section draw our attention to epistemological orientations that demand to be heard, included, and legitimized. Dolores Delgado Bernal and Kenn Gardner Honeychurch offer new epistemological frameworks that are rooted in the experiences of marginalized identities, while Michelle Fine provides a telling example of what happens when research looks beyond explanations based on dominant views of gender and sexuality.

Building on the work of "endarkened" feminists, Delgado Bernal challenges the notion of objectivity and neutrality assumed in mainstream empiricist paradigms that have ignored or subjugated oppressed groups. Instead, she draws on a unique research framework offered by groups that have been "Othered" in framing research. She speaks of a "Chicana feminist epistemology"[11] that allows Chicana scholars to reclaim their subjugated knowledge by acknowledging a "cultural intuition" that not only highlights personal experience, but also includes a collective cultural memory. She appeals to community members to be engaged in analyses and interpretation of research endeavors. Research, from this position, becomes a tool to make certain school issues and community experiences visible. Delgado Bernal not only proposes a strategy to foment the participation of Chicanas in the construction of knowledge from their own experience as women of color, but also urges Chicana scholars to pursue educational research as a political tool for social justice.[12]

In his chapter, Honeychurch argues that approaching social knowledge from a queered position is "a postmodern rejection of epistemological certainty." Posing an important challenge to ways of knowing and producing knowledge that is rooted in a normative view of heterosexuality, he asks us to open up a space where new realities, explanations, and logic can be registered and legitimized. According to Honeychurch, gay and lesbian researchers embracing a queer positionality can reformulate traditional conceptions of culture and, through this challenge, democratize the production of knowledge. "Through the claims of an alternative that expands the sphere of legitimacy applicable to all research," Honeychurch explains, "a queered position provides a unique way of commenting on a social world whose processes and outcomes might otherwise be (in)appropriately measured when constructed against the norm of un-queered perspectives." The potential of social empowerment and transformation from a "queered" position that embraces the body and autobiography as cites of knowledge production underlie the alternatives articulated and promoted in his chapter.[13]

Michelle Fine's article offers an example of what happens when the communal voice of research "subjects" is put in conversation with research findings that echo dominant research orientations. By looking carefully at the grand discourses on female sexuality in public schools while conducting fieldwork with adolescent girls, Fine reinterprets the meanings of earlier research to find a "missing discourse" that falls beyond the boundaries of what is knowable through the empirical and analytic strategies of traditional research. By illuminating the role of desire in the debate around female teenage pregnancy, Fine closes the gaps of understanding around teenage sexual behavior. More importantly, her inclusion of the voices of teenage girls stands in stark opposition to clinical claims of deviance. Fine uncovers the limitations on teenage girls to own their sexual desire where their sexual behavior marks them as "bad." According to Fine, researchers misunderstand the discourse of teenage girls as authentic, when in fact these girls are more likely adhering to an unspoken code.

The three authors in Part Two all pursue their theoretical work in educational contexts, pointing to the possibility of educational research that provides a space for new ways of both understanding and questioning the world around us. From their perspectives, gender and sexual orientation are not only important parts of the identity puzzle, but also the center of analysis and of the pursuit of a shared social justice rationale. Once again, as part of the cultural studies of education, these perspectives contribute to challenge the traditional and hegemonic notions of culture, bringing in other dimensions of a redefined politics of representation.

Notes

1. See, for example, the critique in Carol Gilligan, *In a Different Voice: Psychological Theory and Women's Development* (Cambridge, MA: Harvard University Press, 1982).
2. See, for instance, the analysis offered in Madeleine Grumet, *Bitter Milk: Women and Teaching* (Amherst: University of Massachusetts Press, 1988).
3. Carmen Luke and Jennifer Gore, eds., *Feminisms and Critical Pedagogy* (New York/London: Routledge, 1992); Kathleen Weiler, ed., *Feminist Engagements: Reading, Resisting, and Revisioning Male Theorists in Education and Cultural Studies* (New York: Routledge, 2001). See also bell hooks, *Teaching to Transgress: Education and the Practice of Freedom* (New York: Routledge, 1994).
4. Kate Bornstein, *Gender Outlaw: On Men, Women, and the Rest of Us* (New York: Vintage, 1994); Judith Butler, *Gender Trouble: Feminism and the Subversion of Identity* (New York: Routledge, 1999); Eve Kosofsky Sedgewick, *Tendencies* (Durham, NC: Duke University Press, 1993).
5. See, for example, the influential works of Gloria Anzaldúa, ed., *Making Face, Making Soul — Haciendo Caras: Creative and Critical Perspectives of Feminists of Color* (San Francisco: Aunt Lute Books, 1990); bell hooks, *Ain't I a Women? Black Women and Feminism* (Boston: South End Press, 1981); Audre Lorde, *Sister Outsider: Essays and Speeches* (Trumansburg, NY: Crossing Press, 1984).
6. For more thorough discussions of the evolution of queer theory, see Joseph Boone, ed., *Queer Frontiers: Millennial Geographies, Gender, and Generations* (Madison: University of Wisconsin Press, 2000); Michael Warner, ed., *Fear of a Queer Planet: Queer Politics and Social Theory*

(Minneapolis: University of Minnesota Press, 1993); Monique Wittig, "The Straight Mind," in *Critical Theory: A Reader,* ed. Douglas Tallack (New York: Harvester Wheatsheaf, 1995).

7. See, for example, R. W. Connell, *Masculinities* (Berkeley: University of California Press, 1995); Judith Kegan Gardiner, ed., *Masculinities Studies and Feminist Theory: New Directions* (New York: Columbia University Press, 2002).

8. Carol Gilligan, "In a Different Voice: Women's Conception of the Self and of Morality," *Harvard Educational Review* 47 (1977).

9. Sandra Harding, ed., *Feminism and Methodology: Social Science Issues* (Bloomington: University of Indiana Press, 1987). See also bell hooks, *Talking Back: Thinking Feminist, Thinking Black* (Boston: South End Press, 1989).

10. For a critique from the perspective of a White feminist doing antiracist work, see Becky Thompson, *A Promise and a Way of Life: Anti-Racist White Activists* (Minneapolis: University of Minnesota Press, 2001).

11. Chicana/o is an identifier that many Mexican Americans have claimed to identify themselves with a political project of self-determination, social justice, and identity renovation. See essays in Arturo Aldama and Naomi Qiñonez, eds., *Decolonial Voices: Chicana and Chicano Cultural Studies in the 21st Century* (Bloomington: Indiana University Press, 2002).

12. See also Gloria Anzaldúa, *Borderlands, La Frontera: The New Mestiza* (San Francisco: Aunt Lute Books, 1997); Lorde, *Sister Outsider;* Cherríe Moraga and Gloria Anzaldúa, eds., *This Bridge Called My Back: Writings by Radical Women of Color* (New York: Kitchen Table/Women of Color Press, 1983); Barbara Smith, ed., *Home Girls: A Black Feminist Anthology* (New Brunswick, NJ: Rutgers University Press, 2000).

13. For further explorations of these topics and concepts, see William Pinar, ed., *Queer Theory in Education* (Mahwah, NJ: Lawrence Erlbaum, 1998).

Using a Chicana
Feminist Epistemology
in Educational Research

DOLORES DELGADO BERNAL

> Schools . . . presuppose and legitimate particular forms of history, community, and
> authority. . . . The question is what and whose history, community, knowledge, and
> voice prevails? Unless this question is addressed, the issues of what to teach, how to
> teach, how to engage our students, and how to function as intellectuals becomes re-
> moved from the wider principles that inform such issues and practices. (Giroux,
> 1992, p. 91)

Epistemological concerns in schools are inseparable from cultural hegemonic domination in educational research. The way educational research is conducted contributes significantly to what happens (or does not happen) in schools. In education,
what is taught, how it is taught, who is taught, and whose fault it is when what is
taught is not learned are often manifestations of what is considered the legitimate
body of knowledge. For Chicanas, this is not merely an epistemological issue, but one
of power, ethics, politics, and survival.[1] Employing a Chicana feminist epistemology
in educational research thus becomes a means to resist epistemological racism
(Scheurich & Young, 1997) and to recover untold histories.

In this article, I describe a Chicana epistemological perspective by providing an example of my research, which places Chicanas as central subjects and provides a forum
in which Chicanas speak and analyze their stories of school resistance and grassroots
leadership. I draw from the strong traditions of Black, Native American, and Chicana
feminists in an attempt to articulate a Chicana feminist epistemology in educational
research that reflects my history and that of the women I write about, a unique history
that arises from the social, political, and cultural conditions of Chicanas. Most feminists of color recognize that gender, race, class, and sexual orientation — not gender
alone — determine the allocation of power and the nature of any individual's identity,
status, and circumstance (Collins, 1986; hooks, 1989; Hurtado, 1989; Pesquera &
Segura, 1993). Therefore, "endarkened" feminist epistemologies are crucial, as they
speak to the failures of traditional patriarchal and liberal educational scholarship and

Harvard Educational Review   Vol. 68   No. 4   Winter 1998

examine the intersection of race, class, gender, and sexuality.[2] Endarkened epistemologies in general, and Chicana feminism in particular, inform my perspective.

I first review briefly the failure of traditional mainstream educational scholarship and liberal feminist scholarship to provide a useful paradigm to examine the realities of working-class Chicana students. Second, I outline characteristics of a Chicana feminist epistemology by drawing from the work of Chicana scholars in various disciplines. Next, I use the work of Anselm Strauss and Juliet Corbin (1990) to describe four sources of what I call "cultural intuition" — that is, the unique viewpoints Chicana scholars bring to the research process. In doing so, I provide examples of my own cultural intuition as it relates to my research. In the last sections of this article, I clarify what I mean by a Chicana feminist epistemology and cultural intuition by describing an oral history study that examined a specific example of Chicana students' oppositional behavior as an act of school resistance and grassroots leadership (Delgado Bernal, 1997).[3] I demonstrate how, although not specifically articulated at the time of my study, my research was guided by my own cultural intuition and a Chicana feminist epistemology.

The Failure of Liberal Educational Scholarship

Gender, ethnic, and class oppression contribute to the unique position of working-class Chicana students, yet liberal educational scholarship has failed to provide a useful paradigm to examine this intersection. For example, theories that attempt to understand how schools replicate the social relationships and attitudes needed to sustain the existing relations in a capitalist society have traditionally focused on White, working-class male students and ignored the role of female students (Bowles & Gintis, 1976). The goal of school resistance literature has been to better understand the role of agency in the process of social reproduction; however, most early studies are also grounded in a traditional, patriarchal epistemology that focuses on White working-class males and does not fully explain the resistance of female students (MacLeod, 1987; Willis, 1977). Theories of cognitive development (Piaget, 1952, 1954) still espoused in many teacher education and educational psychology programs are normed on the behaviors of White middle-class male students, and are ignored or misapplied to students of any other identities. Historically, traditional mainstream educational scholarship has not addressed the influence of gender, race/ethnicity, class, and sexuality on education policy and practice.

Most liberal feminist scholarship has also failed to provide a useful paradigm to examine the gender, ethnic, and class oppression that contribute to the unique positions of working-class Chicana students. Liberal feminist scholarship gives primacy to the domination of patriarchy without seriously addressing how institutional and cultural differences based on sexism, racism, and classism create a different range of choices and options for Chicanas (Zambrana, 1994). Another problematic position of liberal feminist scholarship is the notion that an analysis should begin with the commonalties of women's experience. By only looking at commonalties based on gender and omitting issues of race/ethnicity or class, one may overlook how institutional and cultural structures constrain and enable different groups of women differently. For example, very little is known about the educational mobility of women of color in general, and Chicanas in particular. Until recently, the educational paths of Chicanas were rarely explored. Today there are studies that have investigated the barriers to education experienced by Chicanas (Gándara, 1982; Segura, 1993; Vásquez, 1982), the marginality of Chicanas in higher education (Cuádraz, 1996), and in the college choice and resistance of Chicanas (Talavera-Bustillos, 1998). These studies go beyond the commonalties of women's experience and examine how family backgrounds, school practices, male privilege, and class and ethnic discrimination shape Chicanas' educational experiences and choices. More specifically, Denise Segura (1993) found that teachers' and counselors' actions channeled Chicanas into non-academic programs offering a lower quality of instruction, which restricted their range of life chances and options. Segura and other Chicana scholars address the shortcomings of liberal educational scholarship by embracing a Chicana feminist epistemology that examines Chicanas' experiences in relation to an entire structure of domination. Although it is impossible in this article to describe all the nuances of a Chicana epistemology or its evolution, in the next section I outline some of the defining characteristics of a Chicana feminist epistemology.

A Chicana Feminist Epistemology

The relationship between methodology and a researcher's epistemological orientation is not always explicit, but is inevitably closely connected. Sandra Harding (1987) makes a distinction between epistemology, methodology, and method that is helpful in defining a Chicana feminist epistemology. "Method" generally only refers to techniques and strategies for collecting data. Although early feminist arguments defended qualitative approaches to studying and understanding women's lives over quantitative approaches, feminists today have reconsidered the false dichotomy of qualitative and quantitative methods (Maynard, 1994). Though quantitative methods are limited, both methods have been used in Chicana feminist research (e.g., Delgado-Gaitan, 1993; Flores-Ortiz, 1991; Pardo, 1990; Pesquera & Segura, 1990; Soldatenko, 1991), and as numerous educational researchers and feminists have pointed out, both methods have been used to objectify, exploit, and dominate people of color (Fine, 1994; Kelly, Burton, & Regan, 1994; Lather, 1991). A decision of whether to use qualitative or quantitative methods primarily depends on the topic and the research questions asked. Therefore, what becomes crucial in a Chicana feminist epistemology goes beyond quantitative versus qualitative methods, and lies instead in the methodology employed and in whose experiences and realities are accepted as the foundation of knowledge.

Methodology provides both theory and analysis of the research process, how research questions are framed, and the criteria used to evaluate research findings (Harding, 1987). Therefore, a Chicana methodology encompasses both the position from which distinctively Chicana research questions might be asked and the political and ethical issues involved in the research process. Liberal feminists have argued that what distinguishes feminist research from other forms of research is "the questions we have asked, the way we locate ourselves within our questions, and the purpose of our work" (Kelly, 1988, p. 6). However, these feminists (as well as mainstream scholars and Chicano male scholars) have too often failed to ask questions that analyze the interrelationships between classism, racism, sexism, and other forms of oppression, especially from Chicanas' perspectives. Liberal feminist research has insisted "on its political nature and potential to bring about change in women's lives" (Maynard, 1994, p. 16), yet this research has not addressed the lives of Chicanas.

Instead, it has been Chicana scholars who have challenged the historical and ideological representation of Chicanas, relocated them to a central position in the research, and asked distinctively Chicana feminist research questions, all important characteristics of a Chicana feminist epistemology (e.g., Alarcón et al., 1993; de la Torre & Pesquera, 1993; Flores-Ortiz, 1993; Mora & Del Castillo, 1980; Pérez, 1993; Romero, 1989; Zavella, 1993). By shifting the analysis onto Chicanas and their race/ethnicity, class, and sexuality, scholars are able to address the shortcomings of traditional patriarchal and liberal feminist scholarship (Castañeda, 1993; Castillo, 1995; Pardo, 1998; Pérez, 1993; Ruiz, 1998; Trujillo, 1993), thereby giving voice to Chicana experiences and bringing change to their lives. For example, Yvette Flores-Ortiz (1998) points to the need for and begins the process of creating a Chicana psychology. She points out that "the theory and practice of psychology have subjugated Chicanas by measuring their development, personality, and mental health against a male white upper-class model" (p. 102). Even feminist psychology that challenges patriarchal assumptions subsumes Chicanas under the variable of gender, and leaves them appearing deficient or dysfunctional when compared to White middle-class women. Flores-Ortiz's (1998) theoretical framework for a Chicana psychology relocates Chicanas to a central position and is informed by her twenty years as a clinical psychologist and her experience of immigration to the United States. Lara Medina's (1998) research documents the voices of how twenty-two Chicanas learned to substitute "patriarchal religion with their own cultural knowledge, sensibilities, and sense of justice" (p. 190). Her research challenges the spiritual and ideological representation of Chicanas in religion by asking how Chicanas recreate traditional cultural practices and look to non-Western philosophies as part of an ongoing process of spirituality. These and other Chicana scholars embrace and further develop a Chicana feminist epistemology by researching the lives and experiences of Chicanas, and framing their research questions in ways that give voice to these women. Inés Hernández-Avila (1995) speaks candidly about the importance of this kind of scholarship, and though a Chicana feminist epistemology may be unsettling for those operating within traditional research epistemologies, she affirms its importance in the academy:

> When I and other Native American women are central as subjects — as sovereign subjects — we often unsettle, disrupt, and sometimes threaten other people's, particularly many white people's, white scholars', white women feminists' sense of self as subjects. That may not have been my or our primary motivations, but it is necessarily inherent in Native women's claiming our right to speak for ourselves. (p. 494)

Epistemology involves the nature, status, and production of knowledge (Harding, 1987). Therefore, a Chicana epistemology must be concerned with the knowledge about Chicanas — about who generates an understanding of their experiences, and how this knowledge is legitimized or not legitimized. It questions objectivity, a universal foundation of knowledge, and the Western dichotomies of mind versus body, subject versus object, objective truth versus subjective emotion, and male versus female. In this sense, a Chicana epistemology maintains connections to indigenous roots by embracing dualities that are necessary and complementary qualities, and by challenging dichotomies that offer opposition without reconciliation. This notion of duality is connected to Leslie Marmon Silko's (1996) observation of a traditional Native American way of life: "In this universe there is no absolute good or absolute bad; there are only balances and harmonies that ebb and flow" (p. 64).

A Chicana feminist standpoint also acknowledges that most Chicanas lead lives with significantly different opportunity structures than men (including Chicano males) and White women. Patricia Hill Collins (1986) points out that Black feminists (similar to Chicana feminists) rarely describe the behavior of women of color without paying attention to the opportunity structures shaping their lives. Thus, adopting a Chicana feminist epistemology will expose human relationships and experiences that are probably not visible from a traditional patriarchal position or a liberal feminist standpoint. Within this framework, Chicanas become agents of knowledge who participate in intellectual discourse that links experience, research, community, and social change. Adela de la Torre and Beatríz Pesquera (1993) comment on this tradition, which places Chicanas as speaking subjects:

> Rooted in the political climate of the late 1960s and early 1970s, our scholarship, like other currents of dissent, is a Chicana critique of cultural, political, and economic conditions in the United States. It is influenced by the tradition of advocacy scholarship, which challenges the claims of objectivity and links research to community concerns and social change. It is driven by a passion to place the Chicana, as speaking subject, at the center of intellectual discourse. (p. 1)

While acknowledging the diversity and complexity of Chicanas' relationships and experiences, we must also recognize that, as an indigenous/mestiza-based cultural group, our experiences are different from those of African Americans and Native Americans in the United States. A Chicana feminist epistemology is informed by and shares characteristics of endarkened feminist epistemologies (e.g., examinations of the influence of race, class, gender, and sexuality on opportunity structures), but is different from the "Black Feminist Thought" of Collins (1991) or the inter-tribal discourses of Elizabeth Cook-Lynn (1996) and Marmon Silko (1996). A unique characteristic of a Chicana feminist epistemology is that it also validates and addresses experiences that are intertwined with issues of immigration, migration, generational status, bilingualism, limited English proficiency, and the contradictions of Catholicism. In addition, through the process of naming dynamic identities and diverse cultural/historical experiences, these issues have been studied and written about by numerous Chicana feminists in a much different way than most Chicano male scholars (e.g., Alarcón, 1990; Anzaldúa, 1987; Castillo, 1995; Medina, 1998; Sandoval, 1998; Trujillo, 1998).

For example, concepts such as mestiza, borderlands, and Xicanisma are unique to a Chicana epistemology. A mestiza is literally a woman of mixed ancestry, especially of Native American, European, and African backgrounds. However, the term mestiza has come to mean a new Chicana consciousness that straddles cultures, races, languages, nations, sexualities, and spiritualities — that is, living with ambivalence while balancing opposing powers. Gloria Anzaldúa (1987) states that "the new mestiza copes by developing a tolerance for contradictions, a tolerance for ambiguity. She learns to be an Indian in Mexican culture, to be Mexican from an Anglo point of view. She learns to juggle cultures" (p. 79). Within a Chicana feminist epistemology, borderlands refers to the geographical, emotional, and/or psychological space occupied by mestizas. Anzaldúa believes that those individuals who are marginalized by society and are forced to live on the borderlands of dominant culture develop a sixth sense for survival. Therefore, Chicanas and other marginalized peoples have a strength that comes from their borderland experiences. Xicanisma, a term introduced by Ana Castillo (1995), describes Chicana feminisms that are developed from and carried out to "our work place, social gatherings, kitchens, bedrooms, and society in general" (p. 11).

Rather than use an epistemological framework that is based solely on the diverse social histories of other women of color (e.g., Black feminist thought) or the social history of the dominant race (e.g., liberal feminist thought), a Chicana feminist epistemology offers a standpoint that borrows from endarkened feminist epistemologies and is grounded in the unique life experiences of Chicanas. For example, in educational research it is important to remember that Chicana students experience school from multiple dimensions, including their skin color, gender, class, and English-language proficiency. Castillo (1995) reflects on the trauma a Chicana may experience in regard to bilingualism:

> She was educated in English and learned it is the only acceptable language in society, but Spanish was the language of her childhood, family, and community. She may not be able to rid herself of an accent; society has denigrated her first language. By the same token, women may also become anxious and self conscious in later years if they have no or little facility in Spanish. (p. 39)

Bilingualism is often seen as un-American and is considered a deficit and an obstacle to learning. Prohibiting Spanish-language use among Mexican schoolchildren is a social philosophy and a political tool that has been and continues to be used to justify school segregation and to maintain a colonized relationship between Mexicans and the dominant society (Delgado Bernal, 1999). In my own research, I learned how Vickie Castro, a Los Angeles Unified School District board member, was physically separated from peers as a young girl because of the devaluation of Spanish:

> I do recall my first day of school. And I did not speak English. . . . I just recall being frightened and I recall not knowing what to do and I recall being told to just sit over there in the corner. And there was one other little girl and we were just scared out of our minds. (Castro, 1994, pp. 2, 3)

Historically, many Chicana and Chicano students have been segregated and stigmatized, with their perceived language deficiency used as justification. Students today continue to be segregated based on their limited English proficiency. In June 1998, California voters passed Proposition 227, the English Language Education for Immigrant Children initiative. The initiative does away with all bilingual education and English-language development programs that do not meet its rigid 180-day English-only approach.[4] It promotes stigmatization by allowing local schools "to place in the same classroom English learners of different ages but whose degree of English proficiency is similar."

To ground one's research within the experiences of Chicanas means that we deconstruct the historical devaluation of Spanish, the contradictions of Catholicism, the patriarchal ideology that devalues women, and the scapegoating of immigrants. In-deed, the everyday lives of Chicanas demonstrate that they are often at the center of these struggles against cultural domination, class exploitation, sexism, and racism. A Chicana feminist epistemology is therefore grounded in the rich historical legacy of Chicanas' resistance and translates into a pursuit of social justice in both research and scholarship.

A Chicana feminist epistemology that is based on the lives of Chicanas and is dedi-cated to achieving justice and equality combats what James Joseph Scheurich and Michelle Young (1997) call epistemological racism. As they define it, epistemological racism arises out of the social history and culture of the dominant race and is present in the current range of traditional research epistemologies — positivism to postmod-ernism and poststructuralism. Traditional research epistemologies reflect and rein-force the social history of the dominant race, which has negative results for people of color in general and students and scholars of color in particular. A Chicana feminist epistemology arises out of a unique social and cultural history, and demonstrates that our experiences as Mexican women are legitimate, appropriate, and effective in de-signing, conducting, and analyzing educational research. A Chicana cultural stand-point that is located in the interconnected identities of race/ethnicity, gender, class, and sexuality and within the historical and contemporary context of oppressions and resistance can also be the foundation for a theoretical sensitivity (Strauss & Corbin, 1990) that many Chicana scholars bring to their research.

Four Sources of Cultural Intuition

The disciplines of Black and other ethnic studies and women's studies have opened the way for multiple theoretical and epistemological readings in the fields of educa-tional research. A major contribution of these fields is that feminist and scholars of color (and those of us who identify as both) have argued that members of marginalized groups have unique viewpoints on our own experiences as a whole. (Dillard, 1997, p. 5)

I argue that Chicana researchers have unique viewpoints that can provide us with a perspective I call "cultural intuition." A Chicana researcher's cultural intuition is simi-lar in concept to Strauss and Corbin's (1990) "theoretical sensitivity" — a personal quality of the researcher based on the attribute of having the ability to give meaning to data. Their construct of theoretical sensitivity indicates an understanding of the subtle meanings of data, and that "one can come to the research situation with vary-ing degrees of sensitivity depending on one's previous reading and experience with or relevant to the data" (p. 41). They argue that theoretical sensitivity actually comes from four major sources: one's personal experience, the existing literature, one's pro-fessional experience, and the analytical research process itself. Having outlined in the last section important characteristics of a Chicana feminist epistemology, I propose that these four sources contribute to Chicana researchers' cultural intuition and are the foundation of a Chicana feminist epistemology in educational research. However, my concept of cultural intuition is different from theoretical sensitivity because it ex-tends one's personal experience to include collective experience and community memory, and points to the importance of participants' engaging in the analysis of data. In the next sections, I briefly describe the four sources and how each contributes to my cultural intuition as a Chicana researcher. The sources do not include all possibilities, yet they provide a framework that facilitates an understanding of cultural intuition and therefore a Chicana feminist epistemology in educational research. My hope is that this framework helps demonstrate what forces shape a Chicana feminist epistemology without limiting the nuances that must be addressed in future work.

Personal Experience

First, one's personal experience represents a very important source of cultural intuition and is derived from the background that we each bring to the research situation. As many feminists contend, the researcher is a subject in her research and her personal history is part of the analytical process (Maynard, 1994; Stanley & Wise, 1993). Through past life experiences, individuals acquire an understanding of certain situations and why and what might happen in a particular setting under certain conditions. This often implicit knowledge helps us to understand events, actions, and words, and to do so more confidently than if one did not bring these particular life experiences into the research (Strauss & Corbin, 1990). For example, my life experiences as a Chicana, a student, and a participant in protest politics such as campus and community demonstrations and boycotts helped me to understand and analyze my data. The oral histories I collected in my study of Chicana student activists (Delgado Bernal, 1997) were not heard as merely random stories, but as testimonies of authority, preemption, and strength that demonstrate women's participation and leadership in school resistance. In other words, my personal experiences provided insight and a cultural intuition from which to draw upon during my research.

   However, personal experience does not operate in a vacuum. To extend Strauss and Corbin's (1990) notion of personal experience, I argue that personal experience goes beyond the individual and has lateral ties to family and reverse ties to the past. Personal experience is partially shaped by collective experience and community memory, and as Marmon Silko (1996) states, "an individual's identity will extend from the identity constructed around the family" (p. 52). Through the experiences of ancestors and elders, Chicanas and Chicanos carry knowledge of conquest, loss of land, school and social segregation, labor market stratification, assimilation, and resistance. Community knowledge is taught to youth through legends, *corridos*,[5] storytelling, behavior, and most recently through the scholarship in the field of Chicana and Chicano Studies. As a child, my own family experience included learning through my grandmothers' stories, which were sprinkled with religion and mysticism, and my father's stories about the urban challenges of his childhood. As an adult, I began interviewing and recording the stories and knowledge that my family members shared with me. This knowledge that is passed from one generation to the next can help us survive in everyday life by providing an understanding of certain situations and explanations about why things happen under certain conditions. Sara Lawrence-Lightfoot (1994) discusses the unique knowledge that comes from the intertwinement of collective experience and intuition in African American communities:

> The development of this understanding is not rational — it comes from "the gut"; it is based on experience and intuition. There is the idea that this suspicion is passed down from the ancestors who teach the next generation the subtle dangers

— through act and deed — who instruct their offspring in how to walk through treacherous minefields, who show them jungle posture. (p. 60)

Lawrence-Lightfoot writes of the "ancestral wisdom" that is taught from one generation to the next, and calls it "a powerful piece of our legacy" that is "healthy" and "necessary for survival." Likewise, Marmon Silko (1996) writes of how the Pueblo people have depended on the collective memory of many generations "to maintain and transmit an entire culture, a worldview complete with proven strategies for survival" (p. 30). For Chicana researchers, ancestral wisdom, community memory, and intuition influence one's own personal experiences. And it is personal experience that provides one source of cultural intuition from which to draw upon during research.

Existing Literature

Another source of cultural intuition is the existing literature on a topic. Technical literature includes research studies and theoretical or philosophical writings, while non-technical literature refers to biographies, public documents, personal documents, and cultural studies writings (Strauss & Corbin, 1990). Having an understanding of this information provides some insight into what is going on with the events and circumstances we are studying. The technical literature may be used to stimulate theoretical sensitivity by providing concepts and relationships that are checked against actual data. For example, in my study of Chicana student activists, my readings of endark-ened feminist theories, school resistance theories, and the socio-historical politics of Chicano schooling offered me a particular cultural intuition into the phenomenon I was studying by providing possible ways of approaching and interpreting data. My readings of descriptive materials, such as newspaper articles, also enhanced my cultural intuition by making me sensitive to what to look for in my data and helping me generate interview questions.

Professional Experience

One's professional experience can be yet another source of cultural intuition. Years of practice in a particular field often provides an insider view of how things work in that field (Strauss & Corbin, 1990). This knowledge, whether explicit or implicit, is taken into the research and helps one to understand differently than if one did not have this experience. My experiences as a bilingual teacher, a teacher educator, and my work with education programs in Latino community-based organizations have all contributed to the way I understand and analyze my data in educational research on Chicana students. Indeed, Strauss and Corbin (1990) would argue that due to my professional experience I can move into the educational environment and gain insight into the lives of Chicana students more quickly than someone who has never worked in a school setting with Chicana students: "The more professional experience, the richer the knowledge base and insight available to draw upon in the research" (p. 42).

Analytical Research Process

Finally, the analytical research process itself provides an additional source of cultural intuition: "Insight and understanding about a phenomenon increase as you interact with your data" (Strauss & Corbin, 1990, p. 43). This comes from making comparisons, asking additional questions, thinking about what you are hearing and seeing, sorting data, developing a coding scheme, and engaging in concept formation. As one idea leads to another, we are able to look more closely at the data and bring meaning to the research. For example, in my study of Chicana student activists, my increased awareness of concepts, meanings, and relationships were influenced by my interaction with the interview data (e.g., transcribing, reading transcriptions, listening to taped interviews, and coding interviews). In addition, my awareness was also increased by including the women I interviewed in the analytical process of making sense of the data.

Extending Strauss and Corbin's analytical research process, I suggest that including Chicana participants in an interactive process of data analysis contributes to the researcher's cultural intuition. Pizarro (1998) calls for "a new methodological approach to research in Chicana/o communities" (p. 57) that includes participants as equals at all stages of the research. "This requires that researchers and participants deconstruct the epistemology of the participants and use it as the basis for the entire project" (p. 74). In the latter half of this article, I describe in detail how using a focus group strategy allowed me to incorporate the epistemological perspectives of the Chicanas I interviewed. This process allowed me to go beyond a simple feedback loop, and bring meaning to the data based on an interactive process.

Of course, researchers must be careful to not let any of the four sources block them from seeing the obvious or assume everyone's personal and professional experiences are equal to theirs. Early in my research, I learned that the women in my study were very diverse and the life experiences they shared with each other were very different from my own personal experiences. For example, all eight of these women shared the following similarities: they were second- or third-generation Chicanas, first-generation college students, grew up in working-class neighborhoods on the east side of Los Angeles, and were student activists in 1968. As a third-generation Chicana and first-generation college student, I grew up in the suburbs of Kansas City, was in preschool in 1968, and was not introduced to political activism until my early twenties. Therefore, my personal experiences did not automatically designate me an "insider." I, like any researcher, had to be concerned with how I was approaching and interpreting my subject's stories of activism. As hooks (1989) states, we have to consider the purpose and use of our research:

> When we write about the experiences of a group to which we do not belong, we should think about the ethics of our action, considering whether or not our work will be used to reinforce and perpetuate domination. (p. 43)

While I do not argue for an essentialist notion of who is capable of conducting research with various populations based on personal experiences, I do believe that many Chicana scholars achieve a sense of cultural intuition that is different from that of other scholars. Sofía Villenas (1996) indirectly addresses this issue as she examines her own emerging and changing identity as a Chicana researcher. In doing so, she asks what constitutes an insider to a community of research participants and asserts that it is based on "collective experiences and a collective space" at multiple levels, rather than on a singular identity (p. 722). Villenas explains how her practice in the field as a Chicana educational ethnographer cannot be explicated in the same manner as White, middle-class researchers' relationships with their research participants. She therefore argues for a process by which Chicanas "become the subjects and the creators of knowledge" (p. 730), essentially advocating for the use of a Chicana feminist epistemology in educational research.

Likewise, Dillard (1997) speaks of cultural intuition in her discussion of theoretical and conceptual standpoints of Black women educational researchers. She poses that the insights from being and living as African American researchers opens up possibilities for the research community to see phenomena in new ways. She views these standpoints of Black women as achieved rather than inherent in one's singular identity:

> While we will argue vehemently that Black women as a cultural group "theorize" and embody extensive life experiences which, while diverse, shape a coherent body, what we advance here is the notion that, in educational research, such theoretical and conceptual standpoints are achieved; they are not inherent in one's race, class, sex, or other identities. (pp. 5–6)

A Chicana researcher's cultural intuition is achieved and can be nurtured through our personal experiences (which are influenced by ancestral wisdom, community memory, and intuition), the literature on and about Chicanas, our professional experiences, and the analytical process we engage in when we are in a central position of our research and our analysis. Thus, cultural intuition is a complex process that is experiential, intuitive, historical, personal, collective, and dynamic.

Having defined cultural intuition and a Chicana feminist epistemology, I now attempt to illustrate what these concepts mean in educational research. In order to provide a concrete example of this conceptual discussion, the next section describes a research project I worked on over several years. As I describe the oral history project, it is important to point out that I only became attentive to my own cultural intuition and the epistemology I brought to the research after I completed the project and had time to reflect on the research process. Though my theoretical framework was shaped by the school resistance theories in the sociology of education literature and interdisciplinary critical feminist theories, my self-reflections have allowed me to (re)interpret my epistemological framework from a Chicana feminist standpoint.[6] I now realize that the way I asked my research questions, designed the methodology, collected the data, and arrived at conclusions was greatly influenced by my cultural intuition. Even where the individual and focus group interviews were held, and my need to include the women in the data analysis process was unknowingly driven by a shared epistemology we all brought to the research. Therefore, it was both my cultural intuition and my epistemological orientation that served to resist dominant epistemologies and recover an ignored history of Chicana students.

Resistance and Recovery
through an Oral History Research Project

In 1968, people witnessed a worldwide rise in student movements in countries such as France, Italy, Mexico, and the United States. In March of that year, over ten thousand students walked out of schools in East Los Angeles to protest the inferior quality of their education. The event, which came to be known as the East L.A. Blowouts, focused national attention on the K–12 schooling of Chicanas and Chicanos and also set a precedent for school boycotts throughout the Southwest (Acuña, 1988).

Though their stories are often excluded in written historical accounts, my research demonstrates that Chicanas played crucial leadership roles in these mass demonstrations and were intimately involved in the struggles for educational justice. As an educational researcher and a Chicana, I was interested in the women's voices and their unique experiences that had previously been omitted from the diverse accounts of the Blowouts. My historical-sociological case study, informed by my own achieved cultural intuition and a Chicana feminist epistemology, posed the following research question: How does pivoting the analysis onto key Chicana participants provide an alternative history of the 1968 Blowouts? This research question itself is distinctively Chicana, especially when compared to previous research that has examined the Blowouts. Chicano and White males have studied the event from a perspective of protest politics (Puckett, 1971), a spontaneous mass protest (Negrete, 1972), internal colonialism (Muñoz, 1973), the Chicano student movement (Gómez-Quiñones, 1978), and a political and social development of the wider Chicano movement (Rosen, 1973). Indeed, none of their historical accounts locate Chicanas in a central position in the research or address the many factors that restricted or enabled Chicana students to participate. My study, in contrast, examined how women interpret their participation in the Blowouts nearly thirty years later, and how their participation is important to an understanding of transformational resistance, grassroots leadership, and an alternative history of the Blowouts (Delgado Bernal, 1997, 1998).

To gain new perspectives and interpretations of the 1968 Blowouts and Chicana school resistance, my primary methods of data collection were in-depth, semistructured oral history interviews with eight key female participants from the Blowouts, a two-hour semistructured focus group interview, and phone interviews. Following a network sampling procedure (Gándara, 1995), I interviewed eight women who were identified by other female participants or resource individuals as "key participants" or "leaders" in the Blowouts. In scheduling these interviews, I allowed ample time, realizing that the length of each interview would vary. The interviews took place when and where it was most convenient for each woman — in their homes, their mother's home, or at work. I created an interview protocol with open-ended questions in order to elicit multiple levels of data that would address my research questions. Though the interview protocol was used as a guide, I realized that as the women spoke of very personal experiences, a less-structured approach allowed their voices and ways of knowing to come forth. I also asked probing questions to follow up on responses that were unclear or possibly incomplete in order to understand how the women interpreted the reasons and ways in which they participated in the Blowouts.

The oral histories were not merely heard as random stories, but as testimonies of authority, preemption, and strength that demonstrate women's participation and leadership in school resistance. My life experiences as a Chicana provided a source of cultural intuition that helped me both to listen to and to hear the interviewees. For example, in six of the eight individual interviews, religion was discussed in terms of Catholic values, contradictions of Catholicism, or spirituality. I understood Rosalinda Méndez González's feelings of disillusionment and betrayal when she passionately talked to me about the contradictions of her Catholic upbringing and the influence it had on her activism. Having been exposed to these contradictions myself, and still identifying as a "cultural Catholic" (Medina, 1998), I heard her story as a very personal one. She remembers:

And then from my Catholic upbringing we were taught about compassion and charity, and how Jesus healed the ill and took care of the poor, and all of that. . . . And I go to college and find out that every religion in the world claims the same thing, that they're all the only true one, and that all of them have committed atrocities in the name of God, in the name of their religion, that the Catholic church tortured people and killed people in the name of God. (Interview with author)

After conducting individual oral history interviews, I corresponded with each woman twice. The first time I sent a complete copy of the interview transcript with a letter describing their role in the analysis of the data. The following is a portion of that letter:

I've decided to send transcriptions back to the women I've interviewed so that you each have a chance to see my initial interpretation. I believe it's important that you have an opportunity to reflect and respond to what you said in the interview. This will not only strengthen my analysis, but it allows each woman to interact with and "dialogue" with her own interview. The interview transcription with comments and questions in the margins is the one I'd like for you to review. These comments and questions are specific to areas that I'm curious or not quite clear about (that is, other women commented on the same issue, or I've since thought of a related issue). If possible I'd love for you to respond in writing on the transcription and/or a separate page. Please bring this copy and your comments with you to the focus group interview. At that time, we can further address any areas you'd like to elaborate on or additional questions I may have. The second clean copy is for you to hold on to — an interesting keepsake.

Closer to our meeting, I wrote the women informing them where we would be holding the group interview and the agenda for our meeting. Here is a portion of that letter:

Well, the date of our group interview is drawing near and I wanted to send you this update. On Saturday, February 17th we will hold our event in East Los Angeles' Self-Help Graphics from 4:00 to 7:00 p.m. Tomás Benitez, assistant director of Self-Help (and Mita Cuaron's husband) was able to secure space for us in the art gallery. The art gallery will be particularly special given the beautiful exhibit, La Vida Indigena, and the fact that the interview will be filmed. . . .

The agenda for the actual group interview will follow a semi-structured format. That is, based on your responses in the individual interviews, I will identify a few topics I would like to ask the group to respond to. In addition, I would also like each of you to bring up any blowout-related issues or events that are particularly interesting to you. . . . I'm not as interested in reconstructing the "Truth" of what happened as I am interested in your individual experiences and their similarities and differences.

When we met for the two-hour focus group, all but one of the women had read and reflected on their transcripts prior to the group meeting, and three of them returned their transcript with responses to my queries actually written in the margins. Their comments ranged from yes/no responses and name spelling corrections to several emotional sentences elaborating on their activism and a paragraph explaining why someone considered herself a leader. The written reflections were of course helpful to my analysis, as they provided me with additional information and clarified specific points from the individual interviews. The impact of the written reflections, however, was small in comparison to the lessons I gained from the subsequent group dialogue. My real interest in conducting a focus group interview was to incorporate the explicit use of group interaction to produce data and insights that might have been less accessible otherwise (Krueger, 1988).

I now realize that the focus group process seemed natural to me partially because of the cultural intuition I brought to the research project. I was used to my grandmothers' storytelling in which absolute "Truth" was less important to me than hearing and recording their life experiences. It was my familiarity with and respect for ancestral wisdom taught from one generation to the next and a regard for collective knowledge that allowed me to approach the research project with complete respect for each woman's testimony of school resistance. Indeed, the women shared their community knowledge through a form of storytelling in which all the women talked about their resistance by invoking stories about their families, quoting their parents, and mentioning where their parents were born. To make a point about democratic ideals and the right to question authority, Rosalinda contrasted her upbringing and socialization with that of her mother's a generation earlier:

> I remember when I was a kid growing up in Texas and going to school and being taught these things about democracy and how different my response was from my mother's response. My mother was born and raised in Mexico, in Chihuahua. And if you spoke up against the government, the next day your body would be found. . . . And she was terrified of standing up for her rights or speaking against any authority figure, and that included teachers. (unpublished focus group data)

The interaction among the participants also produced new information and differing viewpoints. For instance, several women were reminded of something based on another woman's recollections and made comments such as, "I was listening to Mita talk and I hadn't thought about it till right now . . .". The group interaction also allowed them to compare and contrast their experiences with each other. Three of the women come from politically progressive families who had been concerned with justice struggles for many years, and one of them stated, "I was born into this family of struggle, protest, rebellion, [and] . . . equal rights." In contrast, the other women spoke of coming from a more "traditional family." Whatever their personal family experiences were, they all agreed that during the time of their activism there was a knowledge or "gospel" in Mexican homes in East Los Angeles that did not question the Church or schoolteachers' absolute authority: "The church, whatever they say and the teachers, whatever they say." The women's interactions were a form of storytelling in which they were able to compare and contrast their memories and experiences. Their group dialogue also provided me with invaluable lessons in relation to the data analysis process.

Lessons from the Focus Group

Prior to the focus group interview, I sorted data by integrating key themes that emerged from the women's individual oral histories with the existing literature. During the focus group, I presented four themes related to the women's school resistance and asked them to respond to my preliminary interpretations of how these themes shaped their student activism: dual identity, patriotism, dimensions of leadership, and awareness/agency. Presenting my preliminary findings to the women was one way of including their knowledge and a means of avoiding "authenticity of interpretation and description under the guise of authority" (Villenas, 1996, p. 713). Indeed, my cultural intuition and the women's knowledge helped shape my final analysis.

For example, I was originally attempting to interpret the women's behavior within the common duality of "good girl" and "bad girl" discussed and critiqued by a number of Chicana authors (Anzaldúa, 1987; Castillo, 1995; Hurtado, 1996; Trujillo, 1993). These imposed constructions of Chicanas' identity are couched in women's sexuality and in what is perceived as acceptable and unacceptable behavior. The two polarized roles of Virgin Mary and whore exemplify the ultimate "good girl" and "bad girl." Aida Hurtado (1996) states that these are "social locations that are given cultural space to exist" (p. 50). During the individual interviews the women talked about their "good schoolgirl" behavior in terms of being "college-bound," "real straight-laced," "a star student," "head cheerleader," and in the "goody-goody camp." Yet in the same breath they discussed their very bold resistant behavior that was considered "bad activist student" behavior and deviant by most of society. The women wrote articles for community activist newspapers regarding the poor conditions in their schools, stood up to accusations of being communists, provided testimony about the inferior quality of their education to the U.S. Commission on Civil Rights, and were arrested by police and expelled from school because of their activism. Because shifting from "deviant (and therefore defiant) locations . . . to culturally sanctioned locations is . . . difficult" (Hurtado, 1996, p. 50), I was interested in how they were able to move between these social locations. Therefore, I asked the women how the social, cultural, and sexual realities of their lives were manifested in the duality of "good schoolgirl" and "bad activist student."

The women expressed a belief that my preliminary analysis was slightly off target. In fact, they believed that rather than moving between these two social locations, they were engaging in the same type of behaviors as "good schoolgirls" and as "bad activist students." It was the perceptions of their behaviors that changed. Their good schoolgirl behavior of speaking up in class, asking questions, and offering leadership to sanctioned student organizations was acceptable behavior (and even encouraged). However, when they practiced these same behaviors during the school boycotts, they were perceived as deviant. Their behavior had not changed — others' interpretation of their behavior had. In other words, they helped me to see that their "good schoolgirl" behavior that was so openly rewarded by good grades, student council positions, and respect from teachers was the exact same behavior that was unfairly punished when they used it to protest the inferior quality of their education. Their insight contributed to my reorganization of themes and altered my preliminary analysis.

In another case, the women confirmed my preliminary analysis regarding the complexity of gender's influence on their different dimensions of leadership. For example, during the oral history interviews, women made statements ranging from "Nobody ever said that you couldn't do this because you were a girl" to "I know that the females were not the leaders," and from "Being a female was not an issue, it was just a non-issue" to "I'm sure I knew that there was sexism involved . . . but we probably didn't talk about it." During the focus group interview the influence of gender continued to be perceived in a somewhat nebulous way. The diversity of statements found within interviews, between interviews, and at the focus group interview led me to conclude that there was no one distinct and precise viewpoint on gender's influence. Rather, the women's individual and collective thoughts on gender represent the indeterminate and complex influence of gender within a structure of patriarchy — a system of domination and unequal stratification based on gender.

Including these women in the analytical process of making sense of the data helped shape my research findings and was an important source of my own cultural intuition. Just as importantly, their participation in this process made them not just subjects of research, but also creators of knowledge — an important characteristic of a Chicana feminist epistemology. Thus, contrary to patriarchal historical accounts of the 1968 East L.A. School Blowouts, a Chicana feminist standpoint exposes human relationships and experiences that were previously invisible.

Conclusion

> The issue of subjectivity represents a realization of the fact that who we are, how we act, what we think, and what stories we tell become more intelligible within an epistemological framework that begins by recognizing existing hegemonic histories. . . . [Thus], uncovering and reclaiming of subjugated knowledges is one way to lay claim to alternative histories. (Mohanty, 1994, p. 148)

How educational research is conducted significantly contributes to what and whose history, community, and knowledge is legitimated. A Chicana feminist epistemology addresses the failure of traditional research paradigms that have distorted or omitted the history and knowledge of Chicanas. Though similar endarkened feminist epistemologies exist in specific segments of women's studies and ethnic studies, acknowledging a Chicana feminist epistemology in educational research is virtually unprecedented. And yet, a disproportionate number of all Chicana and Chicano Ph.D.s receive their doctoral degrees in the field of education (Solorzano, 1995). Without an articulated Chicana epistemology or an acknowledgment of cultural intuition within the field of education, these scholars are restricted by cultural hegemonic domination in educational research.

Therefore, one of the major contributions of this article is an emerging articulation of a new epistemology in educational research. This epistemology gives license to both Chicana and Chicano education scholars to uncover and reclaim their own subjugated knowledge. It also allows them to place some trust in their own cultural intuition so that they move beyond traditional areas of research situated in existing paradigms that overlook the particular educational experiences of Chicanas or Chicanos. To illustrate this point, consider the experience of Chicano scholar Octavio Villalpando when he conducted his doctoral dissertation research. Villalpando's (1996) investigation yielded very significant quantitative evidence demonstrating that Chicana and Chicano college students benefit substantially from affiliating primarily with other Chicanas and Chicanos during college. These benefits were particularly noteworthy for Chicano students, spanning a range of several important post-college outcomes. Although these are significant findings in the field of higher education, they could not be completely explained by preexisting higher education paradigms. Villal-pando's analysis might have been taken further had he been able to access his cultural intuition (Villalpando, personal communication, 1998). A Chicana feminist episte-mology gives Chicana and Chicano education scholars some freedom to interpret their research findings outside of existing paradigms, and hopefully develop and pro-pose policies and practices that better meet the needs of Chicanas and Chicanos.

Given the significant and growing Chicana and Chicano student population, par-ticularly in the Southwest, it certainly is not my intent to suggest an end to all educa-tional research on Chicanas that is not conducted by Chicana scholars. Indeed, I hope that others will read this article and think about their own epistemological framework and that of the Chicana and Chicano communities they research. Borrowing from a Chicana epistemology may help all scholars to raise more appropriate research ques-tions and avoid asking questions based on a cultural deficit model or incorrect stereo-types. Chicana sociologist Mary Pardo (1998) provides an insightful example of a White woman colleague who asked an inappropriate question based on stereotypes rather than the knowledge base of the East Los Angeles Chicanas she was reporting on. During Pardo's research, she and her colleague were having a meal with women from Mothers of East Los Angeles (MELA), a group of working-class community ac-tivists. Her colleague asked the group how they might mobilize around a hypothetical case of false imprisonment of an alleged youth gang member. Pardo describes why si-lence engulfed the room:

> Her question about the alleged gang member reflected the media assumption that
> gang activity constituted the most significant problem facing Eastside Los Angeles
> residents. But the women from MELA were long-time, stable home owners, most
> of whose children had already graduated from college. They had . . . directed collec-
> tive efforts at getting summer jobs for youth. . . . Rebuilding a neighborhood park
> and opposing the prison and toxic-waste incinerator consumed most of their time.
> (p. 12)

A new epistemological approach in educational research has the potential to avoid these type of inappropriate questions and focus on questions that may expose impor-tant school issues and community experiences that are otherwise not visible.

A major tenet of cultural intuition and a Chicana feminist epistemology is the in-clusion of Chicana research participants in the analysis of data. This allows Chicana participants — whether they are students, parents, teachers, or school administrators — to be speaking subjects who take part in producing and validating knowledge. A focus group interview is one data collection strategy that helps Chicana scholars and non-Chicana scholars include the epistemology of their research participants in the analysis of data. The example I provide in this article demonstrates how focus groups can be paired with an oral history methodology to include Chicana participants in the interpretation of data. In addition, it seems that focus groups can be effectively used with other qualitative and quantitative research methods and methodologies such as school ethnography, student interviews, survey research, and classroom observations. In the future, we must look for additional strategies that provide opportunities for Chicanas and Chicanos to participate in the construction of knowledge and research that is dedicated to achieving social justice. Hopefully, "an analysis of the Chicana/o experience can . . . assist us in forging a new epistemological approach to academic life and can help us uncover a methodology that is true to and helpful in the struggle of these people as it 'creates' a new knowledge base" (Pizarro, 1998, p. 72).

Notes

1. "Chicana" is a cultural and political identity composed of multiple layers and is often an identity of resistance that we consciously adopt later in life. "Chicana is not a name that women (or men) are born to or with, as is often the case with 'Mexican,' but rather it is consciously and critically assumed and serves as a point of redeparture for dismantling historical conjunctures of crisis, confusion, political and ideological conflict . . ." (Alarcón, 1990, p. 250). The term *Chicana* is used to discuss women of Mexican origin and/or women who identify with this label. While many of the issues addressed in this article apply to Chicano males and other Latinas and Latinos, the focus here is on Chicanas.
2. Cynthia Dillard (1997) proposes that "endarkened feminist ideology described as inherently cultural, positional, political, strategic, relational, and transformative is offered as possible criteria and catalyst for future educational research. In contrast to our common use of the term 'enlightening' as a way of expressing the having of new and important insights, we use the term endarkening to suggest epistemological roots of Black feminist thought which embody a distinguishable difference in cultural standpoint" (pp. 3–4). I use endarkened in a similar way, and include not only Black feminist thought, but the feminist thought of all women of color.
3. In this study, school resistance was defined as students' acknowledging problems in oppressive educational settings and demanding changes.
4. Proposition 227 requires that "all children in California public schools shall be taught English by being taught in English." This requirement counters educational research that demonstrates that English immersion is one of the least effective ways to teach the English language to children with limited English proficiency. The proposition also requires local schools to place students in English immersion classrooms for up to one year, based on their degree of English proficiency (Article 2). Parental exception waivers for the English immersion requirement may only be granted to parents who personally visit the school to apply and whose children meet certain requirements, including children who already know English, are over ten years old, or have special needs (Article 3).
5. The *corrido* is a Mexican ballad and is one means of oral tradition in which history and culture are preserved and shared through song. Corridos often tell stories of the struggles and resistance of Mexican people.
6. My self-reflections have been greatly influenced by earlier and recent Chicana scholars and writers. Unfortunately, much of the early work by Chicanas is difficult to find and has often gone unrecognized — indicative of the Eurocentric culture of academia. In the 1980s there was a reemergence of Chicana scholarship that not only repositioned class and ethnicity in relationship to gender, but also addressed the many aspects of sexuality. In the last few years the work of several progressive Chicana scholars has been particularly influential in helping me develop an articulation of Chicana feminist epistemology in educational research (Castillo, 1995; de la Torre & Pesquera, 1993; Hurtado, 1996; Pardo, 1998; Ruiz, 1998; Trujillo, 1998).

References

Acuña, R. (1988). *Occupied America: A history of Chicanos.* New York: HarperCollins.

Alarcón, N. (1990). Chicana feminism: In the tracks of "the" native woman. *Cultural Studies, 4,* 248–256.

Alarcón, N., Castro, R., Pérez, E., Pesquera, B., Sosa-Riddell, A., & Zavella, P. (Eds.). (1993). *Chicana critical issues.* Berkeley: Third Woman Press.

Anzaldúa, G. (1987). *Borderlands, la frontera: The new mestiza.* San Francisco: Aunt Lute Books.

Bowles, S., & Gintis, H. (1976). *Schooling in capitalist America.* New York: Basic Books.

Castañeda, A. (1993). Sexual violence in the politics and policies of conquest: Amerindian women and the Spanish conquest of Alta California. In A. de la Torre & B. Pesquera (Eds.), *Building with our hands: New directions in Chicano studies* (pp. 15–33). Berkeley: University of California Press.

Castillo, A. (1995). *Massacre of the dreamers: Essays on Xicanisma.* New York: Plume.

Collins, P. H. (1986). Learning from the outsider within: The sociological significance of Black feminist thought. *Social Problems, 33*(6), S14–S32.

Collins, P. H. (1991). *Black feminist thought: Knowledge, consciousness, and the politics of empowerment.* New York: Routledge.

Cook-Lynn, E. (1996). *Why I can't read Wallace Stegner and other essays: A tribal voice.* Madison: University of Wisconsin Press.

Cuádraz, G. (1996). Experiences of multiple marginality: A case study of "Chicana scholarship women." In C. Turner, M. García, A. Nora, & L. Rendón (Eds.), *Racial and ethnic diversity in higher education* (pp. 210–222). New York: Simon & Schuster.

de la Torre, A., & Pesquera, B. (Eds.). (1993). *Building with our hands: New directions in Chicana studies.* Berkeley: University of California Press.

Delgado Bernal, D. (1997). *Chicana school resistance and grassroots leadership: Providing an alternative history of the 1968 East Los Angeles blowouts.* Doctoral dissertation, University of California, Los Angeles.

Delgado Bernal, D. (1998). Grassroots leadership reconceptualized: Chicana oral histories and the 1968 East Los Angeles school blowouts. *Frontiers: A Journal of Women Studies, 19*(2), 113–142.

Delgado Bernal, D. (1999). Chicana/o education from the civil rights era to the present. In J. F. Moreno (Ed.), *The elusive quest for equality: 150 years of Chicano/Chicana education.* Cambridge, MA: Harvard Educational Review.

Delgado-Gaitan, C. (1993). Researching change and changing the researcher. *Harvard Educational Review, 63,* 389–411.

Dillard, C. B. (1997, April). *The substance of things hoped for, the evidence of things not seen: Toward an endarkened feminist ideology in research.* Paper presented at the annual meeting of the American Educational Research Association, Chicago.

Fine, M. (1994). Working the hyphens: Reinventing self and other in qualitative research. In N. Denzin & Y. Lincoln (Eds.), *Handbook of qualitative research* (pp. 70–82). Thousand Oaks, CA: Sage.

Flores-Ortiz, E. (1998). Voices from the couch: The co-creation of a Chicana psychology. In C. Trujillo (Ed.), *Living Chicana theory* (pp. 102–122). Berkeley: Third Woman Press.

Flores-Ortiz, Y. (1991). Levels of acculturation, marital satisfaction, and depression among Chicana workers: A psychological perspective. *Aztlán, 20*(1/2), 151–175.

Flores-Ortiz, Y. (1993). La mujer y la violencia: A culturally based model for the understanding and treatment of domestic violence in Chicana/Latina communities. In N. Alarcón et al. (Eds.), *Chicana critical issues* (pp. 169–182). Berkeley: Third Woman Press.

Gándara, P. (1982). Passing through the eye of the needle: High-achieving Chicanas. *Hispanic Behavioral Sciences, 4,* 167–179.

Gándara, P. (1995). *Over the ivy walls: The educational mobility of low-income Chicanos.* Albany: State University of New York Press.

Giroux, H. A. (1992). *Border crossings: Cultural workers and the politics of education.* New York: Routledge.

Gómez-Quiñones, J. (1978). *Mexican students por La Raza: The Chicano student movement in Southern California 1967–1977.* Santa Barbara, CA: Editorial La Causa.

Harding, S. (Ed.). (1987). *Feminism and methodology.* Milton Keynes, Eng.: Open University Press.

Hernández-Avila, I. (1995). Relocations upon relocations: Home, language, and Native American women's writings. *American Indian Quarterly, 19,* 491–507.

hooks, b. (1989). *Talking back: Thinking feminist, thinking Black.* Boston: South End Press.

Hurtado, A. (1989). Relating to privilege: Seduction and rejection in the subordination of White women and women of color. *Signs: Journal of Women in Culture and Society, 14,* 833–855.

Hurtado, A. (1996). *The color of privilege: Three blasphemies on race and feminism.* Ann Arbor: University of Michigan Press

Kelly, L. (1988). *Surviving sexual violence.* Cambridge, Eng.: Polity Press.

Kelly, L., Burton, S., & Regan, L. (1994). Researching women's lives or studying women's oppression? Reflections on what constitutes feminist research. In M. Maynard & J. Purvis (Eds.), *Researching women's lives from a feminist perspective* (pp. 27–48). Bristol, PA: Taylor & Francis.

Krueger, R. A. (1988). *Focus groups: A practical guide for applied research.* Newbury Park, CA: Sage.

Lather, P. (1991). *Getting smart: Feminist research and pedagogy with/in the postmodern.* New York: Routledge.

Lawrence-Lightfoot, S. (1994). *I've known rivers: Lives of loss and liberation.* New York: Penguin Books.

MacLeod, J. (1987). *Ain't no makin' it: Leveled aspirations in a low-income neighborhood.* Boulder, CO: Westview Press.

Marmon Silko, L. (1996). *Yellow woman and a beauty of the spirit: Essays on Native American life today.* New York: Touchtone.

Maynard, M. (1994). Methods, practice and epistemology: The debate about feminism and research. In M. Maynard & J. Purvis (Eds.), *Researching women's lives from a feminist perspective* (pp. 10–26). Bristol, PA: Taylor & Francis.

Medina, L. (1998). Los espíritus siguen hablando: Chicana spiritualities. In C. Trujillo (Ed.), *Living Chicana theory* (pp. 189–213). Berkeley, CA: Third Woman Press.

Mohanty, C. T. (1994). On race and voice: Challenges for liberal education in the 1990's. In H. A. Giroux & P. McLaren (Eds.), *Between borders: Pedagogy and the politics of cultural studies* (pp. 145–166). New York: Routledge.

Mora, M., & Del Castillo, A. R. (Eds.). (1980). *Mexican women in the United States: Struggles past and present.* Los Angeles: University of California, Los Angeles, Chicano Studies Research Center.

Muñoz, C., Jr. (1973). *The politics of Chicano urban protest: A model of political analysis.* Unpublished doctoral dissertation, Claremont Graduate School.

Negrete, L. R. (1972). Culture clash: The utility of mass protest as a political response. *Journal of Comparative Cultures, 1,* 25–36.

Pardo, M. (1990). Mexican American women grassroots community activists: "Mothers of East Los Angeles." *Frontiers: A Journal of Women Studies, 11,* 1–7.

Pardo, M. (1998). *Mexican American women activists: Identity and resistance in two Los Angeles communities.* Philadelphia: Temple University Press.

Pérez, E. (1993). Speaking from the margin: Uninvited discourse on sexuality and power. In A. de la Torre & B. Pesquera (Eds.), *Building with our hands: New directions in Chicana studies* (pp. 57–71). Berkeley: University of California Press.

Pesquera, B. M., & Segura, D. A. (1990). *Feminism in the ranks: Political consciousness and Chicana/Latina white collar workers.* Paper presented at the annual meeting of the National Association for Chicana and Chicano Studies, Albuquerque, NM.

Pesquera, B. M., & Segura, D. A. (1993). There is no going back: Chicanas and feminism. In N. Alarcón et al. (Eds.), *Chicana critical issues* (pp. 95–115). Berkeley, CA: Third Woman Press.

Piaget, J. (1952). *The origins of intelligence in children.* New York: International Universities Press.

Piaget, J. (1954). *The construction of reality in the child.* New York: Basic Books.

Pizarro, M. (1998). "Chicana/o Power!" Epistemology and methodology for social justice and empowerment in Chicana/o communities. *International Journal of Qualitative Studies in Education, 11*(1), 57–80.

Puckett, M. (1971). *Protest politics in education: A case study in the Los Angeles Unified School District.* Unpublished doctoral dissertation, Claremont Graduate School.

Romero, M. (1989). Twice protected? Assessing the impact of affirmative action on Mexican American women. *Journal of Hispanic Policy, 3,* 83–101

Rosen, G. (1973). The development of the Chicano movement in Los Angeles from 1967–1969. *Aztlán, 4,* 155–183.

Ruiz, V. (1998). *From out of the shadows: Mexican women in twentieth-century America.* Oxford, Eng.: Oxford University Press.

Sandoval, C. (1998). Mestizaje as method: Feminists of color challenge the canon. In C. Trujillo (Ed.), *Living Chicana theory* (pp. 352–370). Berkeley, CA: Third Woman Press.

Scheurich, J. J., & Young, M. D. (1997). Coloring epistemologies: Are our research epistemologies racially biased? *Educational Researcher, 26*(4), 4–16.

Segura, D. (1993). Slipping through the cracks: Dilemmas in Chicana education. In A. de la Torre & B. Pesquera (Eds.), *Building with our hands: New directions in Chicana studies* (pp. 199–216). Berkeley: University of California Press.

Soldatenko, M. A. (1991). Organizing Latina garment workers in Los Angeles. *Aztlán, 20*(1/2), 73–96.

Solorzano, D. G. (1995). The baccalaureate origins of Chicana and Chicano doctorates in the social sciences. *Hispanic Journal of Behavioral Science, 17*(1), 3–32.

Stanley, L., & Wise, S. (1993). *Breaking out again.* London: Routledge.

Strauss, A., & Corbin, J. (1990). *Basics of qualitative research: Grounded theory procedures and techniques.* Newbury Park, CA: Sage.

Talavera-Bustillos, V. (1998). *Chicana college choice and resistance: An exploratory study of first-generation Chicana college students.* Unpublished doctoral dissertation, University of California, Los Angeles.

Trujillo, C. (1993). Chicana lesbians: Fear and loathing in the Chicano community. In N. Alarcón et al. (Eds.), *Chicana critical issues* (pp. 117–125). Berkeley, CA: Third Woman Press.

Trujillo, C. (1998). La Virgen de Guadalupe and her reconstruction in Chicana lesbian desire. In C. Trujillo (Ed.), *Living Chicana theory* (pp. 214–231). Berkeley, CA: Third Woman Press.

Vásquez, M. (1982). Confronting barriers to the participation of Mexican American women in higher education. *Hispanic Journal of Behavioral Sciences, 4,* 147–165.

Villalpando, O. (1996). *The long term effects of college on Chicano and Chicana students: "Other oriented" values, service careers, and community involvement.* Unpublished doctoral dissertation, University of California, Los Angeles.

Villenas, S. (1996). The colonizer/colonized Chicana ethnographer: Identity marginalization, and co-optation in the field. *Harvard Educational Review, 66,* 711–731.

Willis, P. E. (1977). *Learning to labour: How working-class kids got working-class jobs.* Aldershot, Eng.: Gower.

Zambrana, R. (1994). Toward understanding the educational trajectory and socialization of Latina women. In L. Stone & G. M. Boldt (Eds.), *The education feminism reader* (pp. 135–145). New York: Routledge.

Zavella, P. (1993). The politics of race and gender: Organizing Chicana cannery workers in Northern California. In N. Alarcón et al. (Eds.), *Chicana critical issues* (pp. 127–153). Berkeley, CA: Third Woman Press.

I am indebted to the many Chicana scholars, activists, writers, and artists who have influenced my (ongoing) epistemological journey and helped me to better understand my cultural intuition. I am particularly grateful to Adaljiza Sosa-Riddell, Daniel Solorzano, Octavio Villalpando, and Harvard Educational Review Editorial Board members Romina Carrillo and Matthew Hartley for their invaluable insights and suggestions on this article. I take responsibility for my interpretations and, because producing knowledge must be part of an ongoing conversation, I welcome comments and constructive criticism.

Researching Dissident Subjectivities: Queering the Grounds of Theory and Practice

KENN GARDNER HONEYCHURCH

The operations of social research are a means by which cultural knowledges may be confirmed, refuted, or generated. All theories and methods of research, however, presuppose a particular worldview and also determine the ways in which individuals experience, and subsequently privilege, particular knowledges and approaches over others. Hence, the subject(s),[1] processes, and claims of research inquiry are considered, explained, and legitimated through selectively authorized epistemologies, methodologies, and texts that have embedded within them not only the intellectual ideas and assumptions, but also the values, of the culture in which they are produced.

The activities of research cannot be separated from the circumstances in which they are steeped. Through the interimplications of knowledge, culture, and social power, certain discourses are made cogent, while others, through the same peremptory exercise of dominance, are constrained. As an example, in researching matters of sexuality, the denunciative heterosexualizing discourses of powerful cultural institutions, including schools and the Academy, legitimized through the authorities of religion, science, and the law, have long made the subjects of homosexualities a problem.[2] As a consequence, any consideration of the latter cannot be separated from a reflection on the denigrating conceptual frameworks, and the disdainful, sometimes murderous, cultural practices within which such inquiries proceed. "There is no question that the threat of this violent, degrading, and often fatal extrajudicial sanction works even more powerfully than, and in intimately enforcing concert with, more respectably institutionalized sanctions against gay choice, expression, and being" (Sedgwick, 1990, p. 18).

Identities soiled by hegemonic cultural discourses, lesbians and gay men must doubt the imposition of heterosexist knowledges and beliefs, and disobey the conventions that continue to erase or maim the realms of same-sex affiliation and desire.[3] In order to conduct productive autoethnographic research with homosexual subjects, it is particularly imperative that gay and lesbian researchers mobilize an interrogative objection to the epistemological, methodological, and textual assumptions and stipulations of compulsory heterosexualized discourse that may otherwise be inimical to its

Harvard Educational Review   Vol. 66   No. 2   Summer 1996

operations.[4] As an initial response, an antihomophobic stance in researching homo-sexualities is a meritorious posture; as an end, it is short-sighted. Defined as "not het-erosexuality," homosexuality has been explained by what it lacks (Hocquenghem, 1978). Antihomophobic inquiry is similarly restricted, because its onus is also on that which is absent — that is, the distaste for and fear of homosexuals. As a consequence, antihomophobic social research is a claim to particularity through the practice of nu-merous disavowals that represent homosexual subjects only by the shadows of inter-diction.

While a reasonable goal of any research around homosexualities, antihomophobic epistemologies, methods, and texts, because they remain focused on what is lacking, reinscribe the subject(s) as sites of absence. In Freudian terms, homosexuality has been defined as an arrest in development — a stopping short that prevents the full story from unfurling. Antihomophobic inquiry fails also, by default, in that it does not sufficiently demarcate what the narratives of social research by, with, and for gay and/or lesbian subject(s) might become — how they might be productively consti-tuted and expressed by that which is present and different in their conception and ex-ecution rather than by that which is lacking.

Considering Social Research from a Queered Position

For approximately eighteen months, as a gay male theorist/researcher interested in the visual arts education of adults, I was engaged in a descriptive, in-depth study with two gay male artists. The research first considered the relationship of sexual subjectivities to cultural productions, and secondly investigated the relationship of each artist and his work to the organization and practices of the broader culture — including the postsecondary educational institution in which each was enrolled. Data was collected in a series of scheduled interviews, in unscheduled participant-observations, and through a careful examination of each artist's art works and processes. The resultant data was organized and analyzed according to each individual artist and, subse-quently, similarities and differences were noted.

I and other gay male and lesbian academics who choose both to declare our sexualities and to study a subject of homosexualities and/or homosexual subjects must consider perspectives outside of the homogenizing constraints of heterosexualizing models.[5] Any pursuit of a singular homosexual nature or state of mind, however, is clearly an unreasonable (and impossible) intention. The familiar term "gay/lesbian sensibilities" does not adequately account for either the multiplicity of differences (race, class, ethnicity, etc.) within those identities, or the anticipation of common grounds between them.[6] It is perhaps in the more expansive term "queer" that most possibilities emerge for denominating and declaring a range of differences and posi-tions arising from the gamut of sexual diversities.[7]

The "gay" subject is now, at least in some quarters, being rewritten as "queer" (Edelman, 1994). "The word 'queer' itself means *across* — it comes from the Indo-European root — *tewerkw,* which also yields the German *quer* (transverse), Latin *torquere* (to twist), English *athwart*" (Sedgwick, 1993, p. xii). While it is perhaps even more difficult to disentangle the word queer from its pejorative history and the denunciative mythologies that surround it, the term is being reclaimed by those long despoiled by its derogating accusations — individuals and communities now more vigorous in an insistence on ending both narrow categorizations and repressions based on sexual diversity. Further, it is evident that the word queer has a different meaning when hurled on the street as a homophobic epithet than when used in a descriptive conjunctural relationship with evolving epistemologies, methodologies, or texts that it seeks to both reflect and constitute.

While the word queer often refers to lesbians and gay men, it is not restricted to categories of sexual orientation. Sedgwick proffers that the "most exciting work around, 'queer' spins the term outward along dimensions that can't be subsumed under gender and sexuality at all: the ways that race, ethnicity, postcolonial nationality criss-cross with these and other identity-constituting, identity-fracturing discourses" (1993, pp. 8–9). Its adoption is an effort to avoid the "ideological liabilities" of other terms associated with sexual diversity, and is, alternately, a means by which to "transgress and transcend them — or at the very lest, problematize them" (de Lauretis, 1991, p. v).

As a category of contradiction, a queered perspective offers a recognition of both heterogeneity in, and the possibilities of mutual identifications across, difference. For example, my study of gay artists could consider the particularities of gay male sexuality and visual representations from a queered perspective. However, a queered position could also be utilized by a variety of researchers in a wide range of social research undertakings that inquire into an array of eccentric social identities. All could be enunciated under a queer umbrella.

The suggestion of a queered alternative is not merely an interest in the addition of the previously excluded to dominant epistemologies and research practices that otherwise remain unaltered. A queered position requires an ontological shift comprehensively resistant in its exceptions to dominant normativity. A queering of standpoint in social research is a vigorous challenge to that which has constrained what may be known, who may be the knower, and how knowledge has come to be generated and circulated. A queered position first dislocates the agent of its constitution. While homosexuals have largely been defined by the discourse of others, queers participate in positioning themselves through both authoring and authorizing experience. As lesbian and gay (queer) subjects are located in an evolving discourse that preexists and constitutes them, they are, at the same time, its creative agents. Any claim to a queered perspective is therefore an embrace of a dynamic discursive position from which subjects of homosexualities can both name themselves and impact the conditions under which queer identities are constituted.

A queered position, while it may never be fully fixed, can be declared by producing visibility through that which it is, or that which it might become under its own auspices.[8] A queered position insists not only on the partiality of exclusionary heterosexual assertions, but also on the necessity of recognizing the admittedly equally partial yet productive differences of queered presence. Through the claims of an alternative that expands the sphere of legitimacy applicable to all research, a queered position provides a unique way of commenting on a social world whose processes and outcomes might otherwise be (in)appropriately measured when constructed against the norm of un-queered perspectives.

In considering emergent theoretical, methodological, and textual possibilities, I do not intend to suggest that alternate viewpoints and tactics should be abandoned as totally pernicious and irrelevant to queer experiences. Lesbian and gay male social researchers engaged in studying the subjects of homosexualities can escape neither the implications of our sexualities nor the heterosexual prerogatives of the schools, Academy, and cultures in which we are indoctrinated. Similarly, the insights of queered research practices are not only of relevance to queer subjects. While restrictive research practices, such as homophobic inquiry, are damaging to lesbians and gay men in constraining ideas and critical perspectives, such restrictive investigations also have epistemological consequence beyond the gay community, in that they yield partial and distorted knowledges for all inquirers.

To urge the potentialities of a queered position in social research inquiry around homosexualities is also not to suggest equable, coherent, and closed practices that might be organized around its denomination. It is, rather, an endeavor to query and obstruct heterosexist models long enough to engage the pluralities of desire and knowledge in ways that permit lesbians and gay men, among others, to constitute ourselves more positively individually and to contribute to more expansive collective cultural discourses. The possibilities of a queered position in social research, while nascent and tentative, include, but are not limited to: thinking outside of heterosexual epistemologies; issues around objectivity; the queering of language and texts; the implications of the body and the erotic in research practices; the likelihood of raising the hackles of contrary readers; and, finally, the interimplications of the Academy and schooling with the potential for transformative social practices.

Queering Epistemologies: Thinking *through* (Homo)sexualities

Knowledge does not emerge in a cultural vacuum. Rather, it is acquired in particular settings where research is undertaken according to prevailing cognitive structures within which its subjects are conceived and through which claims are made and understood. Because heterosexuality is most often assumed, even a rudimentary consideration outside of the mental categories it constructs becomes arduous; the *straight mind* universalizes all of its ideas and is unable to conceive of a culture that does not order all concepts on the basis of heterosexuality (Wittig, 1992).

Other sexualities are thereby excluded, constrained, or, when they are maintained, fabricated as unspeakably perverse and therefore of no consequence to legitimate knowledge. Lacking sanctioned theories of its own, the *queered mind* has been forced to camouflage itself, to obscure its variance and potence within the puckers of what has been passed off as the seamless fabric of heterosexualized knowledges. Privileged heterosexualized theory and practice has been constituted as the entirety of epistemology and praxis — its meanings so ratified, its claims so assured in their rectitude, so obdurate in their refusals, that nothing other than itself has been envisioned.

Initially, queered inquiry requires a decentering that *drags* theory into the zones occupied by its subjects, rather than otherwise forcing them into the unlikely spaces of heterosexual attention(s). Approaching social knowledge from a queered position is a postmodern rejection of epistemological certainty. A queered tenor calls the bluff of heterosexist epistemology and reveals the arbitrary and mediated nature of its otherwise apparently unquestionable logic.

The nature and extent of possible biomaterial and sociocultural influences in the lives of lesbians, bisexuals, transgendered individuals, and gay men is unknown. In an essentialist argument, sexual orientation is considered a consequence of some immutable factors, independent, at some level, of culture.[9] Conversely, from the non-univocal social constructionist perspectives that are particularly popular in the Academy, sexuality is construed as an artifact of the society in which it is encountered (Butler, 1993; Greenberg, 1988). However, in resisting *any* biological explanations, the role of the social/experiential is overestimated.[10] To concentrate only on the cultural generation of sexualized knowledges and deny any other accounting of sexuality is to forfeit too much. While I resist constraining lesbian or gay identities as already determined, and recognize that cultural discourses produce queer bodies, those inscriptions are not made on empty slates. Sexuality is neither outside, nor born of, ideology. Sexual subjects are the constituted effect of discourse, but they are also its enabling conditions, in which sexual forces are already immanent.[11]

It is likely that a merger of biomaterial and social perspectives will prove advantageous in any adequate understanding of sexuality. As such, sexual identities are constructed in a precarious interstice that draws from both the possibilities of the unwavering truisms of essentialism and the necessities of continual performative reinvention of constructionism. However, until knowledges constituted in a heterosexual order are no longer presumed to be absolute and universal, and until inchoate queer subjects and theories are no longer forced into a "straight-acting" and "straight-looking" guise, the possibilities of queered knowledges will not come out of the epistemological closet. It is only in the long-term incorporation of more congruent considerations and organizations of knowledge that the extent of such queered difference may be productively explored.

While a full articulation of the possibilities of fixed queered knowledges is beyond the scope of this, or any, project, some basic queered theoretical perspectives, with particular respect to sexual orientation and gay males, were assumed and made explicit within the earlier described research inquiry that precipitated interest in the present discussion. Sexual orientations are not a private matter that impacts only personal sexual practices, but are dimensions of subjectivity that infuse all human experience, including higher cognitive functions;[12] are imbricated in that sexuality, gender, class, etc.; are layered and interimplicated and therefore cannot be read monolithically; and are viewed as identities coherent enough to be recognized, but fluid enough to be interrogated. Further, homosexualities are normal variants of human experience; productive subjects of research inquiry; an enacted objection to the demand that all sexuality is reproductive in nature; an expressed alternative to gender-conformity and social order around male and female as those biological/cultural forms have been constituted by an heterosexual regime; and, finally, a visible alternative to cultural sex-negativity or erotophobia.

Objectivity and Queer Inclination(s)

In objectivist paradigms, the object of consideration is envisioned as existing outside the conditions of its perceivability. Historically, the objectivist view is the one afforded by high positions in the social structure where the phenomenon under investigation is apprehended by the observer through a reasoning process that facilitates closer and closer approximation to some *truth* deemed independent of the inquirer (Bourdieu, 1977). Such disembodied rules of scrutiny accentuate the split between the researcher and the researched where objectivity comes to be defined by the measure of the researcher's detachment from the subjects of investigation.

Because the idea of a particularized individual who brings the world into being is suspended, the researcher's own subjectivities are rendered invisible and/or irrelevant. When the researcher was accounted for in traditional inquiry, it was assumed that objectivity was maintained because one subject position was seen as universal and therefore capable of representing every other. In the West, the White male heterosexual view became the purportedly objective perspective that, because it was unmarked and considered unmediated, was deemed to be transcendent of the particularities of its location. The biases of powerful and regulatory regimes were thereby mistaken for knowledge. In legitimizing certain options, heterosexual White males presumptively claimed an objectivity that did not recognize the partiality of that view — a dispassion not afforded to women of all races and sexual orientations, nor to non-White or homosexual men. Until the challenges of feminism, White heterosexual males had pulled a double-take by masquerading that position as a view from nowhere, while at the same time passing it off as the view from everywhere.

With particular respect to sexuality, heterosexist presumptions provide a distorted perception of the social world by assuming and thereby reinforcing the universality of the researcher's experience of desire. Dominant prejudices are thereby mistaken for sexual knowledge.[13] However, the sexual subjects of research cannot be neutered through a universalization that negates the reality that research participants are embodied individuals with specific and differing orientations and desires living in particular cultural contexts. Because the queer researcher, like any researcher, is an inevitable part of the social world under consideration, the possibilities of bias and subjective perceptions cannot be eradicated. As it is not possible to step outside the lived body in particular cultural circumstances, the queer body performs its epistemologies; that is, the theories of social research are embodied and enacted by the sexual bodies of the research coparticipants.

The validity of any social research — that is, the relationship between the account of the inquiry and something other than the account (i.e., an objective reality) — is dependent upon and relative to the individual sexually embodied researcher(s), and also to "some community of inquirers on whose perspective the account is based" (Maxwell, 1992, p. 284). The endeavors of queered research share feminist claims, not only for embodied objectivity, but for a community of inquirers who are "answerable for what we learn how to see" (Haraway, 1988, p. 583). As such, queer inquiry is not value-free. Under queered terms, however, objectivity is not about counterfeit claims to exceeding subjectivities, but, rather, is about specific embodied beliefs and values that situate knowledges in cultural contexts with recognized underlying structures, power relations, and material conditions.[14] In acknowledging and accepting responsibility for its positions, queered inquiry can address how its particular shapes and presumptions may slant and fashion the research process in its entirety. As a result, while objectivism is decreased, objectivity is increased as the beliefs and behaviors of the queer researcher become part of the professions of the inquiry, thereby making available more of the evidence marshalled for any resultant claims.[15]

Queeries of Social Research: *Camping* in the Academy

Until the objections of feminism, the results of social research had been articulated and made meaningful in a language deemed to be reasonably unambiguous.[16] In matters of sexuality, an assumption of univocality had made the relationship between the word and that which it sought to describe appear *straight*. If, however, other-than-straight (queer) researchers are to veraciously chronicle the processes of research and write themselves into their accounts, they must confront the denigrating nature of the language intrinsic to such an undertaking. For example, given a regulative homophobic climate, it is impossible to denominate the gay and lesbian subjects of inquiry without engendering the contempt that penetrates the language to which it must resort. A queer endeavor emerges, therefore, in the shadow of inherited hostilities deeply inscribed in the language that has constituted the moment it seeks to articulate, but, at the same time, that it looks to refuse and unmake.[17]

In opposition, as queer subjects, gay men and lesbians must come to knowledge by speaking in our own terms. The results are inevitably bound to look queer. First, queered texts require that sexual subjects speak out as such: lesbians, bisexuals, gay men, heterosexuals, and others need to be named rather than presumed. Second, texts produced by homosexual subjects, in reflecting the urgencies of sexual variance and the speculations of a generant discourse, are likely to be marked by the imprint of excess. In asserting an ability to see beyond and contest what appears obvious, the *strain(s)* of queered difference may be witnessed through the often immoderate invigoration of *camp*.

There is often disagreement as to what may constitute or qualify as, or for, camp. While noting that homosexuals have constituted its vanguard and most articulate audiences, Sontag (1982), in referring to camp, has also noted that "no one who wholeheartedly shares in a given sensibility can analyze it; he can only, whatever his intention, exhibit it" (p. 276). Sontag's cautions aside, the discussion of camp and what it *means,* some accord seems apparent. Camp is a style of object or of communication and/or perception that often reflects exaggeration and artifice; exists in a state of tension with other cultural practices; is easily recognizable to those marginal to the cultural mainstream; and has historically been associated with homosexual culture and challenges to the naturalization of desire (Bergman, 1993). Robertson (1993) argues for an extension of camp beyond its essential link with gay men and for its adoption by feminists as "a model for critiques of sex and gender roles" (p. 156). Therein, Robertson suggests, lies the potential of camp to assert the "overlapping interests of gay men and women, lesbian and straight" (p. 156).

In speaking autobiographically about sexual orientation, I don't have to look hard for *camp grounds* when I claim that, while only shortly before realizing that I was wearing them, I began dropping my beads in the 1980s. David Bergman (1993) suggests that this phrase, however dated, is an expression that describes an option that makes obvious and exaggerated hints about (homo)sexual orientation. By electing to use this decorative expression to designate my sexual subjectivity, I use the potentialities of camp as a style of communication to impress the revelation on the text and, therefore, on the reader, in a queer way. In an academic presentation defending camp and recognizing the disparity between the serious and the absurd on which camp is based, Long (1993) challenges gender binaries and exclusions and activates a camp perspective by suggesting the audience imagine his essay delivered "by a small, mustachioed man wearing a gold lame cocktail dress, black pumps with three inch stiletto heels, a raven wig, and a beaded cloche with peacock feathers" (Long, 1993). Long's association of a male academic with women's apparel and accessories asserts queerness in a way that speaks beyond a mainstream culture that already constructs gay men as effeminate, and a misogynist climate that discredits the experiences of, and denies critical authority to, the female. Camp, then, is an overall objection through which queers may articulate the (im)possibility of representing queer ontology via the sexual/textual options of heterosexuality. Camp is not only a style or a form of characterization by which queer identities are made visible, but is also a stance of resistance embedded in representational practices by which dominant cultural forms are challenged and dynamic queer identities are constituted.[18] While not always utilizing objections to gender conformity, as the examples may imply, camp is, in part, an effect of sexism and homophobia and emerges as one discernible means both to challenge and to construct more embracing alternatives.

In addition to camp, other textual adaptations that might lead to a sense of obvious and productive queered pitch include extending words of contention to the discourses of the Academy. Language is a means of regulating or silencing the body and desire. Accordingly, research texts of the Academy are often cold and sexually detached — their pages cleansed of any suggestion of the erotic among participants. Especially contentious is any possibility that makes legible a (queer) desire already constructed as offensive. Furthermore, there is even less space to imagine that a reader might feel identification with, and desire for, the writer or for the subjects of inquiry. If queered texts are held to the de-sexualizing conventions of heterosexist academic discourse, the message is necessarily confused by the medium. Lesbians and gay men are both identified and reviled on the basis of sexual practices. In recognizing that diversity in desire through writing, the code of academic convention is shifted as queered texts contest ideological repression through libidinal expression. Queered texts may privilege not only gender and sexuality, but also an eroticism of words, phrases, and perspectives otherwise deemed tense and unacceptable. This is not to suggest that queered texts are imperatively incontinent, nor, at the same time, is it to deny titillation that may pleasurably excite those whom they engage. While speaking of sexuality in frank terms may stimulate, the rousing presence of the erotic in writing is not solely, or necessarily, a function of the introduction of inflaming sexual experiences and vernacular languages. An idea, word, or phrase can simply be stimulating in its unfamiliarity, repetition, ambiguity, location, alterations, flamboyance, or in its pairing with a seemingly incompatible other. As Barthes (1975) has suggested, a word can be erotic "on two opposing conditions, both excessive: if it is extravagantly repeated, or on the contrary, if it is unexpected, succulent in its newness . . . words glisten, they are distracting, incongruous apparitions" (p. 42).

Queered texts, in refusing the anonymity of authorship, draw the texts of the Academy into the more intimate spaces of the body. While many feminist writers have consistently engaged the personal, a man who materializes male subjectivity — who chooses to write in and about his body — is a cross-writer who transgresses the boundaries of gender/text expression. Because man is defined in heterosexual terms that have excluded all that is outside of those bounds, without claiming queer differ- ence, a gay male writer is compelled to lipsynch discourse as a man in drag as a man. By exposing himself, the gay man subverts the power of the hidden male body that has suited the aims of a patriarchy dependent upon a masculine power fueled by phal- lic mystery.

Queered texts are resistant to such discursive binary distinctions as homosexual/ heterosexual, nature/culture, and male/female, and concomitantly refuse to reinscribe the terms of their exclusion and powerlessness. Using the private/public binary as an example, homosexual orientation has been required to describe itself within the sub- jection of the former, while heterosexual orientation rests comfortably in the predom- inance of the latter. To name oneself as homosexual and to discuss homosexuality may reinforce the common complaint that gay men and lesbians simply want to flaunt their sexuality, bringing it to bear on matters where it has no relevance. Conversely, as demonstration that the rules of privacy apply differently to homosexuality and het- erosexuality, to name oneself as heterosexual and discuss heterosexuality is considered to do neither.

Queer academics clearly face a textual challenge. While perhaps no medium can veraciously fully capture any human experience, to speak of homosexuality with a lan- guage that has within it so deeply embedded its denigration or exclusion is to court conundrum. Any reader will engage with the author, the text, and its subjects against a background of other, perhaps mostly heterosexist, or at least heterosexual, experi- ences. To use only familiar and acceptable heterosexualizing terms and syntax to de- scribe what might be perceived by the reader as alien, inappropriate, or perhaps even immoral practices and experiences is to ignore the vigorous informing potentialities of difference. This accommodation inevitably leads to participation in an exercise that can only fall short of its intentions. On the other hand, an insistence on queered cadence or the introduction of any language and strategies located ulterior to the deemed pertinent boundaries of heterosexist academic discourse may sentence it to preterition. For lesbians, gay men, and others so inclined in the production of cultural discourses, the aim, simply put, is to *queer the pitch* without *pitching the queer*.

Carnal Knowledge: The *Seductions* of Research Practice

The corporeal body is gaining currency in academia and popular culture (Frank, 1990). The centrality of the mind is being displaced through a "refiguring of the body so that it moves from the periphery to the center of analysis, so that it can now be un- derstood as the very 'stuff' of subjectivity" (Grosz, 1994, p. ix). As some bodies are constrained and others are more carefully considered, it is clear that culture does not make all bodies matter the same. For example, the dominant heterosexist society still attempts to deny or keep lesbian and gay bodies hidden. As a consequence, queer bodies most often come into view because, in their registration and performance of differences repellent to the dominant culture, they often serve as the culture's gender and/or sexual alarm.

As a lean ten-year-old attempting to weave a body image out of the culture's pre-scriptions for manhood, I was taunted and punched hard by a group of older boys who realized an *outsider* in the perceived failure of my gender. In their obvious and fierce need to master the difference that alarmed them, the masculine anxieties of my tormentors threatened them into bloody exterminating action. Afterwards, I hurled my sissy-boy's body into a relentless struggle to become the male that eluded it, only to fully understand later, in the throes that the fear of what they imagined I was belonged to them and not to me. While it may be, as Grumet (1988) notes, that it is the (heterosexual) old man who "knows like a woman" (p. 65) in a young gay boy's body, the bullies spotted a feared embodied (feminine) knowledge and determined to drive it out of themselves by killing it in me.

A version of this narrative is common to the lives of many lesbians and gay men. As a consequence of never-justifiable offenses of cruelty, we come to knowledge obliged to consider our bodies with a deliberateness not required of heterosexuals. Forced to ponder our bodies by a culture startled by gender nonconformity and sexual diversity, social researchers who claim a queered position may best be suited to interrogating the sexual in social inquiry. Indeed, it is in a contemplation of our variance that lesbians and gay men discover not only a capacity but also a proficiency for innovation that, in turn, affirms both the fortitude and fluidity of queer bodies.

While there have been periodic references to matters of the erotic between participants in social research, the sexual body often still remains illegitimate in the conventions of the Academy.[19] Any sustained interest in the sexual body in social research is still considered degenerate and outside the parameters of serious scholarly endeavor. The lack of acknowledged attention, however, is not an indication of the sexual body's insignificance or irrelevance. Researchers have admitted *embroidering* fantasies or having *impure* thoughts around a research subject (Golde, 1970; Malinowski, 1967). Some have experienced (hetero)sexual relations with members of their study groups, others have described ethnographic encounters in (unadmittedly) homoerotic detail, while others reported receiving sexual advances from male subjects of their research (Rabinow, 1977; Read, 1986; Williams, 1986). Yet, the only open and responsible account of the erotic in research that I am aware of is provided by Newton (1993), a lesbian, who admits that her data collection visits were "full of erotic byplay" and that she and her informant "flirted with the idea of making love" (p. 13). Newton centralizes the lack of attention (in public venues) to the erotic dimension of fieldwork while recognizing the overall significance of sexuality to human experience. Further, Newton not only questions the "erotic equation in fieldwork" (p. 3) and explicitly relates her personal experiences of attraction to a female subject of her research, but questions the impact that eros might have on all aspects of the research process.

In my research with other gay men, the effect of the sexual body was utterly significant and is illustrated by the comments of one participant:

> There was indeed the presence of your physicality here that was really quite disturbing for me . . . the physical presence of someone who could readily occupy my center of subjectivity was really odd . . . when the person (I'm talking with) . . . is another gay man, and one who is capable of perceiving and understanding so bodily all the issues that are affecting me so profoundly. So where does that boundary between affection and care become a site of love and sex? How does one know where that boundary exists? Why do we have a sense that boundaries need to exist? . . . So

here we were doing all this embracing, but the physicalness was being refused. . . .
Was it because you are going to pretend that you are an analytical researcher and I'll
pretend that I'm an interesting subject? If we move off of either of those centers
then we become two gay men in the same room sharing very passionate things with
each other [that] . . . in other circumstances would lead to something probably
quite affectionate, romantic, sexual. (April 1994)

My independently produced notes similarly concluded:

In this particular project the physicality created an *edge* which for me, was very surprising. What do we do about our bodies? And how can it be spoken about? I am
engaged in processes with this man that are passionate. While emotionally and intellectually engaging, at the same time I am disavowing my physical responses to
him and our interaction. What I am thinking is that in not mentioning it, I was
acting in complicity with heterosexist strategies. (April 1994)

During my research, it was clear that sexuality provided an energizing force for the
entire project. Since mood is inevitably a factor to be considered in social inquiry, it is
likely that eros may impact candor, rapport, motivation, and analytic strategies
among other possibilities. Perhaps, most importantly, in admitting the impact of reduced sexual/affective distance between researchers and subjects, the overall account
of the research may become more trustworthy. Clearly, a more complete investigation
and discussion of the implications of the body and sexuality in social research is war-
ranted.[20]

In an examination of the performances of social research, the investigator who
claims a queered position and interest in the role of the sexual body may produce
work that, to appropriate Lyotard's claims for the postmodern artist or writer, is not
"in principle governed by preestablished rules, and . . . cannot be judged according to
a determining judgment by applying familiar categories" (Lyotard, 1984, p. 81). It is
in the acts of social research itself that the rules and categories for the body and sexuality are sought. To attach again the possibilities of research to Lyotard's claim, from a
queered position, the researcher operates "without rules in order to formulate the
rules of what will have been done. Hence the fact that work and text have the character of an event" (Lyotard, 1984, p. 81).

From a queered perspective, the research need not be abandoned as chaotic because
the experience falls outside of expectation. By reflecting on that which has not been
reflected upon, and examining the lived verities of the experience, the researcher gains
access to an understanding of how rules and categories around the sexual body might
be reevaluated and generated through the operations of social research. Further, once
the sexual body's implications are claimed rather than disowned as prurient, the researcher is able to fruitfully explore the constituting effects of its agency. How might
eros motivate and invigorate the process for participants? How might rapport and
candor be influenced by sexual attractions? How might the veracity of results be im-
pacted by desire? What are the differences between heterosexual and homosexual researchers who study others similarly identified? Are sexual relations between researcher and researched always outside the bounds of reasonable possibility?[21]

It is imperative that the sexual body and the erotic be made comprehensible in the
practices of social inquiry. Rather than disclaiming the corporeal as a way of knowing,
the body's knowledges and desires are inescapable and constitutive to research out-

comes. At a minimum, a queered position allows social researchers to address more honestly the impact of desire and the overall ineluctable role of the body in research and knowledge. It is the absence, not the presence, of an accounting for sexual bodies that renders research accounts incomplete and therefore inaccurate. While it is premature to make any cohesive arguments for the impact of the lived-body and the sexual in social research, it is neither too early nor too late to argue for a reexamination of the foundations and terms of their exclusion.

Raising the Hackles of Contrary Readers

Outside of the researcher, the findings of any research inquiry are meaningless without the dialogical intelligence of a reader. In the final analysis, reader subjectivities will ultimately determine the construction of meaning and attribute value to any research. Because any study of homosexualities may fall well outside personal experience, readers unable to believe outcomes that they themselves have not experienced as *truths* may remain unconvinced. In the current cultural climate, to position research inquiry, and oneself, as other than heterosexual is to render all aspects of the inquiry open to entire registers of personal, epistemological, and methodological criticisms not entertained otherwise. To claim the possibilities of queered (auto)ethnography is not, however, intended to distance. Nonetheless, to simply endorse experiences other than heterosexual may offend or alienate a contrary reader. The introduction of queered theories, methodologies, terms, and style may force the non-queer reader into an outsider position. In a discussion of bias, Strathern (1987) notes that any such experiences of the reader are problematic: "What guarantee is there that the description will not feed prejudice, will not, far from enlarging, merely augment a narrow perspective?" (p. 256).

It is perhaps improbable to envision that homosexual subject(s) could challenge universalizing and regulatory heterosexualized epistemologies and practices, without risking further entrenchment in their own marginality. Any endeavor to queer the operations of social research is threatening to conventional theory and practices and may be perceived as epistemologically unsound, methodologically faulty, textually prurient, and perhaps even pathological, illegal, or immoral.

Implicating Social Research Inquiry and Cultural Practice(s)

Schools and the Academy contribute to the production, maintenance, and authorization of cultural discourses. The Academy has been reluctant not only to challenge its own epistemological exclusions, but also to assume responsibility for recognizing their ultimate political impact by placing those epistemologies at the service of cultural practices (Hall, 1990). "Any piece of research with minority groups, especially in field settings, is necessarily an ethical and political intervention with participants . . . [that requires] persistent investigator attention to ensure positive outcomes and to prevent harmful . . . effects" (Walsh-Bowers & Parlour, 1992, p. 109). As such, the intellectual work of the academic researcher is "incomplete unless it self-consciously assumes responsibility for its effects in the larger public culture while simultaneously addressing the most profoundly and deeply inhumane problems of the societies in which we live" (Giroux, 1994, p. 300; see essay reprinted in this volume).

In embracing the potentialities of queered research in the Academy, the relationship of knowledge to *truth* and to social justice for gays, lesbians, bisexuals, and others is recognized. The university, then, as primary site of social inquiry, has an opportunity to contribute to the constitution of inclusionary knowledges and emancipatory projects rather than remaining removed from them. Through the recognition of the possibilities of queered positions in social research and discourse, the Academy can contribute not only to the affirmation of diverse identities and the relevant generation of knowledges, but also to the social empowerment of, and transformation for, all of its subject(s).

Notes

1. While I am uneasy about the use of the term *subject,* a consequence, in part, of separating the word from its associations with the colonizing energies that placed one person or group under the authority of another, other terms such as *respondent, informant, interlocuter,* etc., make me equally concerned. While recognizing its limitations, the term *subject(s)* is employed to refer to both the embodied participants and to the topic of any research interest.

2. The term *homosexualities* is adopted here to include the diverse experiences subsumed as non-heterosexual. Through the use of the plural form, the wide range of dissident sexualities that constitute homosexual desire, behavior, and identity are recognized and inscribed as non-monolithic. By graphically representing plurality, the reification of the heterosexual/homosexual binary, wherein a more unitary and stabilized conception of homosexuality (and heterosexuality) are inappropriately reinforced, is also contested and disrupted. Further, while I am a gay White man speaking as, not on behalf of, other gay men, whose precise sexualities might differ from my own, my intention is not to make one kind of sexuality visible at the expense of, nor to postulate direct applicability to, others. While it is hoped that lesbians, bisexuals, and other gay men, as examples, might consider the matters under discussion relevant to their own interests, I make no effort to speak for those I cannot possibly represent.

3. In common usage, the terms *gay* and *lesbian* are relatively new, and somewhat ambiguous. In practice, the word gay sometimes still refers to both males and females, but it is increasingly applied to the former as the word lesbian is used to describe women's experience. Clearly, lesbian and gay are not terms that have singular meaning or that reflect singular experience. The complexities of lesbian and gay experience may include nonconformity to cultural notions of gender; one, or a combination of, same-sex friendship, love, and expressed or unexpressed erotic desire; as well as the possibilities of particular cognitive, cultural, and political perspectives.

4. "Autoethnography" signals a cultural consideration of one's own people as determined by both self and other identification (Hayano, 1979). Clifford (1986) uses the term *indigenous ethnographer* to describe an insider who studies their own culture and is able to thereby provide a perspective and depth of understanding that, he suggests, yields accounts that are both particularly empowered and restricted.

5. Researchers who study homosexual subject(s) have been reluctant to declare their sexual orientations. In a study of 351 reports on homosexuality between 1974 and 1988, only two studies, both by lesbian researchers, identified the researcher as homosexual (Walsh-Bowers & Parlour, 1992).

6. For a discussion of gay sensibility, see Sontag (1982) and Bronski (1984).

7. While my interest here is particularly in a discussion of sexual difference that uses gay male sexuality to explicate, the word "queer" does not negate other differences, but provides a com-

mon ground for an array of finer distinctions (gender, race, ethnicity, class, etc.) in identities and discursive strategies.

8. For discussions of the temporality of the term *queer,* see Butler (1993) and Sedgwick (1993).

9. While research into biological elements in lesbian sexuality is increasing, much of the biomaterial studies to date have focused on males — some of it made possible by the devastating impact of AIDS (Bailey & Pillard, 1991; LeVay, 1993; LeVay & Hamer, 1994).

10. There remains, however, an extreme contemporary sensitivity to any biological approach to the study of any human behavior (Hrdy, 1990).

11. I recognize that a willingness to accede the significance of the biological may make me prey to accusations of a retrograde yearning for an essentialized identity whose consequence could ultimately support homophobic opposition to sexual diversity. My position is, rather, that the state of our knowledge of sexualities is extremely limited and that we have much to gain by remaining open.

12. Results of tests of spatial ability and fluency in populations of homosexual men, heterosexual men, and heterosexual women suggest differences in the patterns of cognitive ability (McCormick & Witelson, 1991).

13. In supposedly neutralizing the consequences of sexual orientation and desire, a heterosexist perspective actually further fortifies its own predictions. As heterosexual orientations are presumed, but remain unnamed and hidden, they are verified and reproduced. The substantiation and propagation further reinforces and authorizes heterosexual suppositions, which by the license of that authority increases the likelihood that social inquiry will continue to function under its ubiquitous terms.

14. I am significantly indebted to the work of many feminist scholars who have cogently addressed issues relating to research methodologies. In particular, see Roman (1993), Haraway (1988), Harstock (1987), Harding (1987), and Lather (1986).

15. This argument is extended from a feminist perspective. See Harding (1987).

16. There is now a more widespread interest (outside of feminism) in the impact of subjectivity and of language/writing in research. See Clifford (1986). However, in response, Mascia-Lees, Sharpe, and Cohen (1989) suggest that these apparently new postmodern insights have received significant exploration by feminist scholars for the past forty years.

17. Attitudes toward homosexuals, and others who challenge categories of identities, are developed through the culture's masculinist and heterosexist language constructed systems. Terms and phrases, however, mean something from specific positions. As examples, the words "man," "woman," "husband," and "wife," are constructed within heterosexual cognitive and lingual systems where meaning appears fixed in ways that may have no, or certainly different, relevance to the experience of homosexual women and men. As an instance, it has been argued that lesbians are not women because the term "woman" is constructed and has meaning only in a heterosexual system of thought. See Wittig (1992).

18. Meyer (1994) suggests that queer performance is not "expressive of social identity but is, rather, the reverse — the identity is self-reflexively constituted by the performances themselves" (p. 4).

19. The body is prohibited by a long history of injunctions based on the separation of mind and body and a denunciation of the latter; a cultural sex-negativity that views sexuality as disruptive; uneven relationships of power between researcher and researched; and a heterosexual regime that universalizes heterosexuality and regulates sexual behavior as a means of social control.

20. I have more fully detailed the consequences of the sexual body elsewhere (Honeychurch, 1998).

21. My position is that sexual involvements where participants have differential access to power ought always to be avoided. While here neither always recommending or always refusing possible physical sexual relations between research participants, the options cannot be generalized as equally applicable to all populations. The perspectives that demarcate the borders of the acceptable/unacceptable in terms of the erotic in research are multiple, contextual, and qualitative, rather than singular, fixed, and quantitative.

References

Bailey, M., & Pillard, R. (1991). A genetic study of male sexual orientation. *Archives of General Psychiatry, 48,* 1089–1096.

Barthes, R. (1975). *Pleasure of the text.* New York: Hill and Wang.

Bergman, D. (1993). Strategic camp: The art of gay rhetoric. In D. Bergman (Ed.), *Campgrounds: Style and homosexuality* (pp. 92–109). Amherst: University of Massachusetts Press.

Bourdieu, P. (1977). *Outline of a theory of practice.* Cambridge, Eng.: Cambridge University Press.

Bronski, M. (1984). *Culture clash: The making of a gay sensibility.* Boston: South End Press.

Butler, J. (1993). *Bodies that matter: On the discursive limits of sex.* New York: Routledge.

Clifford, J. (1986). Introduction: Partial truths. In J. Clifford & G. Marcus (Eds.), *Writing culture: The poetics and politics of ethnography* (pp. 1–26). Berkeley: University of California Press.

de Lauretis, T. (1991). Queer theory: Lesbian and gay sexualities. An introduction. In T. de Lauretis (Ed.), *Differences: A journal of feminist cultural studies* (pp. iii– xviii). Providence, RI: Brown University Press.

Edelman, L. (1994). *Homographesis: Essays in gay and literary cultural theory.* New York: Routledge.

Frank, A. (1990). Bringing bodies back in: A decade review. *Theory, Culture, and Society, 7,* 131–162.

Giroux, H. (1994). Doing cultural studies: Youth and the challenge of pedagogy. *Harvard Educational Review, 64,* 278–308.

Golde, P. (1970). *Women in the field: Anthropological experiences.* Chicago: Aldine.

Greenberg, D. (1988). *The construction of homosexuality.* Chicago: University of Chicago Press.

Grosz, E. (1994). *Volatile bodies: Toward a corporeal feminism.* Bloomington: Indiana University Press.

Grumet, M. (1988). *Bitter milk: Women and teaching.* Amherst: University of Massachusetts Press.

Hall, S. (1990). The emergence of cultural studies and the crises of the humanities. *October, 53,* 11–23.

Haraway, D. (1988). Situated knowledges: The science question in feminism and the privilege of partial perspectives. *Feminist Studies, 14,* 575–599.

Harding, S. (1987). Introduction: Is there a feminist method? In S. Harding (Ed.), *Feminism and methodology* (pp. 1–14). Bloomington: Indiana University Press.

Harstock, N. (1987). The feminist standpoint: Developing the ground for a specifically feminist historical materialism. In S. Harding (Ed.), *Feminism and methodology* (pp. 157–180). Bloomington: Indiana University Press.

Hayano, D. (1979). Auto-ethnography: Paradigms, problems, and prospects. *Human Organization, 38*(1), 99–104.

Hocquenghem, G. (1978). *Homosexual desire.* London: Allison & Busby.

Honeychurch, K. G. (1998). Carnal knowledge: Re-searching through the sexual body. In W. Pinar (Ed.), *Queer theory in education* (pp. 251–273). Mahwah, NJ: Lawrence Erlbaum Associates.

Hrdy, S. (1990). Sex bias in nature and history: A late 1980's re-examination of the "biological origins" argument. *Yearbook of Physical Anthropology, 33,* 25–37.

Lather, P. (1986). Issues of validity in openly ideological research: Between a rock and a soft place. *Interchange, 17*(4), 63–84.

LeVay, S. (1993). *The sexual brain.* Cambridge, MA: MIT Press.

LeVay, S., & Hamer, D. (1994). Evidence for a biological influence in male homosexuality. *Scientific American, 270*(5), 44–49.

Long, S. (1993). The loneliness of camp. In D. Bergman (Ed.), *Campgrounds: Style and homosexuality* (pp. 78–91). Amherst: University of Massachusetts Press.

Lyotard, J. (1984). *The postmodern condition: A report on knowledge.* Minneapolis: University of Minnesota Press.

Malinowski, B. (1967). *A diary in the strictest sense of the term.* New York: Harcourt, Brace, and World.

Mascia-Lees, F., Sharpe P., & Cohen, C. (1989). The postmodernist turn in anthropology: Cautions from a feminist perspective. *Signs: Journal of Women in Culture and Society, 15*(1), 7–33.

Maxwell, J. (1992). Understanding and validity in qualitative research. *Harvard Educational Review, 62,* 279–300.

McCormick, C., & Witelson, S. (1991). A cognitive profile of homosexual men compared to heterosexual men and women. *Psychoneuroendocrinology, 16,* 459–473.

Meyer, M. (1994). Introduction: Reclaiming the discourse of camp. In M. Meyer (Ed.), *The politics and poetics of camp* (pp. 1–22). London: Routledge.

Newton, E. (1993). My best informant's dress: The erotic equation in fieldwork. *Cultural Anthropology, 8*(1), 3–23.

Rabinow, P. (1977). *Reflections on fieldwork in Morocco.* Berkeley: University of California Press.

Read, K. (1986). *Return to the high valley.* Berkeley: University of California Press.

Robertson, P. (1993). "The kinda comedy that imitates me": Mae West's identification with the feminist camp. In D. Bergman (Ed.), *Campgrounds: Style and homosexuality* (pp. 156–172). Amherst: University of Massachusetts Press.

Roman, L. (1993). Double exposure: The politics of feminist materialist ethnography. *Educational Theory, 43*(3), 279–308.

Sedgwick, E. (1990). *Epistemology of the closet.* Berkeley: University of California Press.

Sedgwick, E. (1993). *Tendencies.* Durham, NC: Duke University Press.

Sontag, S. (1982). *Against interpretation and other essays.* New York: Octagon Books.

Strathern, M. (1987). Out of context: The persuasive fictions of anthropology. *Current Anthropology, 28,* 251–281.

Walsh-Bowers, R., & Parlour, S. (1992). Researcher-participant relationships in journal reports on gay men and lesbian women. *Journal of Homosexuality, 23*(4), 93–113.

Williams, W. (1986). *The spirit and the flesh.* Boston: Beacon Press.

Wittig, M. (1992). *The straight mind and other essays.* Boston: Beacon Press.

Sexuality, Schooling, and Adolescent Females: The Missing Discourse of Desire

MICHELLE FINE

Since late 1986, popular magazines and newspapers have printed steamy stories about education and sexuality. Whether the controversy surrounds sex education or school-based health clinics (SBHCs), public discourses of adolescent sexuality are represented forcefully by government officials, New Right spokespersons, educators, "the public," feminists, and health-care professionals. These stories offer the authority of "facts," insights into the political controversies, and access to un-acknowledged fears about sexuality (Foucault, 1980). Although the facts usually involve the adolescent female body, little has been heard from young women themselves.

This article examines these diverse perspectives on adolescent sexuality and, in addition, presents the views of a group of adolescent females. The article is informed by a study of numerous current sex education curricula, a year of negotiating for inclusion of lesbian and gay sexuality in a citywide sex education curriculum, and interviews and observations gathered in New York City sex education classrooms.[1] The analysis examines the desires, fears, and fantasies which give structure and shape to silences and voices concerning sex education and school-based health clinics in the 1980s.

Despite the attention devoted to teen sexuality, pregnancy, and parenting in this country, and despite the evidence of effective interventions and the wide-spread public support expressed for these interventions (Harris, 1985), the systematic implementation of sex education and SBHCs continues to be obstructed by the controversies surrounding them (Kantrowitz et al., 1987; Leo, 1986). Those who resist sex education or SBHCs often present their views as based on rationality and a concern for protecting the young. For such opponents, sex education raises questions of promoting promiscuity and immorality, and of undermining family values. Yet the language of the challenges suggests an effect substantially more profound and primitive. Gary Bauer, Undersecretary of Education in the U.S. Department of Education, for example, constructs an image of immorality littered by adolescent sexuality and drug abuse:

Harvard Educational Review   Vol. 58   No. 1   February 1988
Copyright © by the President and Fellows of Harvard College

There is ample impressionistic evidence to indicate that drug abuse and promiscuity are not independent behaviors. When inhibitions fall, they collapse across the board. When people of any age lose a sense of right and wrong, the loss is not selective. . . . [T]hey are all expressions of the same ethical vacuum among many teens. . . . (1986)

Even Surgeon General C. Everett Koop, a strong supporter of sex education, recently explained: "[W]e have to be as explicit as necessary. . . . You can't talk of the dangers of snake poisoning and not mention snakes" (quoted in Leo, 1986, p. 54). Such commonly used and often repeated metaphors associate adolescent sexuality with victimization and danger.

Yet public schools have rejected the task of sexual dialogue and critique, or what has been called "sexuality education." Within today's standard sex education curricula and many public school classrooms, we find: 1) the authorized suppression of a discourse of female sexual desire; 2) the promotion of a discourse of female sexual victimization; and 3) the explicit privileging of married heterosexuality over other practices of sexuality. One finds an unacknowledged social ambivalence about female sexuality which ideologically separates the female sexual agent, or subject, from her counterpart, the female sexual victim. The adolescent woman of the 1980s is constructed as the latter. Educated primarily as the potential victim of male sexuality, she represents no subject in her own right. Young women continue to be taught to fear and defend in isolation from exploring desire, and in this context there is little possibility of their developing a critique of gender or sexual arrangements.

Prevailing Discourses of Female Sexuality inside Public Schools

If the body is seen as endangered by uncontrollable forces, then presumably this is a society or social group which fears change — change which it perceived simultaneously as powerful and beyond its control. (Smith-Rosenberg, 1978, p. 229)

Public schools have historically been the site for identifying, civilizing, and containing that which is considered uncontrollable. While evidence of sexuality is everywhere within public high schools — in the halls, classrooms, bathrooms, lunchrooms, and the library — official sexuality education occurs sparsely: in social studies, biology, sex education, or inside the nurse's office. To understand how sexuality is managed inside schools, I examined the major discourses of sexuality which characterize the national debates over sex education and SBHCs. These discourses are then tracked as they weave through the curricula, classrooms, and halls of public high schools.

The first discourse, *sexuality as violence,* is clearly the most conservative, and equates adolescent heterosexuality with violence. At the 1986 American Dreams Symposium on education, Phyllis Schlafly commented: "Those courses on sex, abuse, incest, AIDS, they are all designed to terrorize our children. We should fight their existence, and stop putting terror in the hearts and minds of our youngsters." One aspect of this position, shared by women as politically distinct as Schlafly and the radical feminist lawyer Catherine MacKinnon (1983), views heterosexuality as essentially violent and coercive. In its full conservative form, proponents call for the elimination of sex education and clinics and urge complete reliance on the family to dictate appropriate values, mores, and behaviors.

Sexuality as violence presumes that there is a causal relationship between official silence about sexuality and a decrease in sexual activity — therefore, by not teaching about sexuality, adolescent sexual behavior will not occur. The irony, of course, lies in the empirical evidence. Fisher, Byrne, and White (1983) have documented sex-negative attitudes and contraceptive use to be negatively correlated. In their study, sex-negative attitudes do not discourage sexual activity, but they do discourage responsible use of contraception. Teens who believe sexual involvement is wrong deny responsibility for contraception. To accept responsibility would legitimate "bad" behavior. By contrast, Fisher et al. (1983) found that adolescents with sex-positive attitudes tend to be both more consistent and more positive about contraceptive use. By not teaching about sexuality, or by teaching sex-negative attitudes, schools apparently will not forestall sexual activity, but may well discourage responsible contraception.

The second disclosure, *sexuality as victimization,* gathers a much greater following. Female adolescent sexuality is represented as a moment of victimization in which the dangers of heterosexuality for adolescent women (and, more recently, of homosexuality for adolescent men) are prominent. While sex may not be depicted as inherently violent, young women (and today, men) learn of their vulnerability to potential male predators.

To avoid being victimized, females learn to defend themselves against disease, pregnancy, and "being used." The discourse of victimization supports sex education, including AIDS education, with parental consent. Suggested classroom activities emphasize "saying no," practicing abstinence, enumerating the social and emotional risks of sexual intimacy, and listing the possible diseases associated with sexual intimacy. The language, as well as the questions asked and not asked, represents females as the actual and potential victims of male desire. In exercises, role plays, and class discussions, girls practice resistance to trite lines, unwanted hands, opened buttons, and the surrender of other "bases" they are not prepared to yield. The discourses of violence and victimization both portray males as potential predators and females as victims. Three problematic assumptions underlie these two views:

- First, female subjectivity, including the desire to engage in sexual activity, is placed outside the prevailing conversation (Vance, 1984).
- Second, both arguments present female victimization as contingent upon unmarried heterosexual involvement — rather than inherent in existing gender, class, and racial arrangements (Rubin, 1984). While feminists have long fought for the legal and social acknowledgment of sexual violence against women, most have resisted the claim that female victimization hinges primarily upon sexual involvement with men. The full range of victimization of women — at work, at home, on the streets — has instead been uncovered. The language and emotion invested in these two discourses divert attention away from structures, arrangements, and relationships which oppress women in general, and low-income women and women of color in particular (Lorde, 1980).
- Third, the messages, while narrowly anti-sexual, nevertheless buttress traditional heterosexual arrangements. These views assume that as long as females avoid pre-

marital sexual relations with men, victimization can be avoided. Ironically, however, protection from male victimization is available primarily through marriage — by coupling with a man. The paradoxical message teaches females to fear the very men who will ultimately protect them.

The third discourse, *sexuality as individual morality,* introduces explicit notions of sexual subjectivity for women. Although quite judgmental and moralistic, this discourse values women's sexual decisionmaking as long as the decisions made are for premarital abstinence. For example, Secretary of Education William Bennett (1987) urges schools to teach "morality literacy" and to educate towards "modesty," "chastity," and "abstinence" until marriage. The language of self-control and self-respect reminds students that sexual immorality breeds not only personal problems but also community tax burdens.

The debate over morality in sex education curricula marks a clear contradiction among educational conservatives over whether and how the state may intervene in the "privacy of families." Non-interventionists, including Schlafly and Onalee McGraw, argue that educators should not teach about sexuality at all. To do so is to take a particular moral position which subverts the family. Interventionists, including Koop, Bennett, and Bauer, argue that schools should teach about sexuality by focusing on "good values," but disagree about how. Koop proposes open discussion of sexuality and the use of condoms, while Bennett advocates "sexual restraint" ("Koop AIDS Stand Assailed," 1987). Sexuality in this discourse is posed as a test of self-control; individual restraint triumphs over social temptation. Pleasure and desire for women as sexual objects remain largely in the shadows, obscured from adolescent eyes.

The fourth discourse, a *discourse of desire,* remains a whisper inside the official work of U.S. public schools. If introduced at all, it is as an interruption of the ongoing conversation (Snitow, Stansell, & Thompson, 1983). The naming of desire, pleasure, or sexual entitlement, particularly for females, barely exists in the formal agenda of public schooling on sexuality. When spoken, it is tagged with reminders of "consequences" — emotional, physical, moral, reproductive, and/or financial (Freudenberg, 1987). A genuine discourse of desire would invite adolescents to explore what feels good and bad, desirable and undesirable, grounded in experiences, needs, and limits. Such a discourse would release females from a position of receptivity, enable an analysis of the dialectics of victimization and pleasure, and would pose female adolescents as subjects of sexuality, initiators as well as negotiators (Golden, 1984; Petchesky, 1984; Thompson, 1983).

In Sweden, where sex education has been offered in schools since the turn of the century, the State Commission on Sex Education recommends teaching students to "acquire a knowledge . . . [which] will equip them to experience sexual life as a source of happiness and joy in fellowship with other [people]" (Brown, 1983, p. 88). The teachers' handbook goes on, "The many young people who wish to wait [before initiating sexual activity] and those who have had early sexual relations should experience, in class, [the feeling] that they are understood and accepted" (p. 93). Compare this to an exercise suggested in a major U.S. metropolitan sex education curriculum: "Discuss and evaluate: things which may cause teenagers to engage in sexual relations before they are ready to assume the responsibility of marriage" (see Philadelphia School District, 1986; and New York City Board of Education, 1984).

A discourse of desire, though seldom explored in U.S. classrooms, does occur in less structured school situations. The following excerpts, taken from group and individual student interviews, demonstrate female adolescents' subjective experiences of body and desire as they begin to articulate notions of sexuality.

In some cases young women pose a critique of marriage:

> I'm still in love with Simon, but I'm seeing Jose. He's OK but he said, "Will you be my girl?" I hate that. It feels like they own you. Like I say to a girlfriend, "What's wrong? You look terrible!" and she says, "I'm married!" (Millie, a 16-year-old student from the Dominican Republic)

In other cases they offer stories of their own victimization:

> It's not like last year. Then I came to school regular. Now my old boyfriend, he waits for me in front of my building every morning and he fights with me. Threatens me, gettin' all bad. . . . I want to move out of my house and live 'cause he ain't gonna stop no way. (Sylvia, age 17, about to drop out of twelfth grade)

Some even speak of desire:

> I'm sorry I couldn't call you last night about the interview, but my boyfriend came back from [the] Navy and I wanted to spend the night with him, we don't get to see each other much. (Shandra, age 17, after a no-show for an interview)

In a context in which desire is not silenced, but acknowledged and discussed, conversations with adolescent women can, as seen here, educate through a dialectic of victimization and pleasure. Despite formal silencing, it would be misleading to suggest that talk of desire never emerges within public schools. Notwithstanding a political climate organized around the suppression of this conversation, some teachers and community advocates continue to struggle for an empowering sex education curriculum both in an out of the high school classroom.

Family life curricula and/or plans for a school-based health clinic have been carefully generated in many communities. Yet they continue to face loud and sometimes violent resistance by religious and community groups, often from outside the district lines (Boffey, 1987; "Chicago School Clinic," 1986; Dowd, 1986; Perlez, 1986a, 1986b; Rohter, 1985). In other communities, when curricula or clinics have been approved with little overt confrontation, monies for training are withheld. For example, in New York City in 1987, $1.7 million was initially requested to implement training on the Family Life education curriculum. As sex educators confronted community and religious groups, the inclusion of some topics as well as the language of others were continually negotiated. Ultimately, the Chancellor requested only $600,000 for training, a sum substantially inadequate to the task.[2]

In this political context many public school educators nevertheless continue to take personal and professional risks to create materials and foster classroom environments which speak fully to the sexual subjectivities of young women and men. Some operate within the privacy of their classrooms, subverting the official curriculum and engaging students in critical discussion. Others advocate publicly for enriched curricula and training. A few have even requested that community-based advocates *not* agitate for official curricular change, so "we [teachers] can continue to do what we do in the classroom, with nobody looking over our shoulders. You make a big public deal of this, and it will blow open."[3] Within public school classrooms, it seems that female desire may indeed be addressed when educators act subversively. But in the typical sex education classroom, silence, and therefore distortion, surrounds female desire.

The blanketing of female sexual subjectivity in public school classrooms, in public discourse, and in bed will sound familiar to those who have read Luce Irigaray (1980) and Helene Cíxous (1981). These French feminists have argued that expressions of female voice, body, and sexuality are essentially inaudible when the dominant language and ways of viewing are male. Inside the hegemony of what they call The Law of the Father, female desire and pleasure can gain expression only in the terrain already charted by men (see also Burke, 1980). In the public school arena, this constriction of what is called sexuality allows girls one primary decision — to say yes or no — to a question not necessarily their own. A discourse of desire in which young women have a voice would be informed and generated out of their own socially constructed sexual meanings. It is to these expressions that we now turn.

The Bodies of Female Adolescents: Voices and Structured Silences

If four discourses can be distinguished among the many positions articulated by various "authorities," the sexual meanings voiced by female adolescents defy such classification. A discourse of desire, though absent in the "official" curriculum, is by no means missing from the lived experiences or commentaries of young women. This section introduces their sexual thoughts, concerns, and meanings, as represented by a group of Black and Latina female adolescents — students and dropouts from a public high school in New York City serving predominantly low-income youths. In my year at this comprehensive high school I had frequent opportunity to speak with adolescents and listen to them talk about sex. The comments reported derive from conversations between the young women and their teachers, among themselves, and with me, as researcher. During conversations, the young women talked freely about fears and, in the same breath, asked about passions. Their struggle to untangle issues of gender, power, and sexuality underscores the fact that, for them, notions of sexual negotiation cannot be separated from sacrifice and nurturance.

The adolescent female rarely reflects simply on sexuality. Her sense of sexuality is informed by peers, culture, religion, violence, history, passion, authority, rebellion, body, past and future, and gender and racial relations of power (Espin, 1984; Omolade, 1983). The adolescent woman herself assumes a dual consciousness — at once taken with the excitement of actual/anticipated sexuality and consumed with anxiety and worry. While too few safe spaces exist for adolescent women's exploration of sexual subjectivities, there are all too many dangerous spots for their exploitation.

Whether in a classroom, on the street, at work, or at home, the adolescent female's sexuality is negotiated by, for, and despite the young woman herself. Patricia, a young Puerto Rican woman who worried about her younger sister, relates: "You see, I'm the love child and she's the one born because my mother was raped in Puerto Rico. Her father's in jail now, and she feels so bad about the whole thing so she acts bad." For Patricia, as for the many young women who have experienced and/or witnessed sexual violence, discussions of sexuality merge representations of passions with violence. Often the initiator of conversation among peers about virginity, orgasm, "getting off," and pleasure, Patricia mixed sexual talk freely with references to force and violence. She is a poignant narrator who illustrates, from the female adolescent's perspective, that sexual victimization and desire coexist (Benjamin, 1983).

Sharlene and Betty echo this braiding of danger and desire. Sharlene explained: "Boys always be trying to get into my panties," and Betty added: "I don't be needin' a man who won't give me no pleasure but take my money and expect me to take care of him." This powerful commentary on gender relations, voiced by Black adolescent females, was inseparable from their views of sexuality. To be a woman was to be strong, independent, and reliable — but not too independent for fear of scaring off a man.

Deidre continued this conversation, explicitly pitting male fragility against female strength: "Boys in my neighborhood ain't wrapped so tight. Got to be careful how you treat them. . . ." She reluctantly admitted that perhaps it is more important for Black males than females to attend college, "Girls and women, we're stronger, we take care of ourselves. But boys and men, if they don't get away from the neighborhood, they end up in jail, on drugs or dead . . . or wack [crazy]."

These young women spoke often of anger at males, while concurrently expressing a strong desire for male attention: "I dropped out 'cause I fell in love, and couldn't stop thinking of him." An equally compelling desire was to protect young males — particularly Black males — from a system which "makes them wack." Ever aware of the ways that institutional racism and the economy have affected Black males, these young women seek pleasure but also offer comfort. They often view self-protection as taking something away from young men. Lavanda offered a telling example: "If I ask him to use a condom, he won't feel like a man."

In order to understand the sexual subjectivities of young women more completely, educators need to reconstruct schooling as an empowering context in which we listen to and work with the meanings and experiences of gender and sexuality revealed by the adolescents themselves. When we refuse that responsibility, we prohibit an education which adolescents wholly need and deserve. My classroom observations suggest that such education is rare.

Ms. Rosen, a teacher of a sex education class, opened one session with a request: "You should talk to your mother or father about sex before you get involved." Nilda initiated what became an informal protest by a number of Latino students: "Not our parents! We tell them one little thing and they get crazy. My cousin got sent to Puerto Rico to live with her religious aunt, and my sister got beat 'cause my father thought she was with a boy." For these adolescents, a safe space for discussion, critique, and construction of sexualities was not something they found in their homes. Instead, they relied on school, the spot they chose for the safe exploration of sexualities.

The absence of safe spaces for exploring sexuality affects all adolescents. It was paradoxical to realize that perhaps the only students who had an in-school opportunity for critical sexual discussion in the comfort of peers were the few students who had organized the Gay and Lesbian Association (GALA) at the high school. While most lesbian, gay, or bisexual students were undoubtedly closeted, those few who were "out" claimed this public space for their display and for their sanctuary. Exchanging support when families and peers would offer little, GALA members worried that so few students were willing to come out, and that so many suffered the assaults of homophobia individually. The gay and lesbian rights movement had powerfully affected these youngsters, who were comfortable enough to support each other in a place not considered very safe — a public high school in which echoes of "faggot!" fill the halls.

In the absence of an education which explores and unearths danger and desire, sexuality education classes typically provide little opportunity for discussions beyond those constructed around superficial notions of male heterosexuality (see Kelly, 1986, for a counterexample). Male pleasure is taught, albeit as biology. Teens learn about "wet dreams" (as the onset of puberty for males), "erection" (as the preface to intercourse), and "ejaculation" (as the act of inseminating). Female pleasures and questions are far less often the topic of discussion. Few voices of female sexual agency can be heard. The language of victimization and its underlying concerns — "Say No," put a brake on his sexuality, don't encourage — ultimately deny young women the right to control their own sexuality by providing no access to a legitimate position of sexual subjectivity. Often conflicted about self-representation, adolescent females spend enormous amounts of time trying to "save it," "lose it," convince others that they have lost or saved it, or trying to be "discreet" instead of focusing their energies in ways that are sexually autonomous, responsible, and pleasurable. In classroom observations, girls who were heterosexually active rarely spoke, for fear of being ostracized (Fine, 1986). Those who were heterosexual virgins had the same worry. And most students who were gay, bisexual, or lesbian remained closeted, aware of the very real dangers of homophobia.

Occasionally, the difficult and pleasurable aspects of sexuality were discussed together, coming either as an interruption, or because an educational context was constructed. During a social studies class, for example, Catherine, the proud mother of two-year-old Tiffany, challenged an assumption underlying the class discussion — that teen motherhood devastates mother and child; "If I didn't get pregnant I would have continued on a downward path, going nowhere. They say teenage pregnancy is bad for you, but it was good for me. I know I can't mess around now, I got to worry about what's good for Tiffany and for me."

Another interruption came from Opal, a young Black student. Excerpts from her hygiene class follow.

Teacher: Let's talk about teenage pregnancy.

Opal: How come girls in the locker room say, "You a virgin?" and if you say "Yeah" they laugh and say "Ohh, you're a virgin. . . ." And some Black teenagers, I don't mean to be racial, when they get ready to tell their mothers they had sex, some break on them and some look funny. My friend told her mother and she broke all the dishes. She told her mother so she could get protection so she don't get pregnant.

Teacher: When my 13-year-old (relative) asked for birth control I was shocked and angry.

Portia: Mothers should help so she can get protection and not get pregnant or diseases. So you was wrong.

Teacher: Why not say "I'm thinking about having sex?"

Portia: You tell them after, not before, having sex but before pregnancy.

Teacher (now angry): Then it's a fait accompli and you expect my compassion? You have to take more responsibility.

Portia: I am! If you get pregnant after you told your mother and you got all the stuff and still get pregnant, you the fool. Take up hygiene and learn. Then it's my responsibility if I end up pregnant. . . .

(Field Note, October 23, Hygiene Class)

Two days later, the discussion continued.

Teacher: What topics should we talk about in sex education?

Portia: Organs, how they work.

Opal: What's an orgasm?

[laughter]

Teacher: Sexual response, sensation all over the body. What's analogous to the male penis on the female?

Theo: Clitoris.

Teacher: Right, go home and look in the mirror.

Portia: She is too much!

Teacher: Why look in the mirror?

Elaine: It's yours.

Teacher: Why is it important to know what your body looks like?

Opal: You should like your body.

Teacher: You should know what it looks like when it's healthy, so you can recognize problems like vaginal warts.

(Field Note, October 25, Hygiene Class)

The discourse of desire, initiated by Opal but evident only as an interruption, faded rapidly into the discourse of disease — warning about the dangers of sexuality.

It was in the spring of that year that Opal showed up pregnant. Her hygiene teacher, who was extremely concerned and involved with her students, was also quite angry with Opal: "Who is going to take care of that baby, you or your mother? You know what it costs to buy diapers and milk and afford child care?"

Opal, in conversation with me, related, "I got to leave [school] 'cause even if they don't say it, them teachers got hate in their eyes when they look at my belly." In the absence of a way to talk about passion, pleasure, danger, and responsibility, this teacher fetishized the latter two, holding the former two hostage. Because adolescent females combine these experiences in their daily lives, the separation is false, judgmental, and ultimately not very educational.

Over the year in this high school, and in other public schools since, I have observed a systematic refusal to name issues, particularly issues that caused adults discomfort. Educators often projected their discomfort onto students in the guise of "protecting" them (Fine, 1987). An example of such silencing can be seen in a (now altered) policy of the school district of Philadelphia. In 1985 a student informed me, "We're not allowed to talk about abortion in our school." Assuming this was an overstatement, I asked an administrator at the District about this practice. She explained, "That's not quite right. If a student asks a question about abortion, the teacher can define abortion, she just can't discuss it." How can definition occur without discussion, exchange, conversation, or critique unless a subtext of silencing prevails (Greene, 1986; Noddings, 1986)?

Explicit silencing of abortion has since been lifted in Philadelphia. The revised curriculum now reads:

Options for unintended pregnancy:

(a) adoption
(b) foster care
(c) single parenthood
(d) teen marriage
(e) abortion

A footnote is supposed to be added, however, to elaborate the negative consequences of abortion. In the social politics which surround public schools, such compromises are apparent across cities.

The New York City Family Life Education curriculum reads similarly (New York City Board of Education, 1984, p. 172):

List: The possible options for an unintended pregnancy. What considerations should be given in the decision on the alternatives?

– adoption
– foster care
– mother keeps baby
– elective abortion

Discuss:

– religious viewpoints on abortion
– present laws concerning abortion
– current developments in prenatal diagnosis and their implication for
          abortion issues
– why abortion should not be considered a contraceptive device

List: The people or community services that could provide assistance in the event of an unintended pregnancy

Invite: A speaker to discuss alternatives to abortion; for example, a social worker from the Department of Social Services to discuss foster care.

One must be suspicious when diverse views are sought only for abortion, and not for adoption, teen motherhood, or foster care. The call to silence is easily identified in current political and educational contexts (Fine, 1987; Foucault, 1980). The silence surrounding contraception and abortion options and diversity in sexual orientations denies adolescents information and sends the message that such conversations are taboo — at home, at church, and even at school.

In contrast to these "official curricula," which allow discussion and admission of desire only as an interruption, let us examine other situations in which young women were invited to analyze sexuality across categories of the body, the mind, the heart, and of course, gender politics.

Teen Choice, a voluntary counseling program held on-site by non-Board of Education social workers, offered an instance in which the complexities of pleasure and danger were invited, analyzed, and braided into discussions of sexuality. In a small group discussion, the counselor asked of the seven ninth graders, "What are the two functions of a penis?" One student responded, "To pee!" Another student offered the second function: "To eat!" which was followed by laughter and serious discussion. The conversation proceeded as the teacher asked, "Do all penises look alike?" The students explained, "No, they are all different colors!"

The freedom to express, beyond simple right and wrong answers, enabled these young women to offer what they knew with humor and delight. This discussion ended as one student insisted that if you "jump up and down a lot, the stuff will fall out of you and you won't get pregnant," to which the social worker answered with slight exasperation that millions of sperm would have to be released for such "expulsion" to work, and that of course, it wouldn't work. In this conversation one could hear what seemed like too much experience, too little information, and too few questions asked by the students. But the discussion, which was sex-segregated and guided by the experiences and questions of the students themselves (and the skills of the social worker), enabled easy movement between pleasure and danger, safety and desire, naiveté and knowledge, and victimization and entitlement.

What is evident, then, is that even in the absence of a discourse of desire, young women express their notions of sexuality and relate their experiences. Yet, "official" discourses of sexuality leave little room for such exploration. The authorized sexual discourses define what is safe, what is taboo, and what will be silenced. This discourse of sexuality mis-educates adolescent women. What results is a discourse of sexuality based on the male in search of desire and the female in search of protection. The open, coed sexuality discussions so many fought for in the 1970s have been appropriated as a forum for the primacy of male heterosexuality and the preservation of female victimization.

The Politics of Female Sexual Subjectivities

In 1912, an education committee explicitly argued that "scientific" sex education "should . . . keep sex consciousness and sex emotions at the minimum" (Leo, 1986). In the same era G. Stanley Hall proposed diversionary pursuits for adolescents, including hunting, music, and sports, "to reduce sex stress and tension . . . to short-circuit, transmute it and turn it on to develop the higher powers of men [sic]" (Hall, 1914, pp. 29, 30). In 1915 Orison Marden, author of *The Crime of Silence,* chastised educators, reformers, and public health specialists for their unwillingness to speak publicly about sexuality and for relying inappropriately on parents and peers, who were deemed too ignorant to provide sex instruction (Imber, 1984; Strong, 1972). And in 1921 radical sex educator Maurice Bigelow wrote:

Now, most scientifically-trained women seem to agree that there are no corresponding phenomena in the early pubertal life of the normal young woman who
has good health (corresponding to male masturbation). A limited number of ma-
ture women, some of them physicians, report having experienced in the pubertal
years localized tumescence and other disturbances which made them definitely
conscious of sexual instincts. However, it should be noted that most of these are
known to have had a personal history including one or more such abnormalities
such as dysmenorrhea, uterine displacement, pathological ovaries, leucorrhea, tu-
berculosis, masturbation, neurasthenia, nymphomania, or other disturbances
which are sufficient to account for local sexual stimulation. In short such women
are not normal. . . . (p. 179)

In the 1950s public school health classes separated girls from boys. Girls "learned
about sex" by watching films of the accelerated development of breasts and hips, the
flow of menstrual blood, and then the progression of venereal disease as a result of
participation in out-of-wedlock heterosexual activity.

Thirty years and a much-debated sexual revolution later (Ehrenreich, Hess, &
Jacobs, 1986), much has changed. Feminism, the Civil Rights Movement, the dis-
ability and gay rights movements, birth control, legal abortion with federal funding
(won and then lost), and reproductive technologies are part of these changes (Weeks,
1985). Due both to the consequences of, and the backlashes against, these movements, students today do learn about sexuality — if typically through the representations of female sexuality as inadequacy or victimization, male homosexuality as a
story of predator and prey, and male heterosexuality as desire.

Young women today know that female sexual subjectivity is at least not an inherent
contradiction. Perhaps they even feel it is an entitlement. Yet when public schools resist acknowledging the fullness of female sexual subjectivities, they reproduce a profound social ambivalence which dichotomizes female heterosexuality (Espin, 1984;
Golden, 1984; Omolade, 1983). This ambivalence surrounds a fragile cultural distinction between two forms of female sexuality: *consensual* sexuality, representing consent or choice in sexuality, and *coercive* sexuality, which represents force, victimization, and/or crime (Weeks, 1985).

During the 1980s, however, this distinction began to be challenged. It was acknowledged that gender-based power inequities shape, define, and construct experiences of sexuality. Notions of sexual consent and force, except in extreme circumstances, became complicated, no longer in simple opposition. The first problem
concerned how to conceptualize power asymmetries and consensual sexuality. Could
consensual female heterosexuality be said to exist within a context replete with structures, relationships, acts, and threats of female victimization (sexual, social, and economic) (MacKinnon, 1983)? How could we speak of "sexual preference" when sexual
involvement outside of heterosexuality may seriously jeopardize one's social and/or
economic well-being (Petchesky, 1984)? Diverse female sexual subjectivities emerge
through, despite, and because of gender-based power assymetries. To imagine a female sexual self, free of and uncontaminated by power, was rendered naive (Foucault,
1980; Irigaray, 1980; Rubin, 1984).

The second problem involved the internal incoherence of the categories. Once assumed fully independent, the two began to blur as the varied practices of sexuality
went public. At the intersection of these presumably parallel forms — coercive and

consensual sexualities — lay "sexual" acts of violence and "violent" acts of sex. "Sexual" acts of violence, including marital rape, acquaintance rape, and sexual harassment, were historically considered consensual. A woman involved in a marriage, on a date, or working outside her home "naturally" risked receiving sexual attention; her consent was inferred from her presence. But today, in many states, this woman can sue her husband for such sexual acts of violence; in all states, she can prosecute a boss. What was once part of "domestic life" or "work" may, today, be criminal. On the other hand, "violent" acts of sex, including consensual sadomasochism and the use of violence-portraying pornography, were once considered inherently coercive for women (Benjamin, 1983; Rubin, 1984; Weeks, 1985). Female involvement in such sexual practices historically had been dismissed as nonconsensual. Today such romanticizing of a naive and moral "feminine sexuality" has been challenged as essentialist, and the assumption that such a feminine sexuality is "natural" to women has been shown to be false (Rubin, 1984).

Over the past decade, understandings of female sexual choice, consent, and coercion have grown richer and more complex. While questions about female subjectivities have become more interesting, the answers (for some) remain deceptively simple. Inside public schools, for example, female adolescents continue to be educated as though they were the potential *victims* of sexual (male) desire. By contrast, the ideological opposition represents only adult married women as fully consensual partners. The distinction of coercion and consent has been organized simply and respectively around age and marital status — which effectively resolves any complexity and/or ambivalence.

The ambivalence surrounding female heterosexuality places the victim and subject in opposition and derogates all women who represent female sexual subjectivities outside of marriage — prostitutes, lesbians, single mothers, women involved with multiple partners, and particularly, Black single mothers (Weitz, 1984). "Protected" from this derogation, the typical adolescent woman, as represented in sex education curricula, is without any sexual subjectivity. The discourse of victimization not only obscures the derogation, it also transforms socially distributed anxieties about female sexuality into acceptable, and even protective, talk.

The fact that schools implicitly organize sex education around a concern for female victimization is suspect, however, for two reasons. First, if female victims of male violence were truly a social concern, wouldn't the victims of rape, incest, and sexual harassment encounter social compassion, and not suspicion and blame? And second, if sex education were designed primarily to prevent victimization but not to prevent exploration of desire, wouldn't there be more discussions of both the pleasures and relatively fewer risks of disease or pregnancy associated with lesbian relationships and protected sexual intercourse, or of the risk-free pleasures of masturbation and fantasy? Public education's concern for the female victim is revealed as deceptively thin when real victims are discredited, and when nonvictimizing pleasures are silenced.

This unacknowledged social ambivalence about heterosexuality polarizes the debates over sex education and school-based health clinics. The anxiety effectively treats the female sexual victim as though she were a completely separate species from the female sexual subject. Yet the adolescent women quoted earlier in this text remind us that the female victim and subject coexist in every woman's body.

Toward a Discourse of Sexual Desire and Social Entitlement: In the Student Bodies of Public Schools

I have argued that silencing a discourse of desire buttresses the icon of woman-as-victim. In so doing, public schooling may actually disable young women in their negotiations as sexual subjects. Trained through and into positions of passivity and victimization, young women are currently educated away from positions of sexual self-interest.

If we re-situate the adolescent woman in a rich and empowering educational context, she develops a sense of self which is sexual as well as intellectual, social, and economic. In this section I invite readers to imagine such a context. The dialectic of desire and victimization — across spheres of labor, social relations, and sexuality — would then frame schooling. While many of the curricula and interventions discussed in this paper are imperfect, data on the effectiveness of what *is* available are nevertheless compelling. Studies of sex education curricula, SBHCs, classroom discussions, and ethnographies of life inside public high schools demonstrate that a sense of sexual and social entitlement for young women *can* be fostered within public schools.

Sex Education as Intellectual Empowerment

Harris and Yankelovich polls confirm that over 80 percent of American adults believe that students should be educated about sexuality within their public schools. Seventy-five percent believe that homosexuality and abortion should be included in the curriculum, with 40 percent of those surveyed by Yankelovich et al. (N = 1015) agreeing that 12-year-olds should be taught about oral and anal sex (see Leo, 1986; Harris, 1985).

While the public continues to debate the precise content of sex education, most parents approve and support sex education for their children. An Illinois program monitored parental requests to "opt out" and found that only 6 or 7 of 850 children were actually excused from sex education courses (Leo, 1986). In a California assessment, fewer than 2 percent of parents disallowed their children's participation. And in a longitudinal 5-year program in Connecticut, 7 of 2,500 students requested exemption from these classes (Scales, 1981). Resistance to sex education, while loud at the level of public rhetoric and conservative organizing, is both less vocal and less active within schools and parents' groups (Hottois & Milner, 1975; Scales, 1981).

Sex education courses are offered broadly, if not comprehensively, across the United States. In 1981, only 7 of 50 states actually had laws against such instruction, and only one state enforced a prohibition (Kirby & Scales, 1981). Surveying 179 urban school districts, Sonnenstein and Pittman (1984) found that 75 percent offered some sex education within senior and junior high schools, while 66 percent of the elementary schools offered sex education units. Most instruction was, however, limited to 10 hours or less, with content focused on anatomy. In his extensive review of sex education programs, Kirby (1985) concludes that less than 10 percent of all public school students are exposed to what might be considered comprehensive sex education courses.

The progress on AIDS education is more encouraging, and more complex (see Freudenberg, 1987), but cannot be adequately reviewed in this article. It is important to note, however, that a December 1986 report released by the U.S. Conference of Mayors documents that 54 percent of the 73 largest school districts and 25 state school agencies offer some form of AIDS education (Benedetto, 1987). Today, debates among federal officials — including Secretary of Education Bennett and Surgeon General Koop — and among educators question *when* and *what* to offer in AIDS education. The question is no longer *whether* such education should be promoted.

Not only has sex education been accepted as a function of public schooling, but it has survived empirical tests of effectiveness. Evaluation data demonstrate that sex education can increase contraceptive knowledge and use (Kirby, 1985; Public/Private Ventures, 1987). In terms of sexual activity (measured narrowly in terms of the onset or frequency of heterosexual intercourse), the evidence suggests that sex education does not instigate an earlier onset or increase of heterosexual intercourse (Zabin, Hirsch, Smith, Streett, & Hardy, 1986). The data for pregnancy rates appear to demonstrate no effect for exposure to sex education alone (see Dawson, 1986; Marsiglio & Mott, 1986; Kirby, 1985).

Sex education as constituted in these studies is not sufficient to diminish teen pregnancy rates. In all likelihood it would be naive to expect that sex education (especially if only ten hours in duration) would carry such a "long arm" of effectiveness. While the widespread problem of teen pregnancy must be attributed broadly to economic and social inequities (Jones et al., 1985), sex education remains necessary and sufficient to educate, demystify, and improve contraceptive knowledge and use. In conjunction with material opportunities for enhanced life options, it is believed that sex education and access to contraceptives and abortion can help to reduce the rate of unintended pregnancy among teens (Dryfoos, 1985a, 1985b; National Research Council, 1987).

School-Based Health Clinics: Sexual Empowerment

The public opinion and effectiveness for school-based health clinics are even more compelling than those for sex education. Thirty SBHCs provide on-site health care services to senior, and sometimes junior, high school students in more than 18 U.S. communities, with an additional 25 communities developing similar programs (Kirby, 1985). These clinics offer, at a minimum, health counseling, referrals, and follow-up examinations. Over 70 percent conduct pelvic examinations (Kirby, 1985), approximately 52 percent prescribe contraceptives, and 28 percent dispense contraceptives (Leo, 1986). None performs abortions, and few refer to abortions.

All SBHCs require some form of general parental notification and/or consent, and some charge a nominal fee for generic health services. Relative to private physicians, school-based health clinics and other family planning agencies are substantially more willing to provide contraceptive services to unmarried minors without specific parental consent (consent in this case referring explicitly to contraception). Only one percent of national Planned Parenthood affiliates require consent or notification, compared to 10 percent of public health department programs and 19 percent of hospitals (Torres & Forrest, 1985).

The consequences of consent provisions for abortion are substantial. Data from two states, Massachusetts and Minnesota, demonstrate that parental consent laws result in increased teenage pregnancies or increased numbers of out-of-state abortions.

The Reproductive Freedom Project of the American Civil Liberties Union, in a report which examines the consequences of such consent provisions, details the impact of these statutes on teens, on their familial relationships, and ultimately, on their unwanted children (Reproductive Freedom Project, 1986). In an analysis of the impact of Minnesota's mandatory parental notification law from 1981 to 1985, this report documents over 7,000 pregnancies in teens aged 13–17, 3,500 of whom "went to state court to seek the right to confidential abortions, all at considerable personal cost." The report also notes that many of the pregnant teens did not petition the court, "although their entitlement and need for confidential abortions was as strong or more so than the teenagers who made it to court. . . . Only those minors who are old enough and wealthy enough or resourceful enough are actually able to use the court bypass option" (Reproductive Freedom Project, p. 4).

These consent provisions, with allowance for court bypass, not only increase the number of unwanted teenage pregnancies carried to term, but also extend the length of time required to secure an abortion, potentially endangering the life of the teenage woman, and increasing the costs of the abortion. The provisions may also jeopardize the physical and emotional well-being of some young women and their mothers, particularly when paternal consent is required and the pregnant teenager resides with a single mother. Finally, the consent provisions create a class-based health care system. Adolescents able to afford travel to a nearby state, or able to pay a private physician for a confidential abortion, have access to an abortion. Those unable to afford the travel, or those who are unable to contact a private physician, are likely to become teenage mothers (Reproductive Freedom Project, 1986).

In Minneapolis, during the time from 1980 to 1984 when the law was implemented, the birth rate for 15- to 17-year-olds increased 38.4 percent, while the birth rate of 18- and 19-year-olds — not affected by the law — rose only .3 percent (Reproductive Freedom Project, 1986). The state of Massachusetts passed a parental consent law which took effect in 1981. An analysis of the impact of that law concludes that ". . . the major impact of the Massachusetts parental consent law has been to send a monthly average of between 90 and 95 of the state's minors across state lines in search of an abortion. This number represents about one in every three minor abortion patients living in Massachusetts" (Cartoof & Klerman, 1986). These researchers, among others, write that parental consent laws could have more devastating effects in larger states, from which access to neighboring states would be more difficult.

The inequalities inherent in consent provisions and the dramatic consequences which result for young women are well recognized. For example, twenty-nine states and the District of Columbia now explicitly authorize minors to grant their own consent for receipt of contraceptive information and/or services, independent of parental knowledge or consent (see Melton & Russo, 1987, for full discussion; National Research Council, 1987; for a full analysis of the legal, emotional, and physical health problems attendant upon parental consent laws for abortion, see the Reproductive Freedom Project report). More recently, consent laws for abortion in Pennsylvania and California have been challenged as unconstitutional.

Public approval of SBHCs has been slow but consistent. In the 1986 Yankelovich survey, 84 percent of surveyed adults agree that these clinics should provide birth control information; 36 percent endorse dispensing of contraceptives to students (Leo,

1986). In 1985, Harris found that 67 percent of all respondents, including 76 percent of Blacks and 76 percent of Hispanics, agree that public schools should establish formal ties with family planning clinics for teens to learn about and obtain contraception (Harris, 1985). Mirroring the views of the general public, a national sample of school administrators polled by the Education Research Group indicated that more than 50 percent believe birth control should be offered in school-based clinics; 30 percent agree that parental permission should be sought, and 27 percent agree that contraceptives should be dispensed, even if parental consent is not forthcoming. The discouraging news is that 96 percent of these respondents indicate that their districts do not presently offer such services (Benedetto, 1987; Werner, 1987).

Research on the effectiveness of SBHCs is consistently persuasive. The three-year Johns Hopkins study of school-based health clinics (Zabin et al., 1986) found that schools in which SBHCs made referrals and dispensed contraceptives noted an increase in the percentage of "virgin" females visiting the program as well as an increase in contraceptive use. They also found a significant reduction in pregnancy rates: There was a 13 percent increase at experimental schools after 10 months, versus a 50 percent increase at control schools; after 28 months, pregnancy rates decreased 30 percent at experimental schools versus a 53 percent increase at control schools. Furthermore, by the second year, a substantial percentage of males visited the clinic (48 percent of males in experimental schools indicated that they "have ever been to a birth control clinic or to a physician about birth control," compared to 12 percent of males in control schools). Contrary to common belief, the schools in which clinics dispensed contraceptives showed a substantial postponement of first experience of heterosexual intercourse among high school students and an increase in the proportion of young women visiting the clinic prior to "first coitus."

Paralleling the Hopkins findings, the St. Paul Maternity and Infant Care Project (1985) found that pregnancy rates dropped substantially in schools with clinics, from 79 births/1,000 (1973) to 26 births/1,000 (1984). Teens who delivered and kept their infants had an 80 percent graduation rate, relative to approximately 50 percent of young mothers nationally. Those who stayed in school reported a 1.3 percent repeat birth rate, compared to 17 percent nationally. Over three years, pregnancy rates dropped by 40 percent. Twenty-five percent of young women in the school received some form of family planning and 87 percent of clients were continuing to use contraception at a 3-year follow-up. There were fewer obstetric complications; fewer babies were born at low birth weights; and prenatal visits to physicians increased relative to students in the control schools.

Predictions that school-based health clinics would advance the onset of sexual intimacy, heighten the degree of "promiscuity" and incidence of pregnancy, and hold females primarily responsible for sexuality were countered by the evidence. The onset of sexual intimacy was postponed, while contraception was used more reliably. Pregnancy rates substantially diminished and, over time, a large group of males began to view contraception as a shared responsibility.

It is worth restating here that females who received family planning counseling and/or contraception actually postponed the onset of heterosexual intercourse. I would argue that the availability of such services may enable females to feel they are sexual agents, entitled and therefore responsible, rather than at the constant and terrifying mercy of a young man's pressure to "give in" or of a parent's demands to "save yourself." With a sense of sexual agency and not necessarily urgency, teen girls may be less likely to use or be used by pregnancy (Petchesky, 1984).

Nontraditional Vocational Training: Social and Economic Entitlements

The literature reviewed suggests that sex education, access to contraception, and opportunities for enhanced life options, in combination (Dryfoos, 1985a, 1985b; Kirby, 1985; Select Committee on Children, Youth and Families, 1985), can significantly diminish the likelihood that a teenager will become pregnant, carry to term, and/or have a repeat pregnancy, and can increase the likelihood that she will stay in high school through graduation (National Research Council, 1987). Education toward entitlement — including a sense of sexual, economic, and social entitlement — may be sufficient to affect adolescent girls' views on sexuality, contraception, and abortion. By framing female subjectivity within the context of social entitlement, sex education would be organized around dialogue and critique, SBHCs would offer health services, options counseling, contraception, and abortion referrals, and the provision of real "life options" would include nontraditional vocational training programs and employment opportunities for adolescent females (Dryfoos, 1985a, 1985b).

In a nontraditional vocational training program in New York City designed for young women, many of whom are mothers, participants' attitudes toward contraception and abortion shifted once they acquired a set of vocational skills, a sense of social entitlement, and a sense of personal competence (Weinbaum, personal communication, 1986). The young women often began the program without strong academic skills or a sense of competence. At the start, they were more likely to express more negative sentiments about contraception and abortion than when they completed the program. One young woman, who initially held strong anti-abortion attitudes, learned that she was pregnant midway through her carpentry apprenticeship. She decided to abort, reasoning that now that she has a future, she can't risk losing it for another baby (Weinbaum, personal communication, 1986). A developing sense of social entitlement may have transformed this young woman's view of reproduction, sexuality, and self.

The Manpower Development Research Corporation (MDRC), in its evaluation of Project Redirection (Polit, Lahn, & Stevens, 1985) offers similar conclusions about a comprehensive vocational training and community-based mentor project for teen mothers and mothers-to-be. Low-income teens were enrolled in Project Redirection, a network of services designed to instill self-sufficiency, in which community women served as mentors. The program included training for what is called "employability," Individual Participation Plans, and peer group sessions. Data on education, employment, and pregnancy outcomes were collected at 12 and 24 months after enrollment. Two years after the program began, many newspapers headlined the program as a failure. The data actually indicated that at 12 months, the end of program involvement, Project Redirection women were significantly *less likely* to experience a repeat pregnancy than comparison women; *more likely* to be using contraception; *more likely* to be in school, to have completed school, or to be in the labor force; and twice as likely (20 percent versus 11 percent, respectively) to have earned a Graduate Equivalency Diploma. At 24 months, however, approximately one year out of the program, Project and comparison women were virtually indistinguishable. MDRC reported equivalent rates of repeat pregnancies, dropout, and unemployment.

The Project Redirection data demonstrate that sustained outcomes cannot be expected once programs have been withdrawn and participants confront the realities of a dismal economy and inadequate child care and social services. The data confirm, however, the effectiveness of comprehensive programs to reduce teen pregnancy rates and encourage study or work as long as the young women are actively engaged. Supply-side interventions — changing people but not structures or opportunities — which leave unchallenged an inhospitable and discriminating economy and a thoroughly impoverished child care/social welfare system are inherently doomed to long-term failure. When such programs fail, the social reading is that "these young women can't be helped." Blaming the victim obscures the fact that the current economy and social welfare arrangements need overhauling if the sustained educational, social, and psychological gains accrued by the Project Redirection participants are to be maintained.

In the absence of enhanced life options, low-income young women are likely to default to early and repeat motherhood as a source of perceived competence, significance, and pleasure. When life options are available, however, a sense of competence and "entitlement to better" may help to prevent second pregnancies, may help to encourage education, and, when available, the pursuit of meaningful work (Burt, Kimmich, Goldmuntz, & Sonnenstein, 1984).

Femininity May Be Hazardous to Her Health: The Absence of Entitlement

Growing evidence suggests that women who lack a sense of social or sexual entitlement, who hold traditional notions of what it means to be female — self-sacrificing and relatively passive — and who undervalue themselves, are disproportionately likely to find themselves with an unwanted pregnancy and to maintain it through to motherhood. While many young women who drop out, pregnant or not, are not at all traditional in these ways, but are quite feisty and are fueled with a sense of entitlement (Fine, 1986; Weinbaum, personal communication, 1987), it may also be the case that young women who do internalize such notions of "femininity" are disproportionately at risk for pregnancy and dropping out.

The Hispanic Policy Development Project reports that low-income female sophomores who, in 1980, expected to be married and/or to have a child by age 19 were disproportionately represented among nongraduates in 1984. Expectations of early marriage and childbearing correspond to dramatic increases (200 to 400 percent) in nongraduation rates for low-income adolescent women across racial and ethnic groups (Hispanic Policy Development Project, 1987). These indicators of traditional notions of womanhood bode poorly for female academic achievement.

The Children's Defense Fund (1986) recently published additional data which demonstrate that young women with poor basic skills are three times more likely to become teen parents than women with average or above-average basic skills. Those with poor or fair basic skills are four times more likely to have more than one child while a teen; 29 percent of women in the bottom skills quintile became mothers by age 18 versus 5 percent of young women in the top quintile. While academic skill problems must be placed in the context of alienating and problematic schools, and not viewed as inherent in these young women, those who fall in the bottom quintile may nevertheless be the least likely to feel entitled or in control of their lives. They may feel more vulnerable to male pressure or more willing to have a child as a means of feeling competent.

My own observations, derived from a year-long ethnographic study of a comprehensive public high school in New York City, further confirm some of these conclusions. Six months into the ethnography, new pregnancies began showing. I noticed that many of the girls who got pregnant and carried to term were not those whose bodies, dress, and manner evoked sensuality and experience. Rather, a number of the pregnant women were those who were quite passive and relatively quiet in their classes. One young woman, who granted me an interview anytime, washed the blackboard for her teacher, rarely spoke in class, and never disobeyed her mother, was pregnant by the spring of the school year (Fine, 1986).

Simple stereotypes, of course, betray the complexity of circumstances under which young women become pregnant and maintain their pregnancies. While U.S. rates of teenage sexual activity and age of "sexual initiation" approximate those of comparable developed countries, the teenage pregnancy, abortion, and childbearing rates in the United States are substantially higher. In the United States, teenagers under age fifteen are at least five times more likely to give birth than similarly aged teens in other industrialized nations (Jones et al., 1985; National Research Council, 1987). The national factors which correlate with low teenage birthrates include adolescent access to sex education and contraception, and relative equality in the distribution of wealth. Economic and structural conditions which support a class-stratified society, and which limit adolescent access to sexual information and contraception, contribute to inflated teenage pregnancy rates and birthrates.

This broad national context acknowledged, it might still be argued that within our country, traditional notions of what it means to be a woman — to remain subordinate, dependent, self-sacrificing, compliant, and ready to marry and/or bear children early — do little to empower women or enhance a sense of entitlement. This is not to say that teenage dropouts or mothers tend to be of any one type. Yet it may well be that the traditions and practices of "femininity" as commonly understood may be hazardous to the economic, social, educational, and sexual development of young women.

In summary, the historic silencing within public schools of conversations about sexuality, contraception, and abortion, as well as the absence of a discourse of desire — in the form of comprehensive sex education, school-based health clinics, and viable life options via vocational training and placement — all combine to exacerbate the vulnerability of young women whom schools, and the critics of sex education and SBHCs, claim to protect.

Conclusion

Adolescents are entitled to a discussion of desire instead of the anti-sex rhetoric which controls the controversies around sex education, SBHCs, and AIDS education. The absence of a discourse of desire, combined with the lack of analysis of the language of victimization, may actually retard the development of sexual subjectivity and responsibility in students. Those most "at risk" of victimization through pregnancy, disease, violence, or harassment — all female students, low-income females in particular, and non-heterosexual males — are those most likely to be victimized by the absence of critical conversation in public schools. Public schools can no longer afford to maintain silence around a discourse of desire. This is not to say that the silencing of a discourse of desire is the primary root of sexual victimization, teen motherhood, and the concomitant poverty experienced by young and low-income females. Nor could it be responsibly argued that interventions initiated by public schools could ever be successful if separate from economic and social development. But it is important to understand that by providing education, counseling, contraception, and abortion referrals, as well as meaningful educational and vocational opportunities, public schools could play an essential role in the construction of the female subject — social and sexual.

And by not providing such an educational context, public schools contribute to the rendering of substantially different outcomes for male and female students, and for male and female dropouts (Fine, 1986). The absence of a thorough sex education curriculum, of school-based health clinics, of access to free and confidential contraceptive and abortion services, of exposure to information about the varieties of sexual pleasures and partners, and of involvement in sustained employment training programs may so jeopardize the educational and economic outcomes for female adolescents as to constitute sex discrimination. How can we ethically continue to withhold educational treatments we know to be effective for adolescent women?

Public schools constitute a sphere in which young women could be offered access to a language and experience of empowerment. In such contexts, "well-educated" young women could breathe life into positions of social critique and experience entitlement rather than victimization, autonomy rather than terror.

Notes

1. The research reported in this article represents one component of a year-long ethnographic investigation of students and dropouts at a comprehensive public high school in New York City. Funded by the W. T. Grant Foundation, the research was designed to investigate how public urban high schools produce dropout rates in excess of 50 percent. The methods employed over the year included: in-school observations four days/week during the fall, and one to two days/week during the spring; regular (daily) attendance in a hygiene course for twelfth graders; an archival analysis of more than 1200 students who compose the 1978–1979 cohort of incoming ninth graders; interviews with approximately 55 recent and long-term dropouts; analysis of fictional and autobiographical writings by students; a survey distributed to a subsample of the cohort population; and visits to proprietary schools, programs for Graduate Equivalency Diplomas, naval recruitment sites, and a public high school for pregnant and parenting teens. The methods and preliminary results of the ethnography are detailed in Fine (1986).
2. This information is derived from personal communications with former and present employees of major urban school districts who have chosen to remain anonymous.
3. Personal communication.

References

Bauer, G. (1986). *The family: Preserving America's future.* Washington, DC: U.S. Department of Education.

Benedetto, R. (1987, January 23). AIDS studies become part of curricula. *USA Today,* p. D1.

Benjamin, J. (1983). Master and slave: The fantasy of erotic domination. In A. Snitow, C. Stansell, & S. Thompson (Eds.), *Powers of desire* (pp. 280–299). New York: Monthly Review Press.

Bennett, W. (1987, July 3). Why Johnny can't abstain. *National Review,* pp. 36–38, 56.

Bigelow, M. (1921). *Sex-Education.* New York: Macmillan.

Boffey, P. (1987, February 27). Reagan to back AIDS plan urging youths to avoid sex. *New York Times,* p. A14.

Brown, P. (1983). The Swedish approach to sex education and adolescent pregnancy: Some impressions. *Family Planning Perspectives, 15*(2), 92–95.

Burke, C. (1980). Introduction to Luce Irigaray's "When our lips speak together." *Signs, 6,* 66–68.

Burt, M., Kimmich, M., Goldmuntz, J., & Sonnenstein, F. (1984). *Helping pregnant adolescents: Outcomes and costs of service delivery.* Final Report on the Evaluation of Adolescent Pregnancy Programs. Washington, DC: Urban Institute.

Cartoof, V., & Klerman, L. (1986). Parental consent for abortion: Impact of the Massachusetts law. *American Journal of Public Health, 76* 397–400.

Chicago school clinic is sued over birth control materials. (1986, October 16). *New York Times,* p. A24.

Children's Defense Fund. (1986). *Preventing adolescent pregnancy: What schools can do.* Washington, DC: Author.

Children's Defense Fund. (1987). *Adolescent pregnancy: An anatomy of a social problem in search of comprehensive solutions.* Washington, DC: Author.

Cixous, H. (1981). Castration or decapitation? *Signs, 7,* 41–55.

Dawson, D. (1986). The effects of sex education on adolescent behavior. *Family Planning Perspectives, 18,* 162–170.

Dowd, M. (1986, April 16). Bid to update sex education confronts resistance in city. *New York Times,* p. A1.

Dryfoos, J. (1985a). A time for new thinking about teenage pregnancy. *American Journal of Public Health, 75,* 13–14.

Dryfoos, J. (1985b). School-based health clinics: A new approach to preventing adolescent pregnancy? *Family Planning Perspectives, 17*(2), 70–75.

Ehrenreich, B., Hess, E., & Jacobs, G. (1986). *Re-making love.* Garden City, NY: Anchor Press.

Espin, O. (1984). Cultural and historical influences on sexuality in Hispanic/Latina women: Implications for psychotherapy. In C. Vance (Ed.), *Pleasure and danger* (pp. 149–164). Boston: Routledge & Kegan Paul.

Fine, M. (1986). Why urban adolescents drop into and out of high school. *Teachers College Record, 87,* 393–409.

Fine, M. (1987). Silencing in public school. *Language Arts, 64,* 157–174.

Fisher, W., Byrne, D., & White, L. (1983). Emotional barriers to contraception. In D. Byrne & W. Fisher (Eds.), *Adolescents, sex, and contraception* (pp. 207–239). Hillsdale, NJ: Lawrence Erlbaum.

Foucault, M. (1980). *The history of sexuality* (Vol. 1). New York: Vintage Books.

Freudenberg, N. (1987). The politics of sex education. *HealthPAC Bulletin.* New York: HealthPAC.

Golden, C. (1984, March). *Diversity and variability in lesbian identities.* Paper presented at Lesbian Psychologies Conference of the Association of Women in Psychology.

Greene, M. (1986). In search of a critical pedagogy. *Harvard Educational Review, 56,* 427–441.

Hall, G. S. (1914). Education and the social hygiene movement. *Social Hygiene, 1,* 29–35.

Harris, L., and Associates. (1985). *Public attitudes about sex education, family planning and abortion in the United States.* New York: Author.

Hispanic Policy Development Project. (1987, Fall). *1980 high school sophomores from poverty backgrounds: Whites, Blacks, Hispanics look at school and adult responsibilities,* Vol. 1, No. 2, New York: Author.

Hottois, J., & Milner, N. (1975). *The sex education controversy.* Lexington, MA: Lexington Books.

Imber, M. (1984). Towards a theory of educational origins: The genesis of sex education. *Educational Theory, 34,* 275–286.

Irigaray, L. (1980). When our lips speak together. *Signs, 6,* 69.

Jones, E., Forrest, J., Goldman, N., Henshaw, S., Lincoln, R., Rosoff, J., Westoff, C., & Wulf, D. (1985). Teenage pregnancy in developed countries. *Family Planning Perspectives, 17*(1), 55–63.

Kantrowitz, B., Hager, M., Wingert, S., Carroll, G., Raine, G., Witherspoon, D., Huck, J., & Doherty, S. (1987, February 16). Kids and contraceptives. *Newsweek*, pp. 54–65.

Kelly, G. (1986). *Learning about sex.* Woodbury, NY: Barron's Educational Series.

Kirby, D. (1985). *School-based health clinics: An emerging approach to improving adolescent health and addressing teenage pregnancy.* Washington, DC: Center for Population Options.

Kirby, D., & Sales, P. (1981, April). An analysis of state guidelines for sex education instruction in public schools. *Family Relations*, pp. 229–237.

Koop, C. E. (1986). *Surgeon General's report on acquired immune deficiency syndrome.* Washington, DC: Office of the Surgeon General.

Koop's AIDS stand assailed. (1987, March 15). New York Times, p. A25.

Leo, J. (1986, November 24). Sex and schools. *Time*, pp. 54–63.

Lorde, A. (1980, August). *Uses of the erotic: The erotic as power.* Paper presented at the Fourth Berkshire Conference on the History of Women, Mt. Holyoke College, Holyoke, MA.

MacKinnon, C. (1983). Complicity: An introduction to Andrea Dworkin's "Abortion," Chapter 3, "Right-Wing Women." *Law and Inequality, 1,* 89–94.

Marsiglio, W., & Mott, F. (1986). The impact of sex education on sexual activity, contraceptive use and premarital pregnancy among American teenagers. *Family Planning Perspectives, 18*(4), 151–162.

Melton, S., & Russo, N. (1987). Adolescent abortion. *American Psychologist, 42,* 69–83.

National Research Council. (1987). *Risking the future: Adolescent sexuality, pregnancy and childbearing* (Vol. 1). Washington, DC: National Academy Press.

New York City Board of Education. (1984). *Family living curriculum including sex education. Grades K through 12.* New York City Board of Education, Division of Curriculum and Instruction.

Noddings, N. (1986). Fidelity in teaching, teacher education, and research for teaching. *Harvard Educational Review, 56,* 496–510.

Omolade, B. (1983). Hearts of darkness. In A. Snitow, C. Stansell, & S. Thompson (Eds)., *Powers of desire* (pp. 350–367). New York: Monthly Review Press.

Perlez, J. (1986a, June 24). On teaching about sex. *New York Times*, p. C1.

Perlez, J. (1986b, September 24). School chief to ask mandatory sex education. *New York Times*, p. A36.

Petchesky, R. (1984). *Abortion and women's choice.* New York: Longman.

Philadelphia School District. (1986). Sex education curriculum. Draft.

Polit, D., Kahn, J., & Stevens, D. (1985). *Final impacts from Project Redirection.* New York: Manpower Development Research Center.

Public/Private Ventures. (1987, April). *Summer training and education program.* Philadelphia: Author.

Reproductive Freedom Project. (1986). *Parental consent laws on abortion: Their catastrophic impact on teenagers.* New York: American Civil Liberties Union.

Rohter, L. (1985, October 29). School workers shown AIDS film. *New York Times*, p. B3.

Rubin, G. (1984). Thinking sex: Notes for a radical theory of the politics of sex. In C. Vance (Ed.), *Pleasure and danger* (pp. 267–319). Boston: Routledge & Kegan Paul.

St. Paul Maternity and Infant Care Project. (1985). *Health services project description.* St. Paul, MN: Author.

Scales, P. (1981). Sex education and the prevention of teenage pregnancy: An overview of policies and programs in the United States. In T. Ooms (Ed.), *Teenage pregnancy in a family context: Implications for policy* (pp. 213–253). Philadelphia: Temple University Press.

Schlafly, P. (1986). Presentation on women's issues. American Dreams Symposium, Indiana University of Pennsylvania.

Selected group to see original AIDS tape. (1987, January 29). *New York Times*, p. B4.

Smith-Rosenberg, C. (1978). Sex as symbol in Victorian purity: An ethnohistorical analysis of Jacksonian America. *American Journal of Sociology, 84,* 212–247.

Snitow, A., Stansell, C., & Thompson, S. (Eds.). (1983). *Powers of desire.* New York: Monthly Review Press.

Sonnenstein, F., & Pittman, K. (1984). The availability of sex education in large city school districts. *Family Planning Perspectives, 16*(1), 19–25.

Strong, B. (1972). Ideas of the early sex education movement in America, 1890–1920. *History of Education Quarterly, 12,* 129–161.

Thompson, S. (1983). Search for tomorrow: On feminism and the reconstruction of teen romance. In A. Snitow, C. Stansell, & S. Thompson (Eds.), *Powers of desire* (pp. 367–384). New York: Monthly Review Press.

Torres, A., & Forest, J. (1985). Family planning clinic services in the United States, 1983. *Family Planning Perspectives, 17*(1), 30–35.

Vance, C. (1984). *Pleasure and danger.* Boston: Routledge & Kegan Paul.

Weeks, J. (1985). *Sexuality and its discontents.* London: Routledge & Kegan Paul.

Weitz, R. (1984). What price independence? Social reactions to lesbians, spinsters, widows and nuns. In J. Freeman (Ed.), *Women: A feminist perspective* (3rd ed.). Palo Alto, CA: Mayfield.

Werner, L. (1987, November 14). U.S. report asserts administration halted liberal "anti-family agenda." *New York Times,* p. A12.

Zabin, L., Hirsch, M., Smith, E., Streett, R., & Hardy, J. (1986). Evaluation of a pregnancy prevention program for urban teenagers. *Family Planning Perspectives, 18*(3), 119–126.

Zelnick, M., & Kim, Y. (1982). Sex education and its association with teenage sexual activity, pregnancy and contraceptive use. *Family Planning Perspectives, 14*(3), 117–126.

This paper was originally developed during the Laurie Seminar on Women's Studies at Douglass College, Carol Gilligan, Chair, 1986. The ethnographic research was funded by the W. T. Grant Foundation. The author wishes to thank many individuals for thorough reading, comments, critique, and support: Nancy Barnes, Linda Brodkey, Richard Friend, Carol Gilligan, Henry Giroux, Carol Joffee, Rayna Rapp, David Surrey, and Sandy Weinbaum; additionally, Lori Cornish of Planned Parenthood in Philadelphia provided invaluable research assistance. These individuals bear no responsibility for the final document, but deserve many thanks for their willingness to pursue, unpack, and reconstruct the ideas with me.

PART THREE

Postcolonial and Ethnic Studies

INTRODUCTION

Postcolonial and Ethnic Studies

Imperialism and colonization have always been accompanied by theories about and studies of the people that inhabit conquered lands. The European conquest of the American and African continents, for instance, was followed by an interest in the study of the inhabitants of these lands, whom Europeans considered less than human.[1] By necessity, any imperial project assumes the superiority of the conqueror over the conquered, which is exerted through physical violence and asserted through the imposition of beliefs about the nature of being native.[2] In this process, the colonized are described as incapable of self-study or self-knowledge, except through the gaze of the colonizer. While this gaze and its attendant theories and methodologies are not typically identified as colonial (at least by those who hold and practice them), they are deeply rooted in a colonial project.[3] For example, as Edward Said argues in *Orientalism*,[4] the concept of "the Orient" is a European colonial construct that continues to serve the process of "othering" those outside the boundaries — both political and symbolic — of a "Western" identity. Like Said, postcolonial theorists "suffered the ravages of imperialism and colonialism, and . . . , in challenging the authority, provenance, and institutions of the science that represented them to Europe, were also understanding themselves as something more than what this science said they were."[5]

Frantz Fanon, a Black scholar born in the French colony of Martinique, was among the first "natives" to observe and analyze the effects of colonization on the inhabitants of conquered lands. Fanon delved into the depth of the colonized psyche,[6] sparking a long tradition in the study and theorization of colonial experience by colonized subjects. Fanon also observed the process of colonization as it happened, and theorized about the nature of the conflict between colonizer and colonized through direct observation.[7] Fanon's work, like Said's, is at the heart of contemporary postcolonial theory and the study of ethnicity, which is itself a concept rooted in the experience of colonization.

One of Fanon's most important contributions, which has been at the heart of debates within postcolonial theory, is the belief that once subjects internalize a colonized identity they can never return to a pre-colonized state of being, but rather are condemned to a deeply ambivalent and unstable state of being between what the colonizer tells them about who they are and what they believe and experience themselves to be.[8] Similarly, theorists like Albert Memmi[9] and Paulo Freire[10] have argued that colonization involves a process of dehumanization in the relationship between oppressed and oppressor. Freire draws on Marx's concept of consciousness[11] and Hegel's view of the relationship between master and slave[12] to argue that "full humanity" can only be achieved through a dialogic educative process toward what he calls *conscientização*.[13]

Postcolonial theory does not imply the absence or the end of colonialism. In fact, as authors like Hardt and Negri have argued, colonialism is alive and well,[14] now in the form of globalization and other new versions of the old imperial project.[15] Instead, the term *postcolonial* refers to a shift in the purpose, the actors, and the beneficiaries of the study of culture, ethnicity, race, and other related concepts. Postcolonial theory assumes 1) that the purpose of the study of culture is to strengthen the subjectivity of otherwise colonized subjects, 2) that those who engage postcolonial theory as a lens have themselves experienced and been the subjects of some form of colonization, and 3) that postcolonial theory aims toward the personal, political, intellectual, and even spiritual liberation of colonial subjects.

However, this definition is deceptively simple, and the three essays in Part Three point to many of the traps and the hidden conflicts inherent in various approaches present in postcolonial theory. One such challenge lies in identifying exactly what constitutes a colonial experience and who exactly may qualify as colonized. As Said eloquently explains, "to be one of the colonized is potentially to be a great many different, but inferior things, in many different places, at many different times."[16] This internalized inferiority marks the experience of colonized subjects, whether they are the inhabitants of specific geographic areas, the descendants of slaves dislocated from "ancestral lands," or the emerging generations of various immigrant groups around the world.[17] While potentially confusing and open to grave argument, this aspect of postcolonial theory is essential to understanding its connection to the study of ethnicity, and its attendant social force and twin brother of colonialism — racism.

The three essays included here take different positions and ways of seeing the postcolonial project. Each author takes on a distinct political dilemma, describes different historical and contemporary colonial realities, and outlines a unique approach to the project of postcolonial liberation. Recognizing that colonialism is a contemporary reality, each author suggests a distinct political challenge. Cati Marsh Kennerly describes the Puerto Rican "nation without state" that is struggling for legitimacy as a modern nation through a kind of cultural engineering that does not manage to escape its own premodern fantasy. She points out how colonial subjects end up reifying the contradictions of the modern colonial project by holding on to some of its oppressive discourses, such as sexism, and undermining its political aims.

The essays by Sandy Marie Anglás Grande and Cameron McCarthy illustrate how political projects with similar liberatory ends can assume starkly different stands with regard to defining what it means to "belong" to a particular group and to claim a specific identity. From the standpoint of American Indian liberation projects, Grande carefully demonstrates that belonging or being identified with particular groups can have immediate political and legal consequences. She challenges the concept of *mestizaje*,[18] which has been at the heart of contemporary postcolonial theory,[19] to suggest that indigenous communities cannot afford to see themselves as anything other than stable and coherent cultural entities if they are to survive cultural annihilation through the overwhelming military, cultural, and political power of nation-states like the United States.

In stark contrast, from the standpoint of a radically redefined multiculturalism in the context of U.S. schools, McCarthy proposes nonsynchrony and a deeply subjective process of identification as essential tools for understanding and eradicating racial inequality. Multiculturalism, which has its roots in the emergence of ethnic studies and the civil rights movement, has been at the heart of debates over curriculum and pedagogy in U.S. schools.[20] These debates do not only gravitate around the opposition between multiculturalists and assimilationists,[21] but also encompass a range of definitions of culture, what it means to embrace multiple cultural perspectives, and to what end. McCarthy takes on different understandings of multiculturalism and offers a critique of both liberal and radical views, suggesting that they both fail to capture the nuanced nature of culture and cultural production with enough sophistication. Contrary to Grande, McCarthy's nonsynchrony builds on the fluid and dynamic view of culture and cultural identity. While both of these authors are clearly entrenched in a postcolonial discourse, they speak to each other from distinct political realities, each necessitating diverging strategies, and yet each positioned as a liberatory project for racial, ethnic, and otherwise colonized subjectivities.

As all three essays in Part Three illustrate, postcolonial theory and ethnic studies have a crucial role to play in understanding educational challenges. Whether it is through an analysis of how official educational interventions use popular culture as a way of engineering culture, through a critique of dominant views of race and ethnicity toward a more fluid view of identity, or by reclaiming traditional identities as a source of power and political strength, each essay points to education as a crucial site for the liberation of colonized peoples and the construction of postcolonial subjectivities.

Notes

1. The diaries of Christopher Columbus are good examples of the general attitude of Europeans toward indigenous groups; Christopher Columbus, *The* Diario *of Christopher Columbus's First Voyage to America, 1492-1493*, trans. Oliver Dunn and James Kelley (Norman: University of Oklahoma Press, 1989). Fray Bartolomé de las Casas, one of Columbus' aides, later became an outspoken critic of this view, and is recognized by some as the first non-native advocate for indigenous rights. See Bartolomé de las Casas, *A Short Account of the Destruction of the Indies* (London: Penguin Books, 1992).
2. Linda Tuhiwai Smith, *Decolonizing Methodologies: Research and Indigenous Peoples* (London: Zed Books, 1999).
3. Edward Said, *Culture and Imperialism* (New York: Knopf, 1994); Edward Said, *Orientalism* (New York: Pantheon Books, 1978).
4. Said, *Orientalism.*
5. Edward Said, "Orientalism Reconsidered," in *Reflections on Exile and Other Essays* (Cambridge, MA: Harvard University Press, 2000), 202.
6. Frantz Fanon, *Black Skin, White Masks*, trans. Charles Lam Markman (New York: Grove Press, 1967).
7. Frantz Fanon, *The Wretched of the Earth*, trans. Constance Farrington (New York: Grove Press, 1963).
8. A similar argument can be distilled with regard to African Americans in the United States from the work of W. E. B. Du Bois, *The Souls of Black Folk: Essays and Sketches* (New York: Fawcett, 1961). This dynamic can be closely observed in the literary and artistic production of the inhabitants of colonized lands. The literary criticism of Edward Said has been funda-

mental in this regard. For a collection of his essays, see Edward Said, *Reflection on Exile and Other Essays* (Cambridge, MA: Harvard University Press, 2000). For a more recent analysis of postcolonial art and culture, see Cameron McCarthy and Greg Dimitriadis, "Art and the Postcolonial Imagination: Rethinking the Institutionalization of Third World Aesthetics and Theory," *ARIEL: A Review of International English Literature* 31, No. 1 (2000).

9. Albert Memmi, *The Colonizer and the Colonized*, trans. Howard Greenfeld (Boston: Beacon Press, 1991).

10. Paulo Freire, *Pedagogy of the Oppressed* (New York: Continuum, 1970).

11. See, for instance, Karl Marx, *Economic and Philosophic Manuscripts of 1844*, trans. Martin Milligan (New York: International, 1964). For more on Marx, see Shlomo Avineri, *The Social and Political Thought of Karl Marx* (Cambridge, Eng.: Cambridge University Press, 1968); Robert C. Tucker, ed., *The Marx-Engels Reader*, 2nd ed. (New York: Norton and Co., 1978).

12. G. W. F. Hegel, *Phenomenology of Spirit*, trans. A. V. Miller (Oxford, Eng.: Oxford University Press, 1977). For a helpful introduction to Hegel, see Eric Steinhert, *Master/Slave* (1998). Retrieved May 12, 2001, from http://www.wpunj.edu/cohss/philosophy/COURSES/HEGEL/REASON.HTM

13. This term can be roughly translated as "conscientization" and is closely related to Marx's concept of self-consciousness. For a discussion of conscientização see Antonia Darder, *Reinventing Paulo Freire: A Pedagogy of Love* (Boulder, CO: Westview, 2002); Freire, *Pedagogy of the Oppressed*.

14. Michael Hardt and Antonio Negri, *Empire* (Cambridge, MA: Harvard University Press, 2000).

15. The U.S.-initiated war in Iraq in the spring of 2003 is a vivid example.

16. Edward Said, "Representing the Colonized: Anthropology's Interlocutors," in *Reflections on Exile and Other Essays* (Cambridge, MA: Harvard University Press, 2000), 295.

17. Literary and cultural theorist Homi Bhabha has made important contributions to understanding these overlapping experiences of colonization. See Homi Bhabha, *The Location of Culture* (London: Routledge, 1997). See also the essays in his edited book Homi Bhabha, *Nation and Narration* (London: Routledge, 1990).

18. A Spanish term that references a process of blending cultural forms and identities. For more on mestizaje, see Gloria Anzaldúa, *Borderlands, La Frontera: The New Mestiza* (San Francisco: Aunt Lute Books, 1997).

19. Bhabha's conceptualization of the "interstitial space" has also been important to the postcolonial view of culture and cultural production; see Bhabha, *The Location of Culture*. See also Coco Fusco, *English Is Broken Here: Notes on Cultural Fusion in the Americas* (New York: New Press, 1995); Cameron McCarthy, *The Uses of Culture: Education and the Limits of Ethnic Affiliation* (New York: Routledge, 1998).

20. James A. Banks and Cherry A. McGee Banks, eds., *Multicultural Education: Issues and Perspectives*, 4th ed. (New York: John Wiley, 2001).

21. Multiculturalists are generally those that value the coexistence of multiple cultural experiences and identities, while assimilationists put a premium on homogeneity and argue for the necessary supremacy of one culture over another. On multiculturalism, see Banks and Banks, eds., *Multicultural Education*. For illustrations of the assimilationist perspective, see Lynn Cheney, *America: A Patriotic Primer* (New York: Simon & Schuster, 2002); E. D. Hirsch Jr., *The Schools We Need* (New York: Doubleday, 1996).

Cultural Negotiations: Puerto Rican Intellectuals in a State-Sponsored Community Education Project, 1948–1968

CATI MARSH KENNERLEY

A New Beginning for Puerto Rico: The Institutionalization of Culture

> It was the time of Muñoz Marín. It was the time of hopes that still smelled like new.[1] *

It was a time of magnificent projects, of a modernizing frenzy, when everything "smelled like new." At the dawn of Puerto Rico's contradictory political status in 1952 as an *Estado Libre Asociado* (ELA), or autonomous commonwealth, with U.S. Congressional approval, anything could be built from scratch — even culture.[2] Luis Muñoz Marín, whom many Puerto Ricans viewed as a patriarch *par excellence*, became Puerto Rico's first elected governor in 1948. The experience of *democracia* itself was new for Puerto Ricans, as were industrialization, modernity, and a multitude of new government institutions in charge of everything from hygiene to culture.

Under Muñoz Marín's leadership, the new autonomous state was deeply committed to education beyond mere instruction, and the administration invested a great deal in developing a grand cultural-pedagogical discourse. The state's promotion of a veiled cultural nationalism was part of this discourse: Puerto Rican culture was to be preserved and strengthened, even as the island and its people remained subject to the will of the U.S. Congress and the profit-maximizing strategies of U.S.-based businesses. The island's government told its people that (institutionalized) culture was non-negotiable, even as it was, in fact, negotiating how that culture would be defined with by pro-independence Puerto Rican intellectuals working for the ELA.

With the election of Muñoz Marín, the island entered a period of creating key cultural institutions. The Institute of Puerto Rican Culture was founded in 1955. The

---

*All translations of quotations, titles, and words are by the author.

Harvard Educational Review Vol. 73 No. 3 Fall 2003

University of Puerto Rico continued to host intellectuals from Spain and Latin America, and the Casals Festival was inaugurated by cellist Pablo Casals, one of several prominent Catalonian intellectuals who chose Puerto Rico as their place of refuge from the Spanish dictatorship. The *División de Educación de la Comunidad* (Division of Community Education, or DivEdCo, as it was known) grew out of these efforts. Through these institutions, the state promoted its vision of Puerto Rican culture and legitimated itself in the eyes of its citizens as the primary and authentic representative of their culture, even though it had no political sovereignty.

The Muñoz Marín administration's cultural policy sought to create a basis for conceiving Puerto Rican-ness apart from the island's ambiguously defined political status. Lacking political sovereignty, which was the basis of discourses of "national culture" elsewhere in Latin America, the Puerto Rican state required a new way of understanding and legitimizing its culture. Muñoz Marín recruited intellectuals who defined and imagined the nation in their literary production as a way to institutionalize culture. The national identity, to be built upon the symbols of sovereign nationhood, could exist within the confines of institutionalized culture through the artistic works that writers and artists created and re-created in the printed word and visual image.

The Muñoz Marín administration sponsored experiences that would leave deep imprints on the Puerto Rican people's collective memory. The period of institutionalization of the Estado Libre Asociado marked a watershed in the development of Puerto Rican culture with the number, novelty, and intensity of the cultural projects initiated. It was during this period that *muñocismo* — the political ideology combining populist assertions of cultural nationalism and Puerto Rican autonomy with loyalty to the U.S. government and Constitution, and a commitment to economic development based on market forces and the provision of tax incentives to lure U.S. corporations to the island — became foundational to people's understandings of culture and government, and legitimized itself through educational projects aimed at creating new citizens.

Drawing on Edward Said's distinction between origins and beginnings, it is hard to say if this period, "when everything smelled like new,"[3] can be considered one or the other. For Said, "beginnings" is a more historical term that refers to an activity that repeats itself, rather than to linear-time events; origins, he maintains, refers to the divine. Said states that beginnings cannot come to be without the interplay of the new and the familiar. Conceiving the Muñoz Marín era's cultural projects as beginnings invites different reflections. On the one hand, the government inaugurated a new way of conceiving Puerto Rico through its institutions and its charismatic leader, Muñoz Marín himself. However, it was also creating a populist, quasi-divine generative myth. If anything characterizes the period of Muñoz Marín's governorship, it is the continuous negotiation between the pragmatic and the utopian. The flurry of modernization coincided with the construction of a Puerto Rican culture based as much on the disappearing rural way of life as on elements of modern "democratic" culture. Said explains that "an interest in beginnings is often the corollary result of not believing that any beginning can be located."[4] Indeed, the new state needed a "place" to locate the beginning of the Puerto Rican and symbolic dates for celebrating and legitimating the new nation. The strategy, then, was to use the ELA's founding to create institutions that could construct the culture of the nation-without-a-sovereign-state while the state constituted itself.

As a Puerto Rican born in 1968, I think of my generation as the "grandchildren" of the ELA, born and raised in the contradictions that muñocismo left firmly implanted in the Puerto Rican imagination. Puerto Rican culture, always the object of struggle on an island where the political status and "nationhood" are open issues, was substantially the product of a conscious, pedagogical enterprise conducted by the state. In this article I analyze some of the principal negotiations that gave that pedagogical enterprise its early power, but ultimately limited its options.

I spent eight years away from Puerto Rico, during which I followed events there via the Internet, telephone, printed matter, and my own periodic visits. I was surprised, perhaps aided by distance, to see cultural nationalism being used to sell anything from *Medalla* beer to political candidates, even by the pro-statehood New Progressive Party in its gubernatorial campaign. Advertising — both political and commercial — now makes extensive use of the Puerto Rican flag and other symbols identified with nationhood.[5] Benedict Anderson argues that nations are imagined as bounded, free entities where hopes and purposes are realized in sovereign nationhood.[6] Puerto Rico, where many citizens seem able to imagine the island as a state of the U.S. without fear of cultural assimilation, appears to be an exceptional case. How has Puerto Rico come to be imagined as a nation without a sovereign state? What practices and institutions forged the discourse that has made this possible?

The cultural projects of the ELA, in which many intellectuals and artists have participated over the years, have laid the groundwork for this "lite" cultural nationalism, which affirms the distinctness of Puerto Rican culture without challenging the legal and economic power relationships that mark Puerto Rico's status as unmistakably colonial. While many of those intellectuals have criticized the way Muñoz Marín and his autonomist successors have handled the issue of culture since the 1940s, his cultural projects and the institutions he created to implement them are essential to understanding contemporary popular culture in Puerto Rico.

DivEdCo: Heirs of the New Deal

Founded in 1955, the Institute of Puerto Rican Culture sought to define what ought to be understood as the nation's culture. Prior to this, DivEdCo was the first project in which the state created a relatively autonomous space for a group of Puerto Rican intellectuals to create art that pedagogically enacted that vision of culture.

In 1949, Muñoz Marín himself wrote Law #372, in English and Spanish, which established DivEdCo. The law's preamble states that DivEdCo's pedagogical material ought to be relevant to the Puerto Rican reality. Male and female citizens should recognize themselves as part of the community in which they live. Besides an "imagined community," Muñoz Marín's project could also be said to be searching for a "concrete community." This project did not assume its audience to be a tabula rasa; rather, it had to locate itself in its subjects' reality so as to include them in the process. The language of Law #372 stated, "The community must not be civically unemployed." In fact, democratic community involvement was to be the project's foundation.[7]

DivEdCo had four units: Administration, Field and Training, Analysis, and Production, which included the film, editorial, and graphic arts sections. The formation of DivEdCo consolidated Muñoz Marín's search for a more "modern" way of educating the people, not only about basic problems such as health care, but about what the new citizens of Puerto Rico would be like as the twin processes of industrialization and democratization evolved. The law states:

> The purpose of community education is to communicate basic teaching about the nature of man, his history, his life, his way of working and governing himself in the world and in Puerto Rico. This teaching, aimed at adult citizens meeting in neighborhood groups in rural areas, small towns and cities, will be communicated by means of film, radio, books, pamphlets, posters, phonographic recordings, lectures and group discussions. Its aim is to provide the good hand of popular culture with the tool of a basic education. In practice, this means giving the communities, and the Puerto Rican community as a whole, the desire, the tendency and the means to use its aptitudes for solving many of its own problems in the areas of health, education, cooperation, and social life, through the action of the community itself. The community must not be civically unemployed. The community can be continuously and beneficially employed for itself, in terms of its members' pride and satisfaction.[8]

The modernizing project's starting point would be "the good hand of popular culture" or, rather, a carefully selected sampling of people's beliefs and practices. Muñoz Marín was often concerned about distinguishing his political program from more radical nationalist programs, and he did so by highlighting its peaceful, nonmilitary character.

Although much of the documentation of DivEdCo's internal workings has been lost, a substantial if fragmentary amount of minutes of meetings among the different sections of DivEdCo is available. There are also valuable copies of memoranda that reveal the internal difficulties involved in constructing a pedagogical corpus prepared by artists and intellectuals under state sponsorship. This research draws from a number of these unpublished and hitherto unstudied documents found in the personal archive of René Marqués, chief of DivEdCo's editorial section, as well as interviews with surviving DivEdCo employees (graphic artists Rafael Tufiño and Antonio Maldonado, former director of Field and Training and widow of DivEdCo's director Fred Wale, Carmen Isales, and former organizer Ismael Zapater), and an analysis of the entire surviving collection of films and pamphlets, which were called *Libros para el Pueblo*, or Books for the People.

It is estimated that DivEdCo produced over one hundred films — including feature-length films, short musical numbers, news clips, and documentaries — and more than forty books and pamphlets, plus countless posters and mural-newspapers. Of these, I was able to examine forty films, forty-one books, and seventeen screenplays that did not reach the production stage.[9]

It could be said that DivEdCo's form, and perhaps its seed, may have come from President Franklin Delano Roosevelt's New Deal; its substance, however, reflected Latin American intellectuals' nation-building mission. Roosevelt had established the Works Progress Administration (WPA) to provide employment for many Americans left jobless by the Depression. Under the WPA, the New Deal Arts Project was set up to employ jobless artists and writers; within it, the Federal Writers Project (FWP) employed writers to create "American Guides" intended to promote automotive tourism and local pride. Under fire from congressmen who saw it as a communist threat, the program ended with World War II.

Inspired in part by the New Deal, Muñoz Marín began the popular education project that would later become DivEdCo while he was still president of the Puerto Rican Senate. Muñoz Marín lived in the United States during part of the New Deal era, and Rexford G. Tugwell, the last non–Puerto Rican governor of the island, was a member of Roosevelt's New Deal "Brain Trust." Tugwell was a self-identified socialist who was banished to Puerto Rico as the United States moved toward full participation in World War II.[10] In addition to its New Deal roots, the Puerto Rican project enacted an older tradition, the Latin American intellectuals' involvement in pedagogical institutions as nation builders.[11]

Unlike the FWP writers, DivEdCo's intellectuals were not hired to follow rigid formulas imposed by a central authority. The Puerto Rican project generally allowed much more creativity than FWP, and writers had ample discretion in producing the stories, essays, and screenplays used in Libros para el Pueblo and the films that accompanied them. The state gave them a space and entrusted to them a privileged task — to carry out its cultural-pedagogical mission. For example, Lorenzo Homar and Rafael Tufiño — perhaps the two most famous Puerto Rican graphic artists of the twentieth century — developed and perfected their technique in silk-screening (for movie posters), engraving (for book illustrations), and easel and mural painting at DivEdCo's graphic arts studio. DivEdCo was of crucial importance in the development of Puerto Rican graphic arts — Puerto Rican silk-screening is generally recognized as among the best in the world — and literature.

Ironically, the first people charged with developing Muñoz Marín's brainchild were U.S. liberals, steeped in the more left-leaning currents of New Deal philosophy: Edwin Rosskam was DivEdCo's administrator, and Jack and Irene Delano headed the film and graphic-arts sections, respectively. Rosskam and the Delanos had worked for the U.S. Farm Security Administration (FSA), Rosskam designing publications and exhibits, Jack Delano as a photographer, and Irene as his assistant. The Delanos arrived in Puerto Rico fresh from photographing U.S. rural life. It was through his FSA work that Jack Delano met Muñoz Marín, whom he quickly came to think of as a "New Deal liberal."[12]

In 1946, the division that would become DivEdCo was called the Cinema and Graphic Arts Division of the Parks and Recreation Commission. Jack Delano produced the division's first films and trained young Puerto Ricans in filmmaking for the first time. Meanwhile, Irene Delano introduced the silk-screening techniques with which the first educational and movie-advertising posters were produced. She also insisted on involving all the division's employees in artistic production because of her interest in discovering new Puerto Rican talent.

Rosskam laid the theoretical groundwork for DivEdCo in his "Program of People's Education and Information."[13] This document expressed ideas at odds with the New Deal project that Rosskam knew from first-hand experience. Arguing that a certain freedom for artists was essential for the effectiveness of any popular education undertaking, he also advocated a democratic pedagogy:

> A program using artists to disseminate understanding and information will be successful to the degree to which it offers the artist the opportunity to dedicate himself

to the broadest possible mass of the people — naturally, flowingly, with the least possible correction of commas and re-drawing of lines for purely bureaucratic reasons . . . no language is duller than "governmentese." A small producing unit of devoted people tied together by a common ideology and operating as an intellectual task force can give the people simultaneously what they want and what they need. In a relatively short time it can become an essential weapon in guaranteeing the continuity of a people's government.[14]

Rosskam foresaw the need for Puerto Rican artists and writers to know the audience for whom their material was intended. As a New Deal veteran, Rosskam knew that extreme censorship, centralization, and prescribed formulas would not produce interesting and educational material:

The opportunity for artists and producers to get the "feel" of their subject matter directly from life is an advantage that cannot be exaggerated. . . . You cannot send an artist all over Montana, South Carolina and Massachusetts before you produce each relatively minor publication. The constant contact of the artist with the people who are his audience and subject matter is the basis on which this whole program rests. In it lies the hope of giving Puerto Rico a continuity of its own art production for the people, by its own artists.[15]

Rosskam also recognized the need for a program that would address different social groups and that this need was greatest in the rural areas:

In the rural areas literacy is low, difficulties of distribution and low buying power combine to keep even newspapers at a minimum, not to speak of magazines or books. Here every subject is a new subject . . . the reading habits and formats must be created from scratch, and "How to bathe your baby" or "Why boil your water" is as potentially fascinating a subject as "Puerto Rico and the U.S.A."[16]

In 1947, Rosskam prepared a report on the division's accomplishments and difficulties in its first year of operation. Discussing the successes and mistakes from which DivEdCo would emerge, Rosskam documented details like the short lifespan of a poster in Puerto Rico — due to inclement weather and political opposition — and the need to hire personnel to research public reception of the material. He explained the problems that he and the Delanos faced in communicating with rural people due to their appearance, language, and culture.[17] This report reflected two overarching objectives of these early efforts: publicizing the Puerto Rican government's work and teaching citizenship. The latter meant educating people about the value of their vote and the rights and obligations of citizens in society in the context of "the peculiar position of the island and its peculiar economic conditions."[18]

Rosskam also emphasized the need to create the position of "Informational Writer II," and hoped he could offer adequate remuneration to recruit well-qualified candidates. Rosskam said he would begin the search for such a writer by giving freelance work to Puerto Rican writers. It was not until the time of Rosskam's report that the division received a budget beyond basic payroll expenses. In a letter to Governor Jesus Piñero, Rosskam reported the low cost of producing books in Puerto Rico and how the reception of the books had surpassed his fondest hopes:[19]

So great is the hunger for reading matter, that the cars carrying the *almanaques* are besieged by people, as soon as their cargo becomes known. We have gone into the country ourselves with *almanaques*, and invariably this is what happens: Everybody takes one. Then all conversation stops while the book is examined. Usually everybody looks for his saint's day, and finding it correct, joins somebody else to start discussing the section about hurricanes. This usually takes quite a long time. Sometimes during this period, you can begin to hear the voices of children singing either the *juegos cantados* or the *coplas* at the end of the book. About this time too, somebody generally comes up to the car to ask (pointing to the first page), "Can I put my name here?" or "Is it alright to make a hole in the corner and put a string in it?" And gradually groups form, going through the book slowly, from cover to cover. [20]

Muñoz Marín recruited another U.S. liberal to work for DivEdCo. Fred Wale was a Harvard College graduate recommended by the New School for Social Research in New York City, who had experience in New Deal programs and the Boston Public Schools. In a letter to Wale, Muñoz Marín indicated that he hoped to begin a wide-ranging adult education program. He wrote that those in charge of starting the program were artists rather than teachers, but that they had a great store of optimism. He also said that the program would take the form of "a pretty autonomous division of the Department of Education."[21] Wale accepted Muñoz Marín's invitation to lead the program.

Within its pedagogical mission, DivEdCo would also become an important space of training and experimentation for artists and intellectuals. It produced the first Puerto Rican films, gave an enormous boost to Puerto Rican graphic arts, and employed many writers to work for *el Pueblo*. As an educational undertaking that used images as well as words, DivEdCo created a collection of cultural icons ranging from book illustrations to posters, mural newspapers, and films — images that defined a new citizenry against a carefully selected backdrop of Puerto Rican culture.

The Puerto Rican Bauhaus: *La Generación del Cuarenta* and the Issue of Puerto Rican Culture

There were, together at one time, filmmakers, writers, painters, etc. It was a way of reaching the people through good art. We knew it wouldn't lead to a sovereign republic, but it was a Bauhaus, the Puerto Rican Bauhaus.[22]

Lorenzo Homar, world-renowned Puerto Rican artist, thus explained why many of his DivEdCo colleagues, the writers of the so-called *Generación del cuarenta* (Generation of the Forties), including René Marqués, Pedro Juan Soto, and Emilio Díaz Valcárcel, as well as artists like Rafael Tufiño and Homar himself, decided to work for DivEdCo. In the late 1940s and 1950s, such an artistic and pedagogical project was attractive because of its novel and interdisciplinary nature. Moreover, it was not at odds with the artists' *puertorriqueñista* concerns. The role that these artists and intellectuals would play in the community education project began to be negotiated at the intersection of Muñoz Marín's populism and their concept of Puerto Rican art. As an agency of the *Departamento de Instrucción Pública* (Department of Public Instruction, now called the Department of Education), DivEdCo had relative autonomy, space, and materials with which to create literature, film, and graphic arts. Like the Bauhaus movement in Weimar, Germany, DivEdCo promoted a school of practice that encouraged the integration of artists and society.

DivEdCo's experimental nature, the space it afforded artists' creativity, and the broadness of its charter were, unquestionably, significant incentives to work in the program. During the period of rapid modernization in Puerto Rico (1948 to 1968), DivEdCo was a space of praxis for artists and intellectuals. By all accounts, it was an artists' workshop, a laboratory of democratic practice, and a vehicle for building a Puerto Rican cultural citizenship.[23] More importantly, through DivEdCo they could reach a considerable segment of the island's population and train a new generation of artists.

Among the intellectuals and artists who worked in DivEdCo, René Marqués stands out as the writer who most directly influenced his generation. As an intellectual, Marqués was profoundly pedagogical and moralistic. Arcadio Díaz Quiñones argues that Marqués' "didactic concern" is fundamental to his work, as he sought to "give clear, resounding moral lessons." Díaz Quiñones adds, "One does not 'read' René Marqués: one practically has to obey him."[24] Extremely well known and recognized as an author, Marqués was prepared to rise to the task he had laid out for himself: the defense of Puerto Rican national sovereignty. DivEdCo, born in Muñoz Marín's contradictory cultural nationalism, took shape in the complementary discourse developed under Marqués' guidance.

From DivEdCo, where Muñoz Marín's cultural nationalism protected one of the few spaces for free expression of political dissent in McCarthy-era Puerto Rico, Marqués severely criticized the governor's acceptance of U.S. sovereignty over Puerto Rico, his support of industrialization based on investment by U.S.-based corporations, and the Occidentalism promoted by Jaime Benítez as chancellor of the University of Puerto Rico. Marqués remained for nearly two decades as chief of DivEdCo's editorial section, until a new pro-statehood administration forced him out in 1969.

Although he worked for the Department of Education, Marqués allowed himself the freedom to criticize — and occasionally to caricature — the department's policies concerning Spanish as the vernacular language and the teaching of Puerto Rican history. In a 1960 essay, which the Puerto Rican Nationalist Party published as a pamphlet, Marqués addressed the problem of the language of instruction in Puerto Rico's colonial situation. He concluded: "only the enjoyment of complete national sovereignty will cleanse the pedagogical problem of all extra-pedagogical baggage."[25]

Despite Marqués' bitter criticisms of Muñoz Marín's policies, however, at times his didacticism brought him very close to Muñoz Marín's discourse. Marqués essentially agreed with the project's basic concepts. He knew that the goals of the government's education program went far beyond the preparation of educational pamphlets about how to prevent parasites, or the nutritional value of different foods. The presentation of the material had to be relevant to the Puerto Rican reality, and he was extremely interested in the cultural lode that the project permitted him to mine.

With his own pedagogy laced with absolutes, Marqués affirmed Puerto Ricanness in the agricultural way of life, even as that way of life was quickly disappearing. Whereas Muñoz Marín took great pains to link certain elements of rural culture, which he deemed "authentically Puerto Rican," to the process of modernization,

Marqués, bent on conservation, clung more tightly to what was disappearing. He created "an aesthetic and static vision of man and objects, which of course was an ahistoric vision, to counterpose — implicitly or explicitly — the corruption of the customs of the present day."[26]

At times Marqués tried to bring both tendencies — the education of a democratic citizenry and his struggle to conserve rural values as authentically Puerto Rican in the face of Americanizing modernity — to his work at DivEdCo, but it is apparent that the conservation of rural values was the dominant theme in his educational work. This discursive operation was to become one of the foundations of muñocista cultural nationalism, and it made possible, at least at the outset, a *jíbaro* pedagogy.

Jíbaro Pedagogy: A School for "The Learned City"[27]

"This book has been made in Puerto Rico for Puerto Ricans."[28]

Jíbaro is a term that refers to Puerto Rican peasants; it indexes a whole way of life, now folklorized as "that which is essentially Puerto Rican," since the disappearance — precisely during DivEdCo's heyday in the 1950s and 1960s — of the agricultural economy that was its material basis. The narrative of what could be called jíbaro pedagogy sprang from the marriage of Marqués' transgressive/conservative thought with Muñoz's populism. In a certain way, the writer's literary constructions — charged with binary oppositions such as sin/innocence, docility/heroism, true patria (motherland)/false patria, heroic founders/barbarian invaders[29] — affirmed the muñocista generative myth. In the literary world, agrarian Puerto Rico was still possible and could be preserved. At the same time, the resulting pedagogical narrative required a selection of the most "essential" characteristics of rural life, which might and must be conserved amidst the rapid modernization.

DivEdCo proposed transforming rural communities in a dual, contradictory movement, wanting and not wanting them to modernize, meticulously selecting what might be changed while expressing a longing for it to remain the same. The peasantry became *lo puertorriqueño:* identified as what was essentially Puerto Rican in the face of a modernization process that, though managed and encouraged by Puerto Ricans, inevitably promoted the imitation of U.S. patterns of mass production and consumption. Rural Puerto Rican culture was subjected to a winnowing process, and those elements that were to be preserved were taken and turned into the ideological foundations of *puertorriqueñidad*. The task was to sanitize it — literally and figuratively — eliminate superstition, and create a new democratic citizenship.

DivEdCo's charter was quite broad, permitting the implementation of a pioneering political education in Puerto Rico: a homegrown pedagogy like the Books for the People and, as Tufiño described DivEdCo's films, "*caseras, como hacer arroz y habichuelas*" (home-made, like rice and beans).[30] In DivEdCo's educational materials, the basic lesson was that an informed citizenry took charge of its community and turned authoritarian patterns into collective democratic processes. Initially, at least, there was plenty of incentive for all parties to participate in the project: the intellectuals and artists had a broad audience for their art; Muñoz Marín furthered his cultural nationalism and strengthened his grassroots political base; and the rural communities gained basic education and help in addressing their most immediate problems.

In 1957, Marqués published an article titled "Writing for a Community Educa-tion Programme" for UNESCO, in which he mentioned the DivEdCo writers' aca-demic credentials and solid literary background. However, he noted that they had no special training or experience in the field of education. He said that the ivory tower did not exist for Puerto Rican writers, and that it was necessary to go to the field in or-der to write educational materials:

> Our main objective was to stir the hearts and minds of people so as to help them identify themselves with the truth of our message. The more an individual feels his own dignity as a human being, the more apt is he to feel respect and responsibility toward others and to work with them in the development and improvement of the community. Factual information is of course needed, but facts alone will not move people to re-examine deep-rooted cultural practices and prejudices. We frankly did not know where to go to learn this kind of writing, except perhaps to the rural com-munities in our own country.
>
> The writers in the Editorial Unit go frequently to the country as part of their job, either to do personal research or to make informal interviews, to get first hand information about community recreational meetings in which our books are read and community problems discussed. The direct contact with rural reality is often a preparation for the actual writing; it might be called the educational-writer-being-educated-by-the-people-he-is-writing-for step.[31]

Thus, DivEdCo was a school not only for the recipients of its educational products, but also for the artists, writers, and young college students who worked there. There were discussions about what training ought to be given to students in the film unit. "The Learned City" and its apprentices went forth to the island's countryside to learn its texture, its colors, and its essence, to transform and fix it in images or in words.

DivEdCo's internal workings were complicated by the fact that the artists' work had to be done collectively, following a thematic unit with a clear educational message, and in different media, with books, films, and posters all related to one another. In 1954, although coordination issues among the different sections were the order of the day, there was a sense of great enthusiasm and efforts to organize the program effectively. That year, a program committee was proposed in an attempt to improve DivEdCo's operations. It was to include representation from the different sections: editorial, graphic arts, film, administration, and field and training. At these meetings, there were discussions of the details of filming, how themes ought to be treated, cultural values, and other agencies' interest in DivEdCo products, as well as reports of the products' re-ception in the field. These rich testimonies of everyday effervescence demonstrated how a new agency was being built in an attempt not only to create materials with which to teach democracy, but to actually function democratically in the process.[32]

Some conflicts between the editorial and film units centered on artistic concerns within the program. For example, one filmmaker expressed concern over how the ru-ral areas were being represented. Upon beginning to film *Cuando los Padres Olvidan* (When Parents Forget), filmmaker Amílcar Tirado noted that the film's topic, recre-ation, was not dealt with realistically. He said that in conversations with residents they had told him they liked getting in cars and seeing the lights of the city, not the stereo-typical gathering to make an *asopao* (a thick stew with rice) as Marqués' screenplay proposed. For Tirado, this showed Marqués' ignorance of rural life and highlighted the problem of representation. The discussion also revealed the problem of how to modify the screenplay without abandoning the film's, or any other product's, original pedagogical focus, which had already been agreed upon. The argument between Tirado and Marqués plunged deep into the issue of the agency's fundamental educational purpose and the hope of harmonizing art and education.

DivEdCo's constant negotiations were both artistic and ideological. How artistic could DivEdCo's books and films be? The difficulties of carrying out an educational program with artists and intellectuals (only two of DivEdCo's personnel had formal training in education) were beginning to show. Still, pedagogical considerations were not the only stumbling block; there were also concerns rooted in ideology and day-to-day work. This subject would come up repeatedly and was clearly a source of tension.

> We place art at the service of our educational program, and not our educational program at the service of art. Experience has shown that there have been no truly irreconcilable conflicts between the artistic means and the educational ends. We have succeeded in producing educational products of great literary, graphic and cinematographic value.[33]

The importance of artistic considerations would continue to be the subject of complaints, debates, and constant clarifications — these were the difficulties of creating a jíbaro pedagogy. One of the filmmakers advocated experimental innovations and artistic values, while the director, Fred Wale, was constantly setting boundaries and reminding his colleagues of the program's educational purposes. DivEdCo continued producing despite the coordination problems, the difficulty of reaching consensus, and the constant questioning of goals and purposes. In interviews, graphic artists Rafael Tufiño and Antonio Maldonado both said that they were often unable to remember who created which illustrations in the Libros para el Pueblo. Because they frequently worked closely together, they did not bother to sign the illustrations.[34]

At the outset, the program's populist ideology allowed ample room for artists and intellectuals to work. However, as DivEdCo's canon became established and more of the agency's effort was channeled into organizing communities to contribute sweat equity to public works projects, the negotiations began to stall. In a 1957 letter to Fred Wale, Marqués criticized the recruitment of unpaid labor for rural public works, while no such contribution was being asked of middle-class city residents.[35] A few months later he voiced his frustrations with the limitations that came up time and again in their internal discussions.[36] The project was growing more contradictory and exhausting its possibilities, due to both its statements and its yearnings. What was the result of the negotiations between artists and intellectuals employed by the state? What pedagogies did they create in film, graphic arts, and literature? What memory of these processes can be traced through the cultural production sponsored by Puerto Rican populism?

Cultural Production: The DivEdCo Canon

DivEdCo was created as an urgent effort to teach the basic lessons of a new democracia. The new rural citizenry — "the people who have just come on stage"[37] — had to treasure its roots as it replaced the old authoritarian political habits with modern, democratic ones. The high rate of illiteracy made it impossible at first to rely solely on the printed word. Film, together with the illustrations that gave life to posters and books, would bring vivid examples of democratic practice before the jíbaros in their own communities: neighbors gathering to discuss community problems, making decisions by consensus, overcoming apathy, and forming cooperatives. The screenings were often followed by discussions moderated by the DivEdCo organizers, who also distributed free Libros para el Pueblo on the same subject to all who attended.

By 1947, still under the Parks and Recreation Commission, Rosskam reported that the film unit had produced three documentaries and ten color posters in large quantities.[38] The first pamphlet, designed by Irene Delano, bore the title *Por qué la Piña?* (Why the Pineapple?), and explained the need for this fruit to be cultivated on the island of Vieques, where the U.S. Navy had expropriated some two-thirds of the land.[39] By the time DivEdCo's charter became law in 1949, Jack Delano had already directed several more documentaries, including *La Montaña* (The Mountain),[40] *Una Gota de Agua* (A Drop of Water)[41], and *La Caña* (Sugarcane).[42]

These first documentaries would lay the cornerstones of the new citizenry — health, hygiene, and agriculture — that would be referred to constantly in DivEdCo's narratives. In *Una Gota de Agua*, a drop of water is taken to a laboratory in San Juan to determine its purity. This film communicated scientific health information, such as the need to boil drinking water. Advertisements for the documentaries and other films supported the hygiene messages: "DANGER, flies bring sicknesses. Cover your food or wash their [children's] hands before eating."[43] *La Caña* featured sugarcane as Puerto Rico's most important product and a valuable export. The film stated that today there were unions, a minimum wage law, and a legislated eight-hour working day; it concluded that workers had more rights than yesterday. Yesterday — the dark past of Spanish and later U.S. colonial rule, exploitation by absentee-owned sugar companies, poverty, and ignorance — and today — since Muñoz Marín's peaceful democratic revolution and the advent of modernization that accompanied the founding of the ELA — marked the poles of a simple story that began from a remote, primitive, and unjust origin to contrast it with the recently inaugurated period of progress.

During the transition to the Puerto Rican cadre who would take charge of DivEdCo, Jack Delano produced several more documentaries,[44] including *Desde las Nubes* (From the Clouds),[45] *La Voz del Pueblo* (The People's Voice),[46] and *Las Manos del Hombre* (Man's Hands).[47] He also directed his first feature-length film, *Los Peloteros* (The Baseball Players),[48] now considered a classic in Puerto Rican cinema. This period also saw the publication of the first Libros para el Pueblo and *Almanaques del Pueblo* (People's Almanacs).[49] The cover of the first *Almanaque del Pueblo* 1949 featured a peasant family in front of their house: a woman with a child in her arms and the man with a farming tool. The almanac, profusely illustrated and apparently disorganized in its presentation of the material, might seem to lack a clear purpose. Nonetheless, by virtue of the democratization of its content, it constituted a new pedagogy. Moreover, the material was unmistakably didactic in intent, written for a readership — adults as well as children — with a fourth-grade reading ability.[50] This first almanac is notable for the presentation of a story about the origins of humanity in which the essential elements were the development of transportation, industrialization, and struggles to assert the rights of man. The theme of origins and the contrast between yesterday and today would remain throughout DivEdCo's educational production; the texts' didacticism would complement the muñocista discourse.

In a section titled "How the world is getting smaller," readers learned that

> the world is not so large as it was before. Telegraphs, telephones and radio make New York as close to San Juan as Ponce. The seas are not a wall that man cannot cross. Today, Puerto Rico is closer to New York than the states of Texas and California.[51]

Through *décimas* (a 10-verse form used in popular poetry throughout the Spanish-speaking world), readers were informed of labor legislation that permitted "a more just distribution." The government imitated the *Farmer's Almanac* genre to disseminate information about its cultural and political program. One section, "Puerto Rico moves towards a brighter future," presented achievements in education, health, and recreation, among others:

> Our country has little land and many people. It cannot support its growing population if it does not become part of the industrial world which surrounds it. . . . No nation, no matter how large or powerful, can exist by itself in today's world. What is happening today, is happening to the world, and Puerto Rico is part of the world. [52]

Although all the texts tried to make various connections with the film products, it was the first Libro para el Pueblo that, together with Jack Delano's film *Desde las Nubes* and the poster portraying a map of Puerto Rico, constituted DivEdCo's first formal pedagogical unit of film, book, and poster. Delano recalled in an interview that "the idea was always to have, along with the film, some booklets on the same subject. After seeing the film, the people would take something home with them."[53] *Desde las Nubes* framed the national territory by showing it from the air as it told the story of the origins of the island's major products. It ended with people singing, "with pick and hoe, let all the people work together." As the camera dwelled on the island's landscapes, the narrator stated, "We owe this land everything we are." As the city of San Juan was viewed from the air, the narrator said, "Not everyone can fly in a plane," and therefore maps were necessary. It showed factories, agriculture, dairy production, a new public housing project, and ended with the narrator saying "The task of those of us who live in the island of enchantment" is to "march on toward the future."[54] The film's pilot's-eye view underlined technology and progress, as it affirmed the idea of a "whole" nation.

One of the most characteristic elements in DivEdCo's products was the resolution of conflict through dialogue. This is the case in the films *Belén (La del traje blanco)* (Belén, the one with the white dress),[55] where the protagonist must deal with her father's patriarchal objections to her desire to become a nurse; *Modesta*,[56] in which women unite to confront domestic violence through dialogue; and *Ignacio*,[57] in which the death of the illiterate protagonist's son's makes him speak out against undemocratic leadership. Later, other DivEdCo products would try rather timidly to introduce more complexity into the development of democratic process. This complexity, however, scarcely sprinkled the DivEdCo corpus as a whole. The books made great historical leaps (e.g., René Marqués' treatment of "human rights" in *Los Derechos del Hombre* [the Rights of Man]),[58] and avoided mentioning the conflict inherent in processes of industrialization and urbanization. None of the films dealing with these processes was distributed; most remained as unproduced screenplays, and the only one that was completed, *Un Día Cualquiera* (Any Day), was shelved by Muñoz Marín himself because it "gave no hope."[59] The conventions that governed this didactic literature and the films emphasized the narration of origins, the construction of a past as a series of progressive leaps, and the promise of a prosperous future through democratic dialogue, which proved impossible to represent in the context of urban poverty.

DivEdCo's "foundational" products sought to constitute a sort of modern, democratic citizenry through hygiene, science, and health; the optimism about the march of "progress" toward the future; emphasis on manual labor and the importance of close community ties; and the story of the nation's origin. These starting points were the beginning of the DivEdCo canon, and they shed considerable light on the content of its pedagogy. Every Libro para el Pueblo had a space for writing the family's name, and urged people to create a small family library of books "made by and for Puerto Ricans."[60]

DivEdCo's first products, created by its U.S. founders, Rosskam and the Delanos, were more obvious in their promotion of government projects. The Puerto Rican cadre distanced itself somewhat from the government as it began to take charge of the production. Planting the *pedacito de tierra* (small piece of land) was promoted as an activity for the whole family, the privileged unit that served as the basis for the (local) community, as well as for the nation.[61] The first illustration of the book *La Familia* is illuminating (see Illustration #1): men, women, and children holding up the country, which is made up of countryside, city, and industry. The illustration was explained:

> The family is the smallest group or unit in a society. It is the basis or foundation of a nation. The family is made up of individuals. The community is made up of families. The nation is made up of communities. But the pillars, the *zocos* [posts upon which raised wooden houses were built] that hold up the society, are the families. . . . The virtues, vices, attitudes, prejudices and feelings of individuals will affect the family. And if the family is affected, the community will be affected. And if the community is affected, so will society, in other words, the country or nation. So we can see that the individual cannot act alone, without affecting the other individuals around him. To a greater or lesser degree, the individual affects the structure of the whole society with his attitude and behavior. This is a reality that we can see quite often. Perhaps because we shut ourselves up as individuals in our egotism. And we don't realize the responsibility we have to our family, our community and our nation.[62]

The book ended with the following sentence, centered in the final, otherwise blank, page: "What we are to be as a people, as a nation, depends greatly on how you are, and how your family is."[63] The facing page showed a group of workers with tools in hand, and a lone woman in the center holding a basket of fruits or eggs, flanked by two girls and a boy.

The products emphasized a new citizenry made up of men and women, children, grandmothers, and grandfathers. The populist "democratic circle" included them all. Women were called upon to learn to read, and to speak at meetings even if their husbands opposed it. Physically challenged boys and girls were also among the voices of

ILLUSTRATION 1   *La familia aguanta el país (The family supports the country)*

the new democracy. The new citizens entered into dialogue guided by democratic principles, knew the laws, stayed healthy, loved and worked the land, and created a family.

The inclusive view of citizenship and the teaching of democracy were the outstanding characteristics of DivEdCo's production throughout the 1950s and 1960s. The characters in the cultural products were the people themselves: the members of the rural communities. The stories were their stories, framed by the rural landscape. For example, *El Pueblo en Acción* (The People in Action) was a series of documentaries about different communities' efforts and self-help projects as they built wells or gardens. Despite the different roles assigned to men and women in this system of representation, many of the products portrayed an inclusive community.[64] There were also distinctly experimental film products, with considerable artistic/cultural content. *Nenén de la Ruta Mora* (Little Boy from the Moorish Way), filmed in color by the newly trained filmmaker and screenwriter Oscar Torres, stands out in this sense. This film, Torres' first, is a treatment of the feast of *Santiago Apóstol* (St. James the Apostle), patron saint of the largely Black north coast town of Loíza, from the perspective of a child, Nenén, and his play with a *vejigante,* one of the mischievous masked characters of the yearly carnival procession.[65] Afro-Puerto Rican culture, often shrouded in silence, had been brought to the screen, and the narrator said the carnival was for "*blancos, negros y mulatos,*" inviting all Puerto Ricans to claim African, as well as Spanish (and, much less controversially, indigenous Taíno) heritage. By showing women actively participating in community improvement, and showcasing non-European roots of Puerto Rican culture, the films sought to weaken racial and gender divisions within the community that they invited rural viewers to imagine.

DivEdCo's films, print, and graphic arts products created an archive of words and images that consolidated a collective memory. The people, framed by their landscape, had come on the stage of history. People could see themselves on screen. The movies' protagonists were often residents of the community where the film was shot, as were the extras and lesser characters.

DivEdCo's films would follow certain conventions established by Jack Delano in *Los Peloteros* (The Baseball Players). The camera focused on faces that later films would frame in the windows of rural houses as "the Puerto Rican face." Delano's films were foundational in both image and experience. As Delano said in an interview:

> When we would go to a film screening, for example, we'd leave here at nightfall, and as we approached the place we'd see the posters stuck to trees, announcing the movie. Each poster said, "*Película hecha en Puerto Rico — Entrada gratis*" [Movie made in Puerto Rico — Free admission]. As we got closer, we could hear music from a loudspeaker and see the people gathered there, and people coming down the mountainsides, mostly barefoot, women with children in their arms. There was no seating, everybody had to stand. We'd get to the place, and there'd be 200 or 300 people waiting to see the movie. For many, it was their first experience of film. Some, who had seen movies, had never seen Puerto Rican faces on the screen.[66]

DivEdCo's film and print images reveal a compact set of icons, a visual canon. The community, not individuals, is at the center of this system of representation. The democratic circle is one of the icons that best represents DivEdCo's pedagogical thrust (see Illustration #2) and it was repeatedly used throughout DivEdCo's products. Most of the time it took place in a rural setting. This was the circle Muñoz Marín had inaugurated in his early electoral campaigns — outdoor conversations away from the learned cabinet, in the *batey* (a Taíno word referring to an open meeting or ceremonial gathering place).

Its opposite was the meeting where participants couldn't see each other. This image exemplified, in both texts and movies, anti-democratic proceedings in which decisions are not taken by the community as a whole.

There are two large absences in this first phase of DivEdCo's production: rural-urban migration and emigration to the United States, both massive social processes that were peaking during DivEdCo's most productive years. The Libro para el Pueblo titled *Emigración* (Emigration), the only product to deal with the enormous population movement, was finished in 1954, a year after the emigration peaked.[67] Its implicit message was not to emigrate. Housing units in the United States tended to be too small for large Puerto Rican families and there were examples of prejudice against Puerto Ricans. For example, a sign that read "No Puerto Ricans allowed" led to a claim that racial prejudice was not as bad in Puerto Rico as in the United States, because slavery on the island had been peacefully abolished. Readers were urged not to "trade our customs for the American ones."[68] The book ends with information about the Puerto

ILLUSTRATION 2   *Círculo democrático sencillo (Democratic circle)*

Rican Department of Labor's U.S. offices, which promised to guarantee migrant farmworkers a contract including housing, medical care, and other benefits. It clearly states several times, and with an illustration showing a large X over dollar bills changing hands, that those offices would not provide financial assistance or transportation. Thus, the book embodied the contradiction between DivEdCo's idealization of the rural, and the government's promotion of industrialization and emigration.[69]

Like the film *Un Día Cualquiera* (A Day Like Any Other), the proposed Libro para el Pueblo, *El Arrabal* (The Slum) — both rather bleak depictions of life in the urban slums to which thousands were migrating from the countryside — was not allowed to circulate, ultimately by Muñoz Marín's decision. The disagreement between DivEdCo's promotion of rural community values and the government's policy encouraging industrialization and emigration stands out as a great contradiction in the treatment of these subjects.

DivEdCo's work from the 1940s through the 1960s saw the construction of a particular rhetoric about progress. Its homegrown pedagogy sought to identify modernity not with industrialization, but with a new attitude toward the community itself. Modernity was also marked in the discourse on the power of science to control sickness. Systems of knowledge that might interfere with the discourses of medicine and science — from folk medicine to midwifery — were dismissed.

Citizenship was integral to the democratic polis. The rights of men and women held a place of honor in the democratic circle, which sought to be the basis for the country. Communication and the open discussion of ideas were the foundation of this new Puerto Rico that was on its way to a promising future. War was barbarism that threatened the peaceful people of Puerto Rico, who had made great strides through democracy and avoided the conflicts that had plagued other countries.

DivEdCo's first decade of cultural production, referred to in later memos as the "golden age," was the most innovative. By the late 1960s, themes were becoming repetitive, books were being reprinted, and production dropped off. Interestingly, stories of Taíno and African origins from DivEdCo's early texts resurfaced in the late 1960s, in an apparent attempt to present Puerto Rico as a racially integrated and harmonious society during a time when racial tensions in the United States were at their peak. The images of families were complemented by narratives populated by characters named José and María, like the parents of Jesús, adding yet another originary spin. The rural family was a utopian icon, an idealized moral standard: within the domestic space, a woman serving or making coffee was almost obligatory (see Illustration #3).

This gesture was a ritual, part of the iconologic inventory: the toasting, straining, or serving of coffee. This scene was repeated in many DivEdCo products, and would remain even in a 1976 Libro para el Pueblo. At the center of this iconology was the jíbaro, whose image would become classicized. Films and book illustrations made up an iconologic work that would travel through time to create a visual memory of the nation. For example, Muñoz Marín's Popular Democratic Party's logo is still the *pava* (the jíbaro's straw hat), more than sixty years after its founding. Craft fairs teem with colorful silk-screens of rural houses, and Puerto Ricans in New York have built *casitas* — replicas of Puerto Rican rural houses — on abandoned lots as community gathering places, bearing witness to the power of these images.

Contradictions

In the ELA's institutions, the appeal of populism to a range of social groups simultaneously brought together technocrats and literati as *pueblo,* an enormous fictive family:

> "Populism," as a particular inflection of popular interpellations, can never constitute the articulating principle of a political discourse — even when it constitutes a feature present in it. It is precisely this abstract character of "populism" which permits its presence in the ideology of the most varied classes.[70]

Thus, cultural production that can be called populist may contain, in words and images, multiple contradictions.

By the 1960s, the convergences that Muñoz Marín's populist discourse brought together began to collapse. As people left rural communities for the anonymity of urban life and the allure of material prosperity, DivEdCo tried to keep alive the dream of an idealized citizenry. The identification of the jíbaro, defined by Puerto Rico's mountainous landscape, with the essence of Puerto Ricanness excluded progressively more people, and in the quest for "progress" the term came to be associated as much with backwardness and ignorance as with the values DivEdCo sought to promote.

Locally recruited paid organizers, critically important in DivEdCo's rural educational work, were never portrayed in its cultural production; all their work remained backstage. In DivEdCo's imagery, it was as if communities organized themselves spontaneously, without government intervention. In reality, the DivEdCo organizers brought residents together to view movies, discuss local problems, and start self-help projects. In exchange for the residents' "sweat equity," the organizers mobilized tech-

ILLUSTRATION 3   *Mujer cuela café (Woman making coffee)*

nical support, tools, and materials from government agencies. Though DivEdCo used nonprofessional actors in its films and trained new graphic artists and filmmakers in its San Juan workshop, the agency never fully made the transition to being of the community, as its title suggested. The ideal of "spontaneous organization" of communities may reflect a hope that rural people might not wait for the government to send an organizer to their community, as much as a desire to avoid accusations of "manipulating" the supposedly ignorant jíbaros. It was important, from Muñoz Marín's perspective, to show "the people" taking charge of their lives; showing the role of government employees in that process would weaken this idea. DivEdCo remained an outside influence, albeit a sympathetic and culturally congruent one.

The project's initial contradictions between the rural ideal and modernization grew into impenetrable, fixed limitations. Agrarian utopias had to yield to modernization, and the emphasis on the spirituality of manual labor was more and more illusory as industrialization replaced agricultural activity throughout the island. The stories of returning to the land and developing community life had, as their backdrop, massive emigration. Similarly, DivEdCo's democratic pedagogy existed alongside the *Ley de la Mordaza* (Gag Law), a colonial counterpart to the McCarthyite repression in the United States, which criminalized support for independence in the wake of the Puerto Rican Nationalist Party's 1950 uprising and 1954 attack on the U.S. Congress.[71]

Another important contradiction in DivEdCo's work, and the hardest to resolve, was between gender and citizenship. The democratic discourse proclaimed equality among men and women as citizens, yet DivEdCo's products praised motherhood as women's fundamental role, and all the while the state was aggressively promoting the massive sterilization of women.[72] Similar contradictions occurred in other countries. José Vasconcelos, a Mexican minister of education and one of the great intellectual pedagogues of Latin America, called artist Diego Rivera from exile to paint murals on public buildings, complementing Vasconcelos' messianic national pedagogy that sought to bring "progress" to Mexico after the chaos of the 1910 Revolution. Rivera turned Vasconcelos' ideology of *la raza cósmica* (the all-encompassing race) into striking public images.[73] But outside the ideological canon of Mexicanness lay the work of Rivera's companion, Frida Kahlo, whose images of fragmented bodies, bleeding nakedness, and miscarriages subverted the nationalist discourse; to invoke or include wounds undermined the "unitary" utopian discourse of the nation/*patria.*

Barbara Melosh argues that New Deal art in the United States embodied a strategy of containment of feminism, creating a gendered iconologic system of concessions and limitations. Among the fundamental icons of New Deal art, Melosh identifies "the comradely ideal" among heterosexual couples as a trope for democratic citizenship. Women's strong role in the pioneer family, seen as the basis of agrarian democracy, was recognized, but still seen as supporting "the manly worker."[74]

These two pedagogical projects occurred at times of profound change. As U.S. and Mexican societies made the transition from mostly rural to mostly urban, Vasconcelos' educational program and New Deal public art revealed the need to define the roles of the new citizens, especially marginalized subjects. Whether to avoid any depiction of confrontation between Whites and Natives, to create a comradely ideal, or to subsume the native in a cosmic race, these great projects sought, with their immense faith in education, to create new citizens for the new epoch that was dawning.

As the ELA was established, the Puerto Rican state organized roles, as it organized knowledge, in a moment of national redefinition. It is no coincidence that Muñoz Marín's government sought, with its new political autonomy, to establish the rituals of nationhood and harmoniously blend modernity with tradition. Most of DivEdCo's cultural products that focus on women and offer clear prescriptions as to the role of female citizens appeared after the foundation of the ELA in 1952. However, different discourses were at work that disrupted the space assigned to female subjects. On the one hand, women's traditional roles were reaffirmed, while on the other their participation in democratic community work was called for to help define and solve collective problems. For example, the documentary film *Qué Opina la Mujer?* (What Do Women Think?) showed University of Puerto Rico professor Margot Arce in her home, speaking of herself first and foremost as a mother.[75] Meanwhile, *Modesta* is famous for its assertion of women's rights within the domestic sphere, and an illustration in the Libro para el Pueblo entitled *El Hombre de la Sonrisa Triste* (The Man With the Sad Smile) shows a woman speaking in the "democratic circle."[76] Marqués' *La Mujer y sus Derechos* (Woman and Her Rights) was an explicit treatment of this issue.[77]

Francine Masiello argues that roles are reaffirmed or restructured according to the needs of the state. In the order of discourse, the family is a microcosm of the state and the foundation and stability of the nation. She states that, in the Argentine foundational project, maternity and domesticity played a significant role in the national program; the family was the arena where citizens were trained.[78] In Puerto Rico, a third element was added to the family and the prescribed roles for female citizens: the insistence on developing communal ties and democratic participation for all citizens. Redundant though it might seem, the inclusive character of Puerto Rican democracy was shown extending even into the domestic or private sphere.

One of the discourses that seemed at times to complement the state's project and at others to lead down more conservative paths is seen in DivEdCo's editorial leadership. The state needed to create the idea of a new Puerto Rican woman citizen, and the DivEdCo intellectuals, especially Marqués, took on the task of outlining this archetype for the modern state. Throughout the 1950s, several conflicting dimensions or levels can be identified in the recodification or resignification of the Puerto Rican woman citizen's national role in DivEdCo's educational program. At the macro level, the massive sterilization and birth control campaign defined women's bodies as a site for scientifically controlling the population problem, while DivEdCo simultaneously insisted that women and men become active participants in democracy. These two agendas stand in contrast to the desire expressed in Marqués' and other writers' ideological convictions to dominate the psychology and treatment of their female characters.[79] These conflicting agendas led to a destabilization, a fissure, a rupture in the discourse on what Puerto Rican woman citizens' democratic participation ought to be.

As Agnes Lugo Ortiz has noted, it is in the regulation of the female citizen that the programs of the state and the writers of Marqués' generation fit seamlessly together. Her reading of Marqués' discourse starkly illuminates his role as intellectual leader of his generation and head of DivEdCo's editorial section:

> To discipline the female body — to rationalize its procreative potential, surgically penetrate it to cancel its reproductive capacities — was one of the touchstones of Puerto Rican social modernity. No modernity, whether social or literary, was conceived without the regulation of women.[80]

In his 1959 essay, *El Cuento Puertorriqueño en la Promoción del Cuarenta* (The Puerto Rican Short Story in the Generation of the Forties), Marqués argued that his colleagues of the *generación del cuarenta* had

> lived through precisely the initial upsurge of Anglo-Saxon matriarchy in Puerto Rico and, plausibly, some of them have not been able to accept, as docilely as their North American counterparts, the role of mere breadwinners which the matriarch has assigned them within this cultural pattern which is now common to both societies.[81]

In his most famous essay, *El Puertorriqueño Dócil* (The Docile Puerto Rican), Marqués advocated recovering machismo:

> The young writers seem to take ferocious vengeance on matriarchy — a foreign pattern recently imported to their culture — often portraying women in the most adverse light they can bear, as characters. Apparently, they — the writers — are the only ones in Puerto Rican society who have reacted with aggressiveness and rebelliousness against the disappearance of the last cultural bastion from which the col-

lective docility could, in part, be combated: machismo, the Creole version of the fusion and adaptation of two secular concepts, the Spanish *honra* [honor], and the Roman *pater familiae*.[82]

DivEdCo's cultural nationalism was a gendered discourse that created static national symbols, tropes of femininity, and a masculinized heritage and memory. A body of literature was created specifically to regulate women's role as citizens. The images went from the simple obligatory scene of the woman serving coffee to her role in religion, hygiene, and marriage.

Perhaps the icons that best represent the internal struggle within DivEdCo's pedagogy were the house and the democratic circle. From these recurring images, we can read the outlines of women's space. At first glance DivEdCo might seem to be presenting a homogeneous archetype of female citizenship, but a space was opened between the house and the democratic circle in which the recodification of women's roles was less than clear. Although the state's and the writers' discourses agreed on the need to control women in order to achieve modernization, another subdiscourse destabilized this insistence on control. DivEdCo's pedagogy, by virtue of its charter, emphasized the importance of all citizens' participation in the construction of Puerto Rican democracy. In the web of limitations generated by state projects and intellectual discourse, DivEdCo's program called for the inclusion — albeit limited — of women as citizens. The democratic ideal of the community meeting, the original batey, and, in principle, even the urban plaza and public policy debates required ignoring the marked female body that limited women's entry and circulation in public spheres.

The 1955 film *Modesta* is perhaps the DivEdCo product that presented the greatest breadth of options for women. *Modesta* employed nonprofessional actors from the town of Guaynabo's rural Barrio Sonadora, and won the first prize among short films at the 1956 Venice Film Festival. Festival audiences marveled that this film was an official, state-sponsored production.[83] The movie presents the story of Modesta, who defends herself with a piece of wood against her husband's abuse, and gathers together other women in her community with similar problems to demand their rights. The iconic democratic community meeting changed; now it was women coming together to solve "women's and family" problems, which were also community problems. Modesta, visibly pregnant, becomes the president of the "League of Liberated Women" and asks her daughter to write down the new rights they demand. Modesta proclaims that the *raja de leña* (piece of firewood) with which she defended herself from her husband would be the group's symbol, and announces the following resolution: "Now that we have taken our first step towards our emancipation, we must become vigilant to defend our rights. Therefore, we must join efforts for this to be so."[84]

The decision to make the film originated with DivEdCo field organizer's request. Meléndez Centeno, recounting a 1993 interview with Luis Maisonet, one of DivEdCo's film directors, explains:

> The film Modesta came out of a DivEdCo meeting in which an organizer brought up the subject of machismo. Maisonet told of how, during a community meeting in a rural barrio, a woman was told to shut up by a male peasant, as she was trying to explain her ideas. This required the group organizer's intervention, who brought the incident to the attention of the DivEdCo leadership. This was how the problem

of male dominance came to be one of the problems DivEdCo dealt with, because it was seen as an obstacle to modernizing Puerto Rico, and would therefore be a subject continuously discussed at Division meetings.[85]

In an opening characteristic of DivEdCo films, *Modesta* begins with a narrator evoking the oral tradition, *Había una vez . . .* (Once upon a time . . .) that was one of the recurrent constructions in DivEdCo narratives: time out of time, an imagined country where what was presented no longer took place because democratic progress had been achieved. It was a way of marking a new beginning, in which anything that did not contribute to the recent modernity was forgotten.

These DivEdCo films debated concurrent discourses on the position of women in the new ELA, a discourse of comradely democratic equality next to another expressing longing for patriarchal stability. DivEdCo's writers' treatment of the subject of women in their educational books was similar to that in the films. In one of DivEdCo's basic narratives, promoted by the editorial section, women were portrayed as needing to be in the home, guarding the family's harmony, the essence of Puerto Ricanness. A number of screenplays that were not produced are populated by modern consumer-minded women who destroy family unity. DivEdCo's cultural production would not show many women doing paid work; most female characters appeared doing domestic activities such as housework, sewing, and childrearing. However, the tension produced by the concurrent discourses on the rural house and participation in the democratic circle can be felt in all cultural products. DivEdCo's charter democratic message contended not only with the discourse of its writers, but also with the technocratic discourse of the state that employed them.

Final words: *La Brega*

In all the marvelous plasticity of the term *la brega*, probably the most complex meaning is the one which manifests a special cultural and political affinity for negotiation. That *bregar* has to do with action within the bounds of a restricted freedom, a framework not chosen by the subject, rather than with the transgressive will to revolution. La brega always expresses a necessity, a position of the speaker, or the desire to accomplish a dream.[86]

It was the continuous negotiation, the brega, that characterized the intellectuals' attempt to inhabit a state-provided space. They negotiated their position as employees, who were simultaneously artists and writers, within the process of rapid modernization. They chose to assure their own agency in pedagogical-cultural decisions without ruling out the creation and promotion of alternative forums of criticism. They were initially able to find a space in the common areas created by populist discourse, but their negotiations began to stall as DivEdCo's very nature did not allow it to respond to the period's deepest socioeconomic transformations. DivEdCo was largely dismantled by the pro-statehood administration that took power in 1969, following twenty-eight years (1941–1969, going back to the presidentially appointed governors) of popular hegemony. It endured four more changes in administration before it was finally dissolved in the 1990s, but its cultural production had ended well before Marqués' forced resignation in 1969.

Could the state sponsor a project to develop democratic communities? How could cultural politics be enacted to promote inclusiveness and autonomy? DivEdCo's production, despite the fact that these intellectuals were salaried government employees and that the material had to be relevant to its audiences, signals a more inclusive pedagogy. Traveling from their offices in San Juan to the rural areas, the intellectuals tried to create an art for the people. At the outset, Irene Delano had sponsored the open workshop that, according to Tufiño, allowed Puerto Rican silk-screening to reach such a high level. On the other hand, the film and editorial sections were less open; they could have been more organic, like true workshops. The Division of Community Education, then, never became of the community. Beyond the community organizer, a state employee, and the lessons prepared in the city, rural residents were not invited to construct a pedagogy of their own.

How could intellectuals' participation in state projects be remodeled? The open workshop, the transformation of writers and artists into cultural workers, in the Freirean sense, could constitute the basis of a new project. Puerto Rican intellectuals, men and women, linked to a network of grassroots community organizations, might respond to popular cultural needs from such a workshop. These intellectuals might regularly visit or live in urban and rural communities to develop artistic talent and collaborate with community members in an organic way, as part of rather than for the community. This involvement does not necessarily imply state sponsorship of culture, and certainly not in the service of the development agenda that came to dominate ELA public policy. However, an important state role in cultural promotion, especially in these times of globalization and with the growing prominence of market-based forces in defining Puerto Ricanness, could serve as a counterbalance to the private sector's cultural influence.

The democratic lessons DivEdCo tried to promote in its day-to-day operations, and its attempt to create an autochthonous cultural-pedagogical production, remain viable starting points. For Néstor García Canclini,

> A good cultural policy is not one which merely takes responsibility for organizing cultural development for the utilitarian needs of the masses — an indispensable condition for its being democratic — but which includes moments of play and experimentation, and promotes the conceptual and creative quests through which each society renews itself.[87]

DivEdCo forces us to read culture at its intersections. It leads us to read beyond the letter of the law, to place ourselves in the fissures of the state apparatus. Its cultural-pedagogical project shows, in its attempt to conserve as well as to renew, the structure of populist projects. Its simultaneous proposals help us to understand the educational and cultural institutions — and popular understandings about education and culture, which are the legacies of muñocismo in Puerto Rico. García Canclini argues that "documenting cultural policies remains an indispensable task if one wants to speak of them, or simply to avoid our peoples' loss of memory."[88] This is doubly important, given Puerto Rico's colonial situation.

DivEdCo illuminates the contradictions of the ELA, as well as its possibilities. It frames the transforming and reforming — but not transgressive — dream of Muñoz Marín's cultural politics, and leads us to take notice of the reconstruction of this discourse in the cultural policies of the current, neo-muñocista administration of Governor Sila María Calderón, which has devoted a similar amount of material and ideological resources — mobilizing celebrities and artists — to dozens of low-income areas designated as *comunidades especiales* (special communities). DivEdCo remains as an example of a state's attempt to blend art, education, and popular culture to promote its own community-based pedagogy, with all its contradictions.

The tension between the power of linking intellectual and grassroots activity, on the one hand, and the political and economic limitations that the Puerto Rican state faced during the 1950s and 1960s on the other, makes for an interesting study of individuals and organizations trying to create new solutions to both economic and cultural problems. The experience of the Puerto Rican government in these years, however, suggests possible models for local government, or even nongovernmental or quasigovernmental institutions such as universities, to bring intellectuals together with grassroots leadership as a way of generating new solutions to problems that affect their constituencies.

For instance, if urban social service programs or the community outreach efforts of institutions like universities were linked to a grassroots structure that allowed for community-based decisionmaking, the DivEdCo experience suggests that local results could be quite impressive, even within the context of poverty and urban decay. The critical factor would be the willingness to mobilize rather than to service, to empower and support community leadership in its concerns, rather than attempting to recruit local support for programs generated and designed in offices.

Although U.S. government sponsorship of cultural production has come under heavy attack from conservatives in recent years, other very different dynamics have been taking place in the part of Latin America under direct U.S. control. In Puerto Rico, as in much of Latin America, cultural nationalism has been shaped and used by governments throughout the twentieth century. These projects have had a profound, if unfathomable effect on the development of Puerto Rican popular culture, and on Puerto Ricans' self-recognition as a distinct people.

Notes

1. Magali García Ramis, *Felices Días, Tío Sergio* (San Juan: Editorial Antillana, 1986), 2.
2. Following the U.S. invasion during the Spanish-American war of 1898, Puerto Rico was governed as a colony. Like the Spanish colonial regime, the U.S. president appointed all governors until Congress authorized a popular election in 1948. In the Insular Cases of 1899-1901, the U.S. Supreme Court allowed Puerto Rico to be classified as an "unincorporated territory," giving Congress the power to make any changes in the island's status and to treat it differently from any of the states or "incorporated" territories destined to be states, as Congress deemed appropriate. All subsequent changes to Puerto Rico's status, including the Foraker Act of 1900, the Jones Act of 1917, the Elected Governor Act of 1948, and Public Law 600, which authorized Puerto Rico to draft a constitution (finally ratified in 1952, with the exception of one section of the Bill of Rights guaranteeing free public education, which Congress had found objectionable), have taken place within this constitutional framework.
3. García Ramis, *Felices Días*, 2.
4. Edward Said, *Beginnings: Intention and Method* (New York: Columbia University Press, 1975), 5.
5. Arlene Dávila, *Sponsored Identities: Cultural Politics in Puerto Rico* (Philadelphia: Temple University Press, 1997).

6. Benedict Anderson, *Imagined Communities: Reflections on the Origins and Spread of Nationalism* (New York: Verso, 1993).

7. Ley 372 (Legislature of Puerto Rico, 1949).

8. Ley 372.

9. Many DivEdCo films have been lost or are being restored.

10. Blanca I. Silvestrini and María Dolores Luque de Sánchez Silvestrini, *Historia de Puerto Rico: Trayectoria de un Pueblo* (San Juan: Editorial Cultural Puertorriqueña, 1987).

11. The idea of intellectuals as nation-builders is common currency in the field of Latin American studies. Sarmiento in Argentina, Vasconcelos in Mexico, José Martí in Cuba, Rómulo Gallegos in Venezuela, José Enrique Rodó in Uruguay, and, more recently, Mario Vargas Llosa's presidential candidacy in Peru, are among the more famous examples of a Latin American tradition of leading intellectuals' active involvement in nation-building projects, attempting to define and unify the nation around a cultural-pedagogical discourse.

12. Jack Delano, *Photographic Memories* (Washington, DC: Smithsonian Institution Press, 1997), 113.

13. Edwin Rosskam, "Program of People's Education and Information" (San Juan: Comisión de Parques y Recreos. División de Cinema y Gráfica, c. 1946). Found in the *Archivo General de Puerto Rico*.

14. Rosskam, "Program of People's Education," 5–6.

15. Rosskam, "Program of People's Education," 3.

16. Rosskam, "Program of People's Education," 8.

17. The physical appearance does not refer exclusively to racial phenotype — many rural Puerto Ricans are phenotypically White — but to the *gestalt* of visible signs, including dress, demeanor, and race, which would mark North American intellectuals as outsiders to rural Puerto Rican communities and create barriers to communication.

18. Edwin Rosskam, "Report on the Operation of the Division of Motion Pictures and Graphic of the Commission of Parks and Recreation since December, 1946–July, 1947" (San Juan: Comisión de Parques y Recreos. División de Cinema y Gráfica, 1947), 8. Found in the *Archivo General de Puerto Rico*.

19. Piñero was Tugwell's presidentially appointed successor and Muñoz Marín's immediate predecessor, the island's first Puerto Rican-born governor, and the last to be directly appointed by metropolitan authorities.

20. Edwin Rosskam, letter to Jesús T. Piñero, October 5, 1948 (Unpublished letter, found in the *Archivo General de Puerto Rico*).

21. Luis Muñoz Marín, letter to Fred Wale, November 23, 1948 (Unpublished letter, found at the *Archivo Luis Muñoz Marín*).

22. Lorenzo Homar, personal communication with Erich González Arocho, April 23, 1983.

23. Although Renato Rosaldo's essay "Cultural Citizenship, Inequality, and Multiculturalism" focuses on the situation of Latinos in the United States, this is precisely the type of citizenship that Muñoz Marín sought to create with the legislation that created DivEdCo. Rosaldo and the interdisciplinary Latino Cultural Studies Group recognize how paradoxical the term *cultural citizenship* can be, but they state: "Culture interprets and constructs citizenship, just as the activity of being citizens, in the broad sense of claiming membership in the society, affects how we view ourselves, even in communities that have been branded second-class or 'illegal.'" Thus, we must ask, What role does culture play in citizenry movements? William Flores and Rina Benmayor, eds., *Latino Cultural Citizenship: Claiming Identity, Space, and Rights* (Boston: Beacon Press, 1997), 6.

24. Arcadio Díaz Quiñones, "Los Desastres de la Guerra: Para Leer a René Marqués," in *El Almuerzo en la Hierba (Lloréns, Palés Matos, René Marqués)* (Río Piedras: Ediciones Huracán, 1982), 155.

25. René Marqués, *El Puertorriqueño Dócil y Otros Ensayos, 1953–1971* (Río Piedras: Editorial Antillana, 1977), 147.

26. Díaz Quiñones, "Los Desastres de la Guerra," 164.

27. The phrase belongs to the Uruguayan intellectual Ángel Rama and is the title of his book, *La Ciudad Letrada* (Hanover, NH: Ediciones del Norte, 1984), in which he analyzed the tradition of prominent Latin American intellectuals struggling to give order and definition to the nations they seek to unify and lead, dating back to the sixteenth-century Spanish conquest. In contrast to the U.S. tradition in which intellectuals remain mostly on the sidelines, perhaps as trusted advisors to political leaders, many of the principal Latin American thinkers have assumed positions of political leadership, including head of state.

28. División de Educación de la Comunidad, *De Cómo Llegaron a Puerto Rico la Caña, el Café y Muchas Otras Cosas, Libros Para El Pueblo* (San Juan: Departamento de Instrucción Pública, 1950), 1.

29. Díaz Quiñones, "Los Desastres de la Guerra," 154.

30. Rafael Tufiño, interview by Cati Marsh Kennerley, January 24, 1999.

31. René Marqués, "Writing for a Community Education Programme," *UNESCO: Reports and Papers on Mass Communication*, 24 (1957), 6–8.

32. The surviving copies of minutes of Program Committee meetings are among René Marqués' personal papers, property of the Fundación René Marqués. I was able to review and photocopy them in January 1999. I am grateful to Professor José Lacomba of the Fundación René Marqués and researcher Erich González Arocho for facilitating access to these documents. "Minutas del Comité de Programa. División de Educación de la Comunidad," May 14, June 4, August 6 and 17, September 2, 7, 10, 14, and 27, 1954, October 15 and 18, November 10, and December 28, 1954, January 31, May 20, and August 17, 1955.

33. "Minutas Del Comité De Programa."

34. Antonio Maldonado, interview by Cati Marsh Kennerley, November 28, 1998. Rafael Tufiño, interview by Cati Marsh Kennerley, January 24, 1999.

35. René Marqués, letter to Fred Wale, December 18, 1957 (Unpublished letter, found in René Marqués' personal archive).

36. René Marqués, memorandum to Fred Wale, April 24, 1958 (Unpublished memorandum, found in René Marqués' personal archive).

37. Vicente Geigel Polanco, quoted in Juan Gelpí, *Literatura y Paternalismo en Puerto Rico* (Río Piedras: Editorial de la Universidad de Puerto Rico, 1993), 72.

38. Rosskam, "Report on the Operation of the Division of Motion Pictures."

39. Marimar Benítez, "La Gráfica de Irene Delano," in *Homenaje a Irene Delano*, ed. Ricardo Alegría (San Juan: Casa del Libro, 1988).

40. DivEdCo's films are being archived and restored by the *Archivo de Imágenes en Movimiento*, part of the *Archivo General de Puerto Rico*, San Juan. Videotape and DVD copies of DivEdCo films are available for sale to the public. "La Montaña," directed by Jack Delano (San Juan: DivEdCo, 1946), film.

41. Edwin Rosskam, *Una Gota de Agua*, directed by Jack Delano (San Juan: DivEdCo, 1947), film.

42. Edwin Rosskam, *La Caña*, directed by Jack Delano (San Juan: DivEdCo, 1947), film.

43. Jack Delano, authorless interview in *Investigación en Acción*, 1, No. 1 (1992–1993), 20–26.

44. Joaquín García, *Breve Historia del Cine Puertorriqueño* (San Juan: Editorial Ateneo, 1984).

45. Edwin Rosskam, "*Desde las Nubes*," directed by Jack Delano (San Juan: DivEdCo, 1949), film.

46. Edwin Rosskam, *La Voz del Pueblo*, directed by Jack Delano (San Juan: DivEdCo, 1949), film.

47. Jack Delano, *Las Manos del Hombre*, directed by Jack Delano (San Juan: DivEdCo, 1950), film.

48. Edwin Rosskam, *Los Peloteros*, directed by Jack Delano (San Juan: DivEdCo, 1951), film.

49. División de Educación de la Comunidad, *Almanaque del Pueblo 1949* (San Juan: Departamento de Instrucción Pública). Copies of most DivEdCo publications are available for viewing only at the Puerto Rican Collection of the University of Puerto Rico's José M. Lázaro Library in Río Piedras.

50. División de Educación de la Comunidad, "La Labor de la División de Educación de la Comunidad del Departamento de Instrucción Pública desde el 1ero de julio de 1949 hasta el 15 de octubre de 1951" (San Juan: Departamento de Instrucción Pública, 1951).
51. División de Educación de la Comunidad, *Almanaque del Pueblo 1949*, 51.
52. División de Educación de la Comunidad, *Almanaque del Pueblo 1949*, 51.
53. Jack Delano, authorless interview in *Investigación en Acción*, 1, No. 1 (1992–1993).
54. Edwin Rosskam, *Desde las Nubes*.
55. *Belén (La del traje blanco)*, directed by Michael Alexis (San Juan: DivEdCo, 1961), film.
56. Benjamin Doniger, *Modesta (o la huelga de las mujeres)*, directed by Benjamin Doniger (DivEdCo, San Juan: 1955), film.
57. René Marqués, *Ignacio*, directed by Angel F. Rivera (San Juan: DivEdCo, 1956), film.
58. División de Educación de la Comunidad, "Los Derechos del Hombre," in *Libros Para el Pueblo*, ed. René Marqués (San Juan: Departamento de Instrucción Pública, 1957).
59. Carmen Isales, interview by Cati Marsh Kennerley, August 14, 1998.
60. División de Educación de la Comunidad, *De Cómo Llegaron a Puerto Rico la Caña, el Café y Muchas Otras Cosas*, 16.
61. Edwin Rosskam, *Pedacito de Tierra*, directed by Benjamin Doniger (San Juan: DivEdCo, 1953), film.
62. División de Educación de la Comunidad, *La Familia*, in *Libros Para El Pueblo*, ed. René Marqués (San Juan: Departamento de Instrucción Pública, 1967), 3.
63. División de Educación de la Comunidad, *La Familia*, 17.
64. Examples of this include *El Niño y su Mundo* (The Child and His World) and *Juventud* (Youth), together with the film *Cuando los Padres Olvidan* (When Parents Forget) and the unit on women's rights, which included the books *La Mujer y sus Derechos* (Woman and Her Rights) and *Cuatro Cuentos de Mujeres* (Four Women's Stories), together with the films *Modesta* and *¿Qué Opina la Mujer?* (What Do Women Think?).
65. Oscar Torres, *Nenén de la Ruta Mora*, directed by Oscar Torres (San Juan: DivEdCo, 1955), film.
66. Jack Delano, authorless interview in *Investigación en Acción*, 1, No. 1 (1992–1993).
67. During DivEdCo's first decade of operation, 1940–1950, 230,000 Puerto Ricans emigrated to the United States; between 1950 and 1960, half a million people left the island.
68. División de Educación de la Comunidad, *Emigración, Libros Para El Pueblo*, ed. René Marqués (San Juan: Departamento de Instrucción Pública, 1966), 32.
69. División de Educación de la Comunidad, *Emigración*, 31–35.
70. Ernesto Laclau, *Politics and Ideology in Marxist Theory* (London: Humanities Press, 1977), 195.
71. Ivonne Acosta, *La Mordaza: Puerto Rico 1948–1957* (Río Piedras: Editorial Edil, 1989).
72. Ana María García, *La Operación*, directed by Ana María García (San Juan: DivEdCo, 1982), film. This highly controversial documentary is hard to find, but is available at the *Archivo de Imágenes en Movimiento*.
73. Jean Franco, *Plotting Women: Gender and Representation in Mexico* (New York: Columbia University Press, 1989).
74. Barbara Melosh, *Engendering Culture: Manhood and Womanhood in New Deal Public Art and Theater* (Washington: Smithsonian Institution Press, 1991), 4.
75. René Marqués, *¿Qué Opina la Mujer?*, directed by Oscar Torres (San Juan: DivEdCo, 1957), film.
76. División de Educación de la Comunidad, *El Hombre de la Sonrisa Triste, Libros Para El Pueblo*, ed. René Marqués (San Juan: Departamento de Instrucción Pública, 1963), 23.
77. División de Educación de la Comunidad, *La Mujer y sus Derechos, Libros Para El Pueblo*, ed. René Marqués *(San Juan: Departamento de Instrucción Pública, 1957)*.
78. Francine Masiello, *Entre Civilización y Barbarie: Mujeres, Nación y Cultura Literaria en la Argentina Moderna* (Rosaria, Argentina: Beatriz Viterbo Editora, 1997).
79. René Marqués, *El Puertorriqueño Dócil*.

80. Agnes Lugo-Ortiz, "Sobre el Tráfico Simbólico de Mujeres: Homosocialidad, Identidad Nacional y Modernidad Literaria en Puerto Rico (apuntes para una relectura de *El Puertorriqueño Dócil* de René Marqués)," *Revista de Crítica Literaria Latinoamericana,* 45 (1997), 269.
81. Marqués, *El Puertorriqueño Dócil,* 93–94.
82. Marqués, *El Puertorriqueño Dócil,* 75.
83. García, *Breve Historia del Cine Puertorriqueño.*
84. Benjamin Doniger, *Modesta (o la huelga de las mujeres).*
85. Rosario del Pilar Meléndez Centeno, "Discurso Institucional Feminista en Tres Películas de División de Educación de la Comunidad: *Modesta, Geña la de blas* y *¿Qué opina la mujer?*" (Unpublished dissertation, University of Puerto Rico, 1993), 60.
86. Arcadio Díaz Quiñones, *El Arte de Bregar* (Río Piedras: Editorial Callejón, 2000), 81; translated by author.
87. Néstor García Canclini, "Políticas Culturales y Crisis de Desarrollo: Un Balance Latino-americano," in *Políticas Culturales en América Latina*, ed. Néstor García Canclini Mexico: Editorial Grijalbo.
88. García Canclini, "Políticas Culturals."

American Indian Geographies of Identity and Power: At the Crossroads of Indígena and Mestizaje

SANDY MARIE ANGLÁS GRANDE

> Until Indians resolve for themselves a comfortable modern identity that can be used to energize reservation institutions, radical changes will not be of much assistance. (Deloria & Lytle, 1984, p. 266)

> Our struggle at the moment is to continue to survive and work toward a time when we can replace the need for being preoccupied with survival with a more responsible and peaceful way of living within communities and with the ever-changing landscape that will ever be our only home. (Warrior, 1995, p. 126)

Broadly speaking, this article focuses on the intersection between dominant modes of critical pedagogy[1] and American Indian intellectualism.[2] At present, critical theories are often indiscriminately employed to explain the sociopolitical conditions of all marginalized peoples. As a result, many Indigenous scholars view the current liberatory project as simply the latest in a long line of political endeavors that fails to consider American Indians as a unique population.[3] Thus, while critical pedagogy may have propelled mainstream educational theory and practice along the path of social justice, I argue that it has muted and thus marginalized the distinctive concerns of American Indian intellectualism and education. As such, I argue further that the particular history of imperialism enacted upon Indigenous peoples requires a reevaluation of dominant views of democracy and social justice, and of the universal validity of such emancipatory projects — including critical pedagogy. It is not that critical pedagogy is irrelevant to Indigenous peoples, as they clearly experience oppression, but rather that the deep structures of the "pedagogy of oppression" fail to consider American Indians as a categorically different population, virtually incomparable to other minority groups. To assert this is not to advocate any kind of hierarchy of oppression but merely to call attention to the fundamental difference of what it means to be a sovereign and tribal people within the geopolitical confines of the United States.

Harvard Educational Review Vol. 70   No. 4   Winter 2000

Previous examinations of the potential for critical theory to inform Indigenous pedagogy (Grande, 1997, 2000) expose significant tensions in their deep theoretical structures. For instance, insofar as critical theorists retain "democracy" as the central struggle concept of liberation, they fail to recognize Indigenous peoples' historical battles to resist absorption into the "democratic imaginary"[4] and their contemporary struggles to retain tribal sovereignty. In fact, it could be argued that the forces of "democracy" have done more to imperil American Indian nations then they have to sustain them (e.g., the extension of democracy in the form of civil rights and citizenship has acted as a powerful if not lethal colonizing force when imposed on the intricate tribal, clan, and kinship systems of traditional Native communities).

Compounding the tensions between American Indian intellectualism and critical pedagogy is the fact that American Indian scholars have, by and large, resisted engagement with critical theory,[5] and concentrated instead on the production of historical monographs, ethnographic studies, tribally centered curricula, and site-based research. Such a focus stems from the fact that most American Indian scholars feel compelled to address the political urgencies of their own communities, against which engagement in abstract theory appears to be a luxury and privilege of the academic elite. While I recognize the need for practically based research, I argue that the ever-increasing global encroachment on American Indian lands, resources, cultures, and communities points to the equally urgent need to build political coalitions and formulate transcendent theories of liberation. Moreover, while individual tribal needs are in fact great, I believe that, unless the boundaries of coalition are expanded to include non-Indian communities, Indian nations will remain vulnerable to whims of the existing social order.

The combined effect of internal neglect and external resistance to critical pedagogy has pushed American Indian intellectualism to the margins of critical discourse. This reality raises a series of important questions that help form the basis of this discussion:

1. Insofar as critical theory remains disconnected from the work of American Indian scholars, how do its language and epistemic frames serve as homogenizing agents when interfaced with the conceptual and analytical categories persistent within American Indian educational history and intellectualism?
2. How has the resistance of American Indian intellectuals to critical theory contributed to the general lack of analyses on the impact of racism (and, for that matter, other "isms") within American Indian communities?
3. How have the marginalization of critical scholarship and the concomitant fascination with cultural/literary forms of American Indian writing contributed to the preoccupation with parochial questions of identity and authenticity? And, how have these obsessions about identity concealed the social-political realities facing American Indian communities?

While the above questions provide the foundation for a broad discussion of the intersection of critical theory and American Indian intellectualism, I submit that the main source of tension is embedded in their competing notions of identity — one rooted in Western definitions of the civil society and the other in the traditional structures of tribal society.

In terms of identity, critical theorists aim to explode the concretized categories of race, class, gender, and sexuality and to claim the intersections — the borderlands — as the space to create a new culture — *una cultura mestíza* — in which the only normative standard is hybridity and all subjects are constructed as inherently transgressive.[6] Though American Indian intellectuals support the notion of hybridity, they remain skeptical of the new mestíza as a possible continuation of the colonialist project to fuse Indians into the national model of the democratic citizen. There is, in other words, an undercurrent to the postcolonial lexicon of *mestizaje* that seems to undermine the formation of "a comfortable modern American Indian identity" (Deloria & Lytle, 1984, p. 266). More specifically, I argue that the contemporary pressures of ethnic fraud, corporate commodification, and culture loss render the critical notion of "transgressive" identity highly problematic for Indigenous peoples. As such, the primary argument is that critical efforts to promote mestizaje as the basis of a new cultural democracy does not fully consider Indigenous struggles to sustain the cultural and political integrity of American Indian communities.

That being said, it is important to note that American Indian critical studies are perceived by both Indigenous and non-Indigenous scholars as a "dangerous discourse" equally threatening to the fields of critical pedagogy and American Indian intellectualism.[7] After all, American Indian critical studies would compel "Whitestream" advocates of critical theory to ask how their knowledge and practices may have contributed and remained blind to the continued exploitation of Indigenous peoples. Specifically, it would require a deeper recognition that these are not postcolonial times, that "globalization" is simply the new metaphor for imperialism, and that current constructions of democracy continue to presume the eventual absorption of Indigenous peoples. For American Indian intellectuals, the infusion of critical studies would require a movement away from the safety of unified, essentialized, and idealized constructions of American Indianness toward more complicated readings of American Indian formations of power and identity, particularly those that take into account the existence of internal oppression. Specifically, it would compel American Indian intellectuals to confront the taboo subjects of racism, sexism, and homophobia within American Indian communities.

Ultimately, however, this article is not a call for American Indian scholars to simply join the conversation of critical theorists. Rather, it is an initiation of an Indigenous conversation that can, in turn, engage in dialectical contestation with the dominant modes of critical theory. In this way, I hope that the development of an Indigenous theory of liberation can itself be a politically transformative practice, one that works to transgress tribal divisions and move toward the development of transcendent theory of American Indian sovereignty and self-determination. With this in mind, my discussion of the central tension between critical pedagogy and American Indian intellectualism unfolds in four parts. Part one examines formations of identity that have emerged from the dominant modes of critical discourse, paying special attention to the notion of transgression, and the construction of mestizaje as a counter-discourse of subjectivity. Part two examines American Indian formations of identity and the external forces that work to threaten these formations, namely ethnic fraud, cultural encroachment, corporate commodification, and culture loss. Part three examines the intersection between American Indian identity and mestizaje, as well as other models of hybridity generated by American Indian and other scholars of color. The article concludes with a call for the development of a new Red Pedagogy,[8] or one that is historically grounded in American Indian intellectualism, politically centered in issues of sovereignty and tribal self-determination, and inspired by the religious and spiritual[9] traditions of American Indian peoples.

Part I. Identity, Subjectivity and Critical Theory: Mestizaje and the New Cultural Democracy

"Critical pedagogy is the term used to describe what emerges when critical theory encounters education" (Kincheloe & Steinberg, 1997, p. 24). Rather than offer prescriptions, critical pedagogy draws from the structural critique of critical theory, extending an analysis of school as a site of reproduction, resistance, and social transformation. It examines the ways that power and domination inform the processes and procedures of schooling and works to expose the sorting and selecting functions of the institution. As it has evolved into its current form(s), critical pedagogy has emerged as both a rhetoric and a social movement. Critical educators continue to advocate an increasingly sophisticated critique of the social, economic, and political barriers to social justice, as well as to crusade for the transformation of schools to reflect the imperatives of democracy.

Critical scholars have, over time, provided a sustained critique of the forces of power and domination and their relation to the pedagogical (Kincheloe & Steinberg, 1997). As defined here, "the pedagogical" refers to the production of identity or the way one learns to see oneself in relation to the world. Identity is thus situated as one of the core struggle concepts of critical pedagogy, where the formation of self serves as the basis for analyses of race, class, gender, and sexuality and their relationship to the questions of democracy, justice, and community.

By positioning identity in the foreground of their theories, critical scholars have fueled as many theories of identity as they have varieties of critical pedagogy. While there are differences between and among these formulations, critical constructions of identity are distinct from both liberal and conservative theories of identity. Such theories are viewed as problematic by critical scholars because of their use of "essentialist" or reductionistic analyses of difference (Kinchloe & Steinberg, 1997; McCarthy & Crichlow, 1993; McLaren, 1997). "Essentialist" analysis refers to the treatment of racial and social groups as if they were stable and homogeneous entities, or as if members of each group possessed "some innate and invariant set of characteristics setting them apart from each other and from 'Whites'" (McCarthy & Crichlow, 1993, p. xviii). Critical scholars argue that essentialism not only undertheorizes race but can also result in a gross misreading of the nature of difference, opening the door for the proliferation of deeply cynical theories of racial superiority, such as Richard Herrnstein and Charles Murray's *The Bell Curve* (1994). While conservatives typically invoke essentialist theories, critical scholars acknowledge that some forms of left-essentialism operate in the contemporary landscape to similarly divisive ends.[10]

In response to the undertheorizing of race by both the Left and the Right, critical theorists advocate a theory of difference that is firmly rooted in the "power-sensitive discourses of power, democracy, social justice and historical memory" (McLaren & Giroux, 1997, p. 17). In so doing, they replace the comparatively static notion of identity as a relatively fixed entity that one embodies with the more fluid concept of subjectivity — an entity that one actively and continually constructs. Subjectivity works to underscore the contingency of identity and the understanding that "individuals consist of a decentered flux of subject positions highly dependent on discourse, social structure, repetition, memory, and affective investment" (McLaren & Giroux, 1997, p. 25). In other words, one's "identity" is historically situated and socially constructed, rather than predetermined by biological or other prima facie indicators.

In addition to calling attention to the relational aspects of identity, the critical notion of subjectivity advances a more complex analysis of cultural and racial identity. It shifts race from a passive product of biological endowment to an active "product of human work" (Said, 1993, p. xix). Critical scholars argue that the rupture of previously rigid racial categories reveals contested spaces or borderlands where cultures collide, creating the space to explore new notions of identity in the resulting contradictions, nuances, and discontinuities they introduce into the terrain of racial identity. Thus, where essentialist scholars examine race, class, gender, and sexuality as discrete categories, critical scholars focus on the spaces of intersection between and among these categories.

The emergence of subjectivity as a socially constructed entity spawned a whole new language about identity. Border cultures, border-crossers, mestíza (Anzaldúa, 1987; Delgado Bernal, 1998); *Xicanisma* (Castillo, 1995); postcolonial hybridities, cyborg identities (Harraway, 1991); and mestizaje (Darder, Torres, & Gutierrez, 1997; McLaren & Sleeter, 1995; Valle & Torres, 1995) are just some of the emergent concepts formulated to explain and bring language to the experience of multiplicity, relationality, and transgression as they relate to identity. Moreover, critical scholars contend that the development of transgressive subjectivity not only works to resist essentialist constructions of identity but also acts to counter the hegemonic notion of Whiteness as the normative standard for all subjects. Such efforts represent the hope and possibility of critical pedagogy as they seek to construct a critical democracy that includes multiple cultures, languages, and voices. Critical pedagogy thus serves both to challenge the existing sociocultural and economic relations of exploitation and to strengthen collective work toward peace and social justice, thereby creating a more equitable democratic order and, by definition, more equitable educational institutions.

From Mestizaje to Mestíza back to Mestizaje

The critical notion of mestizaje (Darder, Torres, & Gutierrez, 1997; McLaren & Sleeter, 1995; Kinchloe & Steinberg, 1997; Valle & Torres, 1995) is arguably among the most widely embraced models of multisubjectivity. Historically speaking, the counterdiscourse of mestizaje is rooted in the Latin American subjectivity of the *mestízo* — literally, a person of mixed ancestry, especially of American Indian, European, and African backgrounds (Delgado Bernal, 1998). Mestizaje is the Latin American term for cultural ambiguity, representative of "the continent's unfinished business of cultural hybridization" (Valle & Torres, 1995, p. 141). With regard to this history, Latin American scholars Victor Valle and Rodolfo Torres write:

> In Latin America the genetic and cultural dialogue between the descendants of Eu-
> rope, Africa, Asia, and the hemisphere's indigenous populations has been expressed
> in discourses reflecting and responding to a host of concrete national circum-
> stances. In some cases, mestizaje has risen to the level of a truly critical counter-dis-
> course of revolutionary aspirations, while at other times it has been co-opted by the
> state. (p. 141)

Thus, it could be argued that the political project of mestizaje originated in Latin
America, where the cluster of Spanish, Indian, and Afro-Caribbean peoples were ostensibly "fused" through the violence of genocide into the national model of the
mestízo.

In the northern hemisphere, Chicana scholar Gloria Anzaldúa's seminal text *Borderlands, la Frontera: The New Mestíza* (1987) reinscribed the cultural terrain with the
language and embodiment of mestíza consciousness. Since the book's publication,
mestíza has come to embody a new feminist Chicana consciousness that "straddles
cultures, races, languages, nations, sexualities, and spiritualities" and the experience of
"living with ambivalence while balancing opposing powers" (Delgado Bernal, 1998,
p. 561). Anzaldúa (1987) states, "The new mestíza copes by developing a tolerance
for contradictions, a tolerance for ambiguity. She learns to be an Indian in Mexican
culture [and] to be Mexican from an Anglo point of view" (p. 79). From this base, a
variety of Chicana and other border feminisms have emerged, centered on the social
histories and epistemologies of women of color.

More recently, the intellectual left, particularly critical scholars, has incorporated
the spirit of the Chicana mestíza in its own search for a viable model of subjectivity. It
embraces the emergent discourse of mestizaje and its emphasis on the way in which
all cultures change in relation to one another as the postcolonial antidote to imperial-
ist notions of racial purity (di Leonardo, 1991). This radically inclusive construct
"willfully blurs political, racial, [and] cultural borders in order to better adapt to the
world as it is actually constructed" (Valle & Torres, 1995, p. 149) and embodies the
mestízo's demonstrated refusal to prefer one language, one national heritage, or one
culture at the expense of others. Leading critical scholar Peter McLaren (1997) sum-
marily articulates mestizaje as "the embodiment of a transcultural, transnational subject, a self-reflexive entity capable of rupturing the facile legitimization of 'authentic'
national identities through [the] articulation of a subject who is conjunctural, who is
a relational part of an ongoing negotiated connection to the larger society, and who is
interpolated by multiple subject positionings" (p. 12). In other words, mestizaje
crosses all imposed cultural, linguistic, and national borders, refusing all "natural" or
transcendent claims that "by definition attempt to escape from any type of historical
and normative grounding" (McLaren & Giroux, 1997, p. 117). Ultimately, the critical notion of mestizaje is itself multifunctional, for it signifies a strategic response to
the decline of the imperial West, facilitates the decentering of Whiteness, and undermines the myth of the democratic nation-state based on borders and exclusions (Valle
& Torres, 1995).

Insofar as the notion of mestizaje disrupts the discourse of jingoistic nationalism, it
is indeed crucial to the project of liberation. As McLaren notes, "Educators would do
well to consider Gloria Anzaldúa's (1987) project of creating mestizaje theories that
create new categories of identity for those left out or pushed out of existing ones"
(McLaren, 1997, p. 537). In so doing, however, "care must be taken not to equate

hybridity with equality" (McLaren, 1997, p. 46).[11] As Coco Fusco notes, "The post-colonial celebration of hybridity has (too often) been interpreted as the sign that no further concern about the politics of representation and cultural exchange is needed. With ease, we lapse back into the integrationist rhetoric of the 1960's" (Fusco, 1995, p. 46). These words caution us not to lose sight — in the wake of transgressing borders and building postnational coalitions — of the unique challenges presented to particular groups in their distinct struggles for social justice. In taking this admonition seriously, the following discussion moves into an examination of American Indian tribal identity and some of the current pressures facing Indian communities that, I argue, render the notion of mestizaje somewhat problematic. The question remains whether the construction of a transgressive subjectivity — mestizaje — can be reconciled with the pressures of identity appropriation, cultural commodification, culture loss, and, perhaps more importantly, with Indigenous imperatives of self-determination and sovereignty.

Part II. The Formation of Indígena:
American Indian Geographies of Power and Identity

Whitestream America has never really understood what it means to be Indian and even less about what it means to be tribal. Such ignorance has deep historical roots and wide political implications of not understanding what it means to be tribal, since the U.S. government determined long ago that to be "tribal" runs deeply counter to the notion of democracy and the proliferation of (individual) civil rights. Throughout the centuries, uncompromising belief in this tenet of democratic order provided the ideological foundation for numerous expurgatory campaigns against Indigenous peoples. The Civilization Act of 1819, the Indian Removal Act of 1830, the Dawes Allotment Act of 1886, the Indian Citizenship Act of 1924, the Indian Reorganization Act of 1934, and the Indian Civil Rights Act of 1968 are just a few of the legal mechanisms imposed to "further democracy" and concomitantly erode traditional tribal structures.

Although five centuries of continuous contact may have extinguished the traditional societies of the precontact era, modern American Indian communities still resemble traditional societies enough that, "given a choice between Indian society and non-Indian society, most Indians feel comfortable with their own institutions, lands and traditions" (Deloria & Lytle, 1983, p. xii). Despite such significant differences, tribal America remains curiously difficult to articulate. Vine Deloria Jr., one of the preeminent American Indian scholars, has written over eighteen books and one hundred articles defining the political, spiritual, cultural, and intellectual dimensions of American Indian life. His expansive body of work serves as testimony to the difficulty and complexity of defining tribal life and suggests the impossibility of encompassing the multiple dimensions of Indianness in a single article. To do so would not only minimize Deloria's and other scholars' work, but also presume that centuries of ancestral knowledge could be transcribed into a single literary form. Similarly, to tease out, list, name, and assign primacy to a particular subset of defining characteristics of Indianness would not only serve to objectify and oversimplify the diversity of Native cultures, but would also force what is fundamentally traditional, spatial, and interconnected into the modern, temporal, and epistemic frames of Western knowledge. Accordingly, the following is merely a sample of existing legal, prima facie indicators of what it means to be American Indian in U.S. society, rather than some mythic view of a unified Indigenous culture or an objectified view of Indian "identity":

Sovereignty vs. Democracy: American Indians have been engaged in a centuries-long struggle to have what is legally theirs recognized (i.e., land, sovereignty, treaty rights). As such, Indigenous peoples have not, like other marginalized groups, been fighting for inclusion in the democratic imaginary but, rather, for the right to remain distinct, sovereign, and tribal peoples.

Treaty Rights: These rights articulate the unique status of Indian tribes as "domestic dependent nations." A dizzying array of tribal, federal, and state laws, policies, and treaties creates a political maze that keeps the legal status of most tribes in a constant state of flux. Treaties are negotiated and renegotiated in a process that typically reduces tribal rights and erodes traditional structures (Deloria & Lytle, 1984; Fixcio, 1998).

Dual Citizenship: The Indian Citizenship Act of 1924 extends the rights of full citizenship to American Indians born within the territorial United States, insofar as such status does not infringe upon the rights to tribal and other property. It is a dual citizenship wherein American Indians do not lose civil rights because of their status as tribal members and individual tribal members are not denied tribal rights because of their American citizenship (Deloria & Lytle, 1984).[12]

Federal Recognition: Federal law mandates that American Indians prove that they have continued to exist over time as stable, prima facie entities to retain federal recognition as tribes. Acknowledgment of tribal existence by the Department of the Interior is critical, as it is a prerequisite to the protection, services, and benefits of the federal government available to Indian tribes by virtue of their status as tribes. Therefore, a tribe's existence is contingent upon its ability to prove its existence over time, to provide evidence of shared cultural patterns, and to prove "persistence of a named, collective Indian identity" (USD, Bureau of Indian Affairs, n.d., 83.7).

Economic Dependency: American Indians continue to exist as nations within a nation wherein the relationship between the U.S. government and Indian tribes is not the fictive "government to government" relationship described in U.S. documents, but, rather, one that positions tribes as fundamentally dependent.[13]

Reservations: Roughly two-thirds of American Indians continue either to live on or to remain significantly tied to their reservations and, as such, remain predominantly "tribally oriented" as opposed to generically Indian (Joe & Miller, 1997).

The aggregate of the above indicators positions American Indians in a wholly unique and paradoxical relationship to the United States. These indicators further illuminate the inherent contradictions of modern American Indian existence and point to the gross insufficiency of models that treat American Indians as simply another ethnic minority group. Moreover, the paradox of having to prove "authenticity" to gain legitimacy as a "recognized" tribe and of simultaneously having to negotiate a postmodern world in which all claims to authenticity and legitimacy are dismissed as essentialist (if not racist) conscripts American Indians to a gravely dangerous and precarious space. This reality of Indian existence not only deeply problematizes various postmodern theories' insistence that we move beyond concretized categories, but also reveals their colonizing impulse.[14]

In addition to the (legal) prima facie indicators of American Indianness, there are external forces that further impede and complicate the landscape of American Indian identity. More specifically, the forces of ethnic fraud, cultural encroachment, and corporate commodification work in tandem to call into question the ostensibly liberatory effects of transgression. Such forces pressure Indian communities to define American Indian subjectivity in stable, prima facie measures. In other words, the forces of colonialism and imperialism deeply problematize the postmodern notion of transgression in terms of its abandonment of totality and its emphasis on pluralism and discontinuity. As Steven Best (1989) points out, where critical scholars rightly deconstruct essentialist and repressive wholes, they fail to see how crippling the valorization of difference, fragmentation, and agnostics can be. For the American Indian community, the "crippling" effects have been significant. In particular, the struggle to define "comfortable modern American Indian identities" becomes deeply complicated, enmeshed in the impossible paradox of having to respond to the growing pluralism within their own communities and thus the need to define more fluid constructions of Indianness, while also recognizing that the pressures of identity appropriation, cultural encroachment, and corporate commodification require more restrictive constructions of Indianness. In order to better understand the significance of this paradox, the forces of ethnic fraud, cultural encroachment, and corporate commodification are discussed in greater detail.

Identity Appropriation

In post–*Dances with Wolves* America, it has become increasingly popular to be American Indian. Joane Nagel (1995), a sociologist and expert in the politics of ethnicity, attests that between 1960 and 1990 the number of Americans reporting "American Indian" as their racial category in the U.S. Census more than tripled. Researchers attribute this growth to the practice of "ethnic switching," where individuals previously identifying themselves as "non-Indian," now claim "Indian" as their racial affiliation. She identifies three factors promoting ethnic switching: changes in federal Indian policy; changes in American ethnic politics; and American Indian political activism (Nagel, 1995). Those seminal changes in federal policy referred to by Nagel are the Indian relocation policies of the 1960s and 1970s that led to the creation of urban Indian populations, and the various land-claims settlement of the 1980s, which also led to increases in certain tribal populations.[15] The changes in ethnic politics emanate from the civil rights and Red Power movements that made American Indian identification "a more attractive ethnic option" (Nagel, 1995, p. 956). According to Nagel, these factors helped to raise American Indian ethnic consciousness and encouraged individuals to claim or reclaim their Native American ancestry.

While she makes strong arguments for the three factors she identifies, Nagel ignores the possibility that part of the resurgence may also be due to increasing incidents of identity appropriation, or *ethnic fraud.* Ethnic fraud is the term used to describe the phenomenon of Whitestream individuals who, in spite of growing up far removed from any discernible American Indian community, claim an Indian identity based on the discovery of residuals of Indian blood in their distant ancestries. There is nothing categorically wrong with "discovering" one's ancestral background, but when such claims are opportunistically used to cash in on scholarships, set-aside programs, and other affirmative economic incentives, it becomes highly problematic. Furthermore, there is evidence that such "new Indians" discard their new-found identities as soon as they no longer serve them. For example, studies conducted at UCLA in 1988–1989 and 1993 reveal that of the enrolled 179 American Indian students, 125 did not or could not provide adequate documentation of their tribal affiliation, and that, on average, less than 15 percent of American Indian students were enrolled in federally recognized tribes (Machamer, 1997). More importantly, a significant number of students chose to identify as American Indian only to relinquish this identification by the time of graduation, suggesting that, economic incentives aside, "new Indians" chose to reclaim their Whiteness (Machamer, 1997). Such practices indicate that it is not only popular but profitable to be "Indian" in postmodern America.

In addition to outright identity fraud, American Indian communities also endure the more superficial but equally problematic phenomena of ethnic "vogueing." The seasonal influx of tour buses, church groups, and do-gooders discharges a veritable wave of Whiteness into reservation communities. Armed with their own constructions of Indianness, Whitestream individuals appropriate and try on various elements of Native culture and, in the name of religion, multiculturalism, environmentalism, and radicalism, voyeuristically tour reservation communities like cultural predators loose in Indian theme parks. During these visits, they acquire the usual assemblage of trinkets and souvenirs, and afterwards exit dysconscious[16] of the fact that their adventures have conscripted Native culture as fashion, Indian as exotic, and the sacred as entertainment. While there is a measure of complicity on the part of some American Indians who sell their culture, the overlay of colonialism situates these practices more as products of lost culture, lost economic vitality, and a lost sense of being than as crass indicators of Indian capitalism.

All told, the practice of identity appropriation is believed to have become so widespread that some American Indian organizations have felt compelled to devise statements and enact policies against its proliferation.[17] Even the federal government has recognized the occurrence and ill effects of ethnic fraud. The Indian Arts and Crafts Act, for example, stipulates that all products must be marketed truthfully regarding the Indian heritage and tribal affiliation of the artist or craftsperson. Though this act does more to protect consumers against the purchase of "fraudulent" merchandise, it also protects American Indian artisans from unfair competition by "fraudulent Indian" profiteers.

While such tactics appear to be reasonable in theory, in practice they require the employment of equally problematic essentialist ideology. In other words, in the same moment that particular groups work to determine who is and who is not Indian, they also define fixed parameters of authenticity, reducing the question of Indianness to quantifiable variables and objectified models of culture. It is also difficult to reconcile such contemporary measures with the historical memory that quantifying Indianness is a remnant of the Dawes Allotment Act (1887),[18] in which the U.S. government first introduced blood quantum policies and tribal rolls, and the knowledge that, regardless of how they are defined, measures of authenticity will conjure the same political divisiveness they always have. Finally, insofar as compliance with ethnic fraud policies requires the formation of an Indian Identity Police,[19] enforcement also becomes a dubious enterprise, inviting increased scrutiny from outside agencies.

Cultural Encroachment

The fact that nearly two-thirds of American Indians remain closely tied to their reservations not only points to the continued significance of land in the formation of American Indian identity, but also suggests that a large portion of the Indian population remains fairly segregated from the rest of the nation. Clearly, "Indian Country" persists as both a metaphorical and literal place, undoubtedly shaping the subjectivities of all those who call it home. In other words, living in a physically circumscribed space where literal borders distinguish "us" from "them" must, by definition, shape American Indian consciousness and emergent views of identity and difference. More specifically, the relationship between American Indian communities and the predominantly White border towns not only shapes the ways Indians perceive and construct Whites, but also significantly influences their own views of American Indian identity.

Thus, although reservations exist as a vestige of forced removal, colonialist domination, and Whitestream greed, they have also come to serve as protective barriers and defensive perimeters between cultural integrity and wholesale assimilation. They also serve to distinguish American Indians as the only peoples with federally recognized land claims, demarcating the borders of the only domestic sovereign nations. Though the power of this domestic-dependent-nation status is continually challenged in federal courts, Indians have retained a significant portion of their plenary powers, such as the right to establish tribal courts, tribal governments, and tribal police forces. Ultimately, however, the notion of self-government remains a bit of a farce, since most tribes remain entrenched in untenable relationships with the U.S. government and most reservation economies can only maintain stability with the infusion of outside capital (Deloria & Lytle, 1984).

The dependency on outside capital generates a subordinating effect, leaving American Indians at the virtual mercy of venture capitalists and Whitestream do-gooders. As a result, most reservation communities are overrun by emissaries of White justice, private entrepreneurs, and New Age liberals seeking to forge lucrative careers from predatory practices. Bivouacked in internal and external compounds, enterprising members of the Whitestream wield power and broker services by day, and by night retreat back into the comforts of their bourgeois border towns. As a result, most of the businessmen, teachers, principals, doctors, and health-care providers in reservation communities are White, and most of the laborers, minimum-wagers, underemployed, and unemployed are American Indian.

In spite of the pressures of cultural encroachment, reservation communities continue to work toward becoming sites of political contestation and empowerment. They are learning to survive the dangers of imperialistic forces by employing both proactive strategies that emphasize education, empowerment, and self-determination, and defensive tactics that protect against unfettered economic and political encroachment. Thus, whatever else reservation borders may or may not signify, they serve as potent geographic filters of all that is non-Indian — literal dividing lines between the real and metaphoric spaces differentiating Indian Country from the rest of Whitestream America.

Corporate Commodification

The forces of both ethnic fraud and cultural encroachment operate to create a climate ripe for the corporate commodification of American Indianness. While this commodification takes many forms, it is perhaps most visible in the marketing of Indian narratives, particularly publishing, in which literary/cultural forms of Indian intellectualism have been historically favored over critical forms.

For instance, Indigenous scholar Elizabeth Cook-Lynn (1998) questions why the same editors and agents who solicit her "life story" also routinely reject her scholarly work. She writes, "While I may have a reasonable understanding why a state-run university press would not want to publish research that has little good to say about America's relationship to tribes, . . . I am at a loss to explain why anyone would be more interested in my life story (which for one thing is quite unremarkable)" (p. 121). The explanation, of course, is that the marketable narrative is that which subscribes to the Whitestream notion of Indian as romantic figure, and not Indian as scholar and social critic. Such a predisposition works to favor not only cultural/literary forms of American Indian intellectualism over critical forms, but also the work of "fraudulent" Indians over that of "legitimate" American Indian scholars. Cook-Lynn (1998) argues that, just as the rights to our land remain in the hands of the Whitestream government, the rights to our stories remain in non-Indian enclaves. Deloria (1998) similarly contends that what passes in the academic world as legitimate scholarship on American Indians is often the product of average scholars (often White) advocating a predetermined anti-Indian agenda[20] and "fraudulent" Indians. That such work has been allowed to corner the market raises the question of who controls access to the intellectual property of American Indian peoples. Deloria himself asks, "Who is it that has made such people as Adolph Hungry Wolf, Jamake Highwater, Joseph Epes Brown, Su Bear, Rolling Thunder, Wallace Black Elk, John Redtail Freesoul, Lynn Andrews, and Dhyani Ywahoo the spokespeople of American Indians?" (p. 79). He responds by naming Whitestream America as both patron and peddler of the Hollywood Indian. He writes, "They [the fraudulent Indians] represent the intense desire of Whites to create in their own minds an Indian they want to believe in" (p. 79).

As such, the market is flooded with tragic stories of lost cultures, intimate narratives of "frontier life," and quasi-historic accounts of the Native Americans' plight. Such stories are told and retold as part of America's dark and distant past, a bygone era of misguided faith where cultural genocide is depicted as an egregious but perhaps unavoidable consequence of the country's manifest destiny toward democracy. While I would never argue that stories depicting the truth of Native peoples' tragic experiences (e.g., Indian boarding schools, the Trail of Tears) do not deserve a central place in the telling of American history, such accounts become problematic in the wider context of Whitestream consumption of Indian history.

Why are these stories the ones most often presented as the prime-time programs in the commodified literary network of Indian history? What is gained by focusing on these particular aspects of White domination and Indian subjugation? I argue that such stories serve several purposes, none of which contributes to the emancipatory project of American Indians. First, by propagating the romantic image of American Indians and concomitantly marginalizing the work of Indigenous intellectuals and social critics, Whitestream publishers maintain control over the epistemic frames that define Indians, and thus over the fund of available knowledge on American Indians. Second, such control is underwritten by the understanding that American Indian intellectualism exists as a threat to the myth of the ever-evolving democratization of Indian-White relations, and to the notion that cultural genocide is a remnant of America's dark and distant past. Third, the often oversimplified accounts of Indian history, framed in good-v.-bad-guy terms, allow the consumer to fault rogue groups of dogmatic missionaries and wayward military officers for the slow but steady erosion of Indigenous life, thereby distancing themselves and mainstream government from the ongoing project of cultural genocide. Finally, the focus on Indian history allows the Whitestream to avoid issues facing American Indians in the twenty-first century. As a result, Indians as a modern people remain invisible, allowing a wide array of distorted myths to flourish as contemporary reality — for example, that all the "real" Indians are extinct, that the surviving Indians are all alcoholic-drug addicts who have forsaken traditional ways to become budding capitalists, gaming entrepreneurs, and casino owners — and find their way into public discourse. At the same time these images are circulated, the intensive, ongoing court battles over land, natural resources, and federal recognition are ignored, fueling the great lie of twenty-first century democracy — that America's "Indian problem" has long been solved.

Discussion

The forces of identity appropriation, cultural encroachment, and corporate commodification pressure American Indian communities to employ essentialist tactics and construct relatively fixed notions of identity, and to render the concepts of fluidity and transgression highly problematic. It is evident from the examples above that the notion of fluid boundaries has never worked to the advantage of Indigenous peoples: federal agencies have invoked the language of fluid or unstable identities as the rationale for dismantling the structures of tribal life and creating greater dependency on the U.S. government; Whitestream America has seized its message to declare open season on Indians, thereby appropriating Native lands, culture, spiritual practices, history, and literature; and Whitestream academics have now employed the language of postmodern fluidity to unwittingly transmute centuries of war between Indigenous peoples and their respective nation-states into a "genetic and cultural dialogue" (Valle & Torres, 1995, p. 141). Thus, in spite of its aspirations to social justice, the notion of a new cultural democracy based on the ideal of mestizaje represents a rather ominous threat to American Indian communities.

In addition, the undercurrent of fluidity and sense of displacedness that permeates, if not defines, mestizaje runs contrary to American Indian sensibilities of connection to place, land, and the Earth itself. Consider, for example, the following statement on the nature of critical subjectivity by Peter McLaren:

> The struggle for critical subjectivity is the struggle to occupy a space of hope — a
> liminal space, an intimation of the anti-structure, of what lives in the in-between
> zone of undecidedability — in which one can work toward a praxis of redemption.
> . . . A sense of atopy has always been with me, a resplendent placelessness, a feeling of
> living in germinal formlessness. . . . I cannot find words to express what this border
> identity means to me. All I have are what Georgres Bastille (1988) calls *mots glissants*
> (slippery words). (1997, pp. 13–14)

McLaren speaks passionately and directly about the crisis of modern society and the
need for a "praxis of redemption." As he perceives it, the very possibility of redemption is situated in our willingness not only to accept but to flourish in the "liminal"
spaces, border identities, and postcolonial hybridities that are inherent in postmodern
life and subjectivity. In fact, McLaren perceives the fostering of a "resplendent place-
lessness" itself as the gateway to a more just, democratic society.

While American Indian intellectuals also seek to embrace the notion of transcendent subjectivities, they seek a notion of transcendence that remains rooted in historical place and the sacred connection to land. Consider, for example, the following
commentary by Deloria (1992) on the centrality of place and land in the construction
of American Indian subjectivity:

> Recognizing the sacredness of lands on which previous generations have lived and
> died is the foundation of all other sentiment. Instead of denying this dimension of
> our emotional lives, we should be setting aside additional places that have transcen-
> dent meaning. Sacred sites that higher spiritual powers have chosen for manifesta-
> tion enable us to focus our concerns on the specific form of our lives. . . . Sacred
> places are the foundation of all other beliefs and practices because they represent
> the presence of the sacred in our lives. They properly inform us that we are not
> larger than nature and that we have responsibilities to the rest of the natural world
> that transcend our own personal desires and wishes. This lesson must be learned by
> each generation. (pp. 278, 281)

Gross misunderstanding of this connection between American Indian subjectivity
and land, and, more importantly, between sovereignty and land has been the source of
numerous injustices in Indian country. For instance, I believe there was little understanding on the part of government officials that passage of the Indian Religious Freedom Act (1978) would open a Pandora's box of discord over land, setting up an intractable conflict between property rights and religious freedom. American Indians,
on the other hand, viewed the act as a invitation to return to their sacred sites, several
of which were on government lands and were being damaged by commercial use. As a
result, a flurry of lawsuits alleging mismanagement and destruction of sacred sites was
filed by numerous tribes. Similarly, corporations, tourists, and even rock climbers
filed suits accusing land managers of unlawfully restricting access to public places by
implementing policies that violate the constitutional separation between church and
state. All of this is to point out that the critical project of mestizaje continues to operate on the same assumption made by the U.S. government in this instance, that in a
democratic society, human subjectivity — and liberation for that matter — is conceived of as inherently rights-based as opposed to land-based.

To be fair, I believe that both American Indian intellectuals and critical theorists
share a similar vision — a time, place, and space free of the compulsions of White-

stream, global capitalism and the racism, sexism, classism, and xenophobia it engenders. But where critical scholars ground their vision in Western conceptions of democracy and justice that presume a "liberated" self, American Indian intellectuals ground their vision in conceptions of sovereignty that presume a sacred connection to place and land. Thus, to a large degree, the seemingly liberatory constructs of fluidity, mobility, and transgression are perceived not only as the language of critical subjectivity, but also as part of the fundamental lexicon of Western imperialism. Deloria (1999) writes:

> Although the loss of land must be seen as a political and economic disaster of the first magnitude, the real exile of the tribes occurred with the destruction of ceremonial life (associated with the loss of land) and the failure or inability of white society to offer a sensible and cohesive alternative to the traditions which Indians remembered. People became disoriented with respect to the world in which they lived. They could not practice their old ways, and the new ways which they were expected to learn were in a constant state of change because they were not a cohesive view of the world but simply adjustments which whites were making to the technology they had invented. (p. 247)

In summary, insofar as American Indian identities continue to be defined and shaped in interdependence with place, the transgressive mestizaje functions as a potentially homogenizing force that presumes the continued exile of tribal peoples and their enduring absorption into the American "democratic" Whitestream. The notion of mestizaje as absorption is particularly problematic for the Indigenous peoples of Central and South America, where the myth of the mestizaje (belief that the continent's original cultures and inhabitants no longer exist) has been used for centuries to force the integration of Indigenous communities into the national mestízo model (Van Cott, 1994). According to Rodolfo Stavenhagen (1992), the myth of mestizaje has provided the ideological pretext for numerous South American governmental laws and policies expressly designed to strengthen the nation-state through incorporation of all "non-national" (read "Indigenous") elements into the mainstream. Thus, what Valle and Torres (1995) previously describe as "the continent's unfinished business of cultural hybridization" (p. 141), Indigenous peoples view as the continents' long and bloody battle to absorb their existence into the master narrative of the mestízo.

While critical scholars do construct a very different kind of democratic solidarity that disrupts the sociopolitical and economic hegemony of the dominant culture around a transformed notion of mestizaje (one committed to the destabilization of the isolationist narratives of nationalism and cultural chauvinism), I argue that any liberatory project that does not begin with a clear understanding of the difference of American Indianness will, in the end, work to undermine tribal life. Moreover, there is a potential danger that the ostensibly "new" cultural democracy based upon the radical mestizaje will continue to mute tribal differences and erase distinctive Indian identities. Therefore, as the physical and metaphysical borders of the postmodern world become increasingly fluid, the desire of American Indian communities to protect geographic borders and employ "essentialist" tactics also increases. Though such tactics may be viewed by critical scholars as highly problematic, they are viewed by American Indian intellectuals as a last line of defense against the steady erosion of tribal culture, political sovereignty, Native resources, and Native lands.

The tensions described above indicate the dire need for an Indigenous, revolutionary theory that maintains the distinctiveness of American Indians as tribal peoples of sovereign nations (border patrolling) and also encourages the building of coalitions and political solidarity (border crossing). In contrast to critical scholars McLaren and Kris Gutierrez (1997), who admonish educators to develop a concept of unity and difference as political mobilization rather than cultural authenticity, I urge American Indian intellectuals to develop a language that operates at the crossroads of unity and difference and defines this space in terms of political mobilization and cultural authenticity, thus expressing both the interdependence and distinctiveness of tribal peoples.

Part III. Mestizaje Revisited: Critical Indígena and a New Red Pedagogy

To their credit, Whitestream critical scholars recognize the potential for their own subjectivities and locations of privilege to infiltrate the critical discourse, limiting it in ways they cannot see or anticipate. McLaren (1997) writes, "An individual cannot say he or she has achieved critical pedagogy if he or she stops struggling to attain it. Only sincere discontent and dissatisfaction with the limited effort we exercise in the name of social justice can assure us that we really have the faith in a dialogical commitment to others and otherness" (p. 13). It is perhaps this commitment to self-reflexivity and an ever-evolving pedagogy that represents critical pedagogy's greatest strength. Indeed, critical scholars from other marginalized groups such as Gloria Anzaldúa, Hazel Carby, Antonia Darder, Dolores Delgado Bernal, Kris Gutierrez, bell hooks, Rudy Mattai, Cameron McCarthy, Enrique Murillo, Frances V. Rains, and Sofia Villenas have seized upon its openness, transmuting critical theories to fit their own constructions of culturally relevant praxis. Currently, American Indian scholars are also investigating ways to import the message of critical pedagogy without wholesale adoption of its means. While addressing the impact of racism, sexism, and globalization on American Indian communities, some American Indian intellectuals share underlying principles of mestizaje like reflexivity, hybridity, and multiplicity. However, this notion of a transgressive mestizaje may ultimately undermine American Indian subjectivity. Recognizing the common ground of struggle is an important first step in working to define the ways that critical pedagogy can inform Indigenous praxis.

The following discussion excerpts work by American Indian and other scholars of color who have taken the next step: to define locally and culturally relevant praxis based on a broader critical foundation. I contend that such work represents the possibility and future of both American Indian intellectualism and critical pedagogy.

Voices from the Margin

As might be expected, Latino, Latina, African American, and feminist riffs on Whitestream critical pedagogy speak more directly to the concerns of American Indian intellectuals. In particular, other scholars of color have recognized that the experience of oppression often requires the assertion of hyperauthenticity, and thus have worked to refine critical theorists' hard line against essentialism. For instance, though Chicano scholar Enrique Murillo (1997) rejects the notion of essentialism as a means of recalibrating the balance of power, he employs the term *strategic essentialism* to describe the contradictory experience of many scholars of color caught between the different legitimizing forces of the academy and their own communities. There are times, for example, when scholars of color feel compelled to perform a heightened professional or scholarly identity when seeking legitimacy in the academy, and other times when they feel compelled to perform a hyperauthentic or racialized self to gain or retain legitimacy within their own communities. Murillo's notion of "strategic essentialism" is useful in describing the experience of American Indian intellectuals working to balance the fluidity of the postmodern world with the more stable obligations of their tribal communities. In more concrete terms, this means that, as American Indian scholars work to construct and advocate more complex understandings of American Indian identity, such efforts remain haunted by the knowledge that any failure to continually define and authenticate Indianness in stable and quantifiable terms may result in the loss of everything from school funding to tribal recognition. Within this context, strategic essentialism refers not only to choosing multiple subjectivities where power is located in the self, but also to negotiating between chosen and imposed identities where power continues to be located in the oppressor.

Similar to Murillo's variation on the notion of strategic essentialism, Delgado Bernal (1998) defines a culturally relevant theory of knowledge that brings discussions of power and identity into the realm of epistemology. She argues for a model of identity-based epistemology and develops the notion of "cultural intuition" to validate the centrality of cultural knowledge in the processes of research and in the development of a culture's intellectual history. Specifically, Delgado Bernal employs the notion of cultural intuition to legitimate her unique viewpoint as a Chicana researcher conducting research within the Chicana community.[21] Though similar to Anselm Strauss and Juliet Corbin's concept of "theoretical sensitivity" (1990), Delgado Bernal's paradigm extends the realm of cultural intuition to include collective experience and community memory and to stress the importance of participants' inclusion in the research process, particularly in data analysis. She writes, "While I do not argue for an essentialist notion of who is capable of conducting research with various populations based on personal experiences, I do believe that many Chicana scholars achieve a sense of cultural intuition that is different from other scholars" (p. 567). This insightful articulation of the value and power of cultural intuition brings voice and, more importantly, language to the struggles of Chicano and other scholars of color seeking validation, power, and equity in the domain of academic research. Moreover, the notion of cultural intuition buttresses arguments already made by American Indian scholars on behalf of their own communities; specifically, for the right to speak in their own voices, define their own realities, and develop their own intellectual histories.

Voices from Indian Country

While it is important and beneficial to observe the insights of other critical pedagogies, it is crucial to look to one's own intellectual history and sources of cultural intuition in the development of Indigenous theories and praxis. In this effort, the challenge to American Indian scholars is not merely to "resurrect" these histories and sources of cultural intuition, but to construct meaningful bridges and points of intersection between American Indian intellectualism and Whitestream critical pedagogies.

To this end, while American Indian scholars have, by and large, resisted direct engagement with critical theory, many have begun to theorize their own constructions of Indigenous knowledge and American Indian identity.[22] As a collective effort, such work provides increasingly complex views of American Indian history; of the promise and failures of education; of the struggles for language, agency, and sovereignty; and of the need for political and sociocultural coalitions. Their writings strive to achieve interplay between the past, present, and future, and ride the faultline between continuity, resistance, and possibility.

What follows is a sampling of such works, chosen because of their particular relevance to the topic of American Indian identity and identity formation. The selected scholars differ in their methods and approaches, but they share a thematic undercurrent that includes the interplay of coalition, agency, tradition, and identity; the transformation of curriculum and pedagogy; the retention and reinvigoration of Indigenous languages; the intersection of religion and spirituality; and the quest for sovereignty. While each domain merits extensive discussion, such an effort goes beyond the limits of this work. However, insofar as American Indian "identity" is formulated as an aggregate of the above struggles, they will be discussed interdependently with the understanding that, especially for American Indians, religion/spirituality and sovereignty are inextricably woven into the struggles for identity, education, and language, and vice versa.

The Interplay of Coalition, Agency, and Identity

In the first draft of the final report of the Indian Nations at Risk Task Force, Indigenous scholar and activist Michael Charleston (1994) writes of the importance of coalition and its central role in the development of effective American Indian schools and Indian-centered curricula. Rather than the abstract language of critical pedagogy, however, Charleston invokes the Lakota tradition of the Ghost Dance as a metaphor of the need for healing through community, ceremony, sacrifice, and tradition.[23] He writes:

> The new Ghost Dance calls Native and non-Native peoples to join together and take action. It calls us to be responsible for the future of the people of our tribes. It calls us to protect, revive and restore our cultures, our Native languages, our religions and values. It calls us to heal our people, our families, our tribes, and our societies. It calls for harmony and respect among all relations of creation. It offers a future of co-existence of tribal societies with other American societies . . . indeed domination, oppression, and bigotry are exactly what we are overcoming in the new Ghost Dance as we seek to establish harmony and co-existence of tribes with other societies in the modern world. (p. 28)

This spirit of coalition reflects the growing desire among American Indians to work together and form alliances with Native and non-Native forces in a mutual quest for American Indian sovereignty and self-determination. Though Charleston's rendition of coalition reflects the spirit of mestizaje — that is, the blurring of political, racial, and cultural borders in the service of social justice — he carefully relegates such coalition to the realm of sociopolitical action. In other words, the new Ghost Dance calls to Indian and non-Indian peoples to take collective action against U.S. policies that continue the project of colonization and cultural genocide. It is thus not a call for the embodiment, in critical-theoretical terms, of a transcultural, transnational subject that calls into question the very notion of authentic identities (McLaren, 1997), but rather a metaphor for collective political action.

This is not to say that Charleston or other American Indian scholars do not support the notion that identity is constructed through multiple, intersecting, and contradictory elements. Rather, they remain wary of constructionist understandings of identity that, in the process of providing a corrective to static notions of culture, ignore the real possibility of culture loss — that is, the real existing threat of cultural genocide of Indigenous peoples. Hale (2000) is worth quoting at length:

> When (cultural) transformation is conflated with loss . . . the collective trauma is obscured and the brute historical fact of ethnocide is softened. The culprits in this erasure are the Indians' . . . enemies, but even more centrally . . . elites who embraced classic nineteenth century liberalism cast in the idiom of mestizáje. A homogeneous and individualized notion of citizenship could not be compatible with the rights of Indian communities whose collective histories and identities stood opposed to the dominant mestizo culture. Just beneath the alluring promises to Indians who would accept these individual rights of citizenship was incomprehension, invisibility, and punishing racism for those who would not. (p. 269)

Again, though the contemporary critical project of mestizaje is in many ways antithetical to the Latin American one, both projects ignore the "brute historical fact of ethnocide" and the invisibility of Indians within the broader democratic project. In contradistinction to the critical notion of mestizaje, American Indian scholars seek understandings of identity that not only reflect the multiple and contradictory aspects of contemporary experience, but also maintain a sense of American Indians as historically placed, sovereign peoples. For them, sovereignty is not a political ideology but a way of life (Warrior, 1995). As Charleston (1994) writes, "Our tribes are at a very critical point in our history again. We can stand by and wait for our children and grandchildren to be assimilated into mainstream American society as proud ethnic descendants of extinct tribal peoples. . . . Or, we can protect our tribes, as our ancestors did, and ensure a future for our children and grandchildren as tribal people" (p. 28).

Though it may seem from the above that American Indian intellectuals advocate exclusionary rather than coalitionary tactics, impulses toward isolationism need to be understood in the context of unrelenting threats of cultural appropriation and culture loss. Within this context, it is actually remarkable that American Indian tribal communities remain open and working to define the balance between cultural tradition, cultural shift, and cultural transformation.

Identity Formation and American Indian Tradition(s)

Indigenous scholar Devon Mihesuah (1998) examines the notion of "tradition" in the formation of American Indian identity. Acknowledging that, while traditions are important to maintain, they have always been fluid, she writes:

> An Indian who speaks her tribal language and participates in tribal religious cere-
> monies is often considered traditional, but that term is applicable only within the
> context of this decade, because chances are she wears jeans, drives a car and watches
> television — very "untraditional" things to do. Plains Indians who rode horses in
> the 1860's are considered traditional today, but they were not the same as their tra-
> ditional ancestors of the early 1500's who had never seen a horse. (p. 50)

While contemporary life requires most Indians to negotiate or "transgress" between a multitude of subject positions (i.e., one who is Navajo may also be Catholic,
gay, and live in an off-reservation urban center), such movement remains historically
embedded and geographically placed. Moreover, the various and competing subjectivities remain tied through memory, ceremony, ritual, and obligation to a traditional
identity type that operates not as a measure of authenticity, but rather of cultural continuity and survival. For example, current understanding of a traditional Navajo
(Diné) woman is that she lives in a hogan, speaks her language, participates in cere-
monies, maintains a subsistence lifestyle, nurtures strong clan and kinship ties, serves
as a vast repository of cultural and tribal history, participates in tribal governance,
wears long hair wrapped in traditional cotton cloth, dresses in long skirts and velvet
blouses, and dons the silver jewelry of her family to reside as matriarch of the clan.
Such individuals, along with their male counterparts, are typically held in high esteem
and are granted a great deal of respect and social power. While the Diné recognize this
identity as only one among many accepted as "authentically" Diné, it forms the essence of their tribal identity, serves as the repository of their ancestral knowledge, and
roots them as a historically embedded and geographically placed people.

The struggle for American Indian subjectivity is, in part, a struggle to protect this
essence and the right of Indigenous peoples to live in accordance with their traditional ways. In other words, regardless of how any individual American Indian may
choose to live his or her life as an Indian person, most experience a deep sense of responsibility and obligation to protect the rights of those choosing to live in the ways
of their ancestors. The struggle for identity thus also becomes the struggle to negotiate effectively the line between fetishizing traditional identities and recognizing their
importance to the continuation of American Indians as distinctive tribal peoples. Insofar as American Indian traditional identities remain tethered to "traditional" practices (such as ceremony) and such practices remain interconnected with the land, the
struggle for identity becomes inextricably linked with political struggles for sovereignty and the ongoing battle against cultural encroachment and capitalist desire to
control Native land, resources, traditions, and languages. So, while American Indians
join the struggle against the kind of essentialism that recognizes only one way of being, they also work to retain a vast constellation of distinct traditions that serve as the
defining characteristics of "traditional" ways of being. As Vine Deloria and Clifford
Lytle (1983) note, this allegiance to traditional knowledge has protected American
Indians from annihilation or its modern counterpart, categoric absorption into the
democratic mainstream.

The Transformation of Curriculum and Pedagogy

There is a growing body of work by Indigenous scholars that examines the intersection between the experiences of formal education and tribal culture. Recently, such

work has moved away from comparatively simplistic analyses of "learning style" or curriculum content into deeper examination of the interplay between power, difference, opportunity, and institutional structure (see, for example, Deyhle & Swisher, 1997; Haig-Brown & Archibald, 1996; Hermes, 1998; Lipka, 1994; Pewewardy, 1998). Though such work builds upon the efforts of other scholars of color seeking to define culturally relevant pedagogies (Delpit, 1995; Fordham & Ogbu, 1986; Ladson-Billings, 1995; Trueba, 1988; Watahomigie & McCarty, 1994, for example), American Indian scholars rebuff the undercurrent of democratic inclusion and empowerment that undergirds this work, choosing instead to employ sovereignty as the central struggle in defining relevant praxis.[24]

For example, in her work with Lac Courtie Ojibwe (LCO) reservation schools, Indigenous scholar Mary Hermes (1995, 1998) struggles to define a "culturally based curriculum" where both "culture" and "curriculum" are viewed as fluid, "living" constructs that develop in and through relationship. In her own words, Hermes shifts the research question from "What is the role of culture in knowledge acquisition?" to "What is the role of the school as a site of cultural production?" She argues that research focused on the first question often results in essentialized definitions of culture and the subsequent generation of curricular dichotomies distinguishing "academic" curricula from "cultural" curricula. Instead she seeks answers to the more complicated question, "How can we frame our teaching in an Ojibwe epistemology without representing Ojibwe as a static culture?" (Hermes, 2000). Hermes's question represents a paradigm shift, one that decenters the insertion of a static notion of "culture" into "knowledge" and recenters cultural production as an outcome of the schooling process. In practical terms, such a shift means that community interests not only informed but directed her research methods and outcomes. In her work with Ojibwe schools, she implores educators of American Indian students to recognize culture in the classroom at a deeper level than simply adding content or naming learning styles. She writes:

> I am proposing that we begin to view culture as a complex web of relationships, not just material practices, and enact this in our schools in a way that is central to the curriculum. This could mean, for example, directly teaching tribal history, or simply inviting Elders and community members into the school, regardless of the historical knowledge they bring. (p. 389)

Although Hermes is clearly committed to defining a liberatory praxis based upon a transformative understanding of Ojibwe identity, a goal reminiscent of critical pedagogies, she remains equally committed to the project of American Indian self-determination and sovereignty. Thus, as she advocates an understanding of identity that reflects the fluidity of mestizaje, she also seeks to define a curriculum that remains grounded in the unfolding relationships of tribalness.

In summary, although the development of culturally relevant pedagogy is an objective shared by many marginalized groups, the goal of such efforts for most non-Indian minorities is to ensure inclusion in the democratic imaginary, while the goal for American Indian scholars and educators is to disrupt and impede absorption into that democracy and continue the struggle to remain distinctive, tribal, and sovereign peoples.

The Retention and Reinvigoration of Indigenous Languages

For many American Indian communities, language retention and renewal efforts signify ground zero in the struggle for American Indian sovereignty. Like other aspects of Indigenous experience, there is no single state or uniform condition of Native languages. Some are vibrant like Quechua, which has over one million speakers, and others, like Passamaquoddy, are threatened with extinction. Although ways of speaking and thinking about language shift and language loss may vary within a single community by age, family, life history, gender, and social role, there is a shared sensibility among American Indian peoples that language is inherently tied to cultural continuity — particularly religious and ceremonial continuity — and therefore remains at the core of American Indian identity formation (Anderson, 1998).

Therefore, while many would eschew the oft-implied and "essentialistic" construction of language fluency as a marker of cultural authenticity, there is virtual consensus among American Indian peoples that language loss is tantamount to cultural eradication. Language, in other words, is viewed as a carrier of culture and culture as a carrier of language so that shifts in one reverberate in the other. As such, most tribes work hard to maintain their language through a variety of means, including school, ceremony, community, and family. However, as the traditional structures of community and family erode under the pressures of Whitestream encroachment, tribal members increasingly look to schools to serve as sites of American Indian cultural production and reproduction.

In this effort, American Indian educators looking to develop a critical language of American Indian self-determination and intellectual sovereignty are finding that their own Native languages are replete with metaphors of existence that speak to the lived experience of multiplicity, to the sense of interconnection, and to the understanding that American Indians live not only in relationship with each other, but also with the land. In Quechua, for example, the word for being, person, and Andean person is all the same, *Runa*. This root term has the potential to incorporate the many subcategories of beingness while retaining the same basic reference group, as in *llaqtaruna* (inhabitants of the village) and *qualaruna* (foreigner; literally, naked, peeled). It can be used passively as in *yuyay runa* (one who is knowing or understanding), actively as in *runayáchikk* (that which cultivates a person), or reflexively as in *runaman tukuy* (to complete oneself). Hence, the construct speaks to both the group and the individual and distinguishes in-group from out-group while maintaining the fundamental connection between them. Therefore, it is not a static category or limitation to the sense of Runa as the becoming self (Skar, 1994). Border crossing and the idea of a shifting identity is, thus, neither new nor revolutionary to this Indigenous community, but rather the way of life of Quechua peoples for over five hundred years.

Conclusion

The work outlined above suggests that while American Indian scholars share many of the same concerns as mainstream critical scholars' development of critical agency, construction of political coalition, and transformation through praxis, they reject the construction of the radical mestizaje and work instead to balance their community's needs to both cross and patrol borders of identity and location. They also retain as the central and common goal the perseverance of American Indians as distinctive and sovereign peoples.

Defining that balance is perhaps the quintessential struggle of American Indian peoples today. It is a deeply complicated and contradictory struggle that reflects the colonialist past and portends an uncertain future. In short, American Indians face an identity paradox. At the same time that pressures to respond to internal crises of identity formation — including racism, sexism, and homophobia — require more fluid constructions of Indianness, pressures to respond to external threats to identity formation — cultural encroachment, ethnic fraud, corporate commodification, and culture loss — require more restrictive constructions of Indianness. Hence, as American Indian intellectuals struggle to awaken Indian communities to the "challenges and cultural politics of (their) own ever-burgeoning multiculturalism" (Vizenor, 1999, p. 3), they must also work to ground the ever-changing present in the historical memories of the past while searching for links to an American Indian future.

Though, as I have demonstrated, there is good reason to remain cautious of the constructs that emerge from dominant Whitestream discourses, there is also much to be learned from engagement with such discourse. As Indigenous scholar Robert Allen Warrior (1995) notes, American Indian intellectuals have remained caught in "a death dance of dependence between, on the one hand, abandoning ourselves to the intellectual strategies and categories of white, European thought and, on the other hand, declaring we need nothing outside of ourselves and our cultures in order to understand the world and our place in it" (p. 123). He observes that only when American Indian intellectuals remove themselves from this dichotomy that "much becomes possible" (p. 124).

To this end, I argue that critical scholars need to broaden their own theoretical scopes to consider the different and, at times, competing moral visions of American Indian peoples. Critical engagement with the intellectual histories of Indigenous peoples could only serve to inform discussions of revolutionary theory and praxis. Specifically, such histories call into question the ongoing assumption of conservative and radical ideologies that democracy, as presently constructed in liberal, capitalist terms, presumes the continued absorption or colonization of Indigenous peoples. American Indian scholars also need to enter the critical dialogue and help reimagine the political terrain surrounding identity. They need to create the intellectual space for the struggle for sovereignty and for their efforts to renegotiate the relationship between sovereign American Indian tribal nations and the current democratic order. The challenge to Indigenous scholars is to define the same kind of balance between cultural integrity and critical resistance in their own quest for American Indian intellectual sovereignty. As Warrior (1995) notes, just "as many of the poets find their work continuous with but not circumscribed by Native traditions of story-telling or ceremonial chanting, we can find the work of (critical studies) continuous with Native traditions of deliberation and decision making. Holding these various factors (sovereignty, tradition, community, process and so on) in tension while attempting to understand the role of critics in an American Indian future is of crucial importance" (p. 118).

Ultimately, I am confident that American Indian and non-Indian critical scholars devoted to the remapping of the political project can together define a common ground of struggle and construct an insurgent but poetic moral vision of liberty, sovereignty, and social justice. It is my hope that this discussion will also serve as the foundation for a new critical theory of Indigenous identity and the development of a new Red Pedagogy.

Notes

1. The term *critical pedagogy* will be used interchangeably with *critical theory* to refer to the diverse body of critical educational theories (i.e., postcolonial, feminist, postmodern, multicultural, and Marxist) that advocate an increasingly sophisticated critique of the social, economic, and political barriers to social justice, as well as crusade for the transformation of schools to reflect the imperatives of democracy. The totality of these theories are viewed by critical scholars as the foundation of liberatory discourse and the political project of liberation. *Project* refers to a collectivity of critique and action or solidarity.

2. For the purposes of this article, American Indian intellectualism is distinguished from purely literary or cultural forms of writing, and refers to intellectual activity that engages in substantive critical analysis from an Indigenous perspective.

3. I use the term *American Indians* to refer to the tribal peoples of North America and *Indigenous peoples* as a more inclusive term to relate to global Indigenous peoples.

4. *Democratic imaginary* refers to the notion that democracy is a never-ending project and continuous pursuit — an imagined concept.

5. The comprehensive literature reviews of Robert Allen Warrior (1995), *Tribal Secrets: Recovering American Indian Intellectual Traditions,* and of Donna Deyhle and Karen Swisher (1997), "Research in American Indian and Alaska Native Education: From Assimilation to Self-Determination," provide adequate evidence of the lack of participation of American Indian scholars within the broader field of critical studies.

6. In the critical discourse the notion of transgressive identity takes the postmodern notion of identity — as a highly fluid construct with intersections among the perceived stable categories of race, class, ethnicity, sexuality, and gender — a step further by indicating that even within categories there is "transgression" or strategies of resistance that work to destabilize identity. In other words, it is not only that the categories of race, class, gender, and sexuality intersect but also that the categories (e.g., Lesbian, African American, upper class) themselves are highly contested spaces. Moreover, "transgression" is viewed as an inherently subversive and destabilizing construct, where there is constant resistance to any fixed notion of identity.

7. By "dangerous discourse" I mean that American Indian critical studies is viewed in the same spirit that Black feminism was once perceived by Whitestream feminists and African American intellectuals. (Adapting from the feminist notion of "malestream," critical scholar Claude Denis [1997] defines Whitestream as the idea that, while American society is not White in sociodemographic terms, it remains principally and fundamentally structured on the basis of White, Anglo-European experience.)

8. Though Marxist-feminist scholar Teresa Ebert employs the term *Red Pedagogy* to refer to her own work toward revitalizing the Marxist critique in feminist discourse, I use the term as both a historical reference to such empowering metaphors as "Red Power" and the "Great Red Road." Moreover, in the spirit of such venerable Indian scholars and activists as Vine Deloria and Winona LaDuke, I reappropriate the signifier *Red* as a contemporary metaphor for the ongoing political project of Indigenous peoples to retain sovereignty and establish self-determination.

9. I wish to be clear that the terms *spiritual* and *spirituality* in this text do not refer to New Age constructions of some mythic pan-Indian spirituality but rather to the historical presence and persistence within Indigenous belief systems of life forces beyond human rationality.

10. For example, various race-centric theories and certain forms of feminism. Joe Kincheloe and Shirley Steinberg (1997) state that "left essentialists tend to focus attention on one form of oppression as elemental, as taking precedence over all modes of subjugation. Certain radical

feminists view gender as a central form of oppression, certain ethnic study scholars privilege race, while orthodox Marxists focus on class" (p. 22).

11. Similarly, Cameron McCarthy (1988, 1995), John Ogbu (1978), Chandra Mohanty (1989), and Henry Giroux (1992) — among others — caution against equating hybridity with equality.

12. The very "protection" typically proffered by citizenship rights (i.e., civil liberties) has often worked to erode traditional structures of tribal life, sometimes pitting Indian against Indian and tribe against tribe. For a more complete discussion of the difference between that which is civic and that which is tribal, see Vine Deloria and Clifford Lytle's *The Nations Within: The Past and Future of American Indian Sovereignty*, or Claude Denis's *We Are Not You: First Nations and Canadian Modernity*.

13. As presently constructed, tribal governments retain many powers of nations, some powers greater than those of states, and some governing powers greater than local non-Indian municipalities (Deloria & Lytle, 1984). In spite of their "sovereign" status, Indian tribes currently rely on the federal government for their operating funds, for the right to interpret and renegotiate their own treaty rights, and for access to the natural resources on their own reservations.

14. By "colonizing impulse" I mean the inherent perhaps unconscious impulse to include or conscript Indigenous (tribal) people into the "democratic project."

15. For example, in Maine, with the setting of land claims in the 1970s Carter administration, many people of varying Indian blood quantums "returned" to the reservation since they had a place to call home. The same thing has happened with the Pequot in Connecticut.

16. Joyce King (1991) defines *dysconcious racism* as an uncritical habit of mind; a form of racism that tacitly accepts White norms and privileges. She contends that such unintended racism does not reflect the absence of consciousness, but rather an impaired or distorted way of thinking about race.

17. For example, in response to the growing phenomenon of "ethnic fraud," the Association of American Indian and Alaska Native Professors has issued a position statement urging colleges and universities to follow specific guidelines in their considerations of admissions, scholarships, and hiring practices. Those guidelines are as follows: 1) Require documentation of enrollment in a state or federally recognized nation/tribe, with preference given to those who meet this criterion; 2) Establish a case-by-case review process for those unable to meet the first criterion; 3) Include American Indian/Alaska Native faculty in the selection process; 4) Require a statement from the applicant that demonstrates past and future commitment to American Indian/Alaska Native concerns; 5) Require higher education administrators to attend workshops on tribal sovereignty and meet with local tribal officials, and 6) Advertise vacancies at all levels on a broad scale and in tribal publications. Contrary to the backlash that this statement received, the association does not promote "policing," nor do they employ exclusionary tactics within their own organization, instead relying on self-disclosure.

18. The Dawes Allotment Act (1887) authorized the president of the United States to allot any reservation according to the following formula: 1) To each head of family, one quarter section; 2) To each single person over 18, one-eighth section; 3) To each orphan under eighteen, one-eighth section; 4) To each other single person under eighteen, born prior to the date of the order, one-sixteenth section (Deloria & Lytle, 1983). In order to allot the land, however, government officials required an efficient method by which to determine who was a "legitimate" member of a given community, which resulted in the beginning of widespread use of tribal rolls and blood-quantum policies.

19. The term *Indian Identity Police* is used by M. Annette Jaimes Guerrero (1996).

20. Deloria (1998) includes among such scholars James Clifton, Sam Gill, Elisabeth Tooker, Alice Kehoe, Richard deMille, and Stephen Farca.

21. In an essay reprinted in this volume, Dolores Delgado Bernal (1998) identifies four sources of cultural intuition that together provide the epistemological framework for her analysis of Chicana experience: personal experience, knowledge of existing (academic) literature, professional experience, and the analytical research process itself.

22. See, for example, Elizabeth Cook-Lynn (1998), Michael Charleston (1994); Vine Deloria (1992, 1998); M. Annette Jaimes Guererro (1996); Mary Hermes (1998); K. Tsianina Lomawaima (1994); Devon Mihesuah (1998); Frances Rains (1998, 1999); Karen Swisher (1998); Gerald Vizenor (1999); Robert Warrior (1995).
23. The Ghost Dance was started in 1890 by Chief Big Foot and his band of Lakota as a means of declaring that the Creator would prevent the total destruction of Native people, alleviate their suffering, and return the people to pre-war days of happiness.
24. The Freirean notion of praxis is best understood as action and reflection upon the world in order to change it or simply as intentional action.

References

Anderson, J. (1998). Ethnolonguistic dimensions of northern Arapaho language shift. *Anthropological Linguistics, 40,* 43–108.

Anzaldúa, G. (1987). *Borderlands, la frontera: The new mestíza.* San Francisco: Aunt Lute Books.

Best, S. (1989). Jameson's totality and post-structuralist critique. In D. Kellner (Ed.), *Postmodernism/Jameson/critique* (pp. 233–368). Washington, DC: Maisonneuve.

Castillo, A. (1995). *Massacre of dreamers: Essays on Xicanisma.* New York: Plume.

Charleston, G. M. (1994) Toward true native education: A treaty of 1992 (Final Report of the Indian Nations at Risk Task Force, draft 3). *Journal of American Indian Education, 33*(2), 7–56.

Cook-Lynn, E. (1998). American Indian intellectualism and the new Indian story. In D. A. Mihesuah (Ed.), *Natives and academics: Researching and writing about American Indians* (pp. 111–138). Lincoln: University of Nebraska Press.

Darder, A., Torres, R., & Gutiérrez, H. (Eds.). (1997). *Latinos and education: A critical reader.* New York: Routledge.

Delgado Bernal, D. (1998). Using a Chicana feminist epistemology in educational research. *Harvard Educational Review, 68,* 555–582.

Deloria, V. (1992). *God is Red: A Native view of religion.* Golden, CO: North American Press.

Deloria, V., Jr. (1998). Comfortable fictions and the struggles for turf: An essay review of *The invented Indian: Cultural fictions and government policies.* In D. A. Mihesuah (Ed.), *Natives and academics: Researching and writing about American Indians* (pp. 65–83). Lincoln: University of Nebraska Press.

Deloria, V., Jr. (1999). *For this land: Writings on religion in America.* New York: Routledge.

Deloria, V., Jr., & Lytle, C. (1983). *American Indians, American justice.* Austin: University of Texas Press.

Deloria, V., Jr., & Lytle, C. (1984). *The nations within: The past and future of American Indian sovereignty.* Austin: University of Texas Press.

Delpit, L. (1995). *Other people's children: Cultural conflicts in the classroom.* New York: New Press.

Denis, C. (1997). *We are not you.* Toronto: Broadview.

Deyhle, R., & Swisher, K. (1997). Research in American Indian and Alaskan Native education: From assimilation to self-determination. In *Review of Research in Education* (pp. 113–183). Washington, DC: American Educational Research Association.

di Leonardo, M. (1991). *Gender at the crossroads of knowledge: Feminist anthropology in the postmodernist era.* Berkeley: University of California Press.

Fixcio, D. L. (1998). *The invasion of Indian country in the twentieth century: American capitalism and tribal natural resources.* Niwot: University Press of Colorado.

Fordham, S., & Ogbu, J. (1986). Black students and the burden of "acting White." *Urban Review, 18,* 176–203.

Fusco, C. (1995). *English is broken here: Notes on the cultural fusion in the Americas.* New York: New Press.

Giroux, H. (1992). *Border crossings: Cultural workers and the politics of education.* New York: Routledge.

Grande, S. (1997). *Critical multicultural education and the modern project: An exploratory analysis.* Unpublished doctoral dissertation, Kent State University.

Grande, S. (2000). American Indian identity and intellectualism: The quest for a new Red pedagogy. *Journal of Qualitative Studies in Education, 13,* 373–354.

Guerrero, M. A. J. (1996). Academic apartheid: American Indian studies and "multiculturalism." In A. Gordon & C. Newfield (Eds.), *Mapping multiculturalism* (pp. 49–63). Minneapolis: University of Minnesota Press.

Haig-Brown, C., & Archibald, J. (1996). Transforming First Nations research with respect and power. *International Journal of Qualitative Studies in Education, 9,* 245–267.

Hale, C. R. (2000). Book review of *To die in this way: Nicaraguan Indians and the myth of mestizaje 1880–1965. American Society for Ethnohistory, 47,* 268–271.

Harraway, D. J. (1991). *Simians, cyborgs, and women.* New York: Routledge.

Hermes, M. (1995). *Making culture, making curriculum: Teaching through meanings and identities at an American Indian tribal school.* Unpublished doctoral dissertation, University of Wisconsin–Madison.

Hermes, M. (1998). Research methods as a situated response: Towards a First Nation's methodology. *International Journal of Qualitative Studies in Education, 11,* 155–168.

Hermes, M. (2000). The scientific method, Nintendo, and eagle feathers: Rethinking the meaning of "culture based" curriculum at an Ojibwe tribal school. *International Journal of Qualitative Studies in Education, 13,* 387–400.

Herrnstein, R. J., & Murray, C. (1994). *The bell curve: Intelligence and class structure in American life.* New York: Free Press.

Joe, J. R., & Miller, D. L. (1997). Cultural survival and contemporary American Indian women in the city. In C. J. Cohen (Ed.), *Indigenous women transforming politics: An alternative reader* (pp. 137–150). New York: New York University Press.

Kincheloe, J., & Steinberg, S. (1997). *Changing multiculturalism.* Bristol, PA: Open University Press.

King, J. (1991). Dysconcious racism: Ideology, identity and the miseducation of teachers. *Journal of New Education, 60,* 133–146

Ladson-Billings, G. (1995). "But that's just good teaching!" The case for culturally relevant pedagogy. *Theory Into Practice, 34,* 159–165.

Lipka, J. (1994). Language, power, and pedagogy: Whose school is it? *Peabody Journal of Education, 69,* 71–93.

Lomawaima, K. T. (1994). *They called it prairie light: The story of Chilocco Indian school.* Lincoln: University of Nebraska Press.

Machamer, A. M. (1997). Ethnic fraud in the university: Serious implications for American Indian education. *Native Bruin, 2,* 1–2.

McCarthy, C. (1988). Rethinking liberal and radical perspectives on racial inequality in schooling: Making the case for nonsynchrony. *Harvard Educational Review, 58,* 265–269.

McCarthy, C. (1995). The problem with origins: Race and the contrapuntal nature of the educational experience. In P. McLaren & C. Sleeter (Eds.), *Multicultural education, critical pedagogy and the politics of difference* (pp. 245–268). Albany: State University of New York Press.

McCarthy, C., & Crichlow, W. (1993). *Race and identity and representation in education.* New York: Routledge.

McLaren, P. (Ed.). (1997). *Revolutionary multiculturalism: Pedagogies of dissent for the new millennium.* Boulder, CO: Westview Press.

McLaren, P., & Giroux, H. (1997). Writing from the margins: Geographies of identity, pedagogy and power. In P. McLaren (Ed.), *Revolutionary multiculturalism: Pedagogies of dissent for the new millennium* (pp. 16–41). Boulder, CO: Westview Press.

McLaren, P., & Gutierrez, K. (1997). Global politics and local antagonists: Research and practice as dissent and possibility. In P. McLaren (Ed.), *Revolutionary multiculturalism: Pedagogy of dissent for the new millennium.* (pp. 192–222) Boulder, CO: Westview Press.

McLaren, P., & Sleeter, C. (Eds.). (1995). *Multicultural education, critical pedagogy, and the politics of difference.* Albany: State University of New York Press.

Mihesuah, D. (1998). *Natives and academics: Researching and writing about American Indians.* Lincoln: University of Nebraska Press.

Mohanty, C. (1989). On race and violence: Challenges for liberal education in the 1990s. *Cultural Critique, 14,* 179–208.

Murillo, E. G. (1997, April). *Research under cultural assault: Mojado ethnography.* Paper presented at the annual meeting of the American Educational Studies Association, San Diego.

Nagel, J. (1995). American Indian ethnic renewal: Politics and the resurgence of identity. *American Sociological Review, 60,* 947–965.

Ogbu, J. (1978). *Minority education and caste: The American system in cross-cultural perspective.* New York: Academic Press.

Pewewardy, C. (1998). Fluff and feathers: Treatment of American Indians in the literature and the classroom. *Equity and Excellence in Education, 31,* 69–76.

Rains, F. V. (1998). Is the benign really harmless? Deconstructing some "benign" manifestations of operationalized White privilege. In J. Kinchloe, S. R. Steinberg, & R. E. Chennault (Eds.), *White reign: Deploying Whiteness in America* (pp. 77–101). New York: St. Martin's Press.

Rains, F. V. (1999). Indigenous knowledge, historical amnesia and intellectual authority: Deconstructing hegemony and the social and political implications of the curricular other. In L. M. Semeli & J. Kinchloe (Eds.), *What is Indigenous knowledge? Voices from the academy* (pp. 317–332). New York: Falmer Press.

Said, E. (1985). Orientalism reconsidered. *Race and Class, 26,* 1–15.

Skar, S. L. (1994). *Lives together — worlds apart: Quechua colonization in jungle and city.* New York: Scandinavian University Press.

Stavenhagen, R. (1992). Challenging the nation-state in Latin America. *Journal of International Affairs, 34,* 421–441.

Strauss, A., & Corbin, J. (1990). *Basics of qualitative research: Grounded theory procedures and techniques.* Newbury Park, CA: Sage.

Swisher, K. (1998). Why Indian people should write about Indian education. In D. A. Mihesuah (Ed.), *Natives and academics: Researching and writing about American Indians* (pp. 190–199). Omaha: University of Nebraska Press.

Trueba, E. (1988). Culturally based explanation of minority students' academic achievement. *Minority Achievement, 19,* 270–287.

USD, Bureau of Indian Affairs, 209 manual 8, 83.7. Mandatory Criteria for Federal Recognition. 44 U.S.C. 3501 (et seq.) n.d.

Valle, V., & Torres, R. (1995). The idea of mestizaje and the "race" problematic: Racialized media discourse in a post-Fordist landscape. In A. Darder (Ed.), *Culture and difference: Critical perspectives on the bi-cultural experience in the United States* (pp. 139–153). Westport: Bergin & Garvey.

Van Cott, D. L. (1994). *Indigenous peoples and democracy in Latin America.* New York: St. Martin's Press.

Vizenor, G. (1999). *Postindian conversations.* Lincoln: University of Nebraska Press.

Warrior, R. A. (1995). *Tribal secrets: Recovering American Indian intellectual traditions.* Minneapolis: University of Minnesota Press.

Watahomigie, J., & McCarty, T. L. (1994). Bilingual/bicultural education at Peach Springs: A Hualapai way of schooling. *Peabody Journal of Education, 69,* 26–42.

Rethinking Liberal and Radical Perspectives on Racial Inequality in Schooling: Making the Case for Nonsynchrony

CAMERON McCARTHY

It is not altogether surprising to find a certain uneven development within the various branches of the social science disciplines. . . . It could be argued that race analysis is surprisingly backward in this respect, far more so, for instance, than recent debates within the feminist movement. (Ben-Tovim, Gabriel, Law, & Stredder, 1981, p. 155)

Marxist and other progressive writers on Africa generally approach the issue of "tribalism" as one would approach a minefield. (Saul, 1979, p. 391)

Despite comprehensive evidence of glaring disparities in education in the United States, rigorous, durable, and compelling explanations of the reproduction and persistence of racial inequality in schooling have been slow in coming. In sharp contrast, American curriculum theorists and sociologists of education have been far more forthcoming in their examination of how the variables of class and, more recently, those of gender, have informed the organization and selection of school youth (Anyon, 1979; Apple, 1982; Apple & Weis, 1983; Bowles & Gintis, 1976; Everhart, 1983). As Black sociologists such as Mullard (1985) and Sarup (1986) have pointed out, both mainstream and radical educational researchers have tended to under-theorize and marginalize phenomena associated with racial inequality.

This essay seeks to fulfill three objectives. First, I situate the issue of racial inequality within the context of current data on the status of racial minorities vis-à-vis Whites in U.S. schools and society. Second, I examine how the topic of race is treated in contemporary mainstream and neo-Marxist curriculum and educational research, paying particular attention to the limits and possibilities of the value-oriented thesis of multiculturalism that mainstream liberal educators have championed over the last fifteen years or so as a panacea for racial inequality in schooling. I also offer a critique of neo-Marxist subordination of racial inequality in education to working-class exploitation and the structural requirements of the economy. Third, I present an alternative approach, what I call a nonsynchronous theory of race relations in schooling, in which I argue against the "essentialist" or single-cause explanations of the persis-

Harvard Educational Review Vol. 58   No. 3   August 1988

tence of racial inequality in education currently offered in both mainstream and radical curriculum and educational literatures. Instead, I direct attention to the complex and contradictory nature of race relations in the institutional life of social organizations such as schools. In addition, this nonsynchronous approach attempts to dissolve the unwarranted separation of "values" from considerations of structural constraints on human actions in current accounts of the race/education couplet. I emphasize the materiality of ideology and argue for the codetermination of culture and politics, along with the economy, in radical accounts of the elaboration of the racial character of schooling. Ideology, culture, and politics are as important determinants in shaping race relations in schooling as is the economy. Typically, neo-Marxists emphasize the last of these realms. Racist ideology as a specific set of linked but contradictory ideas manifests itself unevenly in educational structures and the formal and informal practices of school life. In this sense, curricula and programs that seek to address racial antagonism in schooling must take into account, for example, the discriminatory effects of what Kevin Brown (1985) calls "White non-racism" (p. 670). "Non-racism" refers to the covert use of racial evaluation, "apparently" neutral but coded rhetoric or criteria to discuss minorities — for example, the use of code words such as "over-crowding," "welfare mothers," "the lack of experience," or "strain on current resources."

Mounting statistical evidence supplied in government commission reports, census data, and academic journals documents persistent and glaring disparities in the relative economic, social, and educational status of racial minorities and Whites in the United States (Editors, 1986). For instance, unemployment among Black women and men is currently more than twice the level of that among Whites. For Black families, the median income remains at about 56 percent of White families' median income — roughly what it was three decades ago. The Alliance Against Women's Oppression (1983) contends that Black mothers are four times as likely to die in childbirth as White mothers. Black and Native American infant mortality rates are currently higher than those of such Third World countries as Trinidad and Tobago and Costa Rica.

Current data on schooling also present an alarming picture of minority disadvantage. Data from the 1979 Census Bureau study showed that 35 percent of Hispanic and 26 percent of Black youth, ages 18 through 21, had dropped out of school, compared with 15 percent of all Whites of similar ages. Black and Hispanic youth who graduate from high school are less likely than White graduates to enroll in college. At the university level, the percentage of degrees awarded to minority students is also declining. Black students earned only 6.5 percent of all bachelor's degrees awarded in 1981 compared with 10 percent in 1976 (Editors, 1986). These statistics trenchantly underscore the intractability of racial inequality in school and society in the United States. But racial inequality of this sort is by no means peculiar to America; in other urban industrialized societies, such as England, Japan, Canada, and Australia, research has shown that minority youth fare poorly in school and in the labor market (Ogbu, 1978).

Over the years, mainstream and radical sociologists of curriculum and education have provided contrasting explanations for the persistence of racial inequality in schooling. Neo-Marxist sociologists of education such as Berlowitz (1984), Bowles and Gintis (1976), Carnoy (1974), Jakubowicz (1985), and Nkomo (1984) locate the roots of racial domination within the structural properties of capitalism and its elaboration as a world system. In these accounts, racial antagonism is seen as a by-product of the major class contradiction between labor and capital. These radical critics of schooling subsume the problem of racial inequality under the general rubric of working-class oppression. They argue that there is a structural relationship between a racially differentiated school curriculum and a discontinuous labor market. Schools in this view follow the pattern of the economy and serve a narrow reproductive function. As a result, neo-Marxist sociologists of education offer no satisfactory theoretical explanation and no programmatic solution to the problem of racial inequality — the racial dimension is seen as of secondary import, and the inequality is expected to disappear with the abolition of capitalism.

Conversely, mainstream sociologists of schooling reduce the complexities associated with racial inequality to one overwhelming theoretical and programmatic concern: *the issue of educability of minorities.* Their central task has been to explain perceived differences between Black and White students as reflected in differential achievement scores on standardized tests, high school dropout rates, and so on. Their explanations of Black "underachievement" consequently depend upon pathological constructions of minority cognitive capacities (Jensen, 1981), child-rearing practices (Bell, 1975), family structures (Moynihan, 1965), and linguistic styles (Hess & Shipman, 1975). (For an extended discussion of these constructions see Henriques, 1984.) Mainstream theorists have in this sense tended to "blame the victim." Interventions and curriculum practices predicated on these approaches attempt to improve minority school performance through the manipulation of specific school variables, such as teacher behavior, methods of testing, placement, and so on (Atkinson, Morten, & Sue, 1979; Banks, 1981; Ogbu, 1978). As we shall see, multiculturalism represents an important but contradictory inflection on mainstream approaches to racial inequality in schooling.

The Multicultural Solution

Multiculturalism is a body of thought which originates in the liberal pluralist approaches to education and society. Multicultural education, specifically, must be understood as part of a curricular truce, the fallout of a political project to deluge and neutralize Black rejection of the conformist and assimilationist curriculum models solidly in place in the 1960s. Gwendolyn Baker (1977), for instance, cites Black "discontent" as the "catalyst" for the multicultural education movement in the United States: "The school district in Ann Arbor, Michigan, was much like other school districts throughout the country in the late 1960s. Students, particularly Black students, were involved in and responded to the civil rights and ethnic awareness activities of that decade" (p. 163). Barry Troyna (1984) makes similar claims with respect to the origins of multicultural education policies in England: "It is no coincidence that this flurry of [multicultural] activity has taken place in the period since the civil disturbances rocked virtually every major English city in the summer of 1981. . . . Broadly speaking, this educational response parallels what took place in the U.S.A. after the 1965 riots" (p. 76).

Multicultural education as a "new" curricular form attempted to absorb Black radical demands for the restructuring of school knowledge and pedagogical practices and rearticulated them into a reformist discourse of "nonracism." The discourse of nonracism was explicitly aimed at sensitizing White teachers and school administrators to minority "differences" as part of the plurality of differences that percolated through-out the educational system. At the same time, multiculturalism represented an ameliorative advance over rigidly coercive policies and Anglo conformity that had sta-bilized in American education during the first half of the century. The early twenti-eth-century educator Ellwood P. Cubberley summarized the curriculum and policy objectives of the American education system in these terms:

> Our task is to assimilate these people [racial minorities and immigrants] as part of
> the American race, and to implant in their children so far as can be done the Anglo-
> Saxon conceptions of righteousness, law, order, and popular government, and to
> awaken in them reverence for our democratic institutions and for those things
> which we as a people hold to be of abiding worth. (quoted in Grant, Boyle, &
> Sleeter, 1980, p. 11)

Proponents of multicultural education explicitly challenge this assimilationist stance, and urge that we draw more closely to the democratic pulse of egalitarianism and pluralism (Banks, 1981). Grant (1975), for example, argues that "multicultural education assigns a positive value to pluralism" (p. 4). The ideological and profes-sional stance of multiculturalism therefore espouses an emancipatory program with respect to racial inequality in school. First, proponents of multicultural education suggest that the fostering of universal respect for the various ethnic histories, cultures, and languages of the students in American schools will have a positive effect on indi-vidual minority student self-concepts. Positive self-concepts should in turn help to boost academic achievement among minority youth. Second, proponents suggest that through achieving, minority students could break the cycle of "missed opportu-nity" created by a previous biography of cultural deprivation. The labor market is ex-pected to verify multicultural programs by absorbing large numbers of qualified mi-nority youth. This thesis of a "tightening bond" between multicultural education and the economy is suggested in the following claim by James Rushton (1981):

> The curriculum in the multicultural school should encourage each pupil to succeed
> wherever he or she can and strive for competence in what he or she tries. Cultural
> taboos should be lessened by mutual experience and understandings. The curricu-
> lum in the multicultural school should allow these experiences to happen. If it does,
> it need have no fear about the future careers of its pupils. (p. 169)

But, as asserted by Rushton and other multicultural proponents, this linear connec-tion between educational credentials and the economy is problematic. The assump-tion that a more sensitive curriculum will necessarily lead to higher educational attain-ment and achievement and to jobs for Black and minority youth, is frustrated by the existence of racial practices in the job market itself. Troyna (1984) and Blackburn and Mann (1979), in their incisive analyses of the British job market, explode the myth of a necessary "tightening bond" between education and the economy. In his investiga-tion of the fortunes of "educated" Black and White youth in the job market, Troyna concludes that racial and social connections, rather than educational qualifications per se, "determined" the phenomenon of better job chances for White youth even when Black youth had higher qualifications than their White counterparts (1984). The tendency of employers to rely on informal channels or "word of mouth" networks, together represent some of the systematic ways in which the potential for success of qualified Black youth in the labor market is undermined. Carmichael and Hamilton (1967) and Marable (1983) have made a similar argument with respect to the racial obstacles to the employment of qualified Black youth in the job market in the United States. In an analysis of Black unemployment in the 1980s, Chrichlow (1985) concludes that there is no "good fit" between Black educational achievement and the job market. Expanding this argument, he makes the following claim:

> In combination with subtle forms of discrimination, job relocation, and increasing competition among workers for smaller numbers of "good" jobs, rising entry level job requirements clearly underscore the present employment difficulties experienced by young Black workers. Whether they possess a high school diploma or not. Blacks, in this instance, continue to experience high rates of unemployment despite possessing sound educational backgrounds and potential (capital) to be productive workers. (p. 6).

Besides this particular naiveté about the racial character of the job market, a further criticism can be made of the multicultural reformist thesis. As Berlowitz (1984), Carby (1982), and Mullard (1985) have all contended, the underlying assumptions of multicultural education are fundamentally idealistic. As such, the structural and material relations in which racial domination is embedded are underemphasized. This has a costly result. By focusing on sensitivity training and on individual differences, multicultural proponents typically skirt the very problem which multicultural education seeks to address: WHITE RACISM. The A.L.T.A.R.F. (All London Teachers Against Racism and Fascism), in their volume *Challenging Racism* (1984), berate the multicultural education program in London on precisely these grounds:

> These years have witnessed the growing acceptance by LEAs [local educational agencies] of a bland and totally depoliticized form of multicultural education alongside the intensification of state racism in the form of ever increasing deportations, police brutality against Black people, discrimination in employment and harassment in unemployment. (p. 1)

Despite these problems, multicultural education offers a range of ameliorative possibilities to the school curriculum that are not present within an assimilationist framework of Anglo-conformity. For example, in terms of what should be included in the school curriculum, multiculturalism raises the possibility that the plurality of experiences of racial minorities, women, and the socially disadvantaged classes would be taken seriously within a new core curriculum (Banks, 1981). In this sense, multicultural proponents strain their relationship to more mainstream notions of "what every American school child ought to know." This strategic challenge to liberal frameworks over what should constitute the core curriculum represents an important political space within current educational discourses — a political space that must be used to develop more creative and sustained challenges to racial inequality in schooling.

Neo-Marxist Approaches to Race and Education

Left critics provided theoretical arguments and enormous amounts of empirical evidence to suggest that schools were in fact, agencies of social, economic and cultural reproduction. (Giroux, 1985, p. xv)

On the subject of racial inequality in schooling neo-Marxist and radical formulations stand in sharp relief to the formulations of mainstream educational theorists. Neo-Marxist sociologists of education critique mainstream frameworks which depict the relationship between education and social differences and inequality. These radical theorists maintain that attempts to cast the problem of racial oppression in American schooling in terms of attitudes, values, and psychological differences are grossly inadequate. They argue further that liberal emphasis on the domain of values serves to divert our attention from the relationship of schooling to political economy and political power.

Radical educational theorists such as Berlowitz (1984), Bowles and Gintis (1976), and Nkomo (1984) have asserted instead that problems of social difference and inequality are more firmly rooted in the socioeconomic relations and structures generated within capitalist societies such as the United States. Education plays an essentially reproductive role in this story, insofar as it functions to legitimize social disparity and social differences through its selection process and its propagation of dominant values. But in these analyses, racial domination occurs as a tangential distraction to the main drama of class conflict. The whole structure of this radical theoretical framework ultimately rests upon an economic base, from which class relations are derived. All that is non-economic exists in the firmament of the superstructures, namely, the arenas of ideology, culture, consciousness, and so on. Schooling and ethnicity or race are thus dependent variables — epiphenomena relegated to the superstructures.

As C. L. R. James (1980) maintains, neo-Marxist sociologists and educational theorists tend to conceptualize race and racial struggles as episodic rather than determinant. Race, defined as the "otherness" of subordinate groups, manifests itself in neo-Marxist sociological theories only through a proliferation of negatives — "super-exploitation" (Blauner, 1972), "split/labor market" (Bonacich, 1980), and the "divide and conquer" strategies of individual capitalist employers (Roemer, 1979). This emphasis on the negative features of racial dynamics is reproduced in neo-Marxist theories of education. Berlowitz (1984) and Edari (1984), for example, explore the relationship of race to schooling through such taken-for-granted concepts as "minority failure," "underachievement," and "drop-out" rates. But for Berlowitz (1984), Jakubowicz (1985), and others, racial inequality in schooling is at best symptomatic of more powerful class-related dynamics operating within the economy. Edari (1984) summarizes the structuralist definition of race within the neo-Marxist framework: "For this purpose, ethnicity, racism and sexism must be understood in the proper perspective as forms of ideological mystification designed to facilitate exploitation and weaken the collective power of the laboring classes" (p. 8).

In summary, then, neo-Marxist educational theorists explain the specificity of racial domination within the evolution of capitalism in terms of a "structurally convenient form of ideology" (Mullard, 1985, p. 66). Racism as an ideology fulfills capitalism's economic requirements for superexploitation and the creation of a vast reserve army of labor. Racial strife disorganizes the working class and hence weakens working-class resistance to capitalist domination. Schools, as apparatuses of the state, both legitimize racial differences in society and reproduce the kind of racially subordinate subjects who are tracked into the secondary labor market.

But there are significant weaknesses in neo-Marxist theories of racial inequality in general and racial inequality in schooling in particular. First, the specification of the origins of racism within the origins of capitalism seems theoretically and empirically dubious. As both West (1982) and Mullard (1985) have noted, forms of racism existed prior to capitalism in pre-Columbian Latin America, ancient Greece, and elsewhere.

Second, there appears to be neither historical nor contemporary evidence to substantiate that relations established and legitimized on the basis of race were or are identical to those established and legitimized on the basis of class. Historically, for instance, slave labor was constituted by fundamentally different forms of economic, political, and ideological relations from those of wage labor (West, 1982). Slavery involved the exploitation of unfree and politically disenfranchised labor (the slave was the property of her or his employer). On the other hand, the wage-earning worker has the "freedom" within the capitalistic society to sell her or his labor power and the political civil right of mobility — the right to choose employers. It would be very difficult to explain the current incidences of racism against minorities on college campuses across the United States as an effect solely of class differences between different groups of students (Lord, 1987). These examples underscore the fact that the logic and fortunes of race relations are not at all coterminous with those of capitalism, as the persistence of racial antagonism in post-capitalist societies demonstrates (Greenberg, 1980).

Third, the neo-Marxist overemphasis on structural factors associated with the economy underrates the school's role in the production and reproduction of cultural identities and social differences. As such, these formulations trivialize the role of schooling in their accounts of the reproduction and transformation of race relations. In this sense, too, these school critics have ignored or minimized the importance of Black struggles, particularly those struggles conducted on the terrain of education. Black struggles have encouraged and intensified similar efforts with respect to class and gender struggles for political participation and inclusion, and for social and economic amelioration within the United States and in the Third World (McCarthy & Apple, 1988).

Fourth, both neo-Marxist and mainstream educational theorists treat racial groups as monolithic entities, disregarding both differences within groups and the interrelated dynamics of class and gender. As Marable (1985) has insisted, with respect to class dynamics among Black Americans, and Fuller (1980) has maintained, in relation to gender-based forms of resistance within West Indian subcultures in England, the characterization of minority groups in monolithic terms leads to unwarranted generalizations about the social, political, and cultural behavior of racially oppressed groups.

Parallelism and Nonsynchrony: Toward an Alternative Approach to Race and Education

The traditional literature on race and education has failed to reconcile an unwarranted bifurcation. On the one hand, mainstream educational theories assign racial phenomena to the realm of values, beliefs, individual preferences, tastes, and so on; thereby forfeiting a consideration of the structural constraints that limit and regulate human action, and denying the power and materiality of ideology. On the other hand, orthodox and neo-Marxist formulations customarily subordinate human agency and consciousness in their discussion of racial inequality. In significant ways, then, both mainstream and neo-Marxist approaches to racial inequality are "essentialist" in that they eliminate the "noise" of multidimensionality, historical variability, and subjectivity from their explanations of educational differences (Omi & Winant, 1986). The theoretical and practical insights gained from a more relational analysis of racial domination in schooling — one that attempts to show the links between existing social structures (whether economic, political, or ideological) and what real people such as teachers do — have been forfeited.

In recent years, we have witnessed the appearance of more subtle cultural theories and ethnographies of inequality and schooling within Marxist sociology of education paradigms. The work of Apple and Weis (1983), Carby (1982), Giroux (1985), Omi and Winant (1986), Troyna and Williams (1986), and Weis (1985) represents the emergence of a culturalist Marxism that has begun to awaken the radical and liberal school theories with respect to racial and sexual inequality. These educators have drawn attention to the autonomous logics and effects of racial and sexual dynamics in schooling, and to their necessary interaction with class, in lived social and cultural practices in the organization, reproduction, and transformation of social life. These cultural-studies approaches to schooling also call into question the base-superstructure model of society traditionally used by neo-Marxist theorists to explain the relationship between education and the economy and between race and class.

Marxist cultural theorists have therefore argued for a more integrated and synthetic conceptual framework as the basis for researching inequality in schooling. This framework — one that directs our attention to the interrelationships among a number of dynamics and that attempts to illuminate complexity, not wish it away — is known as the *parallelist* position. The case for the parallelist approach to race and schooling is very effectively presented by Michael W. Apple and Lois Weis (1983). Apple and Weis criticize the tendency of mainstream and radical theorists to divide society into separate domains of structure and culture. They argue that this arbitrary bifurcation directly promotes tendencies toward essentialism (single-cause explanations) in contemporary thinking about race. Researchers often "locate the fundamental elements of race, not surprisingly, on their home ground" (Omi & Winant, 1986, p. 52). For neo-Marxists, then, one must first understand the class basis of racial inequality; and for liberal theorists, cultural and social values and prejudices are the primary sources of racial antagonism. In contrast, Apple and Weis contend that race is not a "category" or a "thing-in-itself" (Thompson, 1966) but a vital social process which is integrally linked to other social processes and dynamics operating in education and society. These proponents of the parallelist position therefore hold that at least *three* dynamics — race, class, and gender — are essential in understanding schools and other institutions. None are reducible to the others, and class is not necessarily primary:

> [A] number of elements or *dynamics* are usually present at the same time in any one instance. This is important. Ideological form is not reducible to class. Processes of gender, age, and race enter directly into the ideological moment. . . . It is actually out of the articulation with, clash among, or contradictions among and within, say, class, race, and sex that ideologies are lived in one's day-to-day life. (Apple & Weis, 1983, p. 24)

In addition to this critique of class essentialism, these writers also offer a re-evaluation of economically reductive explanations of unequal social relations. It is acknowledged that the economy plays a powerful role in determining the structure of opportunities and positions in capitalist society. But "the" economy does not exhaust all

FIGURE 1   *The Parallelist Position*

		Economic	Cultural	Political
		Spheres		
	Class			
Dynamics	Race			
	Gender			

Taken from Michael W. Apple and Lois Weis, eds., *Ideology and Practice in Schooling* (Philadelphia: Temple University Press, 1983), p. 25.

existing social relations in society. Rather than using the economy to explain everything, theorists of the parallelist position have argued for an expanded view of the social formation in which the role of ideology and culture is recognized as integral to the shaping of unequal social relations and life chances. Apple and Weis (1983) maintain that there are three spheres of social life: economic, political, and cultural. The dynamics of class, race, and gender operate within each sphere while the spheres themselves continually interact. Unlike base-superstructure models, proponents of parallelist theory assume that action in one sphere can have an effect on action in another (Omi & Winant, 1986). The parallelist position therefore presents us with a theory of *overdetermination* in which the unequal processes and outcomes of teaching and learning and of schooling in general are produced by the constant interactions among three dynamics (race, gender, and class) and in three spheres (economic, political, and cultural). The parallelist model is presented in Figure 1.

The proposition that "each sphere of social life is constituted by the dynamics of class, race, and gender" (Apple & Weis, 1983, p. 25) has broad theoretical and practical merit. For example, it is impossible to understand fully the problem of the phenomenal high dropout rate among Black and Hispanic school youth without taking into account the interrelated race, class, and gender oppressions in U.S. urban centers and the ways in which the intersections of these social dynamics work to systematically "disqualify" inner-city minority youth in educational institutions and in the job market. In a similar manner, theoretical emphasis on gender dynamics complements our understanding of the unequal division of labor in schools and society and directs our attention to the way in which capitalism uses patriarchal relations to depress the wage scale and the social value of women's labor.

At a time when class and economic reductionism still play important roles in our explanations, the thesis of parallelism holds promise. This does not mean, however, that the movement toward a parallelist position is without problems. Its basic drawback is that parallelism has been construed in terms of static, additive models of double and triple oppression in which racial oppression is simply added to class and gender oppression.

Attempts to specify the dynamics of race, class, and gender phenomena in education have often been formulated in terms of a system of linear "additions" or gradations of oppression. Thus, for example, Spencer (1984), in her insightful case study of women schoolteachers, draws attention to their double oppression. Simply stated, these women perform onerous tasks with respect to both their domestic and emotional labor in the home and their instructional labor in the classroom (pp. 283–296). In Spencer's analysis, the oppression of these women in the home is "added" to their oppression as teachers working in the classroom. No attempt is made here to represent the *qualitatively* different experiences of Black women both in the context of the domestic sphere and within the teaching profession itself. In this essentially incremental model of oppression, patriarchal and class forms of oppression unproblematically reproduce each other. Accounts of the intersection of race, class, and gender such as these overlook instances of tension, contradiction, and discontinuity in the institutional life of the school setting (McCarthy & Apple, 1988). Dynamics of race, class, and gender are thus conceptualized as having individual and uninterrupted effects.

Notions of double and triple oppression are not wholly inaccurate. Nevertheless, we need to see these relations as far more complex, problematic, and contradictory than parallelist theory suggests. One of the most useful attempts to conceptualize the interconnections between race, class, and gender has been formulated by Emily Hicks (1981). She cautions critical researchers against the tendency to theorize about the interrelations between social dynamics as "parallel," "reciprocal," or "symmetrical." Instead, Hicks offers the thesis that the operation of race, class, and gender relations at the level of daily practices in schools, workplaces, and so forth, is systematically *contradictory or nonsynchronous*. Hicks's emphasis on nonsynchrony (the production of difference) helps to lay the basis for an alternative approach to thinking about the operation of these social relations and dynamics at the institutional level.

By invoking the concept of nonsynchrony, I wish to advance the position that individuals or groups in their relation to economic, political, and cultural institutions such as schools do not share an identical consciousness and express the same interests, needs, or desires "at the same point in time" (Hicks, 1982, p. 221). In this connection , it is also necessary to attach great importance to the organizing principles of selection, inclusion, and exclusion. These principles operate in ways that affect how marginalized minority youth are positioned in dominant social and educational policies and agendas. Schooling, in this sense, constitutes a site for the production of the politics of difference. The politics of difference or nonsynchrony in the material context of the school expresses "culturally sanctioned, rational responses to struggles over scarce [or unequal] resources" (Wellman, 1977, p. 4).

The concept of nonsynchrony begins to untangle the complexity of causal motion and effects "on the ground," as it were. It also raises questions about the nature, exercise, and multiple determination of power within the middle ground of everyday practices in schooling. The fact is that, as Hicks (1981) suggests, dynamic relations of race, class, or gender do not unproblematically reproduce each other. These relations are complex and often have contradictory effects even in similar institutional settings. It is, therefore, important that we begin to understand the dynamics of the interaction of race, class, and gender in settings inside and outside of schools. The patterns of the social stratification by race, class, and gender emerge not as static variables but as efficacious structuring principles that shape minority/majority relations in everyday life.

In their discussion of educational and political institutions, Gilroy (1982), Omi and Winant (1986), and Sarup (1986) have emphasized the fact that racial and sexual antagonism can, at times, "cut at right angles" to class solidarity. The work of Gilroy (1982) and others directs our attention to the issues of nonsynchrony and contradiction in minority/majority relations in institutional settings, and suggests not only their complexity, but the impossibility of predicting these dynamics in any formulaic way based on a monolithic view of race. For instance, both Omi and Winant (1986) and Sarup (1986) point to examples of the diminution of working-class solidarity outside education, in the context of racial antagonism within North American and British White-dominated labor unions. These unions have had a long history of hostility to minorities and minority causes. On the other hand, Nkomo (1984), in his discussion of the dynamics of race/class relations in South African educational institutions, cites examples of the augmentation of racial solidarity across class lines. He argues that the high levels of cultural alienation experienced in South African Bantu universities by both Black students from urban, professional, middle-class backgrounds and working-class students from the Bantustans heightens the bonds of racial solidarity between these youth of different class backgrounds. Burawoy (1981) has identified the opposite effect of the intersection of race and class in the South African context. In this case, the operation of class contradictions as expressed in the differing material interests and as-pirations of middle-class Black teachers, nurses, state bureaucrats, and their racial counterparts — the Black proletariat from the Bantustans — undermines racial soli-darity between these radically opposed socioeconomic groups. Mary Fuller (1980) points to other contradictions in her study of the subculture of West Indian girls at a British working-class high school. These students exist in a nonsynchronous relation-ship with both their West Indian male counterparts and White working-class girls. While West Indian male youth reject the British school curriculum, the West Indian girls in Fuller's study were among the school's high achievers. However, their apparent compliance with school values of academic success paradoxically constituted the ideo-logical basis for their assertion of their "independence" from West Indian boys as well as their rejection of the racial "underachievement" label that the British school system applies to West Indian youth as a whole.

It is to this literature — literature on the tensions and contradictions among raced, classed, and gendered forms of domination both inside and outside education — that critical scholarship in education should now turn. The key concepts of nonsynchrony and contradiction need to be fully integrated into current research on racial domina-tion in schooling. At the same time, though, we need to be careful not to revert to a totally structural reading of these issues. That is, we need to emphasize the symbolic, signifying, and language dimensions of social interactions and their integral relation-ship both to systems of control and to strategies for emancipation.

This emphasis on symbols, signs, and representations has been particularly impor-tant for advancing our theoretical understanding of the ways racial and sexual antago-nisms operate within cultural, political, and economic institutions such as schools (Carby, 1982). Indeed, we must remember that for a long time Black and feminist writers have argued (much against the tide of dominant research) that racial antago-nism and sexual oppression are mediated through ideology, culture, political and social theories themselves. While neo-Marxist researchers maintained that it was economic exploitation and capitalist need for surplus value that explained the oppression of the socially disadvantaged, Black and feminist writers drew attention to modes of devalua-tion of self-image, culture, and identity. For writers such as James Baldwin (1986),

Ntozake Shange (1983), June Jordan (1980), and Audre Lorde (1982), American schools are principal sites for the production and naturalization of myths and ideologies that systematically disorganize and neutralize minority cultural identities. With the full acknowledgment of the persuasiveness of these claims, race relations theorists such as Cornel West (1982) have argued that it is precisely in these "non-economic" sites of self-production and identity formation, such as the school and the church, that African Americans have sought to struggle against White oppression.

The issues of culture and identity must be seriously incorporated into a nonsynchronous approach to racial domination in schooling — not in the sense of an easy reduction to beliefs and values or the benign pluralism ("We are all the same because we are different.") of the multicultural paradigm, but in terms of a politic that recognizes the strategic importance of the historical struggles over the production of knowledge and the positioning of minorities in social theories and educational policies. Only by taking these issues seriously can we overcome the past and present tendencies in radical scholarship, which, as cultural critics such as Edward Said (1986) argue, obliterate the specific histories and struggles of the oppressed. This, of course, must be done with a full recognition that culture and identity are produced in a material context — one that is completely racial, gendered, and class-defined. The fact that the principles of selection, inclusion, and exclusion that inform the organization of school life have been hitherto understood primarily through class and socioeconomic paradigms says more about the biographies of mainstream and radical neo-Marxist school theorists than about the necessary character of schooling. Critical analysis of inequality in schooling must involve some sober reflection on the racist and sexist character of the production and reproduction of curriculum research itself.

Theories of how race, class, and gender interact, and of how economic, political, and cultural power act in education, need to become increasingly subtle. A non-synchronous theoretical framework remains to be fully articulated. But we need to remember what all of this theoretical labor is about — the political, economic, and cultural lives of real people. Oppressed women and men and children of color are subject to relations of differential power. These relations are not abstract, but are experienced in ways that now help or hurt identifiable groups of people in all-too visible ways.

References

All London Teachers Against Racism and Fascism. (1984). *Challenging racism.* London: Author.

Alliance Against Women's Oppression. (September, 1983). Poverty not for women only: A critique of the "feminization of poverty." *Discussion Paper 3.* San Francisco: Author.

Anyon, J. (1979). Ideology and the United States history textbooks. *Harvard Educational Review, 49,* 361–386.

Apple, M. (1982). *Cultural and economic reproduction in education.* Boston: Routledge & Kegan Paul.

Apple, M., & Weis, L. (Eds.). (1983). *Ideology and practice in schooling.* Philadelphia: Temple University Press.

Atkinson, D., Morten, G., & Sue, D.W. (Eds.). (1979). *Counseling American minorities: A cross-cultural perspective.* Dubuque, IA: William C. Brown.

Baker, G. (1977). Development of the multicultural program: School of Education, University of Michigan. In F. H. Klassen & D. M. Gollnick (Eds.), *Pluralism and the American teacher: Issues and case studies* (pp. 163–169). Washington, DC: Ethnic Heritage Center for Teacher Education of the American Association of Colleges for Teacher Education.

Baldwin, J. (1961). *Nobody knows my name.* New York: Dial.

Banks, J. (1981). *Multiethnic education: Theory and practice.* Boston: Allyn & Bacon.

Bell, R. (1975). Lower class Negro mothers' aspirations for their children. In H. R. Stub (Ed.), *The sociology of education: A sourcebook* (pp. 125–136). Homewood, IL: Dorsey Press.

Ben-Tovim, G., Gabriel, J., Law, I., & Stredder, K. (1981). Race, left strategies and the state. In D. Adlam et al. (Eds.), *Politics and power three: Sexual politics, feminism, and socialism* (pp. 153–181). London: Routledge & Kegan Paul.

Berlowitz, M. (1984). Multicultural education: Fallacies and alternatives. In M. Berlowitz & R. Edari (Eds.), *Racism and the denial of human rights: Beyond ethnicity* (pp. 129–136). Minneapolis: Marxist Educational Press.

Blackburn, R. M., & Mann, M. (1979). *The working class in the labour market.* London: Macmillan.

Blauner, R. (1972). *Racial oppression in America.* New York: Harper & Row.

Bonacich, E. (1980). Class approaches to ethnicity and race. *Insurgent Sociologist, 10,* 9–24.

Bowles, S., & Gintis, H. (1976). *Schooling in capitalist America.* New York: Basic Books.

Brown, K. (1985). Turning a blind eye: Racial oppression and the unintended consequences of white "non-racism." *Sociological Review, 33,* 670–690.

Burawoy, M. (1981). The capitalist state in South Africa: Marxist and sociological perspectives on race and class. In M. Zeitlin (Ed.), *Political power and social theory* (vol. 2, pp. 279–335). Greenwich, CT: JAI Press.

Carby, H. (1982). Schooling in Babylon. In Centre for Contemporary Cultural Studies (Ed.), *The empire strikes back: Race and racism in 70s Britain* (pp. 183–211). London: Hutchinson.

Carmichael, S., & Hamilton, C. (1967). *Black power.* New York: Vintage.

Carnoy, M. (1974). *Education as cultural imperialism.* New York: Longman.

Carnoy, M., & Levin, H. (1985). *Schooling and work in the democratic state.* Stanford: Stanford University Press.

Chrichlow, W. (1985). *Urban crisis, schooling, and black youth unemployment: Case study.* Unpublished manuscript.

Edari, R. (1984). Racial minorities and forms of ideological mystification. In M. Berlowitz & R. Edari (Eds.), *Racism and the denial of human rights: Beyond ethnicity* (pp. 7–18). Minneapolis: Marxist Educational Press.

Editors. (1986, May 14). Here they come ready or not: An *Education Week* special report on the ways in which America's population in motion is changing the outlook for schools and society. *Education Week,* p. 28.

Everhart, R. (1983). *Reading, writing and resistance.* London: Routledge & Kegan Paul.

Fuller, M. (1980). Black girls in a London comprehensive school. In R. Deem (Ed.), *Schooling for women's work* (pp. 52–65). London: Routledge & Kegan Paul.

Gilroy, P. (1982). Steppin' out of Babylon: Race, class, and autonomy. In Centre for Contemporary Cultural Studies (Ed.), *The empire strikes back: Race and racism in 70s Britain* (pp. 278–314). London: Hutchinson.

Giroux, H. A. (1985). Introduction. In P. Freire (Ed.), *The politics of education.* South Hadley, MA: Bergin & Garvey.

Grant, C. (1975). Exploring the contours of a multicultural education. In C. Grant (Ed.), *Sifting and winnowing: An exploration of the relationship between CBTE and multicultural education* (pp. 1–11). Madison: University of Wisconsin-Madison, Teacher Corps Associates.

Grant, C., Boyle, M., & Sleeter, C. (1980). *The public school and the challenge of ethnic pluralism.* New York: Pilgrim Press.

Greenberg, S. (1980). *Race and state in capitalist development: Comparative perspectives.* New Haven: Yale University Press.

Henriques, J. (1984). Social psychology and the politics of racism. In J. Henriques (Ed.), *Changing the subject* (pp. 60–89). London: Methuen.

Hess, R., & Shipman, V. (1975). Early experience and socialization of cognitive modes in children. In H. R. Stub (Ed.), *The sociology of education: A source book* (pp. 96–113). Homewood, IL: Dorsey Press.

Hicks, E. (1981). Cultural Marxism: Non-synchrony and feminist practice. In L. Sargeant (Ed.), *Women and revolution* (pp. 219–238). Boston: South End Press.

Jakubowicz, A. (1985). State and ethnicity: Multiculturalism as ideology. In F. Rizvi (Ed.), *Multiculturalism as an educational policy.* Geelong, Victoria: Deakin University Press.

James, C. L. R. (1980). *Spheres of existence: Selected writings.* Westport, CT: Hill & Co.

Jensen, A. (1981). *Straight talk about mental tests.* New York: Free Press.

Jordan, J. (1980). *Passion.* Boston: Beacon Press.

Lamar, J. V., Jr. (1986, December 1). Today's native sons. *Time,* p. 27.

Lord, M. (1987). Frats and sororities: The Greek rites of exclusion. *The Nation, 245* (1).

Lorde, A. (1982). *Zami: A new spelling of my name.* New York: Crossing Press.

Marable, M. (1985). *Black American politics.* London: Verso.

McCarthy, C. *Beyond intervention: Neo-Marxist theories of racial domination and the state.* Unpublished manuscript.

McCarthy, C., & Apple, M. W. (1988). *Race, class, and gender in American educational research: Toward a Nonsynchronous Parallelist Position.* In L. Weis (Ed.), *Class, Race, and Gender in American Education.* Albany: State University of New York Press.

Moynihan, D. (1965). *The Negro family: The case for national action.* Washington, DC: U. S. Department of Labor, Office of Policy, Planning, and Research.

Mullard, C. (1985). Racism in society and schools: History, policy, and practice. In F. Rizvi (Ed.), *Multiculturalism as an educational policy* (pp. 64–81). Geelong, Victoria: Deakin University Press.

Nkomo, M. (1984). *Student culture and activism in black South African universities.* Westport, CT: Greenwood Press.

Ogbu, J. (1978). *Minority education and caste.* New York: Academic Press.

Omi, M., & Winant, H. (1986). *Racial formation in the United States.* New York: Routledge & Kegan Paul.

Roemer, J. (1979, Autumn). Divide and conquer: Microfoundations of Marxian theory of wage discrimination. *Bell Journal of Economics, 10,* 695–705.

Rushton, J. (1981). Careers and the multicultural curriculum. In J. Lynch (Ed.), *Teaching in the multicultural school* (pp. 163–170). London: Ward Lock.

Said, E. (1986). Intellectuals in the post-colonial world. *Salmagundi, 70/71,* 44–64.

Sarup, M. (1986). *The politics of multiracial education.* London: Routledge & Kegan Paul.

Saul, J. (1979). *The state and revolution in Eastern Africa.* New York: Monthly Review Press.

Shange, N. (1983). *A daughter's geography.* New York: St. Martin's Press.

Spencer, D. (1984). The home and school lives of women teachers. *Elementary School Journal, 84,* 283–298.

Thompson, E. P. (1966). *The making of the English working class.* New York: Vintage Books.

Troyna, B. (1984). Multicultural education: Emancipation or containment? In L. Barton & S. Walker (Eds.), *Social crisis and educational research* (pp. 75–97). London: Croom Helm.

Troyna, B., & Williams, J. (1986). *Racism, education and the state.* London: Croom Helm.

Weis, L. (1985). *Between two worlds.* Boston: Routledge & Kegan Paul.

Wellman, D. (1977). *Portraits of White racism.* Cambridge, Eng.: Cambridge University Press.

West, C. (1982). *Prophecy and deliverance! Toward a revolutionary Afro-American Christianity.* Philadelphia: Westminster.

I would like to thank the following people for their critical support and comments on the various drafts of this article: Michael W. Apple, Marie Brennan, Ron Good, Stuart Hall, Maria Soledad Martinez, Avanthia Milingou, Laura Stempel Mumford, Bill Pinar, Leslie Roman, Fran Schrag, Odaipaul Singh, Ahmad Moruzso Sultan, Tony Whitson, Erik O. Wright, Osvaldo Vazquez, and all the members of the U.W./C.I. Friday Sessions.

PART FOUR

Popular Culture and Youth Studies

INTRODUCTION

Popular Culture and Youth Studies

Popular culture is a transversal element connecting various approaches in the field of cultural studies, and youth have received more attention in the study of popular culture than any other population. As both contributors to Part Four argue, youth are major participants in the production and consumption of popular culture.[1] Many scholars in the fields of popular culture and youth studies see this relationship as central to the actual and potential role of youth in a democratic society.[2] Seeking materials for the construction and definition of their identities and coping with the social forces that have a direct impact on their lives, the collective action of youth in relation to popular culture remains an important context for cultural studies research and points directly to the crucial relationship between education and cultural studies.

Despite its importance, defining what constitutes popular culture is an elusive task. Notions of popular culture have undergone extensive revision in the last twenty-five years.[3] Some specific definitions — all of which are limited — include: those cultural products and practices that different groups of people identify with, hence making them "popular"; all of the images and messages transmitted through mass media like television and mainstream radio; or, even more coarsely, the leisure activities of the "popular masses" as opposed to the cultural preferences of the elite. Other broader definitions assume that all cultural activity that presupposes a public is popular culture. More recent approaches are less interested in determining what is "popular" and more in understanding how the term is assigned to various cultural practices and the political implications of doing so.[4]

Within education, popular culture has been thus far conceptualized broadly in three ways. The curricular approach sees popular culture as useful content to be incorporated into the established school curriculum. Advocates of this approach see popular culture as a tool to engage students in their learning.[5] The critical pedagogical approach deals with the educative function of popular culture itself. It tries to understand both what popular culture teaches and how it teaches, and it is most interested in how popular culture serves as a tool for both reproduction and resistance.[6] Lastly, many educators deal with popular culture as a threat to the development of youth. In this more traditional way of thinking about popular culture and mass media, teachers see these influences as distracting at best, and as dangerous at worst.[7]

Ten years after its first publication in the *Harvard Educational Review,* Henry Giroux's *Doing Cultural Studies: Youth and the Challenge of Pedagogy* has become a milestone for understanding the intersection of popular culture and the education of young people, at least in the United States. In this classic essay, Giroux reformulates the link between critical pedagogy and cultural studies, highlighting the need for a more fluid dialogue between cultural theorists and educators committed to a critical educational project. Giroux points to the various factors that underlie the resistance from the field of education to the general approach of cultural studies. The insistence on interdisciplinary work and the centrality of analyses of power in cultural studies have been sources of great tension between the two fields of study. Arguing against this tendency, Giroux calls for educators to pay close attention to the changing conditions of youth through the conceptual contributions of cultural studies. Popular culture, he argues, is a pedagogical tool on its own terms, one that connects directly to the various struggles for identity and representation in which youth are invested. In this way, understanding youth through their cultural practices allows educators to engage them in a process of critical reflection about their social existence and their role as actors in the making of a public sphere. To conclude, Giroux identifies five theoretical elements to strengthen the link between the study of popular culture and education.

The intellectual contributions of Paul Willis to cultural theory have had a profound effect on how educational researchers study the experiences of students from subordinate groups, particularly in urban public school systems.[8] Willis developed a theory of cultural production by looking closely at youth culture within and outside of schools and analyzing their cultural responses to the changing socioeconomic context. In his chapter, Willis reflects on his analyses of youth culture over the past three decades, and identifies three "waves of modernization" that have risen from radical shifts in technology and economic structures. Each of these shifts has been accompanied by systemic initiatives "from above" that typically fail to consider the experiences of youth and the range of cultural responses "from below" to state and industry sponsored schemes. In this broad analysis, Willis views the school as the "instrument and site" where the cultural responses of young people to changing material conditions are played out. He compels educators and educational researchers to "open new public realms that are seen not as compensating for or attacking commercial imperatives and their erosion of traditional values, but as going along with the flow of actually existing energies and passions." He concludes, "The conditions of existence within these new public realms would make young people more visible and give them more control over what is expressed and how."

Regardless of how educators view the relationship between popular culture and education, it would be difficult to ignore its ubiquity in the lives of youth.[9] Studies of youth and popular culture offer an opportunity to look at the complex dynamic interaction between social institutions (e.g., media producers, schools, families) and the cultural production of young people. As Paul Willis argues in his chapter, schools are not only a public space where youth spend a great deal of time, but also an important site for the development of social identities and forms of cultural resistance to pervasive social conditions. Understanding the underlying power dynamics that shape the interactions between schools and youth culture has been crucial for theorizing the relationship between the social forces that reproduce society and how individuals and groups resist (or at times reinforce) these forces through cultural production.[10] Popular culture is at the heart of these complex processes.

Notes

1. For a deeper development of this positions, see Henry A. Giroux, *Border Crossings: Cultural Workers and the Politics of Education* (New York: Routledge, 1992); Paul Willis, *Common Culture: Symbolic Work at Play in the Everyday Cultures of the Young* (Boulder, CO: Westview Press, 1990).

2. This point is explored in depth by Nadine Dolby, "Popular Culture and Democratic Practice," *Harvard Educational Review* 73 (2003).

3. For a range of disciplinary perspectives and attempts at defining popular culture, see Chandra Mukerji and Michael Schudson, eds., *Rethinking Popular Culture: Contemporary Perspectives in Cultural Studies* (Los Angeles: University of California Press, 1991). Dolby offers a straightforward discussion of various approaches to the study of popular culture in education in "Popular Culture and Democratic Practice."

4. For explorations of these and other definitions, see Stuart Hall, ed., *Representation: Cultural Representation and Signifying Practice* (London: Sage, 1997); Angela McRobbie, *Postmodernism and Popular Culture* (London: Routledge, 1994); Mukerji and Schudson, *Rethinking Popular Culture;* Roy Shuker, *Understanding Popular Music* (London: Routledge, 1994).

5. See, for example, Donna E. Alvermann, Jennifer S. Moon, and Margaret C. Hagood, *Popular Culture in the Classroom: Teaching and Researching Critical Media Literacy* (Newark, DE: International Reading Association, 1999); Anne Haas Dyson, *The Brothers and Sisters Learn to Write: Popular Literacies in Childhood and School Cultures* (New York: Teachers College Press, 2003); Anne Haas Dyson, *Writing Superheroes: Contemporary Childhood, Popular Culture, and Classroom Literacy* (New York: Teacher's College Press, 1997); Renee Hobbs, "The Simpsons Meet Mark Twain: Analyzing Popular Media Texts in the Classroom," *English Journal* 87 (1998); Andrew Huddleston, "Incorporating Popular Culture into the Curriculum," *Educational Horizons,* Winter 2003.

6. Giroux's chapter in this volume exemplifies this approach, which he has been a central figure in developing. See, for example, Henry A. Giroux, *Disturbing Pleasures: Learning Popular Culture* (New York: Routledge, 1994); Henry A. Giroux, *Stealing Innocence: Corporate Culture's War on Children* (New York: Palgrave, 2000). See also Toby Daspit and John A. Weaver, eds., *Popular Culture and Critical Pedagogy: Reading, Constructing, Connecting* (New York: Garland Publishing Group, 1999). For a critique of this perspective, see David Buckingham, *Teaching Popular Culture: Beyond Radical Pedagogy* (London: UCL Press, 1998).

7. See, for example, Tipper Gore, *Raising PG Kids in an X-Rated Society* (Nashville, TN: Abingdon Press, 1987). See also the essays in Diane Ravitch and Joseph Viteritti, eds., *Kid Stuff: Marketing Sex and Violence to America's Children* (Baltimore: Johns Hopkins University Press, 2003).

8. Willis, *Common Culture;* Paul Willis, *Learning to Labour* (Farnborough, Eng.: Saxon House, 1977).

9. The essays in the *Harvard Educational Review* Special Issue on Popular Culture and Education underscore this point and offer compelling examples. See also Greg Dimitriadis, *Friendship, Cliques, and Gangs: Young Black Men Coming of Age in Urban America* (New York: Teachers College Press, 2003); Nadine Dolby, *Constructing Race: Youth, Identity, and Popular Culture in South Africa* (Albany: State University of New York Press, 2001); Glenn Hudak, "The 'Sound' Identity: Music-Making and Schooling," in *Sound Identities: Popular Music and the Cultural Politics of Education,* ed. Cameron McCarthy et al. (New York: Peter Lang, 1999); Sunaina Marr Maira, *Desis in the House: Indian American Youth Culture in New York City* (Philadelphia: Temple University Press, 2002).

10. Lois Weis and Michelle Fine, eds., *Beyond Silenced Voices: Class, Race, and Gender in United States Schools* (Albany: State University of New York Press, 1993); Lois Weis and Michelle Fine, eds., *Construction Sites: Excavating Race, Class, and Gender among Urban Youth* (New York: Teachers College Press, 2000); Yali Zou and Enrique T. Trueba, eds., *Ethnic Identity and Power: Cultural Contexts of Political Action in School and Society* (Albany: State University of New York Press, 1998).

Doing Cultural Studies:
Youth and the Challenge
of Pedagogy

HENRY A. GIROUX

In our society, youth is present only when its presence is a problem, or is regarded as a problem. More precisely, the category "youth" gets mobilized in official documentary discourse, in concerned or outraged editorials and features, or in the supposedly disinterested tracts emanating from the social sciences at those times when young people make their presence felt by going "out of bounds," by resisting through rituals, dressing strangely, striking bizarre attitudes, breaking rules, breaking bottles, windows, heads, issuing rhetorical challenges to the law.[1]

A recent commentary in the *Chronicle of Higher Education* claimed that the field of cultural studies is "about the hottest thing in humanities and social-science research right now, but it's largely peopled by scholars in literature, film and media, communications, and philosophy".[2] Given the popularity of cultural studies for a growing number of scholars, I have often wondered why so few academics have incorporated cultural studies into the language of educational reform. If educators are to take seriously the challenge of cultural studies, particularly its insistence on generating new questions, models, and contexts in order to address the central and most urgent dilemmas of our age, they must critically address the politics of their own location. This means understanding not only the ways in which institutions of higher education play their part in shaping the work we do with students, but also the ways in which our vocation as educators supports, challenges, or subverts institutional practices that are at odds with democratic processes and the hopes and opportunities we provide for the nation's youth. In what follows, I want to explore not only why educators refuse to engage the possibilities of cultural studies, but also why scholars working within a cultural studies framework often refuse to take seriously pedagogy and the role of schools in the shaping of democratic public life.

Educational theorists demonstrate as little interest in cultural studies as cultural studies scholars do in the critical theories of schooling and pedagogy. For educators, this indifference may be explained in part by the narrow technocratic models that

Harvard Educational Review   Vol. 64   No. 3   Fall 1994
Copyright © by the President and Fellows of Harvard College

dominate mainstream reform efforts and structure education programs. Within such a tradition, management issues become more important than understanding and furthering schools as democratic public spheres.[3] Hence, the regulation, certification, and standardization of teacher behavior is emphasized over creating the conditions for teachers to undertake the sensitive political and ethical roles they might assume as public intellectuals who selectively produce and legitimate particular forms of knowledge and authority. Similarly, licensing and assimilating differences among students is more significant than treating students as bearers of diverse social memories with a right to speak and represent themselves in the quest for learning and self-determination. While other disciplines have appropriated, engaged, and produced new theoretical languages in keeping with changing historical conditions, colleges of education have maintained a deep suspicion of theory and intellectual dialogue and thus have not been receptive to the introduction of cultural studies.[4] Other explanations for this willful refusal to know would include a history of educational reform that has been overly indebted to practical considerations that often support a long tradition of anti-intellectualism. Moreover, educators frequently pride themselves on being professional, scientific, and objective. Cultural studies challenges the ideological and political nature of such claims by arguing that teachers always work and speak within historically and socially determined relations of power.[5] Put another way, educators whose work is shaped by cultural studies do not simply view teachers and students either as chroniclers of history and social change or recipients of culture, but as active participants in its construction.

The resistance to cultural studies may also be due to the fact that it reasserts the importance of comprehending schooling as a mechanism of culture and politics, embedded in competing relations of power that attempt to regulate and order how students think, act, and live.[6] Since cultural studies is largely concerned with the critical relationship among culture, knowledge, and power, it is not surprising that mainstream educators often dismiss cultural studies as being too ideological, or simply ignore its criticisms regarding how education generates a privileged narrative space for some social groups and a space of inequality and subordination for others.

Historically, schools and colleges of education have been organized around either traditional subject-based studies (math education) or into largely disciplinary/administrative categories (curriculum and instruction). Within this type of intellectual division of labor, students generally have had few opportunities to study larger social issues. This slavish adherence to structuring the curriculum around the core disciplinary subjects is at odds with the field of cultural studies, whose theoretical energies are largely focused on interdisciplinary issues, such as textuality and representation refracted through the dynamics of gender, sexuality, subordinated youth, national identity, colonialism, race, ethnicity, and popular culture.[7] By offering educators a critical language through which to examine the ideological and political interests that structure reform efforts in education, such as nationalized testing, standardized curriculum, and efficiency models, cultural studies incurs the wrath of mainstream and conservative educators who often are silent about the political agendas that underlie their own language and reform agendas.[8]

Cultural studies also rejects the traditional notion of teaching as a technique or set of neutral skills and argues that teaching is a social practice that can only be understood through considerations of history, politics, power, and culture. Given its concern with everyday life, its pluralization of cultural communities, and its emphasis on multidisciplinary knowledge, cultural studies is less concerned with issues of certification and testing than it is with how knowledge, texts, and cultural products are produced, circulated, and used. In this perspective, culture is the ground "on which analysis proceeds, the object of study, and the site of political critique and intervention."[9] This in part explains why some advocates of cultural studies are increasingly interested in "how and where knowledge needs to surface and emerge in order to be consequential" with respect to expanding the possibilities for a radical democracy.[10]

Within the next century, educators will not be able to ignore the hard questions that schools will have to face regarding issues of multiculturalism, race, identity, power, knowledge, ethics, and work. These issues will play a major role in defining the meaning and purpose of schooling, the relationship between teachers and students, and the critical content of their exchange in terms of how to live in a world that will be vastly more globalized, high tech, and racially diverse than at any other time in history. Cultural studies offers enormous possibilities for educators to rethink the nature of educational theory and practice, as well as what it means to educate future teachers for the twenty-first century.[11]

At the same time, it is important to stress that the general indifference of many cultural studies theorists to the importance of critical pedagogy as a form of cultural practice does an injustice to the politically charged history of cultural studies, one which points to the necessity for combining self-criticism with a commitment to transforming existing social and political problems. It is not my intention here to replay the debate regarding what the real history of cultural studies is, though this is an important issue. Instead, I want to focus on the importance of critical pedagogy as a central aspect of cultural studies and on cultural work as a pedagogical practice. This suggests analyzing cultural studies for the insights it has accrued as it has moved historically from its previous concerns with class and language to its more recent analysis of the politics of race, gender, identity, and ethnicity. This is not meant to suggest that the history of cultural studies needs to be laid out in great detail as some sort of foundational exegesis. On the contrary, cultural studies needs to be approached historically as a mix of founding moments, transformative challenges, and self critical interrogations.[12] And it is precisely the rupturing spirit that informs elements of its interdisciplinary practice, social activism, and historical awareness that prompts my concern for the current lacunae in cultural studies regarding the theoretical and political importance of pedagogy as a founding moment in its legacy.

In what follows, I want to take up these concerns more concretely as they bear on what Dick Hebdige calls the "problem of youth" and the necessary importance of this issue for educators and other cultural workers.[13] In constructing this line of thought, I begin by making the case that pedagogy must become a defining principle of any critical notion of cultural studies. This position is developed, in part, to expand the meaning and relevance of pedagogy for those engaged in cultural work both in and outside of the university. I then argue for the pedagogical practice of using films about youth not only as legitimate objects of social knowledge that offer representations in which youth can identify their desires and hopes, but also as pedagogical texts that play a formative role in shaping the social identities of youth. Through an analysis of four Hollywood films about youth, I hope to show how the more progressive elements of critical pedagogical work can inform and be informed by cultural studies' emphasis on popular culture as a terrain of significant political and pedagogical importance. I will conclude by developing the implications cultural studies might have for those of us who are concerned about reforming schools and colleges of education.

The Absence of Pedagogy in Cultural Studies

It is generally argued that cultural studies is largely defined through its analysis of culture and power, particularly with regard to its "shifting of the terrain of culture toward the popular" while simultaneously expanding its critical reading of the production, reception, use, and effects of popular texts.[14] Texts in this case constitute a wide range of aural, visual, and printed signifiers; moreover, such texts are often taken up as part of a broader attempt to analyze how individual and social identities are mobilized, engaged, and transformed within circuits of power informed by issues of race, gender, class, ethnicity, and other social formations. All of these concerns point to the intellectual and institutional borders that produce, regulate, and engage meaning as a site of social struggle. Challenging the ways in which the academic disciplines have been used to secure particular forms of authority, cultural studies has opened up the possibility for questioning how power operates in the construction of knowledge while simultaneously redefining the parameters of the form and content of what is being taught in institutions of higher education. In this instance, struggles over meaning, language, and textuality have become symptomatic of a larger struggle over the meaning of cultural authority, the role of public intellectuals, and the meaning of national identity. While cultural studies proponents have provided an enormous theoretical service in taking up the struggle over knowledge and authority, particularly as it affects the restructuring of the curriculum in many colleges and universities, such struggles often overlook some of the major concerns that have been debated by various theorists who work within the diverse tradition of critical pedagogy. This is especially surprising since cultural studies draws its theoretical and political inspiration from feminism, postmodernism, post-colonialism, and a host of other areas that have at least made a passing reference to the importance of pedagogy.

I want to argue that cultural studies is still too rigidly tied to the modernist, academic disciplinary structures that it often criticizes. This is not to suggest that it does not adequately engage the issue of academic disciplines. In fact, this is one of its most salient characteristics.[15] What it fails to do is critically address a major prop of disciplinarity, which is the notion of pedagogy as an unproblematic vehicle for transmitting knowledge. Lost here is the attempt to understand pedagogy as a mode of cultural criticism for questioning the very conditions under which knowledge and identities are produced. Of course, theorists such as Gayatri Spivak, Stanley Aronowitz, and others do engage the relationship between cultural studies and pedagogy, but they constitute a small minority.[16] The haunting question here is, What is it about pedagogy that allows cultural studies theorists to ignore it?

One answer may lie in the refusal of cultural studies theorists either to take schooling seriously as a site of struggle or to probe how traditional pedagogy produces particular social histories, how it constructs student identities through a range of subject positions. Of course, within radical educational theory, there is a long history of developing critical discourses of the subject around pedagogical issues.[17]

Another reason cultural studies theorists have devoted little attention to pedagogy may be due to the disciplinary policing that leaves the marks of its legacy on all areas of the humanities and liberal arts. Pedagogy is often deemed unworthy of being taken up as a serious project; in fact, even popular culture has more credibility than pedagogy. This can be seen not only in the general absence of any discussion of pedagogy in cultural studies texts, but also in those studies in the humanities that have begun to engage pedagogical issues. Even in these works there is a willful refusal to acknowledge some of the important theoretical gains in pedagogy that have gone on in the last twenty years.[18] Within this silence lurks the seductive rewards of disciplinary control, a refusal to cross academic borders, and a shoring up of academic careerism, competitiveness, and elitism. Of course, composition studies, one of the few fields in the humanities that does take pedagogy seriously, occupies a status as disparaging as the field of education.[19] Hence, it appears that the legacy of academic elitism and professionalism still exercises a strong influence on the field of cultural studies, in spite of its alleged democratization of social knowledge.

Cultural Studies and Pedagogy

In what follows, I want to make a case for the importance of pedagogy as a central aspect of cultural studies. In doing so, I first want to analyze the role that pedagogy played in the early founding stages of the Birmingham Centre for Contemporary Cultural Studies.[20] I then want to define more specifically the central dimensions of pedagogy as a cultural practice. But before I address these two important moments of critical pedagogy as a form of cultural politics, I think it is important to stress that the concept of pedagogy must be used with respectful caution. Not only are there different versions of what constitutes critical pedagogy, but there is also no generic definition that can be applied to the term. At the same time, there are important theoretical insights and practices that are woven through various approaches to critical pedagogy. It is precisely these insights, which often define a common set of problems, that serve to delineate critical pedagogy as a set of conditions articulated within the shifting context of a particular political project. These problems include, but are not limited to, the relationship between knowledge and power, language and experience, ethics and authority, student agency and transformative politics, and teacher location and student formations.

Richard Hoggart and Raymond Williams addressed the issue of pedagogy in a similar manner in their early attempts to promote cultural studies in Britain. As founding figures in the Birmingham Centre for Contemporary Cultural Studies, Hoggart and Williams believed that pedagogy offered the opportunity to link cultural practice with the development of radical cultural theories. Not only did pedagogy connect questions of form and content, it also introduced a sense of how teaching, learning, textual studies, and knowledge could be addressed as political issues that bring to the foreground considerations of power and social agency. According to Williams, the advent of cultural studies in the 1930s and 1940s emerged directly out of the pedagogical work that was going on in adult education. The specificity of the content and context of adult education provided cultural studies with a number of issues that were to direct its subsequent developments in Birmingham. These included the refusal to accept the limitations of established academic boundaries and power structures, the demand for linking literature to the life situations of adult learners, and the call that schooling be empowering rather than merely humanizing.[21]

For Williams there is more at stake here than reclaiming the history of cultural studies; he is most adamant in making clear that the "deepest impulse [informing cultural studies] was the desire to make learning part of the process of social change itself."[22] It is precisely this attempt to broaden the notion of the political by making it more pedagogical that reminds us of the importance of pedagogy as a cultural practice. In this context, pedagogy deepens and extends the study of culture and power by addressing not only how culture is produced, circulated, and transformed, but also how it is actually negotiated by human beings within specific settings and circumstances. In this instance, pedagogy becomes an act of cultural production, a process through which power regulates bodies and behaviors as "they move through space and time."[23] While pedagogy is deeply implicated in the production of power/knowledge relationships and the construction of values and desires, its theoretical center of gravity begins not with a particular claim to new knowledge, but with real people articulating and rewriting their lived experiences within rather than outside of history. In this sense, pedagogy, especially in its critical variants, is about understanding how power works within particular historical, social, and cultural contexts in order to engage and, when necessary, to change such contexts.[24]

The importance of pedagogy to the content and context of cultural studies lies in the relevance it has for illuminating how knowledge and social identities are produced in a variety of sites in addition to schools. For Raymond Williams, one of the founding concepts of cultural studies was that cultural education was just as important as labor, political, and trade union education. Moreover, Williams believed that limiting the study of culture to higher education was to run the risk of depoliticizing it. Williams believed that education in the broad, political sense was essential not only for engaging, challenging, and transforming policy, but was also the necessary referent for stressing the pedagogical importance of work shared by all cultural workers who engage in the production of knowledge. This becomes clear in Williams's notion of permanent education. He writes:

> This idea [permanent education] seems to me to repeat, in a new and important idiom, the concepts of learning and of popular democratic culture which underlie the present book. What it valuably stresses is the education force of our whole social and cultural experience. It is therefore concerned, not only with continuing education, of a formal or informal kind, but with what the whole environment, its institutions and relationships, actively and profoundly teaches. To consider the problems of families, or of town planning, is then an educational enterprise, for these, also, are where teaching occurs. And then the field of this book, of the cultural communications which, under an old shadow, are still called mass communications, can be integrated, as I have always intended, with a whole social policy. For who can doubt, looking at television or newspapers, or reading the women's magazines, that here, centrally, is teaching, and teaching financed and distributed in a much larger way than in formal education?[25]

Building upon Williams's notion of permanent education, pedagogy in this sense provides a theoretical discourse for understanding how power and knowledge mutually inform each other in the production, reception, and transformation of social identities, forms of ethical address, and "desired versions of a future human community."[26] By refuting the objectivity of knowledge and asserting the partiality of all forms of pedagogical authority, critical pedagogy initiates an inquiry into the relationship between the form and content of various pedagogical sites and the authority they legitimate in securing particular cultural practices.

I want to be more specific about the importance of pedagogy for cultural studies and other emerging forms of interdisciplinary work by analyzing how youth are increasingly being addressed and positioned through the popular media, changing economic conditions, an escalating wave of violence, and the emergence of discourse that Ruth Conniff has aptly called "the culture of cruelty."[27] I will then address, both through theory and through examples of my own teaching, how the pedagogy implicit in a spate of Hollywood films about youth culture reinforces dominant racist and cultural stereotypes, but in so doing also creates the conditions for rewriting such films through diverse critical pedagogical strategies.

Mass Culture and the Representation of Youth(s)

Youth have once again become the object of public analysis. Headlines proliferate like dispatches from a combat zone, frequently coupling youth and violence in the interests of promoting a new kind of causal relationship. For example, "gangsta rap" artist Snoop Doggy Dogg was featured on the front cover of an issue of *Newsweek*.[28] This message is that young Black men are selling violence to the mainstream public through their music. But according to *Newsweek,* the violence is not just in the music — it is also embodied in the lifestyles of the rappers who produce it. The potential victims in this case are a besieged White majority of male and female youth. Citing a wave of arrests among prominent rappers, the story reinforces the notion that crime is a racially coded word for associating Black youth with violence.[29]

The statistics on youth violence point to social and economic causes that lie far beyond the reach of facile stereotypes. On a national level, U.S. society is witnessing the effects of a culture of violence in which

> close to 12 U.S. children aged 19 and under die from gun fire each day. According to the National Center for Health Statistics, "Firearm homicide is the leading cause of death of African-American teenage boys and the second-leading cause of death of high school age children in the United States."[30]

What is missing from these reports is any critical commentary on underlying causes that produce the representations of violence that saturate the mass media. In addition, there is little mention of the high numbers of infants and children killed every year through "poverty-related malnutrition and disease." Nor is the U.S. public informed in the popular press about "the gruesome toll of the drunk driver who is typically White."[31] But the bad news doesn't end with violence.

The representations of White youth produced by dominant media within recent years have increasingly portrayed them as lazy, sinking into a self-indulgent haze, and oblivious to the middle-class ethic of working hard and getting ahead. Of course, what the dominant media do not talk about are the social conditions that are producing a new generation of youth steeped in despair, violence, crime, poverty, and apathy. For instance, to talk about Black crime without mentioning that the unemployment rate for Black youth exceeds 40 percent in many urban cities serves primarily to conceal a major cause of youth unrest. Or to talk about apathy among White youth without analyzing the junk culture, poverty, social disenfranchisement, drugs, lack of educational opportunity, and commodification that shape daily life removes responsibility from a social system that often sees youth as simply another market niche.

A failing economy that offers most youth the limited promise of service-sector jobs, dim prospects for the future, and a world of infinite messages and images designed to sell a product or to peddle senseless violence as another TV spectacle, constitutes, in part, the new conditions of youth. In light of radically altered social and economic conditions, educators need to fashion alternative analyses in order to understand what is happening to our nation's youth. Such a project seems vital in light of the rapidity in which market values and a commercial public culture have replaced the ethical referents for developing democratic public spheres. For example, since the 1970s, millions of jobs have been lost to capital flight, and technological change has wiped out millions more. In the last twenty years alone, the U.S. economy lost more than five million jobs in the manufacturing sector.[32] In the face of extremely limited prospects for economic growth over the next decade, schools will be faced with an identity crisis regarding the traditional assumption that school credentials provide the best route to economic security and class mobility for a large proportion of our nation's youth. As Stanley Aronowitz and I have pointed out elsewhere:

> The labor market is becoming increasingly bifurcated: organizational and technical changes are producing a limited number of jobs for highly educated and trained people-managers, scientific and technological experts, and researchers. On the other hand, we are witnessing the disappearance of many middle-level white collar subprofessions. . . . And in the face of sharpening competition, employers typically hire a growing number of low paid, part-time workers. . . . Even some professionals have become free-lance workers with few, if any, fringe benefits. These developments call into question the efficacy of mass schooling for providing the "well-trained" labor force that employers still claim they require.[33]

In light of these shattering shifts in economic and cultural life, it makes more sense for educators to reexamine the mission of the school and the changing conditions of youth rather than blaming youth for the economic slump, the culture of racially coded violence, or the hopelessness that seems endemic to dominant versions of the future.

But rethinking the conditions of youth is also imperative in order to reverse the mean-spirited discourse of the 1980s, a discourse that has turned its back on the victims of U.S. society and has resorted to both blaming and punishing them for their social and economic problems. This is evident in states such as Michigan and Wisconsin, which subscribe to "Learnfare" programs designed to penalize a single mother with a lower food allowance if her kids are absent from school. In other states, welfare payments are reduced if single mothers do not marry. Micky Kaus, an editor at the *New Republic,* argues that welfare mothers should be forced to work at menial jobs, and if they refuse, Kaus suggests that the state remove their children from them. Illiterate women, Kaus argues, could work raking leaves.[34] There is an indifference and callousness in this kind of language that now spills over to discussions of youth. Instead of focusing on economic and social conditions that provide the nation's youth, especially those who are poor and live on the margins of hope, with food, shelter, access to decent education, and safe environments, conservatives such as former Secretary of Education William Bennett talk about imposing national standards on public schools, creating voucher systems that benefit middle-class parents, and doing away with the concept of "the public" altogether. There is more at work here than simply ignorance and neglect.

It is in the dominant discourse on values that one gets a glimpse of the pedagogy at work in the culture of mean-spiritedness. Bennett, for instance, in his new book, *The Book of Virtues: A Treasury of Great Moral Stories,* finds hope in "Old Mr. Rabbit's Thanksgiving Dinner" in which the rabbit instructs us that there is more joy in being helpful than being helped. This discourse of moral uplift may provide soothing and inspirational help for children whose parents send them to private schools, establish trust-fund annuities for their future, and connect them to the world of political patronage, but it says almost nothing about the culture of compressed and concentrated human suffering that many children have to deal with daily in this country. In part, this can be glimpsed in the fact that over seventy percent of all welfare recipients are children. In what follows, I want to draw from a number of insights provided by the field of cultural studies to chart out a different cartography that might be helpful for educators to address what might be called the changing conditions of youth.

Framing Youth

The instability and transitoriness characteristically widespread among a diverse generation of 18- to 25-year-old youth is inextricably rooted in a larger set of postmodern cultural conditions informed by the following: a general loss of faith in the modernist narratives of work and emancipation; the recognition that the indeterminacy of the future warrants confronting and living in the immediacy of experience; an acknowledgment that homelessness as a condition of randomness has replaced the security, if not misrepresentation, of home as a source of comfort and security; an experience of time and space as compressed and fragmented within a world of images that increasingly undermine the dialectic of authenticity and universalism. For many youth, plurality and contingency — whether mediated through media culture, or through the dislocations spurred by the economic system, the rise of new social movements, or the crisis of representation and authority — have resulted in a world with few secure psychological, economic, or intellectual markers. This is a world in which one is condemned to wander within and between multiple borders and spaces marked by excess, otherness, and difference. This is a world in which old certainties are ruptured and meaning becomes more contingent, less indebted to the dictates of reverence and established truth. While the circumstances of youth vary across and within terrains marked by racial and class differences, the modernist world of certainty and order that has traditionally policed, contained, and insulated such difference has given way to a shared postmodern culture in which representational borders collapse into new hybridized forms of cultural performance, identity, and political agency. As the information highway and MTV condense time and space into what Paul Virilio calls "speed space," new desires, modes of association, and forms of resistance inscribe themselves into diverse spheres of popular culture.[35] Music, rap, fashion, style, talk, politics, and cultural resistance are no longer confined to their original class and racial locations. Middle-class White kids take up the language of gangsta rap spawned in neighborhood turfs far removed from their own lives. Black youth in urban centers produce a bricolage of style fashioned from a combination of sneakers, baseball caps, and oversized clothing that integrates forms of resistance and style later to be appropriated by suburban kids whose desires and identities resonate with the energy and vibrancy of the new urban funk. Music displaces older forms of textuality and references a terrain of cultural production that marks the body as a site of pleasure, resistance, domination, and danger.[36] Within this postmodern culture of youth, identities merge and shift rather than become more uniform and static. No longer belonging to any one place or location, youth increasingly inhabit shifting cultural and social spheres marked by a plurality of languages and cultures.

Communities have been refigured as space and time mutate into multiple and overlapping cyberspace networks. Bohemian and middle-class youth talk to each other over electronic bulletin boards in coffee houses in North Beach, California. Cafes and other public salons, once the refuge of beatniks, hippies, and other cultural radicals, have given way to members of the hacker culture. They reorder their imaginations through connections to virtual reality technologies and produce forms of exchange through texts and images that have the potential to wage a war on traditional meaning, but also run the risk of reducing critical understanding to the endless play of random access spectacles.

This is not meant to endorse a Frankfurt School dismissal of popular culture in the postmodern age.[37] On the contrary, I believe that the new electronic technologies with their proliferation of multiple stories and open-ended forms of interaction have altered not only the pedagogical context for the production of subjectivities, but also how people "take in information and entertainment."[38] Produced from the centers of power, mass culture has spawned in the name of profit and entertainment a new level of instrumental and commodified culture. On the other hand, popular culture offers resistance to the notion that useful culture can only be produced within dominant regimes of power. This distinction between mass and popular culture is not meant to suggest that popular culture is strictly a terrain of resistance. Popular culture does not escape commodification, racism, sexism, and other forms of oppression, but it is marked by fault lines that reject the high/low culture divide while simultaneously attempting to affirm a multitude of histories, experiences, cultural forms, and pleasures. Within the conditions of postmodern culture, values no longer emerge unproblematically from the modernist pedagogy of foundationalism and universal truths, or from traditional narratives based on fixed identities with their requisite structure of closure. For many youths, meaning is in rout, media has become a substitute for experience, and what constitutes understanding is grounded in a decentered and diasporic world of difference, displacement, and exchanges.

The intersection among cultural studies and pedagogy can be made more clear through an analysis of how the pedagogy of Hollywood has attempted in some recent films to portray the plight of young people within the conditions of a postmodern culture. I will focus on four films: *River's Edge* (1986), *My Own Private Idaho* (1991), *Slacker* (1991), and *Juice* (1992). These films are important as arguments and framing devices that in diverse ways attempt to provide a pedagogical representation of youth. They point to some of the economic and social conditions at work in the formation of different racial and economic strata of youth, but they often do so within a narrative that combines a politics of despair with a fairly sophisticated depiction of the alleged sensibilities and moods of a generation of youth growing up amid the fracturing and menacing conditions of a postmodern culture. The challenge for progressive educators is to question how a critical pedagogy might be employed to appropriate the more radical and useful aspects of cultural studies in addressing the new and different social, political, and economic contexts that are producing the twenty-something generation. At the same time, there is the issue of how a politics and project of pedagogy might be constructed to create the conditions for social agency and institutionalized change among diverse sectors of youth.

White Youth and the Politics of Despair

For many youth, showing up for adulthood at the fin de siècle means pulling back on hope and trying to put off the future rather than taking up the modernist challenge of trying to shape it.[39] Popular cultural criticism has captured much of the ennui among youth and has made clear that "what used to be the pessimism of a radical fringe is now the shared assumption of a generation."[40] Cultural studies has helped to temper this broad generalization about youth in order to investigate the more complex representations at work in the construction of a new generation of youth that cannot be simply abstracted from the specificities of race, class, or gender. And yet, cultural studies theorists have also pointed to the increasing resistance of a twenty-something generation of youth who seem neither motivated by nostalgia for some lost conservative vision of America nor at home in the New World Order paved with the promises of the expanding electronic information highway.[41] While "youth" as a social construction has always been mediated, in part, as a social problem, many cultural critics believe that postmodern youth are uniquely "alien," "strange," and disconnected from the real world. For instance, in Gus Van Sant's film *My Own Private Idaho,* the main character, Mike, who hustles his sexual wares for money, is a dreamer lost in fractured memories of a mother who deserted him as a child. Caught between flashbacks of Mom, shown in 8-mm color, and the video world of motley street hustlers and their clients, Mike moves through his existence by falling asleep in times of stress only to awaken in different geographic and spatial locations. What holds Mike's psychic and geographic travels together is the metaphor of sleep, the dream of escape, and the ultimate realization that even memories cannot fuel hope for the future. Mike becomes a metaphor for an entire generation of lower middle-class youth forced to sell themselves in a world with no hope, a generation that aspires to nothing, works at degrading McJobs, and lives in a world in which chance and randomness rather than struggle, community, and solidarity drive their fate.

A more disturbing picture of White, working-class youth can be found in *River's Edge.* Teenage anomie and drugged apathy are given painful expression in the depiction of a group of working-class youth who are casually told by John, one of their friends, that he has strangled his girlfriend, another member of the group, and left her nude body on the riverbank. The group at different times visits the site to view and probe the dead body of the girl. Seemingly unable to grasp the significance of the event, the youth initially hold off from informing anyone of the murder and with different degrees of concern initially try to protect John, the teenage sociopath, from being caught by the police. The youth in *River's Edge* drift through a world of broken families, blaring rock music, schooling marked by dead time, and a general indifference. Decentered and fragmented, they view death, like life itself, as merely a spectacle, a matter of style rather than substance. In one sense, these youth share the quality of being "asleep" that is depicted in *My Own Private Idaho*. But what is more disturbing in *River's Edge* is that lost innocence gives way not merely to teenage myopia, but also to a culture in which human life is experienced as a voyeuristic seduction, a video game, good for passing time and diverting oneself from the pain of the moment. Despair and indifference cancel out the language of ethical discriminations and social responsibility while elevating the immediacy of pleasure to the defining moment of agency. In *River's Edge,* history as social memory is reassembled through vignettes of 1960s types portrayed as either burned-out bikers or as the ex-radical turned teacher whose moralizing relegates politics to simply cheap opportunism. Exchanges among the young people in *River's Edge* appear like projections of a generation waiting either to fall asleep or to commit suicide. After talking about how he murdered his girlfriend, John blurts out, "You do shit, it's done, and then you die." Another character responds, "It might be easier being dead." To which her boyfriend replies, "Bullshit, you couldn't get stoned anymore." In this scenario, life imitates art when committing murder and getting stoned are given equal moral weight in the formula of the Hollywood spectacle, a spectacle that in the end flattens the complex representations of youth while constructing their identities through ample servings of pleasure, death, and violence.

River's Edge and *My Own Private Idaho* reveal the seamy and dark side of a youth culture while employing the Hollywood mixture of fascination and horror to titillate the audiences drawn to these films. Employing the postmodern aesthetic of revulsion, locality, randomness, and senselessness, the youth in these films appear to be constructed outside of a broader cultural and economic landscape. Instead, they become visible only through visceral expressions of psychotic behavior or the brooding experience of a self-imposed comatose alienation.

One of the more celebrated White youth films of the 1990s is Richard Linklater's *Slacker*. A decidedly low-budget film, *Slacker* attempts in both form and content to capture the sentiments of a twenty-something generation of middle-class White youth who reject most of the values of the Reagan/Bush era but have a difficult time imagining what an alternative might look like. Distinctly non-linear in format, *Slacker* takes place in a twenty-four-hour time frame in the college town of Austin, Texas. Building upon an anti-narrative structure, *Slacker* is loosely organized around brief episodes in the lives of a variety of characters, none of whom are connected to each other except to provide the pretext to lead the audience to the next character in the film. Sweeping through bookstores, coffee shops, auto-parts yards, bedrooms, and rock music clubs, *Slacker* focuses on a disparate group of young people who possess little hope in the future and drift from job to job speaking a hybrid argot of bohemian intensities and New Age pop-cult babble.

The film portrays a host of young people who randomly move from one place to the next, border crossers with little, if any, sense of where they have come from or where they are going. In this world of multiple realities, youth work in bands with the name "Ultimate Loser" and talk about being forcibly put in hospitals by their parents. One neo-punker even attempts to sell a Madonna pap smear to two acquaintances she meets in the street: "Check it out, I know it's kind of disgusting, but it's like sort of getting down to the real Madonna." This is a world in which language is wedded to an odd mix of nostalgia, popcorn philosophy, and MTV babble. Talk is organized around comments like: "I don't know . . . I've traveled . . . and when you get back you can't tell whether it really happened to you or if you just saw it on TV." Alienation is driven inward and emerges in comments like "I feel stuck." Irony slightly overshadows a refusal to imagine any kind of collective struggle. Reality seems too despairing to care about. This is humorously captured in one instance by a young man who suggests: "You know how the slogan goes, workers of the world, unite? We say workers of the world, relax?" People talk, but appear disconnected from themselves and each other, lives traverse each other with no sense of community or connection. There is a pronounced sense in *Slacker* of youth caught in the throes of new information technologies that both contain their aspirations and at the same time hold out the promise of some sense of agency.

At rare moments in the films, the political paralysis of narcissistic forms of refusal is offset by instances in which some characters recognize the importance of the image as a vehicle for cultural production, as a representational apparatus that can not only make certain experiences available but can also be used to produce alternative realities and social practices. The power of the image is present in the way the camera follows characters throughout the film, at once stalking them and confining them to a gaze that is both constraining and incidental. In one scene, a young man appears in a video apartment surrounded by televisions that he claims he has had on for years. He points out that he has invented a game called a "Video Virus" in which, through the use of a special technology, he can push a button and insert himself onto any screen and perform any one of a number of actions. When asked by another character what this is about, he answers: "Well, we all know the psychic powers of the televised image. But we need to capitalize on it and make it work for us instead of working for it." This theme is taken up in two other scenes. In one short clip, a graduate history student shoots the video camera he is using to film himself, indicating a self-consciousness about the power of the image and the ability to control it at the same time. In the concluding scene, a carload of people, each equipped with their Super 8 cameras, drive up to a large hill and throw their cameras into a canyon. The film ends with the images being recorded by the cameras as they cascade to the bottom of the cliff in what suggests a moment of release and liberation.

In many respects, these movies largely focus on a culture of White male youth who are both terrified and fascinated by the media, who appear overwhelmed by "the danger and wonder of future technologies, the banality of consumption, the thrill of brand names, [and] the difficulty of sex in alienated relationships."[42] The significance of these films rests, in part, in their attempt to capture the sense of powerlessness that increasingly affects working-class and middle-class White youth. But what is missing from these films, along with the various books, articles, and reportage concerning what is often called the "Nowhere Generation," "Generation X," "13thGen," or "Slackers," is any sense of the larger political, racial, and social conditions in which youth are being framed, as well as the multiple forms of resistance and racial diversity that exist among many different youth formations. What in fact should be seen as a social commentary about "dead-end capitalism" emerges simply as a celebration of refusal dressed up in a rhetoric of aesthetics, style, fashion, and solipsistic protests. Within this type of commentary, postmodern criticism is useful but limited because of its often theoretical inability to take up the relationship between identity and power, biography and the commodification of everyday life, or the limits of agency in an increasingly globalized economy as part of a broader project of possibility linked to issues of history, struggle, and transformation.[43]

In spite of the totalizing image of domination that structures *River's Edge* and *My Own Private Idaho,* and the lethal hopelessness that permeates *Slacker,* all of these films provide opportunities for examining the social and cultural context to which they refer in order to enlarge the range of strategies and understandings that students might bring to them to create a sense of resistance and transformation. For instance, many of my students who viewed *Slacker* did not despair over the film, but interpreted it to mean that "going slack" was viewed as a moment in the lives of young people that, with the proper resources, offered them a period in which to think, move around the country, and chill out in order to make some important decisions about their lives. Going slack became increasingly more oppressive as the slack time became drawn out far beyond their ability to end or control it. The students also pointed out that this film was made by Linklater and his friends with a great deal of energy and gusto, which in itself offers a pedagogical model for young people to take up in developing their own narratives.

Black Youth and the Violence of Race

With the explosion of rap music into the sphere of popular culture and the intense debates that have emerged around the crisis of Black masculinity, the issue of Black nationalism, and the politics of Black urban culture, it is not surprising that the Black cinema has produced a series of films about the coming of age of Black youth in urban America. What is unique about these films is that, unlike the Black exploitation films of the 1970s, which were made by White producers for Black audiences, the new wave of Black cinema is being produced by Black directors and aimed at Black audiences.[44] With the advent of the 1990s, Hollywood has cashed in on a number of talented young Black directors such as Spike Lee, Allen and Albert Hughes, Julie Dash, Ernest Dickerson, and John Singleton. Films about Black youth have become big business — in 1991 *New Jack City* and *Boyz N the Hood* pulled in over 100 million dollars between them. Largely concerned with the inequalities, oppression, daily violence, and diminishing hopes that plague Black communities in the urban war zone, the new wave of Black films has attempted to accentuate the economic and social conditions that have contributed to the construction of "Black masculinity and its relationship to the ghetto culture in which ideals of masculinity are nurtured and shaped."[45]

Unlike many of the recent films about White youth whose coming-of-age narratives are developed within traditional sociological categories such as alienation, restlessness, and anomie, Black film productions such as Ernest Dickerson's *Juice* (1992) depict a culture of nihilism that is rooted directly in a violence whose defining principles are homicide, cultural suicide, internecine warfare, and social decay. It is interesting to note that just as the popular press has racialized crime, drugs, and violence as a Black problem, some of the most interesting films to appear recently about Black youth have been given the Hollywood imprimatur of excellence and have moved successfully as crossover films to a White audience. In what follows, I want briefly to probe the treatment of Black youth and the representations of masculinity and resistance in the exemplary Black film, *Juice.*

Juice (street slang for respect) is the story of four young Harlem African-American youth who are first portrayed as kids who engage in the usual antics of skipping school, fighting with other kids in the neighborhood, clashing with their parents about doing homework, and arguing with their siblings over using the bathroom in the morning. If this portrayal of youthful innocence is used to get a general audience to comfortably identify with these four Black youth, it is soon ruptured as the group, caught in a spiraling wave of poverty and depressed opportunities, turn to crime and violence as a way to both construct their manhood and solve their most immediate problems. Determined to give their lives some sense of agency, the group moves from ripping off a record store to burglarizing a grocery market to the ruthless murder of the store owner and eventually each other. Caught in a world in which the ethics of the street are mirrored in the spectacle of TV violence, Bishop, Quincy, Raheem, and Steel (Tupac Shakur, Omar Epps, Kahalil Kain, and Jermaine Hopkins) decided, after watching James Cagney go up in a blaze of glory in *White Heat,* to take control of their lives by buying a gun and sticking up a neighborhood merchant who once chased them out of his store. Quincy is hesitant about participating in the stick-up because he is a talented disc jockey and is determined to enter a local deejay contest in order to take advantage of his love of rap music and find a place for himself in the world.

Quincy is the only Black youth in the film who models a sense of agency that is not completely caught in the confusion and despair exhibited by his three friends. Trapped within the loyalty codes of the street and in the protection it provides, Quincy reluctantly agrees to participate in the heist. Bad choices have major consequences in this typical big-city ghetto, and Quincy's sense of hope and independence is shattered as Bishop, the most violent of the group, kills the store owner and then proceeds to murder Raheem and hunt down Quincy and Steele, since they no longer see him as a respected member of the group. Quincy eventually buys a weapon to protect himself, and in the film's final scene, confronts Bishop on the roof. A struggle ensues, and Bishop plunges to his death. As the film ends, one onlooker tells Quincy, "You got the juice," but Quincy rejects the accolade ascribing power and prestige to him and walks away.

Juice reasserts the importance of rap music as the cultural expression of imaginable possibilities in the daily lives of Black youth. Not only does rap music provide the musical score that frames the film, it also plays a pivotal role by socially contextualizing the desires, rage, and independent expression of Black male artists. For Quincy, rap music offers him the opportunity to claim some "juice" among his peers while simultaneously providing him with a context to construct an affirmative identity along with the chance for real employment. Music in this context becomes a major referent for understanding how identities and bodies come together in a hip-hop culture that at its most oppositional moment is testing the limits of the American dream. But *Juice* also gestures, through the direction of Ernest Dickerson, that if violence is endemic to the Black ghetto, its roots lie in a culture of violence that is daily transmitted through the medium of television. This is suggested in one powerful scene in which the group watch on television both the famed violent ending of James Cagney's *White Heat,* and the news bulletin announcing the death of a neighborhood friend as he attempted to rip off a local bar. In this scene, Dickerson draws a powerful relationship between what the four youth see on television and their impatience over their own lack of agency and need to take control of their lives. As Michael Dyson points out:

> Dickerson's aim is transparent: to highlight the link between violence and criminality fostered in the collective American imagination by television, the consumption of images through a medium that has replaced the Constitution and the Declaration of Independence as the unifying fiction of national citizenship and identity. It is also the daily and exclusive occupation of Bishop's listless father, a reminder that television's genealogy of influence unfolds from its dulling effects in one generation to its creation of lethal desires in the next, twin strategies of destruction when applied in the black male ghetto.[46]

While Dyson is right in pointing to Dickerson's critique of the media, he overestimates the importance given in *Juice* to the relationship between Black-on-Black violence and those larger social determinants that Black urban life both reflects and helps to produce. In fact, it could be argued that the violence portrayed in *Juice* and similar films, such as *Boyz N the Hood, New Jack City,* and especially *Menace II Society,* "feeds the racist national obsession that Black men and their community are the central locus of the American scene of violence."[47]

Although the violence in these films is traumatizing as part of the effort to promote an anti-violence message, it is also a violence that is hermetic, sutured, and sealed within the walls of the Black urban ghetto. While the counterpart of this type of violence, in controversial White films such as *Reservoir Dogs* is taken up by most critics as part of an avant garde aesthetic, the violence in the recent wave of Black youth films often reinforces for middle-class viewers the assumption that such violence is endemic to the Black community. The only salvation gained in portraying such inner-city hopelessness is that it be noticed so that it can be stopped from spreading like a disease into the adjoining suburbs and business zones that form a colonizing ring around Black ghettoes. Because films such as *Juice* do not self-consciously rupture dominant stereotypical assumptions that make race and crime synonymous, they often suggest a kind of nihilism that Cornel West describes as "the lived experience of coping with a life of horrifying meaninglessness, hopelessness and (most important) lovelessness."[48]

Unfortunately, West's notion of nihilism is too tightly drawn and while it may claim to pay sufficient attention to the loss of hope and meaning among Black youth, it fails to connect the specificity of Black nihilism to the nihilism of systemic inequality, calculated injustice, and moral indifference that operates daily as a regime of brutalization and oppression for so many poor youth and youth of color in this country. Itabari Njeri forcefully captures the failure of such an analysis and the problems that films such as *Juice,* in spite of the best intentions of their directors, often reproduce. Commenting on another coming-of-age Black youth film, *Menace II Society,* he writes:

The nation cannot allow nearly 50% of black men to be unemployed, as is the case in many African-American communities. It cannot let schools systematically brand normal black children as uneducable for racist reasons, or permit the continued brutalization of blacks by police, or have black adults take out their socially engendered frustrations on each other and their children and not yield despair and dysfunction. This kind of despair is the source of the nihilism Cornel West described. Unfortunately, the black male-as-menace film genre often fails to artfully tie this nihilism to its poisonous roots in America's system of inequality. And because it fails to do so, the effects of these toxic forces are seen as causes.[49]

In both pedagogical and political terms, the reigning films about Black youth that have appeared since 1990 may have gone too far in producing narratives that employ the commercial strategy of reproducing graphic violence and then moralizing about its effects. Violence in these films is tied to a self-destructiveness and senselessness that shocks but often fails to inform the audience about either its wider determinations or the audience's possible complicity in such violence. The effects of such films tend to reinforce for White middle-class America the comforting belief that nihilism as both a state of mind and a site of social relations is always somewhere else — in that strangely homogenized social formation known as "Black" youth.

Of course, it is important to note that *Juice* refrains from romanticizing violence, just as it suggests at the end of the film that Quincy does not want the juice if it means leading a life in which violence is the only capital that has any exchange value in African-American communities. But these sentiments come late and are too underdeveloped. One pedagogical challenge presented by this film is for educators and students to theorize about why Hollywood is investing in films about Black youth that overlook the complex representations that structure African-American communities. Such an inquiry can be taken up by looking at the work of Black feminist film makers such as Julie Dash, and the powerful and complex representations she offers Black women in *Daughters of the Dust,* or the work of Leslie Harris, whose film *Just Another Girl on the IRT* challenges the misogyny that structures the films currently being made about Black male youth. Another challenge involves trying to understand why large numbers of Black, urban, male youth readily identify with the wider social representations of sexism, homophobia, misogyny, and gaining respect at such a high cost to themselves and the communities in which they live. Films about Black youth are important to engage in order to understand both the pedagogies that silently structure their representations and how such representations pedagogically work to educate crossover White audiences. Most importantly, these films should not be dismissed because they are reductionist, sexist, or one dimensional in their portrayal of the rite of passage of Black male youth; at most, they become a marker for understanding how complex representations of Black youth get lost in racially coded films that point to serious problems in the urban centers, but do so in ways that erase any sense of viable hope, possibility, resistance, and struggle.

Contemporary films about Black youth offer a glimpse into the specificity of otherness; that is, they cross a cultural and racial border and in doing so perform a theoretical service in making visible what is often left out of the dominant politics of representations. And it is in the light of such an opening that the possibility exists for educators and other cultural workers to take up the relationship among culture, power, and identity in ways that grapple with the complexity of youth and the intersection of race, class, and gender formations.

Combining cultural studies with pedagogical theory would suggest that students take these films seriously as legitimate forms of social knowledge that reveal different sets of struggles among youth within diverse cultural sites. For White youth, these films mimic a coming-of-age narrative that indicts the aimlessness and senselessness produced within a larger culture of commercial stupification; on the other hand, Black youth films posit a *not* coming-of-age narrative that serves as a powerful indictment of the violence being waged against and among African-American youth. Clearly, educators can learn from these films and in doing so bring these different accounts of the cultural production of youth together within a common project that addresses the relationship between pedagogy and social justice, on the one hand, and democracy and the struggle for equality on the other. These films suggest that educators need to ask new questions, and develop new models and new ways of producing an oppositional pedagogy that is capable of understanding the different social, economic, and political contexts that produce youth differently within varied sets and relations of power.

Another pedagogical challenge offered by these films concerns how teachers can address the desires that different students bring to these popular cultural texts. In other words, what does it mean to mobilize the desires of students by using forms of social knowledge that constitute the contradictory field of popular culture? In part, it means recognizing that while students are familiar with such texts, they bring different beliefs, political understandings, and affective investments to such a learning process. Hence, pedagogy must proceed by acknowledging that conflict will emerge regarding the form and content of such films and how students address such issues. For such a pedagogy to work, Fabienne Worth argues that "students must become visible to themselves and to each other and valued in their differences."[50] This suggests giving students the opportunity to decenter the curriculum by structuring, in part, how the class should be organized and how such films can be addressed without putting any one student's identity on trial. It means recognizing the complexity of attempting to mobilize students' desires as part of a pedagogical project that directly addresses representations that affect certain parts of their lives, and to acknowledge the emotional problems that will emerge in such teaching.

At the same time, such a pedagogy must reverse the cycle of despair that often informs these accounts and address how the different postmodern conditions and contexts of youth can be changed in order to expand and deepen the promise of a substantive democracy. In part, this may mean using films about youth that capture the complexity, sense of struggle, and diversity that marks different segments of the current generation of young people. In this case, cultural studies and pedagogical practice can mutually inform each other by using popular cultural texts as serious objects of study. Such texts can be used to address the limits and possibilities that youth face in different social, cultural, and economic contexts. Equally important is the need to read popular cultural texts as part of a broader pedagogical effort to develop a sense of agency in students based on a commitment to changing oppressive contexts by understanding the relations of power that inform them.

The pedagogical challenge represented by the emergence of a postmodern generation of youth has not been lost on advertisers and market research analysts. According to a 1992 study by the Roper Organization, the current generation of 18- to 29-year-olds have an annual buying power of $125 billion. Addressing the interests and tastes of this generation, "McDonald's, for instance, has introduced hip-hop music and images to promote burgers and fries, ditto Coca-Cola, with its frenetic commercials touting Coca-Cola Classic."[51] Benetton, Esprit, The Gap, and other companies have followed suit in their attempts to identify and mobilize the desires, identities, and buying patterns of a new generation of youth.[52] What appears as a despairing expression of the postmodern condition to some theorists becomes for others a challenge to invent new market strategies for corporate interests. In this scenario, youth may be experiencing the indeterminacy, senselessness, and multiple conditions of postmodernism, but corporate advertisers are attempting to theorize a pedagogy of consumption as part of a new way of appropriating postmodern differences among youth in different sites and locations. The lesson here is that differences among youth matter politically and pedagogically, but not as a way of generating new markets or registering difference simply as a fashion niche.

What educators need to do is to make the pedagogical more political by addressing both the conditions through which they teach and what it means to learn from a generation that is experiencing life in a way that is vastly different from the representations offered in modernist versions of schooling. This is not to suggest that modernist schools do not attend to popular culture, but they do so on very problematic terms, which often confine it to the margins of the curriculum. Moreover, modernist schools cannot be rejected outright. As I have shown elsewhere, the political culture of modernism, with its emphasis on social equality, justice, freedom, and human agency, needs to be refigured within rather than outside of an emerging postmodern discourse.[53]

The emergence of the electronic media coupled with a diminishing faith in the power of human agency has undermined the traditional visions of schooling and the meaning of pedagogy. The language of lesson plans and upward mobility and the forms of teacher authority on which it was based has been radically delegitimated by the recognition that culture and power are central to the authority/knowledge relationship. Modernism's faith in the past has given way to a future for which traditional markers no longer make sense.

Cultural Studies and Youth: The Pedagogical Issue

Educators and cultural critics need to address the effects of emerging postmodern conditions on a current generation of young people who appear hostage to the vicissitudes of a changing economic order, with its legacy of diminished hopes on the one hand, and a world of schizoid images, proliferating public spaces, and an increasing fragmentation, uncertainty, and randomness that structures postmodern daily life on the other. Central to this issue is whether educators are dealing with a new kind of student forged within organizing principles shaped by the intersection of the electronic image, popular culture, and a dire sense of indeterminacy.

What cultural studies offers educators is a theoretical framework for addressing the shifting attitudes, representations, and desires of this new generation of youth being produced within the current historical, economic, and cultural juncture. But it does more than simply provide a lens for resituating the construction of youth within a shifting and radically altered social, technological, and economic landscape: it also provides elements for rethinking the relationship between culture and power, knowledge and authority, learning and experience, and the role of teachers as public intellectuals. In what follows, I want to point to some of the theoretical elements that link cultural studies and critical pedagogy and speak briefly to their implications for cultural work.

First, cultural studies is premised on the belief that we have entered a period in which the traditional distinctions that separate and frame established academic disciplines cannot account for the great diversity of cultural and social phenomena that has come to characterize an increasingly hybridized, post-industrial world. The university has long been linked to a notion of national identity that is largely defined by and committed to transmitting traditional Western culture.[54] Traditionally, this has been a culture of exclusion, one that has ignored the multiple narratives, histories, and voices of culturally and politically subordinated groups. The emerging proliferation of diverse social movements arguing for a genuinely multicultural and multiracial society have challenged schools that use academic knowledge to license cultural differences in order to regulate and define who they are and how they might narrate themselves. Moreover, the spread of electronically mediated culture to all spheres of everyday intellectual and artistic life has shifted the ground of scholarship away from the traditional disciplines designed to preserve a "common culture" to the more hybridized fields of comparative and world literature, media studies, ecology, society and technology, and popular culture.

Second, advocates of cultural studies have argued strongly that the role of culture, including the power of the mass media with its massive apparatuses of representation and its regulation of meaning, is central to understanding how the dynamics of power, privilege, and social desire structure the daily life of a society.[55] This concern with culture and its connection to power has necessitated a critical interrogation of the relationship between knowledge and authority, the meaning of canonicity, and the historical and social contexts that deliberately shape students' understanding of accounts of the past, present, and future. But if a sea change in the development and reception of what counts as knowledge has taken place, it has been accompanied by an understanding of how we define and apprehend the range of texts that are open to critical interrogation and analysis. For instance, instead of connecting culture exclusively to the technology of print and the book as the only legitimate academic artifact, there is a great deal of academic work going on that analyzes how textual, aural, and visual representations are produced, organized, and distributed through a variety of cultural forms such as the media, popular culture, film, advertising, mass communications, and other modes of cultural production.[56]

At stake here is the attempt to produce new theoretical models and methodologies for addressing the production, structure, and exchange of knowledge. This approach to inter/post-disciplinary studies is valuable because it addresses the pedagogical issue of organizing dialogue across and outside of the disciplines in order to promote alternative approaches to research and teaching about culture and the newly emerging technologies and forms of knowledge. For instance, rather than organize courses around strictly disciplinary concerns arising out of English and social studies courses, it might be more useful and relevant for colleges of education to organize courses that broaden student's understanding of themselves and others by examining events that evoke a sense of social responsibility and moral accountability. A course on "Immigration and Politics in Fin de Siècle America" could provide a historical perspective on the demographic changes confronting the United States and how such changes are being felt within the shifting dynamics of education, economics, cultural identity, and urban development. A course on the Los Angeles uprisings could incorporate the related issues of race, politics, economics, and education to address the multiple conditions underlying the violence and despair that produced such a tragic event.

Third, in addition to broadening the terms and parameters of learning, cultural studies rejects the professionalization of educators and the alienating and often elitist discourse of professionalism and sanitized expertise. Instead, it argues for educators as public intellectuals. Stuart Hall is instructive on this issue when he argues that cultural studies provides two points of tension that intellectuals need to address:

> First, cultural studies constitutes one of the points of tension and change at the frontiers of intellectual and academic life, pushing for new questions, new models, and new ways of study, testing the fine lines between intellectual rigor and social relevance. . . . But secondly . . . cultural studies insist on what I want to call the vocation of the intellectual life. That is to say, cultural studies insists on the necessity to address the central, urgent, and disturbing questions of a society and a culture in the most rigorous intellectual way we have available.[57]

In this view, intellectuals must be accountable in their teaching for the ways in which they address and respond to the problems of history, human agency, and the renewal of democratic civic life. Cultural studies strongly rejects the assumption that teachers are simply transmitters of existing configurations of knowledge. As public intellectuals, academics are always implicated in the dynamics of social power through the experiences they organize and provoke in their classrooms. In this perspective, intellectual work is incomplete unless it self-consciously assumes responsibility for its effects in the larger public culture while simultaneously addressing the most profoundly and deeply inhumane problems of the societies in which we live. Hence, cultural studies raises questions about what knowledge is produced in the university and how it is consequential in extending and deepening the possibilities for democratic public life. Equally important is the issue of how to democratize the schools so as to enable those groups who in large measure are divorced from or simply not represented in the curriculum to be able to produce their own representations, narrate their own stories, and engage in respectful dialogue with others. In this instance, cultural studies must address how dialogue is constructed in the classroom about other cultures and voices by critically addressing both the position of the theorists and the institutions in which such dialogues are produced. Peter Hitchcock argues forcefully that the governing principles of any such dialogic exchange should include some of the following elements:

> 1) attention to the specific institutional setting in which this activity takes place; 2) self-reflexivity regarding the particular identities of the teacher and students who collectively undertake this activity; 3) an awareness that the cultural identities at stake in "other" cultures are in the process-of-becoming in dialogic interaction and are not static as subjects; but 4) the knowledge produced through this activity is al-

ways already contestable and by definition is not the knowledge of the other as the other would know herself or himself.[58]

Fourth, another important contribution of cultural studies is its emphasis on studying the production, reception, and use of varied texts, and how they are used to define social relations, values, particular notions of community, the future, and diverse definitions of the self. Texts in this sense do not merely refer to the culture of print or the technology of the book, but to all those audio, visual, and electronically mediated forms of knowledge that have prompted a radical shift in the construction of knowledge and the ways in which knowledge is read, received, and consumed. It is worth repeating that contemporary youth increasingly rely less on the technology and culture of the book to construct and affirm their identities; instead, they are faced with the task of finding their way through a decentered cultural landscape no longer caught in the grip of a technology of print, closed narrative structures, or the certitude of a secure economic future. The new emerging technologies that construct and position youth represent interactive terrains that cut across "language and culture, without narrative requirements, without character complexities. . . . Narrative complexity [has given] way to design complexity; story [has given] way to a sensory environment."[59] Cultural studies is profoundly important for educators in that it focuses on media not merely in terms of how it distorts and misrepresents reality, but also on how media plays "a part in the formation, in the constitution, of the things they reflect. It is not that there is a world outside, 'out there,' which exists free of the discourse of representation. What is 'out there' is, in part, constituted by how it is represented."[60]

I don't believe that educators and schools of education can address the shifting attitudes, representations, and desires of this new generation of youth within the dominant disciplinary configurations of knowledge and practice. On the contrary, as youth are constituted within languages and new cultural forms that intersect differently across and within issues of race, class, gender, and sexual differences, the conditions through which youth attempt to narrate themselves must be understood in terms of both the context of their struggles and a shared language of agency that points to a project of hope and possibility. It is precisely this language of difference, specificity, and possibility that is lacking from most attempts at educational reform.

Fifth, it is important to stress that when critical pedagogy is established as one of the defining principles of cultural studies, it is possible to generate a new discourse for moving beyond a limited emphasis on the mastery of techniques and methodologies. Critical pedagogy represents a form of cultural production implicated in and critically attentive to how power and meaning are employed in the construction and organization of knowledge, desires, values, and identities. Critical pedagogy in this sense is not reduced to the mastering of skills or techniques, but is defined as a cultural practice that must be accountable ethically and politically for the stories it produces, the claims it makes on social memories, and the images of the future it deems legitimate. As both an object of critique and a method of cultural production, it refuses to hide behind claims of objectivity, and works effortlessly to link theory and practice to enabling the possibilities for human agency in a world of diminishing returns. It is important to make a distinction here that challenges the liberal and conservative criticism that, since critical pedagogy attempts both to politicize teaching and teach politics, it represents a species of indoctrination. By asserting that all teaching is profoundly political and that critical educators and cultural workers should operate out of a project of social transformation, I am arguing that as educators we need to make a distinction between what Peter Euben calls political and politicizing education.

Political education, which is central to critical pedagogy, refers to teaching "students how to think in ways that cultivate the capacity for judgment essential for the exercise of power and responsibility by a democratic citizenry. . . . A political, as distinct from a politicizing education would encourage students to become better citizens to challenge those with political and cultural power as well as to honor the critical traditions within the dominant culture that make such a critique possible and intelligible."[61] A political education means decentering power in the classroom and other pedagogical sites so the dynamics of those institutional and cultural inequalities that marginalize some groups, repress particular types of knowledge, and suppress critical dialogue can be addressed. On the other hand, politicizing education is a form of pedagogical terrorism in which the issue of what is taught, by whom, and under what conditions is determined by a doctrinaire political agenda that refuses to examine its own values, beliefs, and ideological construction. While refusing to recognize the social and historical character of its own claims to history, knowledge, and values, a politicizing education silences in the name of a specious universalism and denounces all transformative practices through an appeal to a timeless notion of truth and beauty. For those who practice a politicizing education, democracy and citizenship become dangerous in that the precondition for their realization demands critical inquiry, the taking of risks, and the responsibility to resist and say no in the face of dominant forms of power.

Conclusion

Given its challenge to the traditional notion of teachers as mere transmitters of information and its insistence that teachers are cultural producers deeply implicated in public issues, cultural studies provides a new and transformative language for educating teachers and administrators around the issue of civic leadership and public service. In this perspective, teacher education is fashioned not around a particular dogma, but through pedagogical practices that address changing contexts, creating the necessary conditions for students to be critically attentive to the historical and socially constructed nature of the locations they occupy within a shifting world of representations and values. Cultural studies requires that teachers be educated to be cultural producers, to treat culture as an activity, unfinished and incomplete. This suggests that teachers should be critically attentive to the operations of power as it is implicated in the production of knowledge and authority in particular and shifting contexts. This means learning how to be sensitive to considerations of power as it is inscribed on every facet of the schooling process.

The conditions and problems of contemporary youth will have to be engaged through a willingness to interrogate the world of public politics, while at the same time appropriating modernity's call for a better world but abandoning its linear narratives of Western history, unified culture, disciplinary order, and technological progress. In this case, the pedagogical importance of uncertainty and indeterminacy can be rethought through a modernist notion of the dream-world in which youth and others can shape, without the benefit of master narratives, the conditions for producing new ways of learning, engaging, and positing the possibilities for social struggle and solidarity. Critical educators cannot subscribe either to an apocalyptic emptiness or to a politics of refusal that celebrates the abandonment of authority or the immediacy of experience over the more profound dynamic of social memory and moral outrage forged within and against conditions of exploitation, oppression, and the abuse of power.

The intersection of cultural studies and critical pedagogy offers possibilities for educators to confront history as more than simulacrum and ethics as something other than the casualty of incommensurable language games. Educators need to assert a politics that makes the relationship among authority, ethics, and power central to a pedagogy that expands rather than closes down the possibilities of a radical democratic society. Within this discourse, images do not dissolve reality into simply another text: on the contrary, representations become central to revealing the structures of power relations at work in the public, in schools, in society, and in the larger global order. Pedagogy does not succumb to the whims of the marketplace in this logic, nor to the latest form of educational chic; instead, critical pedagogy engages cultural studies as part of an ongoing movement towards a shared conception of justice and a radicalization of the social order. This is a task that not only recognizes the multiple relationships between culture and power, but also makes critical pedagogy one of its defining principles.

Notes

1. Dick Hebdige, *Hiding in the Light* (New York: Routledge, 1988), pp. 17–18.
2. "Footnotes," *Chronicle of Higher Education,* December 1, 1993, p. A8.
3. I provide a detailed critique of this issue in Henry A. Giroux, *Schooling and the Struggle for Public Life* (Minneapolis: University of Minnesota Press, 1988). See also Stanley Aronowitz and Henry A. Giroux, *Education Still Under Siege* (Westport, CT: Bergin & Garvey, 1993).
4. I take this issue up in detail in Henry A. Giroux, *Disturbing Pleasures: Learning Popular Culture* (New York: Routledge, 1994).
5. Feminist theorists have been making this point for years. For an example of some of this work as it is expressed at the intersection of cultural studies and pedagogy, see the various articles in *Between Borders: Pedagogy and the Politics of Cultural Studies,* ed. Henry A. Giroux and Peter McLaren (New York: Routledge, 1993).
6. The relationship between cultural studies and relations of government are taken up in Tony Bennett, "Putting Policy into Cultural Studies," in *Cultural Studies,* ed. Lawrence Grossberg, Cary Nelson, and Paula Treichler (New York: Routledge, 1992), pp. 23–37.
7. For representative examples of the diverse issues taken up in the field of cultural studies, see Grossberg et al., *Cultural Studies;* Simon During, ed., *The Cultural Studies Reader* (New York: Routledge, 1993).
8. This is especially true of some of the most ardent critics of higher education. A representative list includes: William J. Bennett, *To Reclaim a Legacy: A Report on the Humanities in Higher Education* (Washington, DC: National Endowment for the Humanities, 1984); Stephen H. Balch and Herbert London, "The Tenured Left," *Commentary, 82,* No. 4 (1986), 41–51; Lynne V. Cheney, *Tyrannical Machines: A Report on Education Practices Gone Wrong and Our Best Hopes for Setting Them Right* (Washington, DC: National Endowment for the Humanities, 1990); Roger Kimball, *Tenured Radicals: How Politics Has Corrupted Our Higher Education* (New York: Harper & Row, 1990); Dinesh D'Souza, *Illiberal Education: The Politics of*

Race and Sex on Campus (New York: Free Press, 1991). For a highly detailed analysis of the web of conservative money, foundations, and ideologies that connect the above intellectuals, see Ellen Messer-Davidow, "Manufacturing the Attack on Liberalized Higher Education," *Social Text, 11,* No. 3 (1993), 40–80.

9. Cary Nelson, Paula Treichler, and Lawrence Grossberg, "Cultural Studies: An Introduction," in Nelson, Treichler, and Grossberg, *Cultural Studies,* p. 5.

10. Bennett, "Putting Policy into Cultural Studies," p. 32.

11. I take up these issues in more detail in Henry A. Giroux, *Border Crossings: Cultural Workers and the Politics of Education* (New York: Routledge, 1992) and in Giroux, *Disturbing Pleasures.*

12. Cary Nelson, "Always Already Cultural Studies," in *Journal of the Midwest Language Association, 24,* No. 1 (1991), p. 32.

13. Hebdige, *Hiding in the Light,* pp. 17–18.

14. Stuart Hall, "What is this 'Black' in Popular Culture?" in *Black Popular Culture,* ed. Gina Dent (Seattle: Bay Press, 1992), p. 22.

15. As a representative example of this type of critique, see any of the major theoretical sources of cultural studies, especially the Centre for Contemporary Cultural Studies at the University of Birmingham [England]. For example, Stuart Hall, "Cultural Studies: Two Paradigms," in *Media, Culture, and Society,* ed. Richard Collins et al. (London: Sage Publications, 1986), pp. 34–48, and Stuart Hall, "Cultural Studies and the Center: Some Problematics and Problems," in *Culture, Media, Language: Working Paper in Cultural Studies,* ed. Stuart Hall et al. (London: Hutchinson, 1980); Richard Johnson, "What is Cultural Studies Anyway?" *Social Text, 6,* No. 1 (1987), 38–40; Meaghan Morris, "Banality in Cultural Studies," *Discourse, 10,* No. 2 (1988), 3–29.

16. See Stanley Aronowitz, *Roll Over Beethoven: Return of Cultural Strife* (Hanover, NH: University Press of New England, 1993); Gayatri C. Spivak, *Outside in the Teaching Machine* (New York: Routledge, 1993). See also a few articles in Grossberg et al., *Cultural Studies.* Also, see various issues of *College Literature* under the editorship of Kostas Mrysiades. It is quite revealing to look into some of the latest books on cultural studies and see no serious engagement of pedagogy as a site of theoretical and practical struggle. In David Punter, ed., *Introduction to Contemporary Cultural Studies* (New York: Longman, 1986), there is one chapter on identifying racism in textbooks. For more recent examples, see: Patrick Brantlinger, *Crusoe's Footprints: Cultural Studies in Britain and America* (New York: Routledge, 1990); Graeme Turner, *British Cultural Studies* (London: Unwin Hyman, 1990); John Clarke, *New Times and Old Enemies* (London: Harper Collins, 1991); Sarah Franklin, Celia Lury, and Jackie Stacey, eds., *Off-Centre: Feminism and Cultural Studies* (London: Harper Collins, 1991). In neither of the following books published in 1993 is there even one mention of pedagogy: During, *The Cultural Studies Reader;* Valda Blundell, John Shepherd, and Ian Taylor, eds., *Relocating Cultural Studies: Developments in Theory and Research* (New York: Routledge, 1993).

17. While there are too many sources to cite here, see R. W. Connell, D. J. Ashenden, S. Kessler, and G. W. Dowsett, *Making the Difference* (Boston: Allen & Unwin, 1982); Julian Henriques, Wendy Hollway, Cathy Urwin, Couze Venn, and Valerie Walkerdine, *Changing the Subject* (London: Methuen, 1984); James T. Sears, *Growing Up Gay in the South: Race, Gender, and Journeys of the Spirit* (New York: Harrington Park Press, 1991); Michelle Fine, *Framing Dropouts* (Albany: State University of New York Press, 1991); Roger I. Simon, *Teaching Against the Grain* (New York: Bergin & Garvey, 1992); James Donald, *Sentimental Education* (London: Verso Press, 1992).

18. For instance, while theorists such as Jane Tompkins, Gerald Graff, Gregory Ulmer, and others address pedagogical issues, they do it solely within the referenced terrain of literary studies. Moreover, even those theorists in literary studies who insist on the political nature of pedagogy generally ignore, with few exceptions, the work that has gone on in the field for twenty years. See, for example, Shoshana Felman and Dori Lamb, *Testimony: Crisis of Witnessing in Literature, Psychoanalysis, and History* (New York: Routledge, 1992); Bruce Henricksen and Thais E. Morgan, *Reorientations: Critical Theories & Pedagogies* (Urbana: University of Illinois

Press, 1990); Patricia Donahue and Ellen Quahndahl, eds., *Reclaiming Pedagogy: The Rhetoric of the Classroom* (Carbondale: Southern Illinois University Press, 1989); Gregory Ulmer, *Applied Grammatology* (Baltimore: Johns Hopkins University Press, 1985); Barbara Johnson, ed., *The Pedagogical Imperative: Teaching as a Literary Genre* (New Haven: Yale University Press, 1983).

19. One interesting example of this occurred when Gary Olson, the editor of the *Journal of Advanced Composition,* interviewed Jacques Derrida. He asked Derrida, in the context of a discussion about pedagogy and teaching, if he knew of the work of Paulo Freire. Derrida responded, "This is the first time I've heard his name" (Gary Olson, "Jacques Derrida on Rhetoric and Composition: A Conversation," in *[Inter]views: Cross-Disciplinary Perspectives on Rhetoric and Literacy,* ed. Gary Olson and Irene Gale [Carbondale: Southern Illinois University Press, 1991], p. 133). It is hard to imagine that a figure of Freire's international stature would not be known to someone in literary studies who is one of the major proponents of deconstruction. So much for crossing boundaries. Clearly, Derrida does not read the radical literature in composition studies, because if he did he could not miss the numerous references to the work of Paulo Freire and other critical educators. See, for instance, C. Douglas Atkins and Michael L. Johnson, *Writing and Reading Differently: Deconstruction and the Teaching of Composition and Literature* (Lawrence: University of Kansas Press, 1985); Linda Brodkey, *Academic Writing as a Social Practice* (Philadelphia: Temple University Press, 1987); C. Mark Hurlbert and Michael Blitz, eds., *Composition & Resistance* (Portsmouth, NH: Heinemann, 1991).

20. It is worth noting that the term "cultural studies" derives from the Centre for Contemporary Cultural Studies at the University of Birmingham. Initially influenced by the work of Richard Hoggart, Raymond Williams, and E. P. Thompson, the Centre's ongoing work in cultural studies achieved international recognition under the direction of Stuart Hall in the 1970s and later under Richard Johnson in the 1980s. For a useful history of the Centre written from the theoretical vantage point of one of its U.S. supporters, see Lawrence Grossberg, "The Formations of Cultural Studies: An American in Birmingham," in Blundell et al., *Relocating Cultural Studies,* pp. 21–66.

21. Williams is quite adamant in refuting "encyclopedia articles dating the birth of Cultural Studies from this or that book in the late 'fifties." He goes on to say that: "the shift of perspective about the teaching of art and literature and their relation to history and to contemporary society began in Adult Education, it didn't happen anywhere else. It was when it was taken across by people with that experience to the Universities that it was suddenly recognized as a subject. It is in these and other similar ways that the contribution of the process itself to social change itself, and specifically to learning, has happened" (cited in Raymond Williams, "Adult Education and Social Change," *What I Came to Say* [London: Hutchinson-Radus, 1989], pp. 157–166). See also, Raymond Williams, "The Future of Cultural Studies," in *The Politics of Modernism,* ed. Tony Pickney (London: Verso, 1989), pp. 151–162.

22. Williams, "The Future of Cultural Studies," p. 158.

23. John Fiske, *Power Plays, Power Works* (London: Verso Press, 1994), p. 20.

24. Larry Grossberg goes so far as to argue that cultural studies "sees both history and its own practice as the struggle to produce one context out of another, one set of relations out of another." Lawrence Grossberg, "Cultural Studies and/in New Worlds," *Critical Studies in Mass Communications* (Annandale, VA: Speech Communication Association, forthcoming), p. 4.

25. Raymond Williams, *Communications,* rev. ed. (New York: Barnes & Noble, 1967), pp. 14–15.

26. Simon, *Teaching Against the Grain,* p. 15.

27. Ruth Conniff, "The Culture of Cruelty," *The Progressive,* September 16, 1992, pp. 16–20.

28. See the November 29, 1993, issue of *Newsweek.* Of course, the issue that is often overlooked in associating "gangsta rap" with violence is that "gangsta rap does not appear in a cultural vacuum, but, rather, is expressive of the cultural crossing, mixing, and engagement of black youth culture with the values, attitudes, and concerns of the white majority." bell hooks, "Sexism and Misogyny: Who Takes the Rap?" *Z Magazine,* February 1994, p. 26. See also

Greg Tate's spirited defense of rap in Greg Tate, "Above and Beyond Rap's Decibels," *New York Times,* March 6, 1994, pp. 1, 36.

29. This is most evident in the popular media culture where analysis of crime in the United States is almost exclusively represented through images of Black youth. For example, in the May 1994 issue of *Atlantic Monthly,* the cover of the magazine shows a Black urban youth, without a shirt, with a gun in his hand, staring out at the reader. The story the image is highlighting is about inner-city violence. The flurry of articles, magazines, films, and news stories about crime produced in 1994 focuses almost exclusively on Black youth, both discursively and representationally.

30. Camille Colatosti, "Dealing Guns," *Z Magazine,* January 1994, p. 59.

31. Holly Sklar, "Young and Guilty by Stereotype," *Z Magazine,* July/August 1993, p. 52.

32. Stanley Aronowitz, "A Different Perspective on Educational Inequality," *The Review of Education/Pedagogy/Cultural Studies* (University Park, PA: Gordon & Breach, forthcoming), p. 15.

33. Aronowitz and Giroux, *Education Still Under Siege,* pp. 4–5.

34. These quotes and comments are taken from a stinging analysis of Kaus in Jonathan Kozol, "Speaking the Unspeakable," Unpublished manuscript (1993). The context for Kaus's remarks are developed in Mickey Kaus, *The End of Equality* (New York: Basic Books, 1992).

35. Paul Virilio, *Lost Dimension,* trans. Daniel Moshenberg (New York: Semiotext[e], 1991).

36. Andrew Ross and Tricia Rose, eds., *Microphone Fiends: Youth Music and Youth Culture* (New York: Routledge, 1994), and Jonathon Epstein, ed., *Adolescents and Their Music: If It's Too Loud, You're Too Old* (New York: Garland, 1994).

37. Theodor Adorno and Max Horkheimer, writing in the 1940s, argued that popular culture had no redeeming political or aesthetic possibilities. See Max Horkheimer and Theodor Adorno, *Dialectic of Enlightenment* (New York: Herder & Herder, 1944/1972), especially "The Culture Industry: Enlightenment as Mass Deception," pp. 120–167.

38. Walter Parkes, "Random Access, Remote Control," *Omni,* January 1994, p. 54.

39. This section of the paper draws from Henry A. Giroux, "Slacking Off: Border Youth and Postmodern Education," *Journal of Advanced Composition* (forthcoming).

40. Carol Anshaw, "Days of Whine and Poses," *Village Voice,* November 10, 1992, p. 27.

41. For a critique of the so-called "twenty-something generation" as defined by *Time, U.S. News, Money, Newsweek,* and the *Utne Reader,* see Chris de Bellis, "From Slackers to Baby Busters," *Z Magazine,* December 1993, pp. 8–10.

42. Andrew Kopkind, "Slacking Toward Bethlehem," *Grand Street, 11,* No. 4 (1992), 183.

43. The contours of this type of criticism are captured in a comment by Andrew Kopkind, a keen observer of slacker culture, in "Slacking Toward Bethlehem":

> The domestic and economic relationships that have created the new consciousness are not likely to improve in the few years left in this century, or in the years of the next, when the young slackers will be middle-agers. The choices for young people will be increasingly constricted. In a few years, a steady job at a mall outlet or a food chain may be all that's left for the majority of college graduates. Life is more and more like a lottery — is a lottery — with nothing but the luck of the draw determining whether you get a recording contract, get your screenplay produced, or get a job with your M.B.A. Slacking is thus a rational response to casino capitalism, the randomization of success, and the utter arbitrariness of power. If no talent is still enough, why bother to hone your skills? If it is impossible to find a good job, why not slack out and enjoy life? (p. 187)

44. For an analysis of Black American cinema in the 1990s, see Ed Guerrero, "Framing Blackness: The African-American Image in the Cinema of the Nineties," *Cineaste, 20,* No. 2 (1993), 24–31.

45. Michael Dyson, "The Politics of Black Masculinity and the Ghetto in Black Film," in *The Subversive Imagination: Artists, Society, and Social Responsibility,* ed. Carol Becker (New York: Routledge, 1994), p. 155.

46. Dyson, "The Politics of Black Masculinity," p. 163.

47. Itabari Njeri, "Untangling the Roots of the Violence Around Us — On Screen and Off," *Los Angeles Times Magazine*, August 29, 1993, p. 33.

48. Cornel West, "Nihilism in Black America," in Dent, *Black Popular Culture*, p. 40.

49. Itabari Njeri, "Untangling the Roots," p. 34.

50. Fabienne Worth, "Postmodern Pedagogy in the Multicultural Classroom: For Inappropriate Teachers and Imperfect Spectators," *Cultural Critique*, No. 25 (Fall, 1993), 27.

51. Pierce Hollingsworth, "The New Generation Gaps: Graying Boomers, Golden Agers, and Generation X," *Food Technology, 47*, No. 10 (1993), 30.

52. I have called this elsewhere the pedagogy of commercialism. See Giroux, *Disturbing Pleasures*.

53. For an analysis of the relationship among modernist schooling, pedagogy, and popular culture, see Henry A. Giroux and Roger I. Simon, "Popular Culture as a Pedagogy of Pleasure and Meaning," in *Popular Culture, Schooling, and Everyday Life,* ed. Henry A. Giroux and Roger Simon (Granby, MA: Bergin & Garvey, 1989), pp. 1–30; Henry A. Giroux and Roger I. Simon, "Schooling, Popular Culture, and a Pedagogy of Possibility," in Giroux and Simon, *Popular Culture*, pp. 219–236.

54. Anyone who has been following the culture wars of the past eight years is well aware of the conservative agenda for reordering public and higher education around the commercial goal of promoting economic growth for the nation while simultaneously supporting the values of Western civilization as a common culture designed to undermine the ravages of calls for equity and multiculturalism. For a brilliant analysis of the conservative attack on higher education, see Ellen Messer-Davidow, "Manufacturing the Attack on Liberalized Higher Education," *Social Text, 11,* No. 3 (1993), 40–80.

55. This argument is especially powerful in the work of Edward Said, who frames the reach of culture as a determining pedagogical force against the backdrop of the imperatives of colonialism. See Edward Said, *Culture and Imperialism* (New York: Alfred A. Knopf, 1993); see also, Donaldo Macedo, *Literacies of Power* (Boulder, CO: Westview Press, 1994).

56. Selective examples of this work include: Carol Becker, ed., *The Subversive Imagination* (New York: Routledge, 1994); Giroux and McLaren, *Between Borders;* Simon, *Teaching Against the Grain;* David Trend, *Cultural Pedagogy: Art/Education/Politics* (Westport, CT: Bergin & Garvey, 1992); James Schwoch, Mimi White, and Susan Reilly, *Media Knowledge: Readings in Popular Culture, Pedagogy, and Critical Citizenship* (Albany: State University of New York Press, 1992); Lawrence Grossberg, *We Gotta Get Out of This Place: Popular Conservatism and Postmodern Culture* (New York: Routledge, 1992). See also, Douglas Kellner, *Media Culture* (New York: Routledge, forthcoming); Jeanne Brady, *Schooling Young Children* (Albany: State University of New York Press, forthcoming).

57. Stuart Hall, "Race, Culture, and Communications: Looking Backward and Forward at Cultural Studies," *Rethinking Marxism, 5,* No. 1 (1992), 11.

58. Peter Hitchcock, "The Othering of Cultural Studies," *Third Text, No. 25 (Winter, 1993–1994),* 12.

59. Walter Parkes, "Random Access, Remote Control: The Evolution of Story Telling," *Omni,* January 1994, p. 50.

60. Hall, "Race, Culture, and Communications," p. 14.

61. Peter Euben, "The Debate Over the Canon," *Civic Arts Review, 7,* No. 1 (1994), 14–15.

I would like to thank Susan Searls, Doug Kellner, and Stanley Aronowitz for their critical reading of this manuscript.

Foot Soldiers of Modernity:
The Dialectics of Cultural Consumption
and the 21st-Century School

PAUL WILLIS

Young people are unconscious foot soldiers in the long front of modernity, involuntary and disoriented conscripts in battles never explained. In particular, subordinate and working-class students are rendered by state-mandated education into the compulsory living materials of future imaginings and moldings. These institutional imaginings have immense social power but are usually undertaken by one generation for the next without the rudiments of a sociological or ethnographic imagination. The theories and qualitative methods of the social sciences are necessary to represent local experience at the grassroots and to understand its connections to the operations of larger institutional and macro forces. Power brokers and policy planners are transfixed by the internal logic of their "top-down" practices and initiatives; however, they fail to ponder the frequently ironic and unintended consequences of these practices and the creative cultural ways in which subordinate and working-class groups respond to them. These "bottom-up" responses are often informed by quite different social perceptions, practices, and assumptions.

What is crucial but missed is the recognition that the waves of attempted economic and technical modernization "from above" are often antagonistically related to waves of cultural modernization "from below," which are usually misunderstood. In part, technical modernization is fighting not chaos, a recalcitrant past, or the wrong type of future, but its own alter ego of late cultural modernism as articulated by working-class, dominated, and subordinated groups — what I will henceforth refer to as the popular classes. While often appearing to stand in the way of progress, the latter most often tend to believe in this goal and they profoundly condition, in unexpected ways, how it is played out socially and culturally.

Youth are always among the first to experience the problems and possibilities of the successive waves of technical and economic modernization that sweep through capitalist societies. Young people respond in disorganized and chaotic ways, but to the best of their abilities and with relevance to the actual possibilities of their lives as they see, live, and embody them. These responses are actually embedded in the flows of

Harvard Educational Review Vol. 73 No. 3 Fall 2003

cultural modernization, but to adult eyes they may seem to be mysterious, troubling, and even shocking and antisocial. Schools are one of the principal sites for the dialectical playing out of these apparent disjunctions and contradictions, which, while misunderstood, underlie some of the most urgent education debates — from traditionalism versus progressivism to the canon versus multiculturalism.

In this article, I argue that a social understanding of education needs to consider both top-down practices and bottom-up responses, and the ways in which they interact "on the ground" to produce the complex eddies, waves, and flows of modernization. The activities and processes I discuss in this article have currency throughout Western industrialized countries and exist in highly varied and often compressed versions in newly industrialized and industrializing countries. However, I draw on ethnographic arguments taken primarily from my own research in England. I deal with three waves of what I am calling cultural modernization "from below," which I discuss in the chronological order of my work. This order does not necessarily reflect their real occurrence in time, certainly not across all countries.

The first wave of modernization from below is based on the cultural responses of working-class and subordinate groups to "top-down" state programs and initiatives aimed at competitive modernization. The most important feature of these schemes has been the vastly expanded scale of compulsory education. This wave of modernization is disrupted by the effects of the second and third waves described below, and the subsequent responses of the popular classes to these waves. The social and cultural dislocations and crises resulting from the emergence of a postindustrial society drive the second wave of modernization. This wave brings a catastrophic decline in the demand for manual labor in industrialized Western countries and transforms the role of the state in the regulation of the youth labor market. We can understand this deindustrialization as one aspect of globalization whereby economic restructuring triggers the brutal arrival of the postindustrial society in the "first" world as industrial society finally takes root — unevenly — in the "third." The third wave of modernization from below arises from the common cultural responses of young people to the arrival of the global "commodity and electronic society." Young people creatively respond to a plethora of electronic signals and cultural commodities in ways that surprise their makers, finding meanings and identities never meant to be there and defying simple nostrums that bewail the manipulation or passivity of "consumers."

Although my main focus here will be on the third wave, all aspects and themes of the three waves continue as simultaneous and intertwined forces. In different ways, they continue to have broad relevance to the current conjunctures in various countries. The basic argument of this article is that the third wave cannot be understood except within the context of, and dialectical links with, the first two waves. Common cultural forms must be understood with respect to their interaction with other major forces sweeping through society and with the responses of the popular classes to these forces.

First Wave: Cultural Responses to Universal Schooling

Part of the political settlement between forces representing "capital" and "labor" in the United Kingdom (U.K.) after World War II was to give, at least theoretically, equal education rights to all children. In 1972, the U.K. raised the minimum school-leaving age from fifteen to sixteen. This marked the coming to full fruition of the early modernist drive to secure compulsory full-time education for all. Emile Durkheim (1956) comments on education as the instrument of modernization *par excellence* that is mobilized to raise the skill levels of workers in an internationally competitive industrial world. Always inherent in this drive is the tension between the socially integrative ideologies of aspiration and egalitarianism and the obvious practical logic of the continuing delivery of social agents into gendered hierarchies severely divided by skill, remuneration, and disposition. This tension helps us understand that even the extended support across the organized left in the U.K. for raising the school-leaving age failed to hide the disappointing response of a good section of the working class to the prospect of another year of enforced school attendance. Many working-class kids did not accept their new privilege with good grace. Instead, they simply wanted the earliest possible access to the wage. They did not want to be in school at all, never mind another year of it (Willis, 1977).

The Lads

Learning to Labour describes the informal school culture and interactions of a group of young White working-class boys in an English industrial midlands school in the mid-1970s (Willis, 1977). The "lads" resisted the mental and bodily inculcations of the school and rejected students who showed conformist attitudes to the school authorities. Their culture borrowed and recycled elements of traditional working-class culture and embodied an assertive masculine style, which was often aggressive and predicated on being able to "handle yourself" in a fight. The lads deployed a particularly concrete and sharp way of speaking and were devoted to a certain kind of omni-present humor — "having a laff" — often directed cruelly against conformists and teachers. Their devotion to "the laff" was central to the culture, and its deployment was an ubiquitous form capable of turning almost any situation into material for jokes and ribbing: "It's the most important thing in life, even communists laff" (p. 29).

In *Learning to Labour*, I wanted to get at the inside story of this phenomenon, to try to see the world as the lads did, to get a feel for their social games and their fields of power from their point of view. They had little or no interest in studying and were not interested in gaining academic qualifications.[1] Vigorous opposition to the teachers' authority was the central vertical dynamic organizing the lads' lived culture: "Who are they, tellin' us what to do when they're no better than us?" The central horizontal dynamic that organized and arranged their cultural assumptions and practices was a rejection of conformist pupils labeled as "ear'oles":[2] "They'm prats, they never get any fun do they?" This rejection was felt as a kind of distinction and superiority: "We can make them laff, they can't make us laff." These positions and orientations were enacted and embodied through a strong "rough" masculine set of strategies, embellished in various ways through smoking, drinking, and stylish dressing.

From an educational point of view, the strangest thing about the lads' attitudes and behavior was their low interest in and/or hostility toward academic work and the gaining of qualifications. From a sociological point of view, the most interesting thing about their culture was the indifference it induced among the lads to the actual kind of work they thought of undertaking, ranging from readily available factory work to tire fitting and bricklaying. I argued in *Learning to Labour* that their own culture helped induct them voluntarily into the low-status jobs that most would shun. Their own culture was involved in processes of social reproduction, understood as the generational replacement of individuals in unequal class positions. There was a tragic irony at the heart of their culture; it was surprisingly more effective than any intended ideological mechanism aimed at promoting social reproduction.[3]

"Modern" Social Functions of Resistance

Although resistant cultures continue to be condemned in schools with teachers and administrators increasingly seeing them as pathological, they actually show some clear elements of rationality. In particular, these resistant cultures supply cultural forms and shields from stigma to blunt the cruel edge of individualism and meritocracy in capitalist societies. These ideologies and their associated mechanisms and practices can have only limited meaning for the majority of the working class who cannot all hope to attain the privilege of well-paid and high-prestige jobs at the end of the educational process. Individual logic says that it is worth working hard at school to gain qualifications to get a good job. However, this cannot be the case for all working-class individuals, even though all are asked to behave as if it were so.[4] Only a substantial minority from the working class can hope for mobility, and their cultures and dispositions are adapted accordingly. No one else discusses this, but the lads' culture, despite its disorders and chaos, tells them that no amount of extra qualification will improve the position of the whole class; that would constitute, in fact, the dismantling of the whole class society.

Meanwhile, the dominance of the individualistic and meritocratic ideology produces for the middle class a functional legitimacy for enjoying their privilege — they are there because they have passed exams. The capacities of the popular classes are subject to stultification in hopeless obedience to an impossible dream. Credentialism, or the proliferation of educational qualifications, works to prevent the working class from pursuing either alternative flowerings of their capacities or subversive courses of growth. It seeks to enslave their powers and trap them in the foothills of human development and can stand only as a fraudulent offer to the majority of what can really mean something only to the few. The student population is graded in a descending status order, from whose lowest ranks escape is usually impossible. The educational offer is to join an ever-multiplying classificatory system in which every increase further depresses its bottom layers (Gilborn & Mirza, 2000). The lads' culture exposes this dynamic, releasing them from collusion in their own exclusion and freeing up their potential for an alternative cultural expressivity.

Ironically, the lads' culture also had a stabilizing effect on the hierarchical social order. In their "tumble out of" and "escape" from what they felt was the oppressive atmosphere of the school, they went into manual work quite voluntarily, subsequently helping to reproduce the whole social order at its most difficult point. The lads also found a "culture of the shop floor" on arrival at work that was welcoming and familiar to them because it displayed many of the same qualities as their own counter-school culture. It gave them a collective and human means — even if sexist, anti-intellectual, and often racist — of surviving the harsh conditions and authority regimes of work.

The lads' transition from school to work was, in part, a cultural vote with their feet for the working-class adult world of work. In this informal socialization process, there was also an enthusiastic taking up of rights to the only working-class inheritance bequeathed upon the lads — the wage. The power of the wage created possibilities for which their own culture had already precociously and only too well prepared them: smart dressing, pubbing and clubbing, and crosstown driving.

Hugely important to understand here is the antimental animus of the counter-school culture. While highly relevant in opposing and penetrating the demands of the school, it also becomes a kind of second nature that continues to orient bodily style, attitudes, and values during the transition from school to work and long after. This pattern impels them toward a certain kind of culturally mediated and experiential form of meaning-making throughout their lives. The danger is that this antimental attitude could lead to the whole world being divided into two — the mental and the manual. This makes hope for a "second chance" return to higher education much more difficult and unlikely. The lads' antimentalism reconciles them and those like them to manual work and often to job-hopping between dead-end jobs — now interspersed with long spells of unemployment, or even permanent unemployment — for the rest of their lives. It makes all jobs involving mental work, now and for the future, seem to be simply boring paperwork — "Who wants to spend their day pushing paper around?"

The Articulations of Gender with Antimentalism

Gender meanings and resources are also important elements within the articulations of cultural forces and practices resistant to the school. Symbolic structures of masculinity in the lads' culture help to embody and give an extra force to their school resistance. Masculinity gives them an axis of power over women, but it also gives them a realistic basis for feeling at least some ambiguous superiority over other less successful males, such as teachers and ear'oles. This response has a definite logic and is effective against the attempted domination of the school, and it gives alternative nonmental grounds for valuing the self and a whole solid, sometimes formidable, presence to resist belittling. As I argue in *Learning to Labour*, once formed, "hard" or "tough" masculine identities and the patterning of social relations that follow prove highly inflexible, intractable, and durable. This is perhaps especially so when they have been formed through the winning back of identity and dignity lost in inescapable institutional tensions in which they are trapped on the losing/receiving end. Masculinity and its reflexes henceforth help to organize the same repertoire of defensive/offensive responses no matter what the situation — as if all social sites and social relations contained somehow a mandatory threat. This produces an obvious danger for women in and out of the home, where a compensatory masculinity may seek proof and to exercise a felt superiority. Furthermore, shop floor and manual work relations are suffused with masculinity and masculinized social relations. These relations blunt the oppositional possibility of recognizing how specifically capitalist forms subordinate labor power.

There is a further twist here where the antimentalism and masculinity of the lads become intertwined with their sense of themselves and their own vital powers. For the lads, a manual way of acting in the world is a manly way, while a mental way is effeminate. These gendered associations reinforce and lock each other, producing a disposition and sensibility that may, quite literally, last a lifetime. In a final sealing of their subordinate future, mental work becomes not only pointless "paper pushing" but also "sissy" work for the lads. Teachers are seen as inferior because they are "sissies." Even higher paid mental work is considered sissy from the lads' point of view. Exhausting, exploited, and increasingly low paid, manual work can still somehow be seen in a masculine register, which prevents its true brutality from showing through.

Learning to Labour gives an account of the cultures of White, male, working-class resistance in school. It offers a perspective for understanding a particular stability in the first wave of cultural modernization in the U.K. and its contribution to the maintenance of a relatively peaceful class-divided society. Even after the advent of the Welfare State and formal educational equality for all, there was a settled — though unequal — relation between classes, where no over-ambition from the working class threatened either capitalist organization or the interests of the middle class. At the same time there was some real autonomy allowed to students and young workers, including, at least for an important section, their own transitions from childhood to adulthood. Arguably, this limited autonomy effectively sidelined, or at least profoundly modified, "modernizing" institutional attempts at controlling and regulating the passage into adulthood. Working-class and informal cultural forms and activities, while seen as antisocial by some, could take root and flower in inhospitable circumstances. This made those circumstances more livable and provided collective and mutual relations, communications, and meanings that sustained working-class identity and informal activity on a wider scale.

Although the social and political landscape has changed over the last twenty-six years, there continues to be very hard and persistent elements of resistant culture in schools. Despite their sometimes antisocial nature and the undoubted difficulties they produce for classroom teachers, these cultures continue to pose, in living form, crucial and collective questions from the point of view of the working class: What is "progress" for? What can I/we expect from the sacrifice of hard work and obedience in school? Why am I/are we compelled to be in school if there appears to be nothing in it for me/us?

Second Wave: Responses to the Postindustrial Society

In the early 1980s the U.K. became the first industrialized country to experience massive losses of the manual industrial work that had previously been available to the working classes. This trend is now firmly established across the old industrialized world. In the U.K., over half of the manufacturing jobs that existed in the 1970s have been destroyed with a slightly larger reduction in related trade union membership (Roberts, 2001). At the same time, there has been a virtually epochal restructuring of the kind of work available. From the point of view of the working class, work opportunities have shifted away from well to reasonably paid skilled or semi-skilled industrial work to much lower paid service and out-of-reach white-collar work.

Taken together, the new customer service call centers and the hotel and catering industries now employ more than double the number of workers as the old "smokestack" industries — cars, ship building, steel, engineering, coal mining (Roberts, 2001). The whole working class has been badly affected by the diminution in both the quality and quantity of jobs available, especially young people, older workers, and ethnic minorities. Recently, unemployment has dropped considerably to a general rate of 5.1 percent (Office of National Statistics, 2003). This figure, however, conceals a high turnover in part-time, casual, and insecure low-paid work. It also masks huge geographic variations, with large, predominantly middle-class areas enjoying virtually full employment while the older industrial areas and inner cities suffer from overall unemployment rates of 20 percent and more. One in two less-skilled men are without work and one in five households lack access to earned income (Gregg & Wadsworth, 1999; Willis, Bekenn, Ellis, & Whitt, 1988). Clearly, not everyone will find a role in the new weightless economy, and many continue to expect, against increasing odds, to be remunerated and respected for an ability and disposition to work in traditional manual ways.

The objective probabilities of a reliable and decent wage through manual work have been radically decreased for substantial parts of the working class, and the threat of its removal has become a permanent condition for all workers. This has to be understood as a threat, not only to the wage as an amount of money, but also to the wage as a particular kind of social inheritance and cultural, even moral, enfranchisement (Willis, 2000; Willis, Jones, Canaan, & Hurd, 1990). The wage provides access to cultural commodities and services and to the forms of informal meaning-making that these commodities and services frame and facilitate. It also provides the means to independent living, a place separate from the patriarchal dependencies of the parental home, and from the vicissitudes of the marketplace. The wage enables the formation of the couple and preparation for the nuclear family. Gaining access to the male family wage is still one of the important material bases for the courtship dance, romance, and "love-pairing."

In the U.K., we have been suffering from the breaking of these transitions for over two decades. The old processes and expectations often continue in some form but have been thrown into permanent crisis. There are still plenty of male working-class kids, like the lads, who are perhaps more willing than ever to take on exploited manual work in traditional masculine and antimentalist ways, but there is not enough work to go around, and many are left in suspended animation.[5] The lucky ones, at least to start with, feel grateful for any work. Even though the uncertainties associated with job insecurity — or the deceptive lure of job hopping —may seem like an antidote to the wearing down of repetitive or heavy labor, they threaten to throw workers back into a stagnant pool of labor at any moment. Nevertheless, simple gratitude and escape from vertiginous despair have become important reproductive mechanisms for those finding or holding on to work (Willis et al., 1988). The dramatic changes brought about by this second wave of modernization have destroyed or substantially weakened traditional forms of transition from school to work and have shaken the material foundations of traditional working-class cultural forms. While unemployment is seen from above as a price worth paying for competitive economic restructuring, economic adaptation produces continuing social and cultural crises at the bottom of social space.

The View from Below [6]

The young unemployed are much less physically mobile than the employed. They cannot afford cars and, therefore, have no access to the "crosstown car culture" of visits to pubs, clubs, and friends. In the Wolverhampton survey conducted for the *Youth*

Review (Willis et al., 1988), half of the unemployed say that their activities are limited by the costs of travel, while three-quarters say that they are limited by lack of cash. A good proportion of them visit town centers and shopping malls during the day. They are attracted to the consumer meccas but have no economic role to play. Rather, they simply hang out or engage in activities that put them into conflict with shoppers, shop owners, and the police.

The dominant experience of the young unemployed is one of very limited sociability. They are isolated and homebound, traversing acres of boredom by themselves or in conflict with parents for whom their enforced dependence is often wholly unwelcome. The young unemployed have more free time than any other social group but, ironically, they are excluded from leisure activities, which overwhelmingly now require consumption and commercial power. For instance, whether we like it or not, drinking is by far the most popular activity among young people in the U.K., where three-quarters of them go to pubs nearly four times a week. However, only one-third of the long-term unemployed go drinking, and much less often. Furthermore, they do not spend the extra time engaging in sports or outdoor hobbies, nor do they participate in state-provided community and sports infrastructures any more than the employed. Another vivid aspect of this isolation, according to the *Youth Review* findings, is that, for the unemployed, courtship seems to lose the centrality that it holds for the employed. The young unemployed are much less likely to have a "steady" relationship, and thoughts of marriage or settling down seem very far away for most of them. They are prone to alienation, depression, and pessimism about their future prospects and are plagued by feelings of social shame and suspicions that other people blame them for their condition. Young people who experience long-term unemployment are uniquely open to drug abuse, often seen in distorted ways as forms of self-medication.

A whole succession of training programs and special labor market measures have been developed by the state to bridge the gaping wholes left by the collapse of the old transitions between school and work. In 1998, the British government introduced the New Deal program, which provides unemployed young people with two years of work experience, training, or work in the voluntary and charitable sector (Unemployment Unit, 1999). For the first time with such schemes, refusal to participate is not an option, and benefits are withdrawn if a young person fails to commit to one of these options. Essentially, the means of subsistence are made contingent upon flexibility and obedience, a qualitatively new coercive stage in the disciplining of labor power and attitude.

A significant minority of young people refuses this contractual submission to their own subordination. They are not accounted for in official figures and become invisible to the programs and to the state (Unemployment Unit, 1999; "One in Five Young People," 2003). Despite such refusal and widespread discontent, there is surprisingly little outright public or organized opposition. This may be explained in part by some bleak, internalized, and individualistic additions to the reproduction repertoire whereby many individuals blame themselves for their lack of work and for the lack of success attendance to state schemes brings. Individualizing and internalizing a structural problem, they shamefully reproach themselves for their inability to find work. Having been given so many training opportunities to develop their individual employability and having been told repeatedly that finding work is a question of permanent individual job search, it must be their individual fault when they cannot find work.

These are just some of the forces that corrode the main elements of the first wave modernist cultural settlement. The pride, depth, and independence of a collective industrial cultural tradition, forged from below and neither reliant on patronage nor punished for its cultural impertinence, is giving way to the regulated indignities of becoming a client to a reprimanding state. As the research for the *Youth Review* illustrates, young workers are forced into a reenvisioned reserve army of flexible and obedient labor. This army of workers is supposed to stand ready to occupy, at rock-bottom wages, the new menial functions of the postindustrial economy and to service the growing personal and domestic needs of a newly ascendant middle class. For those who refuse to join state schemes and the legitimate labor market, begging from parents and others, drug dealing, prostitution, hustling, and benefit fraud offer some income. They also lead to entanglements with youth justice systems and possible incarceration, which finally destroys any hope of a "proper" job. But for some, the highly ambiguous and self-defeating freedoms of the streets seem to offer a viable alternative to the mental incarceration of endless state schemes.

Schools in the Second Wave

The school is and will be a principal site for the early playing out of these contradictions and social tensions, thus placing students at the frontlines of these conflicts. A further condition is now added to devalue and question the role of schools at the level of cultural practice. Not only are young people able to challenge its underlying individualistic and meritocratic ideologies, but they can also expose the practical inability of schooling to connect many students to real prospects in the world of work. In these conditions, it is no longer possible to believe in a universal and positive role for the educational system in promoting benign and emancipatory effects for the popular classes. Are schools to prepare their students for unemployment? Are they to engage in remedial programs to equip individuals to fight each other for the very chance of low-paid service work? Are they to abandon altogether any hope of interrupting processes of social reproduction?

Meanwhile, many of the cultural experiences and disarticulations of the late adolescent or early adult unemployed find their way back into the school, importing with them their own hidden and not so hidden injuries and reinforcing attitudes of cynicism, detachment, and gender crisis. These cultural expressions are articulated within different formations of school culture, heightening the negative potential of an already existing atmosphere of disorder, violence, and social fear (Devine, 1997; Johnson, 1999; Paulle, 2003). Singular racial oppressions, exacerbated and magnified through even higher expected unemployment rates, can add further impulses of anger and opposition (Sewell, 1997). School cultural practices have to be understood within this general context of disaffection with oppositional forms termed and understood as displaying "disassociated" or "disaffected" resistance, rather than the "simple" resistance of wave one. Resistance takes on a kind of futility, even potential pathology, when disassociated from traditional first wave cultural resources, from their sense of a future. After all, first wave resistance is solidified by a well-grounded social bet on capital's need for labor. It assumes and relies on a future of collective labor albeit actively and culturally formed to be relatively free from individualistic and meritocratic distortions and false promises. Even if not fitting official templates, there is a consequent materiality here to be worked on for economic, social, and cultural betterment, which still gives continuity to working-class forms. Second wave modernization deconstructs this working-class inheritance, and resistance spins freely without the context of any socially imagined future. It is hard to detect any link of disaffected or disassociated resistance with any kind of emancipatory political project.

Second Wave Gender Articulations

As in the first wave, gender registers and plays a part in these fundamental social and cultural shifts. In particular, forms of working-class masculinity are being thrown into crisis by the second wave of modernization, uprooted from their secure and central lodgings within proletarian relations of manualism, "pride in the job," and breadwinner power. This shift in the meaning of masculinity undermines the specific logic of masculinized resistance in school, as well as the continuities between male counter-school culture and what remains of shop floor culture. Further, the antimentalism of the counter-school culture cannot be securely cloaked in traditional proletarian masculinity. Antimentalism loses the counterpoint with a viable predictable future in manual work.

As the relationship between the wage and traditional meaning of masculinity shifts, the material base for the courtship dance disappears. For many young women, there is no longer the realistic prospect of gaining access to the family wage and to transition into a separate household through male earning power.[7] Questions of gender identity and sexuality may be rendered into matters of immediate attraction or non-attraction, rather than being informed by long-term expectations of commitment. Where a collective apprenticeship to a respectable future fails, for some young men a strategy for maintaining a sense of manhood may entail, and perhaps demand, immediate gender tributes extracted through heavy sexist language and humor and physical intimidation or its threat. This practice can be taken up into whole bodily dispositions, attitudes, and presence. Where masculinity cannot be about assuming the mantle and power of the wage, it can become a claim for power in its own right.[8]

Under conditions of chronic unemployment, social stability and reproduction may require that some of the young and potentially most disruptive of the unemployed of both sexes withdraw themselves into more or less self-pacified or marginalized positions. By excluding themselves permanently from the labor market, they withdraw from society the seeds of non-cooperation and rebellion. The development of an "underclass" (especially the degeneracies of its public imagery; see Adair, 2002), vastly expanding prison populations (the new "welfare" means for the poor), and the further economic victimization of single mothers may also provide socially reproductive object lessons in destitution *pour encourager les autres,* thereby enabling coercive control of working populations, present and future, without the use of explicit force. Substantial proportions of the student body may be influenced by oppositional cultures, but calculate that a state-regulated chance of a low-paid job beats incarceration or the tender mercies of the street. These are raw and open forms of social reproduction that are very different from the more settled, if mystified, forms associated with first wave modernization. But even through ambiguous and disassociated means, collective questions gain cultural articulation again: What's the point of school if there ain't no jobs to follow? If "progress" is so great, why is all I/we see at school, and in the schemes to follow, increased containment and discipline?

Third Wave: Commodity and Electronic Culture

Along with the upheavals in the material conditions of the subordinate classes described above come enormous changes at the cultural level that bring about disorganization to settled forms of working-class culture. New global electronic forms of communication are sidelining old sensuous communities — face-to-face interactions with known others — with now literally hundreds of TV channels available through digitalization. This is furthered by the huge growth of commercial leisure forms and the mass availability of cultural commodities. The postmodern cultural epoch is characterized by this qualitative expansion of commodity relations from the meeting of physical needs — food, warmth, and shelter — to the meeting and inflaming of mental, emotional, expressive, and spiritual needs and aspirations. You could say that the predatory productive forces of capitalism are now unleashed globally not only on nature but also on human nature.

At the level of culture, young people are becoming less defined by neighborhood and class than they are by these new relations of commodity and electronic culture. Even as their economic conditions of existence falter, most young working-class people in the U.K. would not thank you now for describing them as working class. They find more passion and acceptable self-identity through music on MTV, wearing baseball caps and designer shoes, and socializing in fast-food joints than they do through traditional class-based cultural forms.[9]

We should not underestimate the cultural offensive of capitalism against the young consumer. Young people may believe that they are free to choose, but the marketers have different ideas. Simon Silvester, executive planning director for Young & Rubicon Europe, writes recently in the "Creative Business" section of the *Financial Times*, "Marketers have concentrated on youth for 50 years for good reason — they [young people] are forming their brand preferences and trying out new things. . . . In 40 years, there'll be a generation of pierced grannies telling you they're brand-promiscuous and adventurous" (Silvester, 2002, p. 6). Ralph Nader (1996) writes in *Children First*:

> A struggle different than any before in world history is intensifying between corporations and parents over their children. It is a struggle over the minds, bodies, time and space of millions of children and the kind of world in which they are growing up. . . . The corporate marketing culture stresses materialism, money, sex, the power of violence, junk food and the status they bring; its power crowds out or erodes the values of the inherent worth and dignity of the human being. (p. iii, vii)

Common Culture and the Expressive Subject

Such arguments are well known and, oddly enough, made with equal vigor from the Left and the Right. There is much to be agreed with in Nader's pungently expressed views. However, my purpose is not so much to join a moral crusade as to establish the nature of an epochal shift in the symbolic order and its forms. It is crucial to better understand the consequences of these shifts on young people from a social scientific and ethnographic perspective.

The market, which provides an encompassing and saturating cultural environment through its electronic forms, supplies the most attractive and useable symbolic and expressive forms that are consumed by teenagers and early adults. Perhaps political parties, public cultures, or even properly functioning educational institutions should be the principal and principled source of symbolic forms and meanings. It is certainly necessary to continue to battle for the maintenance of the roles and influence of these institutions, but as Margaret Thatcher once said, "You cannot buck the market." Once penetrating the realm of culture and consciousness, a market economy of commodity relations must exert the same formative powers there as it does in the material realm. It drives out craft production and feudal relations of symbolic dependence and brings in an avalanche of commodity goods for consumers constituted as citizens (so long as they have money) who are free to choose and consume as they wish — now with their spirits as well as their bodies. It is not possible to throw out this influence without now throwing out market relations tout court.

My position is that the undoubted market power of capitalist cultural provision certainly determines the forms of production of cultural commodities, but that this cannot be seen as necessarily enforcing an isomorphic consumption reflecting only intended uses or meanings as coded within the production, advertising, and distribution of commodities. As the research reported in *Common Culture* (Willis et al., 1990) illustrates, the commodity form is certainly dominant. But while constricting and structuring the field, the commodity form does not determine it. Within bounds, the commodity form's built-in desperation to find use at any price incites and provokes certain kinds of appropriation. This appropriation is also not necessarily along standard lines: no two people look the same; no two living rooms look the same; no two people think the same; and yet they are all products of a social existence within a market economy.

What the production-oriented pessimists overlook is the other half of the equation — the processes and activities of the acculturation of consumer items. Acculturation refers to the processes and activities whereby human beings actively and creatively take up the objects and symbols around them for their own situated purposes of meaning-making. This process is well known to cultural anthropologists who have observed and commented on it in other contexts (see Clifford, 1997). But while anthropological dignity is accorded to the uses and contextual meanings of objects and artifacts in societies beyond far shores, the proximity and banality of commodity forms "at home" seem to have robbed them of such dignity. I would insist that no matter how disreputable their provenance, commodities and electronic messages are still subject to grounded processes, not only of passive consumption but also of active appropriation. Against the grain of dominant assumptions that aesthetics belong only to High Art and legitimate culture, I have argued that there is a "grounded aesthetics" in everyday practice whereby meanings are attributed to symbols and artifacts, now mostly commodities, in creative ways that produce new orders of symbolic meaning (Willis et al., 1990). These grounded aesthetics reset the possibilities for how every day is experienced and how the selection and appropriation of cultural materials will take place in the future.

Young and working-class people are caught up in the front line of engagement. They acculturate the materials of commodity culture almost as a matter of cultural life and death, not least because they find themselves with ever-diminishing inherited folk cultural resources and with little or no access to legitimate and bourgeois forms of cultural capital. In light of the multiple and complex possibilities of the grounded uses of new environmental resources — commodity and electronic — there is a strange emergence from subordinate cultural relations of a new kind of expressive subject. I would argue that it would have been better if this had occurred without exploitation and in planned developmental ways with more democratic control at the point of formal cultural production. But our hopes for an institutionally led and mutually cooperative cultural program for the popular classes have been rendered quaint and parochial by the new relations of desire brokered through the commodity.

The emergence of a subordinate expressive subject concerns members of the majority popular classes taking for themselves — on the alien and profane grounds of the commodity — something that only the elite have enjoyed as part of their sacred privilege. This privilege entails the formation of sensibilities to mark oneself culturally as a certain kind of person — rather than simply an unconscious carrier of traditional markers of class, race, and gender — or to "choose" to belong to these categories in distinctive, mannered, celebratory, or self-conscious ways. This is to take part in self-formation on relatively autonomous expressive grounds, rather than to be formed from outside on automatically ascribed grounds. The connection of the "given self" to variable external symbolic forms reflects the desire not just to take up social or material space in a way governed by others, but to matter culturally (Willis, 2000). Without some cultural marking, youth feel in danger of being culturally invisible, which increasingly means socially invisible. The choice to wear body jewelry may well last a lifetime, but it is a choice furnished in the conditions of a whole experienced life and life stage. It marks the self-consciousness of one's biography, a sense of self and specific social situation that simply cannot be reduced to the successful marketing of earrings.

It is crucial here to recognize the blurring of the lines between production and consumption in what I call *Common Culture* (Willis et al., 1990). Active consumption is a kind of production. Formal production — as in learning to play an instrument by listening to CDs — often arises first in relation to creative consumption. This is part of what separates the acculturation of popular cultural items from the usual notion of popular culture as materials that have their own inherent meanings and values. Selecting and appropriating popular cultural items for one's own meanings is a kind of cultural production. Though mediated through alien commodity materials, the attachment of an expressive identity to — or its workings through — a socially given mere existence is now a popular, and in its own way democratic, aspiration. While the continuing educational question for first wave modernization concerns whether state education is a means of liberation or ideological confinement for the unprivileged majority, the late modernist question for the same social group concerns whether the commodification and electrification of culture constitute a new form of domination or a means of opening up new fields of semiotic possibility. Are the young becoming culturally literate and expressive in new ways, or are they merely victims of every turn in cultural marketing and mass media manipulation?

However we judge the general tide of influence on this new front, it is incontestable that all school students are drawn in to the field of force of popular cultural provision. The basic point I want to make with respect to the overall theme of this Special Issue is that commodity-related expressive consumption — or common culture — does not take place in a vacuum or simply repeat the exploited meanings of commodity production. Furthermore, the acculturations that arise have to be understood as grounded in and informing other inherited social categories and positions as well as antagonisms between them. We must grant the freedoms of consumption that pedagogists begrudge, political economists deride, and antihumanists deny, but we must locate them at material and social interconnections and historical conjunctures that constrain and channel these freedoms in all kinds of ways. In the school, this points to the importance of understanding popular cultural consumption with respect to previously existing themes of school conformism, resistance, disaffection, variations, and points between them.

We must be alive to how cultural commodities are used to "body out" — give specific bodily expression to — the nature and practice of previously existent or socially articulated positions still organized ultimately by elementary class, race, and gender factors. Of particular importance is how the body-oriented and somatic emphasis of common cultural practices chime with, resonate with, and show an elective affinity with the antimentalism and manual emphases of working-class and subordinate bodily cultures. Bodybuilding, rave, and hip-hop dancing are some of the fields being opened up for the cultural exercise of the body, emphasizing its physical presence and showing its expressivity and superiority over desiccated mental ways of being. Commodity related cultural practices are also producing new fields for the expression of gender in and out of the school. These practices include the trying on of new cloaks for the expression of masculinized resistance or independence from the school. This masculinity is no longer guaranteed by a proletarian industrial inheritance but is still targeted toward the school.

Common cultural practices can also wrap themselves up with second wave disaffected resistance producing a doubly articulated emphasis on the "now" of immediate consumer gratification to go along with the heavy extra weight placed on the present by the lack of a predictable social future. Where the moral and cultural benefits that flow from the proletarian inheritance of the wage are denied, a cultural expressivity through commodities may supply an instant social and cultural imaginary for resistance and alternatives to the felt oppressions of the school, providing, so to speak, something to resist "with." We must recognize that these practices include amplifications and resonances of misogyny and homophobia, as well as criminal and violent themes (hooks, cited in Marriott, 1993). The apparently boundless horizons of consumption have done little to remove the unconscious foot soldiers from their struggles, and have only added another front on which to contend.

These amplifications and resonances of opposition through common cultural means carry their own ironies for social reproduction and negation of subordinate interests. They remove students farther from what school might offer them and diminish the chances of a shot at a "proper" job (Sewell, 2002). Meanwhile, many students from less privileged backgrounds are inexorably drawn to exploited, dead-end, low-paid, intermittent, and part-time work in order to gain or maintain access to this world. The interest in any kind of paid work, no matter how exploited, can be motivated not by any intrinsic interest or delayed gratification, but by the necessity to earn the wages that allow access to the things that really energize and impassion them beyond the boring world of work. Unemployment, or the prospect of it, produces oppression by excluding young people from forms of identity-making and satisfaction provided by these new leisure and consumption fields. The old categories of judging a fair wage and a decent job are being capsized. The individualism inspired by cultural market relations can give a generalized sense of power and autonomy, often entirely misplaced with respect to the objective lack of real choice on youth labor markets, therefore concealing and mystifying it.[10]

Status Systems and Schools

Like the other authors in this Special Issue, I argue that popular culture should be understood in relation to the strong urge of young people to make and maintain a viable informal cultural identity acknowledged by others in shared social space. Commodity consumption and display (trainers, music, appearance, etc.) are major raw materials for the development of such expressive subjectivity and for the symbolic public marking of identity for self and others. But these forms of cultural expression are not simply about developing identity; they are also about putative, comparative, and hierarchical social placing of identity.[11] However, this comparative social dimension cannot be achieved within consumer relations themselves. Knowledgeable manipulations of symbolic markers of identity do not confer status on their own. While a necessary condition, these manipulations need to be part of an identity founded on other grounds. The school is a crucial site for these grounds where an over-mapping of distinctions takes place, with common culture positions and identities mapping onto distinctions within the school and these distinctions themselves mapping onto wider social distinctions.

There is not necessarily an automatic connection between basic social elements (class, race, and gender), school resistance or nonresistance (first wave), disaffection (second wave), and particular kinds of common cultural expression (third wave). Within the site of the school, each of these factors has a relatively independent life and can attach itself to other elements so that there is the possibility, among other things, for class and "ethnic cross-dressing" (McCarthy, 2002). However, there are likely to be some tendencies of strong association, which is the ethnographer's task to uncover. For instance, lower-working-class students are likely to be located at the bottom of the official school status system. From this position they are likely to be inclined to exploit popular culture and other resources to embody their resistance or disaffection with alternative status markers, mobilizing cultural "positional goods" that they can control.

Perhaps it is the singular nature of the modernist school, where people of the same age are forced into a common arena, that compels individuals and groups to find a place and identity within a single complex matrix. No matter how heterogeneous their backgrounds or how different their cultural destinies would have played out without the unnatural social atmospherics of the school, it is within the constraints of this institution that young people negotiate their identities. The previous section looked at some elements of the common cultural status system within the school and some of its points of contact with other systems. There are, in fact, several status systems in play at once in the school. The urgent and sometimes sulphurous social pressures built up in the pressure cooker of the school fuse and force into lived articulation a number of status-conferring symbolic relations derived from without and within the school. For example, the official academic status measures within the school create hierarchical levels among students, which reinforce the external cultural capital systems that confer likely status and advantage on middle-class students. Team sports provide a powerful system of status measurement and achievement,[12] and perceptions of sexual attractiveness provide a status system both inside and outside of schools. Furthermore, systems based on perceived bodily hardness and toughness provide working-class and Black students greater chances for privilege, while opposition to authority, derived from both the resistance of the first wave and the disassociation of the second, produce their own kinds of status systems. Lastly, but by no means least, new patterns of popular cultural consumption confer separate bases for evaluation and prestige.

Though forced into a common matrix, these symbolic relations are not aligned and do not point uniformly to common high-status positions. Conflict is ensured in the cauldron of the school, where students are competing for place and identity with reference to all of these positionalities. To change the metaphor, here is a complex cultural microecology, requiring considerable bravery and skill. On the one hand, failure in navigation skills may lead to victimhood, suffering, and even tragedy, while on the other, it may lead to involvement in serious crime and violence stretching beyond the school.

All schools are likely to manifest all or most of the themes discussed here, although there is likely to be wide variability in the cultural microecologies of particular schools and variation in the combination and alignment of systems. In different ways, common cultural systems are likely to become more central, inflecting how variations in the mix of social class, race, and ethnicities take root and grow in school ecologies. None of this can be read out automatically from social determinants, which again indicates a wide research agenda for ethnographic study.

There is a real autonomy and unpredictable chemistry in how status systems will mix in any given school. Successive and continuing waves of modernization and responses to them have added new layers of pressure and confusion. The contemporary school has been turned into a strange kind of hybrid, incorporating, under the same roof, the very different past and likely future trajectories of their very different students and the weighting of their stakes in different kinds of modernization, and whether these come from above or from below.

"Dominant Populars" in Schools

In predominantly working-class schools there is likely to be a polarization of the official culture and its hierarchies of status from the subterranean one. The latter develops and maintains its dominance by gathering for itself privileged positions within informal status systems that would include, most importantly, the status system of common culture. For instance, "popular" boys are likely to be tough, oppose the school, and be seen as stylish in their music and clothing tastes. To drop one of these attributes would be to drop out of the "dominant popular" — the status system configuration that commands the most student prestige in a given school. To a greater or lesser extent, other social groups are likely to seek justifications for their own positions in relation to the dominant popular in the magnification of the mappings of distinction that are beneficial to them.

Of course, such dominant populars are socially subordinate in the wider frame. They invert not only the school's official hierarchies, but also some of the wider social hierarchies by appearing to confer on students deceivingly dominant roles even when they occupy subordinate economic and social positions outside the school. Unless they can convert informal skills and knowledge to market advantage in the informal or formal cultural industries, marked reproductive consequences are likely to continue for the members of such inverted fixings of the official cultural systems of the school. They may enjoy the ambiguous superiority of symbolic dominance only as a short prelude to and ironic preparation for extended economic disadvantage in the labor market. Middle-class students in predominantly working-class schools may take up positions within such subordinate dominant populars. If so, interesting competitions of influence will ensue between likely poor academic performance and effects flowing from inherited economic and cultural capital.

In schools with predominantly middle-class students, the weight of cultural capital is likely to give informal qualitative and quantitative ballast to the official system and its status prizes. Other systems are more likely to be aligned with this official system so that "popular" boys, for instance, are likely to achieve at least some academic success, get along with staff, and be seen as attractive and stylish. This produces a dominant popular more aligned with the school and with hierarchies outside of it, so to speak, a truly dominant dominant popular. Status systems that are out of line with the official system are likely to be attenuated in their power. A central point I wish to make is that the contents and meanings of the common cultural status system are likely to be very different when aligned with a dominant popular articulated in line with, rather than in opposition to, the school. In general, though, the conflicts and overlaps of various symbolic systems result in a cumulatively rising social atmosphere within the singular institution of the school. There are likely to be negative social and psychological effects associated with being excluded from the dominant popular in any given school.[13]

The School as Instrument and Site

The school is the direct instrument of the first wave; it suffers disorientation from the second wave; and it is an important site for the playing out of the third wave of modernization. You could say that all cultural forms and experiences now have an element of cultural diaspora. Even if you stop in the same place, change flows over you; when the young are still, symbolic borders pass them.

In this article, I have described three themes of cultural modernity "from below": continuing threads of institutionally based informal cultural resistance; responses of disaffection and depression to the continuing effects of postindustrial unemployment and tougher forms of state-regulated school-to-work transitions; and the new cultural and bodily relations and possibilities arising from grounded consumption and leisure.

The combinations of these three themes are unstable and different in their implications for different social groups. Each wave affects the others and has to be understood in light of the others. In particular, issues of popular culture are too often treated for themselves and in their own vectors of effect on identity. These issues can be seen much more productively through the play and effect of preceding and continuing cultural and structural forces of modernization. These forces continue to play over particular groups still constituted in traditional categories of class, race, and gender. Thus there are multiple ways in which resistance (first wave) and disaffection (second wave) are given expression and development within common cultural practices (third wave).

It is true that in the last wave of modernization we can observe the cultural unconscious pushing back; that which was automatic seems willed. The tragedy is that what is sometimes called the aesthetization of experience does not actually change the material relation between freedom and necessity, between the chosen and the determined. These relations are actually tightening for the worse in the life space of the subordinate classes at the hands of second wave modernization, even as third wave modernization indicates symbolic space without borders. Cultural and material vectors seem to be out of kilter as never before. We must not overlook that the super-abundance of images and imaginary possibilities of apparently free-floating and classless forms of consumption intersect with materially worsening conditions for large sections of the working class. This is especially true, given the brute facts of youth unemployment and exploitative underemployment in low-wage service jobs for masses of young people. The blurring of consumption and production in third wave modernization might offer some young people hope of embarking on alternative "twilight" careers in the provision of cultural goods and services. But second wave conditions also produce heightened attractions to crime and to illegal activities in the informal economy. Meanwhile, schools continue to struggle, still formed by the ambitions and illusions of the first wave of modernization now breaking on very different shores.

In schools we can see a blunt, culturally mediated form of negotiation between young people and adults, both uncomprehending the meaning and effects of modernity. Antisocial behavior and associated common cultural forms can be vehicles for expression and for seizing space and autonomy where words fail. It must be understood that schooling is not only an instrument for producing modernity, but is also a site for the playing out of its contradictory forces and forms. Accepting popular culture does not mean a lazy throwing open of the school doors to the latest fad, but rather committing to a principled understanding of the complexity of contemporary cultural experience.

There is a wider set of issues here concerning the fullest understandings of cultural formations and the determinants of their direction for emancipation or alienation. The school is a social field as well as an instrument of social development. Therefore, educators, educational organizations, and their progressive allies should speak up unequivocally on behalf of young people in the middle and bottom of social space who are embroiled in the flux of this dialectical modernization. They can take up clues and themes from young peoples' emergent cultures, pains, and experience. If the consciousness, actions, and cultures of students need to change, so do the wider conditions and structural possibilities that help to structure those very responses. As this article addresses throughout, consciousness and structure are the two intertwined poles of continuous cultural processes. If consciousness has to change, so does structure. At the very least there are firm "voluntarist" limits on how far consciousness can be asked to change if questions of structure are firmly off the agenda. Rather than ever-more individualistic economic competition for the good life driven by the first wave, where are the means for the majority to find a collective place in the sun free from ideological straightjackets? Rather than shaming individualized insecurity and the state disciplining of working poverty described in the second wave, where are the guarantees for enhanced security and greater choice that globalized economic advance is supposed to bring? Rather than predatory market provisions of the third wave enflaming immediate desire, where are the means for the democratic production of new symbolic and informational goods?

The social impulses embodied in these arguments may have an ideological and utopian tinge. Although in different ways, this is no more so than in the idealist figures of the top-down imaginary — dutiful students, an ever-retraining reserve army of the unemployed, passive grateful consumers — forced to progress through educational and economic institutions. These top-down efforts seek to bend consciousness to unremittingly inflexible and harsh structural conditions. It is the internal contradictions and social impossibility of these idealist figurations that unleash cultural modernization from below to forcibly demonstrate in return that everything cannot be as tidy and convenient for the powerful as the official ledger would have it. In this article, I have examined the counter effects, folding loops of irony, and unintended consequences unleashed from dominant imaginings and moldings of "progress," unavoidably set in motion by the institutional and economic power that backs them up. Maintaining a critique and indicating alternative views of "progress" are fundamental educational issues that are umbilically connected to debates over the canon and multiculturalism, or traditionalism and progressivism.

As for the specific questions of how to address issues of popular culture in the curriculum, I would argue that we should look beyond the products of popular culture to their uses in context — to the field of what I term common culture. Educators fret over the predatory view of popular culture, fearing the exploitations of the vulnerabilities and immoderate desires of the young. I am certainly not endorsing the ways market production scales away the remnants of organic community and institutional responsibility with imaginary relations and desires. Rather, I am trying to understand the processes of common culture to shed light on the grounded forms in which the young acculturate commodities into their everyday lives. In this way we may be able to separate the predatory from the creative and entertain a practical hope for practical action.

For all the predatory dangers of popular culture, within common cultural practices lies a new growth of awareness and identity within the individual or group. This growing awareness is a kind of variable and unpredictable mind-full-ness about individual choices and their limits and lodgings within complex social relations and structural determinants. These new, yet nondominant, forms of identity and expression are precarious and open to further rounds of commodification. They also turn within new complexities and flows of social reproduction in situ. But there is nevertheless a dialectical site to be mined for clues to new kinds of public sphere. Within these public spheres, the subordinate mind-full-ness associated with consumer culture might become a purposeful self-conscious mindfullness of individual and collective action.

Educators and researchers within informal settings might explore a variety of ways that cultural consumption and production might be encouraged to operate in less exploitative ways. Their exploration might open new public realms that are seen not as compensating for or attacking commercial imperatives and their erosion of traditional values, but as going along with the flow of actually existing energies and passions. The conditions of existence within these new public realms would make young people more visible and give them more control over what is expressed and how.

Within formal settings, educators and researchers can use the resource of critical ethnographic texts to explore the meanings and rationalities of common cultural practices close to home. They may consider the products of popular culture not simply for their fetishized, immediate identities, but for their common cultural histories, and ask: How did these expressions become commodities and with what effects? How are they de-fetishized and turned into cultural possessions in situ? What do these appropriated expressions say about social position and location?

Pedagogic voices can be shockingly quiet about issues of social context, as if the four walls of the classroom, sanctuary-making as they can be, contain all that is necessary to understand and direct what goes on within them. Educators and researchers should utilize the cultural experiences and embedded bodily knowledge of their students as starting points, not for bemoaning the failures and inadequacies of their charges, but to render more conscious for them what is unconsciously rendered in their cultural practices. The experiences and knowledge of the students — foot soldiers of modernity — can help us, and them, to understand their own place and formation within flows of cultural modernization. This knowledge provides practical grounds for critical self-understandings of social reproduction and even perhaps for an appreciation of how far, under what conditions, and for whom Bourdieu's elusive enigma might hold true: "Resistance can be alienating and submission can be liberating" (quoted in Bourdieu & Wacquant, 1992, p. 24). While celebrating the "freedoms" of consumption, we must always locate them on the front lines where they are exercised.

Notes

1. Not all working-class students failed. However, like today, middle-class students were about six times more likely to go into higher education than were working-class pupils.
2. "Ear'oles" is slang for the exterior bit of the human ear; the lads saw them as always listening and never doing.
3. Other forms of resistance and behavior leading to social reproduction have since been documented. Working-class girls perform more "silent" forms of resistance and disaffection, with similarly ironic processes of reproduction to be observed with respect to their destiny in unpaid domestic work and within low-paid "feminized" occupations (e.g., Anyon, 1983; Llewellyn, 1980; Payne, 1980). In the era of politically driven diaspora following and merging with continuing economic migration, other variants of informal and resistant cultures of school borrow from, recycle, and adapt to elements of various traditional race, ethnic, and national cultures (e.g., Fordham, 1996; Mac an Ghaill, 1988; Portes, 1995; Raissiguier, 1995).
4. Despite a marked spreading out and increase in the "nominal rate" of paper qualifications in the U.K. over the last twenty-five years, patterns of unequal attainment between the classes have remained remarkably constant (Arnot, 2002).
5. This job trend is compelling evidence of the inflexibility and long duration of locked cultural forms.

6. The following is based mainly on my work in *The Youth Review* (1988), Furlong and Cartmel's (1997) *Young People and Social Change*, and Starrin, Rantakeisu, and Hagquist's (1997) "In the Wake of Recession."

7. Single mothers may or may not find some mileage in the manipulation of an increasingly mean, disciplining, and coercive state to provide bare housing and subsistence, but various kinds of limitations on total lifetime welfare entitlements mean that they are running out of road on their way to a crossroads of enforced choice between workfare subservence and the dubious freedoms of subsistence in the informal economy (see Hofferth, Stanhope, & Harris, 2002).

8. On "hyper-masculinity" see Mac an Ghaill (1994).

9. For an overview of popular culture in the United States, see Traube (1996).

10. See discussion of the "epistemological fallacy of late modernity" in Furlong and Cartmel (1997)

11. For an interesting parallel argument about the comparative importance of subcultural capital, see Thornton (1995).

12. This is especially true in the United States (see Holland & Andre, 1994; Spady, 1970).

13. For a biographic and life history ethnographic exploration of some of these issues, see Ortner (2002).

References

Adair, V. C. (2002). Branded with infamy: Inscriptions of poverty and class in the United States. *Signs: Journal of Women in Culture and Society, 27,* 451–471.

Anyon, J. (1983). Intersections of gender and class: Accommodation and resistance by working-class and affluent females to contradictory sex-role ideologies. In S. Walker & L. Barton (Eds.), *Gender, class and education* (pp. 19–37). Lewes, Eng.: Falmer Press.

Arnot, M. (2002). *Reproducing gender? Essays on educational theory and feminist politics.* London: Routledge Falmer.

Bourdieu, P., & Wacquant, L. (1992). *An invitation to reflexive sociology.* Chicago: University of Chicago Press.

Clifford, J. (1997). *Routes: Travel and translation in the late twentieth century.* Cambridge, MA: Harvard University Press.

Devine, J. (1997). *Maximum security: The culture of violence in inner-city schools.* Chicago: Chicago University Press.

Durkheim, E. (1956). *Education and sociology.* New York: Free Press.

Fordham, S. (1996). *Blacked out: Dilemmas of race, identity, and success in Capital High.* Chicago: University of Chicago Press.

Furlong, A., & Cartmel, F. (1997). *Young people and social change.* Philadelphia: Open University Press.

Gilborn, D., & Mirza, H. (2000). *Educational inequality: Mapping race, class and gender.* London: Office for Standards in Education.

Gregg, P., & Wadsworth, J. (Eds.). (1999). *The state of working Britain.* Manchester, Eng.: Manchester University Press.

Hofferth, S. L., Stanhope, S., & Harris, K. M. (2002). Exiting welfare in the 1990s: Did public policy influence recipients' behavior? *Population Research and Policy Review, 21,* 433–472.

Holland, A., & Andre, T. (1994). Athletic participation and the social status of adolescent males and females. *Youth and Society, 25,* 388–407.

Johnson, M. (1999). *Failing school, failing city: The reality of inner city education.* Charlbury, Eng.: Jon Carpenter.

Llewellyn, M. (1980). Studying girls at school: The implications of confusion. In R. Deem (Ed.), *Schooling for women's work* (pp. 42–51). Boston: Routledge & Kegan Paul.

Mac an Ghaill, M. (1988). *Young, gifted and Black.* Milton Keynes, Eng.: Open University Press.

Mac an Ghaill, M. (1994). *The making of men: Masculinities, sexualities and schooling.* Buckingham, Eng.: Open University Press.

Marriott, M. (1993, August 15). Hard core rap lyrics stir backlash. *New York Times*, p. 1.

McCarthy, C. (2002, April). *Understanding the work of aesthetics in modern life: Thinking about the cultural studies of education in a time of recession.* Paper presented at the annual meeting of the American Educational Research Association, New Orleans.

Nader, R. (1996). *Children first: A parent's guide to fighting corporate predators.* Washington, DC: Corporate Accountability Research Group.

Office of National Statistics. (2003). Work and joblessness. June assessment: Claimant count up. In *National Statistics Online.* Retrieved July 2, 2003 from http://www.statistics.gov.uk/cci/nugget.asp?id=12 [Last updates June 11, 2003].

One in five young people may drop out, says OFSTED. (2003, March 6). *London Times Higher Education Supplement*, p. 6.

Ortner, S. (2002). Burned like a tattoo: High school social categories and "American culture." *Ethnography, 3*, 115–148.

Paulle, B. (2003). Contest and collaboration: Embodied cultural responses of adolescents in an "inner city" school in the Bronx (New York) and a "zwarte" school in the Bijlmer (Amsterdam). In J. C. C. Rupp & W. Veugelers (Eds.), *Moreel-politieke heroriëntatie in het onderwijs* (pp. 17–51). Leuven, Belgium: Garant.

Payne, I. (1980). A working-class girl in a grammar school. In D. Spender & E. Sarah (Eds.), *Learning to lose: Sexism and education* (pp. 12–19). London: Women's Press.

Portes, A. (Ed.). (1995). *The economic sociology of immigration: Essays on networks, ethnicity and entrepreneurship.* New York: Russell Sage.

Raissiguier, C. (1995). The construction of marginal identities: Working-class girls of Algerian descent in a French school. In M. H. Marchand & J. L. Parpart (Eds.), *Feminism/postmodernism/development* (pp. 79–93). London: Routledge.

Roberts, K. (2001). *Class in modern Britain.* Basingstoke, Eng.: Palgrave.

Sewell, T. (1997). *Black masculinities and schooling: How Black boys survive modern schooling.* London: Trentham Books.

Sewell, T. (2002, December 15). I know why black boys fail at school – and racism isn't to blame. London: *Mail on Sunday*, p. 59.

Silvester, S. (2002, October 8). Grey hair, wrinkles, and money to burn. *Financial Times,* p. 6

Spady, W. G. (1970). Lament for the letterman: Effects of peer status and extracurricular activities on goals and achievement. *American Journal of Sociology, 75*, 680–702

Starrin, B., Rantakeisu, U., & Hagquist, C. (1997). In the wake of recession – economic hardship, shame and social disintegration. *Scandinavian Journal of Work and Environmental Health, 23*(4), 47–54.

Thornton, S. (1995). *Club cultures.* Cambridge, Eng.: Polity Press.

Traube, Elizabeth G. (1996) "The popular" in American culture. *Annual Review of Anthropology, 25*, 127–151.

Unemployment Unit. (1999). *Working brief 107 August/September.* London: Unemployment Unit and Youth-aid Research, Information, Campaigning.

Willis, P. (1977). *Learning to labour.* Aldershot, Eng: Saxon House.

Willis, P. (2000). *The ethnographic imagination.* Cambridge, Eng: Polity Press.

Willis, P., Bekenn, A., Ellis, T., & Whitt, D. (1988). *The youth review.* Aldershot, Eng.: Avebury.

Willis, P., Jones, S., Canaan, J., & Hurd, G. (1990). *Common culture.* Buckingham, Eng.: Open University Press.

I am extremely grateful for close and detailed critical comments on an earlier draft and suggestions generously offered by Philip Corrigan and Bowen Paulle. Thanks also for the detailed comments and suggestions from editors at *HER,* and especially for the close editorial attentions of Rubén Gaztambide-Fernández and Lionel C. Howard.

About the Contributors

Dolores Delgado Bernal is an assistant professor at the University of Utah, with a joint appointment in the Department of Education, Culture, and Society and the Ethnic Studies Program. Her research draws from critical race theory, Latina/o critical theory, and U.S.-Third World feminist theories to examine and improve the educational experience of Chicanas/os and other students of color. Her recent publications include "An Apartheid of Knowledge in the Academy: The Struggle over 'Legitimate' Knowledge for Faculty of Color" in *Equity and Excellence in Education* (with O. Villalpando, 2002), and "Chicana/o Education from the Civil Rights Era to the Present" in *The Elusive Quest for Equality: 150 Years of Chicano/ Chicana Education* (Harvard Education Publishing Group, 1999).

Michelle Fine is Distinguished Professor of Social Psychology, Women's Studies, and Urban Education at the Graduate Center of the City University of New York, where she has taught since 1990. Her professional interests center on how youth view distributive and procedural justice in schools, prisons, the economy, and in local communities. She is coauthor of "Participatory Action Research: Behind Bars and Under Surveillance" in *Qualitative Methods* (edited by P. Camic and J. Rhodes, 2003), and *Keeping the Struggle Alive: Studying Desegregation in Our Town* (2002).

Ramón Flecha is professor of sociology at the University of Barcelona and director of CREA at the Science Park of Barcelona. His research is dedicated to overcoming social inequalities of marginalized groups. He is author of *Contemporary Sociological Theory* (2003) and coauthor of *Critical Education in the New Information Age* (with M. Castells, P. Freire, H. Giroux, D. Macedo, and P. Willis, 1999).

Henry A. Giroux is the Waterbury Chair Professor and director of the Waterbury Forum in Education and Cultural Studies at Pennsylvania Sate University. His primary areas of research are cultural studies, youth studies, critical pedagogy, and popular culture. His most recent books include *The Abandoned Generation: Democracy beyond the Culture of Fear* (2003) and *Breaking into the Movies: Film and the Culture of Politics* (2002).

Sandy Marie Anglás Grande, assistant professor at Connecticut College in New London, is interested in American Indian education and antiracist pedagogy. She is coauthor of "Critical Theory and American Indian Geographies of Identity, Power, and Pedagogy: A Dialogue with Sandy Marie Anglás Grande" in *International Journal of Educational Reform* (with P. McLaren, 2000), and author of "Beyond the Ecologically Noble Savage: Deconstructing the White Man's Indian" in *Journal of Environmental Ethics* (1999).

Kenn Gardner Honeychurch is vice president (academic and research) at NSCAF University in Halifax, Nova Scotia. He is a mixed-media artist and researcher, with interests in art and cultural diversity, as well as the role of technology in art, culture, and education. His recent publications include "Queen of the Class: Sexual Identities in Pedagogical Spaces" in *Cultural Studies: A Research Volume* (2000), and "Staying Straight: Wanting in the Academy" in *Discourse: Studies in the Cultural Politics of Education* (2000).

Cati Marsh Kennerley is an assistant professor of humanities at the University of Puerto Rico at Rio Piedras. Her professional interests focus on Latin American literature and cultural studies. She is author of "La otra cara de la asimilacion: Norteamericanos en Puerto Rico" ("The Other Face of Assimilation: North Americans in Puerto Rico") in *Diálogo* (1996) and a contributor to several textbooks for grades 1–12.

Patti Lather is a professor in the School of Educational Policy and Leadership at Ohio Sate University. She is interested in qualitative research and theories of feminism. Her published works include *Troubling the Angels: Women Living with HIV/AIDS* (with C. Smithies, 1997) and "Troubling Clarity: The Politics of Accessible Language" in *Harvard Educational Review* (1996).

Cameron McCarthy is a research professor and university scholar at the Institute of Communications Research at the University of Illinois at Urbana-Champaign. His major areas of research are cultural studies and mass communication. His recent published works include "Mobile Identities, Mobilized Knowledges: Technology and Culture in a Global Society" in a special issue of *Information, Theory, and Society* (edited with J. Bratich and M. Leger, in press), and *Foucault, Cultural Studies, and Governmentality* (edited with J. Bratich and J. Packer, 2003).

Gary Thomas is professor of education at Oxford Brookes University in the United Kingdom. His areas of professional interest are in research methodology, inclusive education, and the relation between these two. He is author of *Strangers in Paradigms: Education and Theory in the 20th Century* (forthcoming) and coeditor of *Evidence-Based Practice in Education* (with R. Pring, 2004).

Paul Willis is a professor of social and cultural ethnography at Keele University in Staffordshire, England. His research interests center around conceptual and methodological ways of connecting a concern with identity/culture to economic structure. His best-known book is *Learning to Labour: How Working Class Kids Get Working Class Jobs* (1977); his more recent works include *The Ethnographic Imagination* (2000). He co-founded the journal *Ethnography* in 2000.

About the Editors

Rubén A. Gaztambide-Fernández is an advanced doctoral student and an instructor of education at the Harvard Graduate School of Education, where he teaches curriculum theory. He is a former co-chair of the *Harvard Educational Review* and of the *HER* Special Issue on Popular Culture and Education (2003), and is co-editor of *Curriculum Work as a Public Moral Enterprise* (with J. T. Sears, 2004). The recipient of a Spencer Foundation Research Training Grant, Gaztambide-Fernández's current research focuses on the construction of social identities in elite independent schools. He lives with his wife and daughter in Cambridge, Massachusetts.

Heather A. Harding is an advanced doctoral student at the Harvard Graduate School of Education, where she is a teaching fellow for courses in educational policy, school reform, and race, and is a former co-chair of the *Harvard Educational Review*. She currently supervises campus leaders at Citizen Schools, an afterschool program that provides adult-led apprenticeships for middle school students. She has worked as a rural secondary teacher, a professional development coordinator, and an organizational change consultant for several Boston-area education reform organizations. Harding's research uncovers the motivation and classroom practice of successful White teachers of students of color.

Tere Sordé-Martí is a sociologist and a doctoral student at the Harvard Graduate School of Education. Her main research interests are social theory from a critical perspective, the processes of change in current society, and education as a tool for social transformation. She has been working with the Romà in Europe, and her studies are focused on the Romà Rights Movement. She has published and presented her work at national and international forums.